How to access the supplemental web resource

We are pleased to provide access to a web resource that supplements your textbook, *Leisure Services Financial Management*. This resource offers case studies, sample financial reports to understand and analyze, chapter overviews, glossary terms, and more.

Accessing the web resource is easy! Follow these steps if you purchased a new book:

1. Visit **www.HumanKinetics.com/LeisureServicesFinancialManagement**.
2. Click the first edition link next to the book cover.
3. Click the Sign In link on the left or top of the page. If you do not have an account with Human Kinetics, you will be prompted to create one.
4. If the online product you purchased does not appear in the Ancillary Items box on the left of the page, click the Enter Key Code option in that box. Enter the key code that is printed at the right, including all hyphens. Click the Submit button to unlock your online product.
5. After you have entered your key code the first time, you will never have to enter it again to access this product. Once unlocked, a link to your product will permanently appear in the menu on the left. For future visits, all you need to do is sign in to the textbook's website and follow the link that appears in the left menu!

→ Click the Need Help? button on the textbook's website if you need assistance along the way.

How to access the web resource if you purchased a used book:

You may purchase access to the web resource by visiting the text's website, **www.HumanKinetics.com/LeisureServicesFinancialManagement**, or by calling the following:

800-747-4457	U.S. customers
800-465-7301	Canadian customers
+44 (0) 113 255 5665	European customers
08 8372 0999	Australian customers
0800 222 062	New Zealand customers
217-351-5076	International customers

For technical support, send an e-mail to:

support@hkusa.com	U.S. and international customers
info@hkcanada.com	Canadian customers
academic@hkeurope.com	European customers
keycodesupport@hkaustralia.com	Australian and New Zealand customers

HUMAN KINETICS
The Information Leader in Physical Activity & Health

07-2012

Product: Leisure Services Financial Management web resource

Key code: EMANUELSON-HTE3KB-OSG

This unique code allows you access to the web resource.

Access is provided if you have purchased a new book. Once submitted, the code may not be entered for any other user.

LEISURE SERVICES FINANCIAL MANAGEMENT

David Emanuelson

Human Kinetics

Library of Congress Cataloging-in-Publication Data

Emanuelson, David, 1949-
Leisure services financial management / David Emanuelson.
p. cm.
Includes bibliographical references and index.
ISBN 978-0-7360-9641-6 (hard cover) -- ISBN 0-7360-9641-8 (hard cover) 1.
Service industries--Management. 2. Leisure industry. I. Title.
HD9980.5.E43 2013
790.06'91--dc23

2012011056

ISBN-10: 0-7360-9641-8 (print)
ISBN-13: 978-0-7360-9641-6 (print)

The web addresses cited in this text were current as of April 4, 2012, unless otherwise noted.

Acquisitions Editor: Gayle Kassing, PhD; **Developmental Editor:** Ray Vallese; **Assistant Editor:** Derek Campbell; **Copyeditor:** Alisha Jeddeloh; **Indexer:** Sharon Duffy; **Permissions Manager:** Dalene Reeder; **Graphic Designer:** Fred Starbird; **Graphic Artist:** Yvonne Griffith; **Cover Designer:** Bob Reuther; **Photographer (interior):** © Human Kinetics, unless otherwise noted; **Photo Asset Manager:** Laura Fitch; **Visual Production Assistant:** Joyce Brumfield; **Photo Production Manager:** Jason Allen; **Art Manager:** Kelly Hendren; **Associate Art Manager:** Alan L. Wilborn; **Illustrations:** © Human Kinetics, unless otherwise noted; **Printer:** Sheridan Books

Printed in the United States of America

10 9 8 7 6 5 4 3 2 1

The paper in this book is certified under a sustainable forestry program.

Human Kinetics
Website: www.HumanKinetics.com

United States: Human Kinetics
P.O. Box 5076
Champaign, IL 61825-5076
800-747-4457
e-mail: humank@hkusa.com

Canada: Human Kinetics
475 Devonshire Road Unit 100
Windsor, ON N8Y 2L5
800-465-7301 (in Canada only)
e-mail: info@hkcanada.com

Europe: Human Kinetics
107 Bradford Road
Stanningley
Leeds LS28 6AT, United Kingdom
+44 (0) 113 255 5665
e-mail: hk@hkeurope.com

Australia: Human Kinetics
57A Price Avenue
Lower Mitcham, South Australia 5062
08 8372 0999
e-mail: info@hkaustralia.com

New Zealand: Human Kinetics
P.O. Box 80
Torrens Park, South Australia 5062
0800 222 062
e-mail: info@hknewzealand.com

E5213

Contents

Preface

Leisure services in the United States began as the hospitality industry, with food and lodging as its primary service. Public-sector agencies were created to provide park services to a nation that cried out for a clean environment that offered a refuge from the filth of the cities. But these agencies also focused on profitability of leisure services.

Many nonprofit organizations began as philanthropic ventures to help the poor, relying on donations to cover their costs. Eventually, agencies such as the YMCA realized that people had other needs, including food, lodging, and the opportunity to enjoy themselves.

Leisure services financial management is a diverse topic, as complex as the leisure services industry itself. The leisure services industry contains millions of businesses, nonprofit organizations, and governmental units. The business sector, also called the *private sector*, comprises more than 20 million privately owned businesses. The nonprofit sector comprises nearly 1 million nonprofit organizations, and the government sector, also commonly referred to as the *public sector*, comprises over 87,000 governmental units. Many of these private, nonprofit, and public organizations provide leisure services. These agencies have financial management systems that account for and report their revenues and expenses. Each of these agencies has a unique way of dealing with its finances.

Leisure Services Financial Management was written to describe how these complex systems work and to prepare you as a leisure services professional to manage any system that you may confront. It covers a multitude of topics, from financial management to accounting to politics.

Chapter 1 begins with an overview of the leisure services environment, including how the industry exists in the private, nonprofit, and public sectors, which often compete with each other for clients. Chapter 2 considers the importance of learning technical skills, including economics, accounting, finance, and marketing. It discusses how and why leisure services professionals should develop a philosophy in order to be competent financial managers. To provide the financial skills necessary for this development, chapter 3 offers an overview of accounting, including a discussion of why accounting is so complex and why it is getting more complex as time goes on.

Chapter 4 discusses the private sector, and chapter 5 introduces private-sector accounting. Chapter 6 lays the foundation for private-sector reporting and analysis. Then chapter 7 introduces the often misunderstood nonprofit sector, identifying the differences between the private and government sectors. The stage is then set to introduce the topic of nonprofit accounting and reporting in chapter 8.

A similar systematic approach is taken to the topic of government accounting. In chapter 9, the unique character of the government sector is discussed. In chapter 10, the complexities of government-sector accounting and reporting are described.

The topic of chapter 11 is capital financing as it applies to all three sectors, an area of the leisure services field that many professionals will experience during their careers. Finally, chapter 12 considers future trends in terms of how they will influence the evolution of the field.

Leisure Services Financial Management also includes a student web resource that provides an overview and objectives for each chapter, key terms, case studies that present situations for you to consider and resolve, and sample financial reports for you to read and analyze. The web resource is available online at www.HumanKinetics.com/LeisureServicesFinancialManagement.

Throughout the book and online resource, a discussion of ethical standards takes place. This topic is important and there are many professional guidelines to consider. For instance, the National Recreation and Park Association (NRPA) has a code of ethics, as do the American Society of Public Administration (ASPA), International City/County Management Association (ICMA), Government Finance Officers Association (GFOA), and others. Sometimes these codes contradict each other, and leisure professionals need to determine which one to follow. This book provides case studies to help you navigate ethical dilemmas and avoid making wrong decisions that could tarnish or end your career.

Accounting processes are important for professionals to understand, so *Leisure Services Financial Management* shows how manual accounting originally occurred and how electronic accounting exists today. Selecting the right software provider today is just as important as selecting the right bookkeeper was years ago.

The ability of leisure professionals to create and interpret financial reports is an essential skill and one of your major responsibilities when you become a manager. This text and the web resource provide several examples of financial reports and analyses. The diversity of financial reporting methods in the private, nonprofit, and public sectors is also discussed, beginning with how and why the private sector values its relationship with its customers more than the public sector does.

The political elements of financial management in the private sector are covered in the context of relationships with stockholders and boards of directors. How relationships with bankers and financiers affect your ability to raise capital also is explored. A similar understanding is provided of the political skill sets required of nonprofit leisure services managers. The importance of fund-raising and development is a major focus, as is the relationship between the manager and the members of the board of directors, many of whom are on the board for the purpose of fund-raising.

Public-sector leisure services managers require a unique political skill set. As this book discusses, park and recreation professionals in the public sector have direct relationships with the elected officials who set their tax rates, approve their budgets, and issue their debt. In some states, voters also can approve debt. The politics of passing public referenda are covered as well.

Throughout the book, the differences in accounting methodologies are presented. Financial accounting standards are contrasted against government accounting standards. How nonprofits adopt a permutation of both methodologies is also considered. This book presents many sample financial reports as illustrations of how these reports can look so different yet still be so similar. As a leisure services professional, you should be prepared to create and interpret all types of financial reports, which makes leisure services management as complicated as any other profession. Examples of budgets, financial reports, and management case studies and insights into the realities of economic, political, and financial environments are what make this text so useful. By understanding the forces that have shaped the past and current state of the leisure services industry, managers can determine the direction of the industry for the future.

Unlike most other books on the topic, *Leisure Services Financial Management* pulls together in one place philosophy, ethical standards, politics, accounting, and financial management skills for the field. This is a book that should not be sold back to the bookstore at the end of the semester but rather kept for future reference.

As a permanent reference, this textbook serves the needs of undergraduates in the leisure services field by teaching the language of financial management, the ability to read financial statements, and the knowledge of how to use financial statements to manage financial responsibilities. This textbook also serves graduate students destined for upper-management positions, giving them the ability to create financial statements and use them as tools to manage agencies.

Because this textbook covers private, nonprofit, and public financial management, undergraduate and graduate students can use it as a tool to move from one sector to another during their careers. And since the language of each of these three sectors has been fairly stable over the years, this textbook should be useful for the foreseeable future.

chapter 1

The Leisure Services Environment

Learning Outcomes

After completing this chapter, students will be able to do the following:

- Explain the difference between leisure and recreation.
- Define *leisure services management* and its influences on the economic, political, and social environment.
- Summarize the history of how the three sectors of leisure services were created and developed.
- Compare the financial management similarities and differences among the three sectors.
- Articulate the financial management challenges for each sector.

The leisure services industry falls into three categories: **public sector**, **nonprofit sector**, and **private sector**. Certain financial and accounting principles are unique to each sector, but many similarities exist. No matter which sector you work in, you will need to know how to prepare a budget, how to predict and manage expenses and income to prevent losses, and how to read and understand reports, whether they are for the public, a board of directors, or investors. To be prepared for a management career, leisure services professionals need to understand the business of managing money and the accounting principles for each sector. They also need an understanding of the political forces that exist in each sector and the importance of ethics in decision making.

The premise of this textbook is that a command of sound business practices is essential in all sectors, but each sector has unique characteristics, challenges, and practices. Because the word *business* is commonly used to describe enterprises that operate for profit, the terms *business*, *for profit*, *commercial*, and *private* will be used interchangeably throughout this textbook. *Government* and *tax-supported* will be used interchangeably when discussing the public sector. Terminology for the nonprofit sector is straightforward.

LEISURE AND *LEISURE SERVICES FINANCIAL MANAGEMENT* DEFINED

Let's start with an understanding of the difference between leisure and recreation. Leisure and recreation are often considered the same thing. That may be why some academic programs have the word *leisure* in their names and others use the word *recreation*. Technically, though, leisure and recreation are different concepts. **Leisure** is the time when people can play, but it is not playing in and of itself, and academic programs that call themselves *leisure studies* should, therefore, be studying free time. **Recreation**, on the other hand, is a pastime, diversion, exercise, or other resource affording relaxation and enjoyment, suggesting that recreation is an activity.

Many people interpret recreation activities as just sports and games. An activity such as going to a nightclub, although passing time and being a diversion that affords relaxation and enjoyment, does not seem to qualify. But a nightclub is considered a leisure service and thus is part of the leisure services industry. In fact, the number of activities considered to be recreation is greater than the number of those defined as work.

The term **leisure services** better defines the park and recreation field because it allows for a multitude of pastimes that afford relaxation and enjoyment. That's why this textbook uses the term *leisure services* instead of *recreation*. Doing so frees the reader to understand that the profession is more than the administration of youth baseball, adult softball, and classes for hobbyists. This book is about financial administration of a broad range of leisure services via spreadsheets, written reports, and verbal communications.

The field of leisure services management is complex because of the variety of government entities, nonprofit agencies, and private businesses that deliver leisure services. Some of these agencies are large enough to employ professionals who have a background in business or financial management. However, to be a good leisure services manager regardless of sector or size, you need a solid understanding of leisure services financial management.

Leisure services financial management is the administration of accounting and reporting systems. Each sector has its own generally accepted accounting principles (GAAP) and its own reporting responsibilities to the Internal Revenue Service (IRS) and state revenue departments, as will be discussed in subsequent chapters. Leisure services managers need to understand not only financial management but also the role that politics and ethics play across all sectors in making financial decisions.

The history of how the leisure services field developed in the United States is a study of sociology, politics, and economics. The history sheds light on the social and political influences that created the three distinct leisure services sectors and the principles that define leisure services financial management in the 21st century. As shown by the history that follows and other chapters in this book, politics, ethics, and financial management are often intertwined. Although financial management is largely about following the rules, the rules can be different for each sector and subject to interpretation and amendment depending on the political environment and ethical judgment of those in charge.

Politics is much more than fighting between Republicans and Democrats, liberals and conservatives. Webster's online dictionary defines *politics* as the art or science of government or influencing government (www.merriam-webster.com/dictionary/politics). But this textbook uses a much broader definition crossing all three leisure services sectors: the acquisition and use of power to determine outcomes. It is who gets what, when, and how. Politics exist wherever human beings interact. Thus, if you plan a career in any of the three leisure services management arenas, you must understand how to function in a political environment, and you must realize that you will be a political figure.

Ethics involves codes of conduct that professions create based on their fundamental understanding of right from wrong. Some professions, such as elected officials, have no official ethical standards that govern their behaviors; therefore, there must be laws that do. But ethics often transcends the law and the rules. Ethics is all about making the right decision in the face of political and moral dilemmas.

The history of leisure services in the United States is punctuated by politics, no matter what the sector. Subsequent chapters discuss the codes of conduct for financial management in each of the sectors and provide examples to prepare you for ethical decision making. The examples illustrate the complexity of leisure services financial management but also show that it is understandable and manageable.

HOW LEISURE SERVICES BEGAN IN THE UNITED STATES

European immigrants saw the United States as a wilderness that needed to be tamed. At first, there wasn't much leisure time. Food needed to be gathered and homes needed to be built. For the first 100 years of the United States, work took all of a person's waking hours in order to provide the necessities of life.

As the Industrial Revolution began in the mid-1800s, society was not very efficient at doing its work. The wealthy had leisure time, but the rest of the population, who ended up working for the wealthy, did not. That changed as industry became more efficient and work could be done more quickly. From that point on, workers no longer had to make all of their worldly goods; they could buy them with their paychecks. That created leisure time, and ordinary citizens began to think of themselves as worthy of the diversions of the wealthy. Americans started to play.

Urban Park Movement

In the United States, it is generally held that the leisure services profession began around 1854, when a group of **horticulturalists** and **environmentalists** led by **Andrew Jackson Downing** convinced the New York Legislature to permit the creation of **Central Park**, a place for New Yorkers to play. Horticulturalists are experts in the science of cultivating plants, especially gardens, and environmentalists are people who work to protect the environment from destruction or pollution. Downing was a landscape designer and the editor of *The Horticulturalist* magazine in New York. He had traveled extensively in Europe and was surprised at how much more livable European cities were compared with U.S. cities.

At the time, U.S. cities were horrible places, with factories belching smoke into the air, animals soiling streets, open sewers draining into water supplies, and crowded tenements packing people into housing units as if they were sardines. People needed to get away from the filth and congestion, and influential New Yorkers, such as Downing, thought it was time for parks in Manhattan just as there were parks in London and Paris.

Downing lobbied the New York Legislature to create a **special taxing district** for constructing a park in the center of Manhattan. A special taxing district is a geographic area within which property owners pay a tax to support a service or improvement specific to that area. The park was intended to be built and run by an independent commission, the members of which were initially appointed by a judge. What has been somewhat

Boss Tweed and Tammany Hall

Andrew Jackson's motto of "To the victor belongs the spoil" was adopted as the philosophy of political patronage from 1830 to 1880. This philosophy was based on the view that newly elected officials should not be saddled with government employees from previous administrations; instead, newly elected officials need their own people to carry out their policies. This philosophy filtered down from the national level to state and local governments, but it went bad as time went on.

During the 1850s and 1860s, in no place was that philosophy more apparent than the City of New York. In New York, a Democratic political machine known as Tammany Hall, named after the location where it was housed, was led by a man known as Boss Tweed. Tweed used political patronage at the city level as a political army that worked tirelessly to get Tweed's candidates elected. Controlling the city government from the outside permitted Tweed to enrich himself and other party officials through kickbacks from contractors and through outright theft from city coffers, creating a level of corruption whereby about the only thing city government was able to do effectively was keep itself in power.

Eventually, Tweed was indicted, convicted, and sent to prison, and eventually political reforms led to changes in how government was run and elections were conducted. But during its heyday, Tammany Hall created an atmosphere that discouraged the urban park movement from taking root in municipal government. In New York City, a special district was created to avoid the Tammany Hall machine (Bailey, Kennedy, and Cohen 1998).

lost in history is the importance of the arguments made by Downing and his allies to create the Central Park Commission. They recognized that the Central Park Commission needed **financial autonomy** (independence) from the City of New York, which was run by the **political machine** called **Tammany Hall**, and they understood that many New York legislators believed that public parks were too costly and were not an essential function of local government. To circumvent the opposition, Downing and his supporters argued that the park could be created at little cost to the taxpayers of New York by using a **business model**, a plan for generating income to support a product or service, in this case the park.

The Central Park Commission was created shortly after Downing's untimely death in a boating accident. Its creation was, for all practical purposes, the precipitating event that made **leisure services administration** a profession. Leisure services administration was made possible because the Central Park Commission was a special-purpose government, not part of the municipal government of New York City. As a separately operated **governmental unit**, the Central Park Commission had its own sources of revenue, its own authority to hire staff, and its own authority to disburse tax money for improvements and operations.

One of the commission's first acts was to appoint **Frederick Law Olmsted** as its superintendent. Olmsted was a strong-willed individual who knew how to get things done, including how to manage money. He knew how to resist the influence of Tammany Hall, fiscal corruption, and **political patronage**, or giving favors to supporters, such as giving jobs, appointments, and contracts to those who support a particular political party or elected official. Olmsted applied his will to running the commission as an independent financial unit of government. As a result, he was able to oversee the successful construction of Central Park.

With the immediate and immense popularity of Central Park, Olmsted became an influential public figure. His successful design of Central Park put him in demand, and he became a noted park designer. Other cities hired him to design their parks, and other states, such as California, sought his advice in designing their state parks. Olmsted became a national figure, businessman, and advocate for municipal parks. He influenced the creation of three **park districts** in Chicago, in essence special taxing districts to support the development and upkeep of park and recreation services. He also was asked to help plan several cities and to be a designer for the 1893 World's Columbian Exposition in Chicago.

Olmsted's legacy to the profession of leisure services management was that the financial model of the Central Park Commission worked. Only private property immediately around the park was taxed, because property owners would benefit from the park visitors needing food and lodging, souvenirs, and carriage rides to make their visits fun. Central Park became a 19th-century version of Disneyland. People went there to get away from their troubles and to refresh themselves from the filth and congestion of the city. In doing so, the surrounding property owners benefited financially, more than recovering the extra property taxes they paid.

Some Eastern cultures say that by your success, you can become undone. That is precisely what happened in New York after the creation of Central Park. The park was so popular with the public that Tammany Hall wanted to own it. Seeing the park's 250 employees and political largess from construc-

© emeraldphoto - Fotolia

The creation of New York City's Central Park and the plan to have it run by an independent commission helped to make leisure services administration a profession.

tion contracts, Tammany Hall appealed to the state legislature to disband the commission and turn it over to the city. Traveling around the country as a park designer, Olmsted failed to see that Tammany Hall coveted the jobs and political benefits of operating the park. In 1868, when Olmsted was out of town, the New York Legislature turned the park over to the city, disbanding the Central Park Commission as a separate financial entity.

Other states took notice. East Coast cities with their own political machines became advocates of municipal park departments, making sure that special districts providing parks could not be created. That way, the municipal political machine, the group that controlled the activities of the ruling political party, could control the money and jobs that parks and recreation provided. Many Eastern cities took over their school districts as well.

Under Olmsted's leadership, states in the West and Midwest, such as Ohio, Illinois, North Dakota, Colorado, California, Utah, Washington, and Oregon, created park districts with their own financial autonomy, similar to the Central Park Commission. Instead of political patrons, many of these special districts sought professional administration. The parks profession grew from the creation of these separate financial entities.

Olmsted's vision of public parks as a profession had its limitations; he believed that professionals existed only to provide municipal, state, and national parks. The horticulturalists and environmentalists who eventually became park management professionals had the same rigid view of their **mission** or purpose. For instance, when groups wanted to hold horse races in Central Park, the horticulturalists and environmentalists who helped create the park opposed these sports and games. Parks were viewed as gardens, not active play spaces. No races were permitted.

Urban Recreation Movement

About the same time that Central Park was being created in New York in the mid-1850s, George Williams moved his Young Men's Christian Association concept in England to Springfield, Massachusetts. The concept was that young men would come to the YMCA and worship. Built on a financial model similar to churches, these organizations survived from donations made by parishioners.

At first the idea worked, but as the United States became more developed in the late 1800s, financial support from donations waned. YMCAs needed a new financial model, and Williams had another idea. He and other YMCA leaders believed men would come to the YMCA if there was fun to be had. He created camps as an extension of his ministry, used outdoor recreation as a reason for men to go there, and charged fees for participation.

Williams and others also saw another opportunity. Under the belief that indoor recreation centers with swimming pools, boxing rings, and gymnasiums would draw young men to the Y, the first **nonprofit organizations** were born. YMCAs began charging fees for memberships, expanding their mission to include non-Christians and families, and grew to be facility-based agencies that managed substantial revenue streams. YMCAs have flourished in the United States ever since.

Missions don't just define organizations; missions also limit them. Early park professionals believed their mission was to provide outdoor sites where people could refresh themselves. Early recreation professionals believed their mission was to provide recreation programs as a vehicle to teach Christian values and to help people in need of assistance. Both worked for a while, but eventually there was nowhere for them to grow because activities were limited to either passive parks or YMCA programs. People had more leisure time and the money to spend playing, and they wanted more.

Commercial Recreation

After World War I, immigration slowed to a trickle. Labor unions emerged. There was less need for social engineering, and people had more leisure time for playing. In the 1920s, a prosperous American citizenry decided they needed a lot more fun. An emerging middle class went on vacations and to sporting events and bought themselves expensive toys. With a financial model completely different from previous public and nonprofit models for financing of leisure services, the private sector came to meet the public's needs. The private sector provided leisure services of any kind for a price. And when the private sector wouldn't provide the leisure services people wanted in the 1920s and early 1930s, such as alcohol and gambling, illegal leisure services providers, such as organized crime, did.

The Great Depression put many leisure services on hold for a while, but there was no going back. After World War II, the leisure services industry became big business once and for all. Whether people visited parks, joined their local YMCA, or went to Las Vegas, they were spending their time and money on the largest industry in the country. Leisure was king.

LEISURE SERVICES SECTORS

Today, the public and nonprofit sectors have expanded their missions. Governmental units now own and operate hotels, golf courses, stadiums, and sport programs, although they do not adhere to business financial models where profits are made. Nonprofit organizations provide a wide range of services that focus on revenue generation. In some ways, the three sectors of leisure services have grown together and now overlap, but they do not operate under the same accounting principles. The three sectors have different tax laws to follow and different levels of transparency to which they need to adhere.

Commercial Organizations Today

To understand financial management in the commercial leisure services industry, you need to grasp the massive size of the U.S. private sector. It is huge—the largest industry in the world. Today there are more than 22.5 million businesses in the United States. It has been estimated that leisure services is the largest sector, composing more than 8 percent of the gross domestic product of the United States and including nearly 2 million commercial recreation businesses.

Part of the reason the leisure services industry is so large is that it is broadly defined as an industrial category. The industry is composed of several subsets, including

- travel and tourism,
- hospitality,
- resorts,
- gaming,
- amusement parks,
- restaurants,
- professional sport,
- sporting goods manufacturers and retailers,
- movie and entertainment,
- camping and outdoor recreation, and
- video games.

These industries provide 6.5 million jobs in the United States and generate $88 billion annually in national and state tax revenue. In the U.S. economy, $1 in every $12 is from spending in the leisure services industry.

Walt Disney Company

An example of a leisure services corporation that spans many soft and hard products is the Walt Disney Company. Disney began during the Great Depression of the 1930s, when the American unemployment rate approached 25 percent. High unemployment imposed a large amount of forced leisure time upon the workforce. Not only did people have time on their hands, but they also felt bad about not having jobs.

Walt Disney saw that need and knew that people were going to the movies to fill their time. Because he couldn't compete with big movie studios, he decided to make cartoons that could be shown to movie viewers before feature-length movies. He invented Mickey Mouse and other cartoon characters.

Disney's cartoons became so popular that he opened his own studio, which today is one of the biggest and most popular in the world, making feature-length cartoons and movies. Using profit as his motivation, Walt Disney created a movie studio to entertain people, filling their leisure with enjoyment.

Disney thought of another way of entertaining people and making money at the same time. In 1955, he took the idea of the amusement park a big step further and opened Disneyland in Anaheim, California. The park had rides, but it also had a theme: the Magic Kingdom. Disneyland provided children and adults with a place to escape to a world of fantasy, all for an admission price of just under $100 for "children over 10 years old."

Leisure services are part of the soft sector of the U.S. economy, called the *services industry*. Subparts include insurance, banking, retail, education, and health care. The service industry is not thought to produce any hard products such as appliances or furniture. It is assumed that the leisure services industry buys and sells hard products, even though it doesn't actually produce them.

Such would be the case for most sectors in the service industry, but what makes leisure services unique is its diversity. Other than health care, where hospitals can be operated for profit, not for profit, or by governmental units, no other profession spans all three sectors. And no other profession except health care requires the diversity of financial skills required in the leisure services profession. The leisure services industry is vast and diversified, often defying definition. Its hard products are produced by the sporting goods retail industry, recreation vehicle industry, and souvenir industry.

The cruise industry is an example of how difficult it has become to define the leisure services industry. Part of the travel and tourism industry, the cruise industry provides destination voyages to the four corners of the world. For as little as $500 per person, cruisers can live on a ship for a week, eat gourmet meals, see shows, purchase jewelry and other retail goods, and visit exotic ports of call, including adventure excursions. To keep up with the need, Royal Caribbean International launched a massive ship, the Oasis of the Seas, costing over $1.2 billion and holding in excess of 5,000 passengers and 1,500 crew members. Its maiden voyage began December 9, 2009, from Ft. Lauderdale, Florida ("Oasis of the Seas: Is a combination of arts, science and technology" n.d.). The cruising industry alone involves at least 10 other industries, including ship building, retail, electronics, and communications.

Creativity has become the hallmark of private-sector leisure services today. Las Vegas, founded as a place where gamblers could go with no fear of breaking the law, is now a major convention center and family vacation destination. It has amusement parks, food, entertainment, luxury resorts, and, of course, gambling, raking in billions of dollars per year. Las Vegas also does a large and diversified retail business, but it is difficult to determine how to categorize that retail.

Should retail in vacation destinations be considered part of the overall retail industry, or is it a retail business that would not have taken place without the visit to the vacation destination? The answer to the question is both; retail sales can be part of the general retail sales industry or can be considered part of the leisure services industry. That's one way how the leisure services industry can morph to other portions of the private sector, making it difficult to determine whether businesses that sell retail in vacation destinations should be considered part of the leisure services industry or part of the retail industry as a whole.

The point is that it's not really important which businesses are pure leisure services and which are not. The important point is that the private sector of the leisure services industry is big and getting bigger. The industry has been predicted to grow as the middle classes grow in other countries. With the burgeoning international middle class learning to play throughout every stage of life, from their youth through their golden years, and with the disposable income to do so, leisure services worldwide has the potential to be a growth industry over the long haul, just as it has been in the United States.

With the forecast that the leisure services industry will continue to grow, including in exports, it may be one of the bright spots of the U.S. economy. The United States exports its culture to other countries around the world, especially through restaurant franchises and entertainment. Hamburgers were invented in Germany, yet we open McDonald's franchises in Europe. A British writer storms the literary world with her Harry Potter novels, yet it is the U.S. film industry that generates millions of dollars worldwide with the Harry Potter movies.

What might stop the U.S. leisure services industry from growing, though only temporarily, would be economic downturns. During economic

© MOKreations - Fotolia

The leisure service industry can be hard to define. Cruise ships are part of travel and tourism but include many other industries, including ship building, retail, electronics, and communications.

downturns, such as the one that occurred after the terrorist attacks of September 11, 2001, there were temporary setbacks in the growth of the industry. For instance, the golf segment of the leisure services industry stopped growing after September 11 and has been in decline ever since. The growth of the outdoor adventure industry also began to decline after September 11 (RoperASW 2004). Overall, though, the filling of leisure time with fun has become such a way of life that it is affecting the world economy. The world now has leisure services needs and the U.S. industry stands ready to meet them, for a profit of course.

The essence of the private sector is that it identifies customer needs. For a price, customers pay businesses to meet those needs. Financial management in the private sector is a straightforward process. Transactions take place when customers willingly hand over their money for products and services they want (or perhaps didn't even know they wanted).

Nonprofit Organizations Today

An organization called *GuideStar*, which gathers and analyzes data on nonprofit organizations and makes this information available to the public online, has information on 1.8 million nonprofit organization in the United States (www2.guidestar.org/rxg/analyze-nonprofit-data/index.aspx). GuideStar includes the following:

- 1.8 million IRS-recognized tax-exempt organizations
- 5.4 million IRS Form 990 images
- 3.2 million digitized Form 990 records
- 6.6 million people in the nonprofit sector

In addition, a vast number of organizations operate as **quasi-businesses**, where they make a profit but reinvest that money into expanding the organization.

Nonprofit organizations are exempt from paying federal taxes under IRS Internal Revenue Code 501(c) and must file annual reports with the IRS to substantiate their tax exemption. There are numerous categories under this section, but the most pertinent for leisure services are social and recreational clubs allowed under section 501(c)(7) and charitable organizations allowed under section 501(c)(3).

According to the IRS code, to receive exempt status, a social club must be organized for pleasure, recreation, and other similar purposes and cannot discriminate against any person based on race, color, or religion. "A club may, however, in good faith limit its membership to members of a particular religion in order to further the teachings or principles of that religion and not to exclude individuals of a particular race or color" (IRS 2012a).

Charitable organizations, the other category of tax-exempt organizations, exist for advancing religious, educational, scientific, or literary purposes; performing testing for public safety; fostering national or international amateur sport competition; or preventing cruelty to children or animals. Further, the tax code defines *charitable* as including "relief of the poor, the distressed, or the underprivileged; advancement of religion; advancement of education or science; erecting or maintaining public buildings, monuments, or works; lessening the burdens of government; lessening neighborhood tensions; eliminating prejudice and discrimination; defending human and civil rights secured by law; and combating community deterioration and juvenile delinquency" (IRS 2012b).

Whereas commercial organizations exist to earn and redistribute taxable wealth to owners and shareholders, nonprofit corporations cannot distribute excess revenues to shareholders or owners because there are none. Both commercial and nonprofit organizations are able to retain **surplus money** and use this money as capital for expansion, however. Commercial organizations call this surplus money **profit**, while nonprofits call it **excess revenue over expenditures**. If revenues fall short of covering expenses, both commercial and nonprofit organizations may struggle to survive.

Some nonprofit organizations put substantial funds into hiring and rewarding their corporate leadership, middle-management personnel, and workers. Others use unpaid volunteers, and even executives may work for no compensation, particularly for small, nonprofit, youth athletic organizations.

Some nonprofit leisure services providers do charitable work as defined by the IRS, such as Boys and Girls Clubs. Other nonprofits, such as country clubs, don't do charitable work. Both types have nonprofit status as approved by the IRS, which allows them to make a profit as long as they remain true to their purpose and reinvest the profit into the organization.

Today, tens of thousands of U.S. youth sport organizations are organized as nonprofits so they can accept revenue and not have profits taxed. Some youth sport organizations maintain 501(c)

YMCA

Initially, the religious community was willing to support the missionary objectives of YMCAs, which were charitable organizations operating strictly from donations. Gradually, with the introduction of recreation programs, that changed. Today YMCAs receive almost no funding from religious institutions. Instead, they rely on their entrepreneurial skills for survival and on donations for capital improvements. But they still have 501(c)(3) status because of the charitable work they do.

YMCAs are chartered by states. Some chartered organizations, such as the Chicago YMCA system, have branches that generate revenues in excess of their expenses and other branches that cannot begin to cover their expenses. Cumulatively, these YMCAs break even. Others, such as the Geneva Lakes YMCA in Lake Geneva, Wisconsin, have only one branch, which breaks even as a unit.

YMCAs have developed their own management education and training programs, teaching senior managers methods for providing services and financial skills for managing funds, including fund-raising for capital development. Emanating from the George Williams College (Williams Bay, WI) senior leadership certification program, these education and training programs train YMCA managers according to the YMCA management model.

(3) status and others do not, depending on the organizational mission and whether the organization does something that could be considered as charitable work. For instance, Pony Baseball is a national organization that has **charitable status** because it serves children regardless of their ability to pay. Local club teams generally do not have charitable status because they exist to serve the needs of a small group of children whose parents pay a substantial fee for their participation.

The IRS permits states to allow nonprofit organizations to exist through the corporate chartering process. Nonprofits, therefore, have two governmental reporting relationships. They must answer to state governments through the chartering process and to the federal government through the tax reporting process. Some states require income tax reports as well, further complicating the process.

Nonprofit organizations often compete against commercial and governmental units for clients. For instance, the local YMCA might sell fitness club memberships, competing with a private fitness club or the local park and recreation department. A youth club athletic team might compete with the park district for young baseball players.

Nonprofit leisure services providers exist in many communities to fill the void when neither governmental nor private leisure services are available. Others exist because residents want their leisure needs met in ways that governmental or charitable providers cannot meet. Country clubs, tennis clubs, swimming clubs, and other athletic clubs fall into this category because of their exclusivity.

As in the commercial sector, there are many opportunities for leisure services managers in the nonprofit sector. Some nonprofit providers, such as local youth baseball programs, might not employ full-time staff, but larger providers, such as Scouting, Camp Fire Girls, and YMCAs, do.

In chartered nonprofit organizations, financial management focuses on managing revenues and expenses so the organization will generate enough excess revenue (i.e., profit) to invest back into the organization and sustain its purpose. Accounting rules have to be followed and reports have to be submitted to governmental agencies to make sure this is the case.

Government Units Today

Government spending in the leisure services industry makes up about 1 percent of the entire amount of money spent. However, leisure services provided by the government are a cornerstone of employment in the leisure services field. Many graduates from academic leisure services programs are drawn to the public sector, particularly at the county and municipal levels. State and federal leisure services professionals attain their positions by political appointment or competitive testing.

Federal and State Systems

The federal government and the 50 states provide leisure services, but they represent only a small percentage of the government sector. There are 86,949 other governmental units in the United States, many of which provide leisure services. Let's take a look at how leisure services management differs at the federal, state, and local levels.

The federal government is primarily in the business of maintaining national forests, parks, and recreation areas. Most recreation services are oriented toward park and nature conservation, and most of the user fees come from admissions, parking, and use of camping, food, and accommodation facilities. The federal government provides outdoor services through a number of agencies in various departments. In 1876, Congress created the U.S. Forest Service (USFS) as a special agent of the U.S. Department of Agriculture (USDA). In 1881, the Division of Forestry was created, renamed in 1901 as the Bureau of Forestry, still under the USDA. With a budget of $5.5 billion, over 40 percent of which is spent fighting fires, the USFS has 34,250 employees in 750 locations, including 10,050 firefighters, 737 law enforcement personnel, and 500 scientists managing 193 million acres (78 million hectares).

Under the National Park Service Act, the National Park Service (NPS) was created in 1916 as part of the Department of the Interior. Today, the service manages over 84 million acres (34 million hectares) in 58 park sites throughout the United States, receiving 270 million visitors each year. Other federal agencies that provide park and nature conservation services include the Bureau of Land Management, the Fish and Wildlife Service, and the Bureau of Reclamation. In 2008, the House Subcommittee on Interior, Environment, and Related Agencies asked the Government Accounting Office if all of the park and nature conservation agencies, including the Forest Service, should be managed by the Department of the Interior. At this time, they remain separate.

The 50 state governments provide services similar to the NPS. State departments of natural resources primarily manage their state park systems, some of which have restaurants, hotels, campgrounds, boat rentals, and other supplemental services. Some parks charge admission. For instance, in Illinois, the Department of Natural Resources operates a state park system that includes camping facilities where fees are charged as well as a hotel on Lake Michigan at Illinois Beach State Park and a hotel and conference center at Starved Rock State Park. The NPS operates campgrounds at many national parks and charges fees for admission to Yosemite and other national parks, controlling the number of visitors that are there at any one time.

Federal and state park services could be considered competitors for the same clientele groups, except they have different missions. The federal government had the vision and funding to purchase and conserve areas considered natural wonders long before most states had the will to do so. As a result, most of the best park sites were acquired by the federal government.

The majority of state park systems were created in the 1930s during the Great Depression, when the Civilian Conservation Corps made large numbers of workers available to states to make improvements to properties that states owned but couldn't sell. Since the 1930s, states have been actively acquiring land for conservation and use by the public.

County Park and Recreation Systems

Within states, county governments own and operate parks and open space areas for public usage. These sites fill in gaps that federal and state parks are not capable of filling, providing similar services but on a smaller scale. They generally don't charge fees, but there are exceptions. For instance, county parks might rent boats, operate restaurants, and provide campsites for fees. The Milwaukee County Parks system is a good example. In Milwaukee County, the park department leases marina space for boats, rents soccer fields and picnic shelters, and operates golf courses, traditional swimming pools, and aquatic centers. The system also charges fees for usage of its parking garage in downtown Milwaukee.

The process of managing county park and recreation systems will be considered in this text because it differs greatly from place to place. In some states, like Ohio and Illinois, county park systems are permitted to operate as special districts, separate from county government. In other states, county park systems are departments of the county government. There are more than 4,000 units of county government in the 50 states. Of those, about half operate park systems, either as departments of the general-purpose government or as special taxing districts.

In most of the county systems, the provision of parks and conservation areas is the only mission of the agencies. There are exceptions, however. The Milwaukee County Parks Department, a recent winner of the Gold Medal Award for Excellence in Park and Recreation Management, operates swimming pools, athletic fields, golf courses, and marinas in addition to parks and conservation areas.

Special taxing districts also have been created by state governments that own athletic stadiums and convention centers. These sport authorities use property, sales, excise, and hotel taxes to construct and maintain their facilities. The facilities can be rented to professional and university sport programs, generating millions of dollars in revenue.

Municipal Park and Recreation Systems

At the local level there are over 25,000 municipalities in the United States. A municipality is a city or town with a local government elected by those who live within the boundaries of the city or town. At the municipal level, a multitude of government structures provide park and recreation services. The most common are park and recreation departments of cities, villages, and towns.

Municipal parks are usually created when a town is small, sometimes with as few as 200 residents. By the time a town reaches 1,000 people, it has a park in the center of the community. Because the town is too small to have revenues to sustain a park department, the community park is usually maintained by the public works staff. When a community reaches sufficient size for there to be demands for recreation programs, it hires a few staff to provide these programs. A sufficient town size can be as few as 2,000 people or as many as 50,000, but at some point, political pressure is brought to bear to consider parks and recreation as worthwhile governmental services.

A few states allow park districts to be created at the local level. Ohio has been operating county park districts for 80 years. It also has provisions within state law to create park districts at the local level. States that allow park districts also allow municipalities to provide park and recreation services. Only in Illinois and North Dakota do park districts outnumber park and recreation departments. With the exception of California, which has more than 175 park districts, municipalities and voters in other states that allow park districts have been reluctant to create them.

Financial management of governmental units has unique challenges. Whereas leisure services managers in the commercial sector need to generate profits for their owners, and managers in the nonprofit sector need to generate profits to sustain the purpose of the organization, managers in government need to be transparent—in other words, open to public scrutiny. Because governmental units are permitted to tax the public to provide services, leisure services managers in the public sector must show they are spending that tax money wisely, with accounting systems reflecting **transparency** first and foremost. Transparency in financial management is discussed in detail in chapters 5, 8, and 10. Suffice it to say there are penalties and the potential for ending careers when government leisure services managers try to hide things from the public.

CHALLENGES FACING MANAGERS TODAY

Leisure services managers have their challenges, making them no different than managers in other professions. Leisure services managers, however, are especially vulnerable to changes in the economy and the political environment. When the economy is bad, people defer their vacations until times are better and the government cannot afford to spend money on publicly provided leisure services. This provides challenges to leisure services professionals, particularly financial managers who have the task of funding the services. Unfortunately, when the economy is bad, more people have forced leisure time on their hands because of high unemployment, but the government is not in a position to accommodate their leisure needs because there is no money to do so.

Managing Commercial Leisure Services

As a leisure services manager, you need to understand that each of the leisure sectors—commercial, nonprofit, and public—has its own rules for financial management, some of them formal and others informal. These sectors have their own traditions, rules, and standard operating procedures that not only make them different from each other but also make them different from other services in their sector.

For-profit leisure services need to identify human needs and offer services to meet those needs. These businesses must focus on the customer because it is the transaction between the business and the customer that provides the business its lifeblood. This is known as taking a **marketing approach**.

This singular focus on the customer provides challenges to commercial leisure services that don't exist in the public and nonprofit sectors. With no taxes or donations to sustain commercial leisure services, there is no safety net. These managers walk a tightrope without a net. Stockholders and owners expect a return on their capital, and lenders need to be repaid with interest. Customer needs change and there is a constant threat of competition. Like their counterparts in the other two sectors, commercial leisure services are susceptible to economic downturns and must comply with government regulations.

Leisure services managers in the commercial sector also have advantages compared with managers of nonprofit and public organizations. For instance, much less transparency is required of businesses. The media do not have access to the financial records of privately owned companies, and they have limited access to those of publicly traded companies.

Another advantage for managers in the private sector is that their employees have fewer rights than do employees in the public sector. The salaries and wages of corporate employees can be kept secret from other employees. In some cases, it is actually possible to terminate corporate employees for divulging their pay, allowing managers to use pay as a motivational tool.

Leisure services providers in the private sector do not have public board meetings like governmental units do. There is no state open meetings act requiring that their business be done in public; in fact, to do so would be providing competitors with strategic information. Therefore, setting prices for services is not open to debate in the private sector the way it is in the public sector. And board members of commercial leisure services can be paid substantial amounts of money for attending meetings, but board members of nonprofit and public leisure services agencies are not compensated.

Another advantage of being a commercial manager is the compensation. If a manager is the owner of the company, she is entitled to all of the profits. If the manager works for a corporation that he does not own, there is an opportunity for pay to be commensurate with performance. It has been said that there are only two ways of acquiring wealth in the United States: one is investing well, and the other is owning or being the senior manager of a business. That's the upside. The downside is that the majority of businesses fail.

It takes a business-minded person to manage in the private sector. With a focus on the needs of the customer and the art of the deal, managing in the commercial recreation sector can be rewarding. But walking a high wire without a net has its risks.

Managing Nonprofit Leisure Services

With their primary source of income coming from fees and donations, nonprofit organizations need to focus on revenues to remain financially viable. Just like commercial endeavors, this focus causes nonprofits to be creative in the services they provide to their clients.

Transparency is another issue for nonprofit organizations. Although freedom of information and open meetings acts do not apply to nonprofits, charitable organizations must file IRS reports that reveal financial information and some salaries. These reports are available to the public by request or through Internet sites such as GuideStar. Because they solicit donations from the public and their membership, nonprofits also have an ethical obligation to be transparent about their finances.

Boards of directors for nonprofits are usually appointed or nominated by other board members and then approved by a vote of the board. Sometimes nonprofits have annual membership meetings, where all in attendance approve or elect

The manager of a commercial leisure service, such as a ski resort and lodge, is faced with financial rules and procedures that are different than those in the nonprofit and public sectors.

those nominated for the board or even nominate a different person. Also, board meetings are not open to the public or regulated by state open meetings acts, so replacing board members can be done without public scrutiny. Nonprofit board members are rarely compensated for their service to the organization. In fact, their primary responsibility may be to bring money into the agency through their fund-raising efforts.

Nonprofit leisure services managers share the challenge of customer relations with their business counterparts. But for managers of charitable nonprofits, there's a political dimension of maintaining the goodwill of customers who also may be donors. For example, you may feel it's time to raise prices, but in order to maintain the donor or customer relationship, you do not.

Managing employees can be different from the other sectors as well. Because employees are generally not rewarded by sharing profits, managing nonprofit employees is similar to managing public employees. It is generally done using sociological principles of group motivation, which suggest that people behave differently in groups than they do as individuals.

Nonprofit managers focus on how their agency generates revenues from fund-raising and fees, who receives free services, how the agency judiciously spends its money, and how the agency maintains an environment where clients can be donors and employees only have nice things to say about the organization.

The good news is that nonprofit leisure services organizations usually succeed. Of the new nonprofit organizations created each year, it is estimated that less than 2.3 percent fail each year (Bowen, Nygren, Turner, and Duffy 1994). This is partly due to the stability of their revenue streams and the safety net that donors provide. When nonprofits are chartered by states, the people who charter them usually have established a need for their services and sources of revenues for their operations. People who pursue a career in nonprofit leisure services often are intrinsically motivated, wanting the security of a stable environment while performing a service to the community.

Managing Government Leisure Services

It has been said that public administration is like managing in a fishbowl—nothing is private. Part of the reason is that government taxes its citizens. Unlike businesses or nonprofit organizations where revenues are exchanged through transactions that both parties agree upon, taxation is not voluntary.

To protect its citizens, the United States has built a system of checks and balances that permit taxpayers to see how their tax money is spent. Called *transparency*, these laws require all but personnel information to be public. In addition, meetings must be announced and take place in public, and individuals or companies doing business with the governmental unit must bid competitively for that business. The salaries of public leisure services managers are public information, as are the salaries of everyone within the governmental unit, whereas salaries in corporate leisure services are private.

Another challenge in managing governmental units is that public employees have greater rights than do business and nonprofit employees. In most states, public employees cannot be hired and fired by managers without the consent of the elected board. This means employees have the right to a board hearing before termination.

Boards in the public sector are unique as well. The governing boards levying taxes and approving budget expenditures must be elected. Appointed park and recreation department boards may have advisory authority, but only the elected boards have the power to decide. This means that directors of park and recreation departments have two boards as their bosses, the city council and the appointed advisory board. Sometimes leisure services managers have three bosses: the city council, the park board, and the city manager. This can make managing a public leisure services agency the most difficult of all assignments.

Working for an elected board in an environment where everything a manager does is public information adds a dimension of politics to the management process. Nonprofit leisure services managers might worry about offending potential donors, but if governmental leisure services managers offend a member of the public, that person can run for election to the governing board, as can a disgruntled employee.

Another challenge of managing governmental leisure agencies is the need for two types of financial management skills. One is the management of tax-supported services, typically parks, which are used for free and supported entirely from tax revenues. The other is the operation of recreation programs and facilities, which generate self-sustaining revenues from user fees. Managers in the

Rockford Park District

In recent years, *Money Magazine* has repeatedly rated Rockford, Illinois, at the bottom of the list of livable cities in the United States. One reason is that the Rockford school district has been under a court-supervised desegregation order since the 1980s, underscoring the racial divide and tensions that have given the city a bad reputation. Another is that the Rockford economy has been dependent on manufacturing jobs, a sector in decline, and the unemployment rate has been higher than the national average in most years.

A bright spot is the Rockford Park District. Established as a special-purpose governmental unit under the Illinois Park District Code, the district has been a shining example of how governmental units can work. During the tenure of the district's recently retired executive director Webs Norman, the Rockford Park District has amassed leisure services that are the envy of other governmental units. Having been a Gold Medal Award for Excellence in Park and Recreation Management finalist 12 times and having won the award 6 of those times, the park district has reached a level of national recognition that only two other agencies of its population size have achieved.

The formula for success in the Rockford Park District is its business model. Because its property tax base has been at a plateau for decades, the park district has built, bought, or otherwise acquired revenue-generating facilities, including five community golf courses, a championship golf course, five neighborhood swimming pools, a destination water park, a racket club, a fitness center, two ice rinks, an outdoor soccer and softball complex, an indoor soccer facility, and a riverboat. It also has numerous neighborhood and community parks. Except for the parks, all of these facilities operate at or close to a break-even basis, dependent on fees for their operating support.

In the management system of the park district, each facility has a department head who is accountable for its financial performance. There is a central marketing department, which oversees most of the facilities' promotional efforts. But the staff members of each facility take responsibility for promotional efforts as well, knowing that the financial health of their department is directly related to them having a job.

Based on the theory that there is a dichotomy between politics and administration, new board members are oriented in their role as policy makers, allowing staff the responsibility of implementing board policies. When Norman retired, the finance director, Tim Dimke, was the natural selection as a successor. The skills required to oversee multiple governmental and enterprise funds would have made any other candidate for the position virtually unqualified to oversee the business model that the Rockford Park District operates. Dimke has added a dimension of professional financial management that many districts would be wise to emulate.

public sector are, therefore, running governmental units, providing tax- and fee-supported services in a transparent arena where disgruntled employees or members of the public can run for their boards.

Governmental units that provide leisure services have had their tax funding reduced in recent years, forcing their managers to take a more businesslike approach to revenue generation. But taking a businesslike approach does not change the legal requirements of being transparent, adding another level of complexity to their management responsibilities.

Skills Needed for Managing Leisure Services

Managers in all the sectors need to be good communicators and knowledgeable about accounting, marketing, and organizational theory. Coursework should be broad, including economics, finance, political science, psychology, sociology, and organizational behavior. If you want to own or manage a large leisure services business, you might want to focus on business administration. If you want to be a manager in the public sector, you should take courses in public administration and park and recreation management. Some universities have niche programs in sport management, tourism, and nonprofit administration. Universities with programs in parks and recreation or leisure services administration should give you the skills and knowledge base to work in any of the three sectors, including coursework that provides a solid understanding of financial management.

To work in the public sector, you need to understand government accounting, which is different from business or nonprofit accounting. To maintain the required levels of transparency, governmental units have much more complex accounting rules compared with business and nonprofit accounting. If you oversee the operation of parks, your skills need to include those related to park maintenance and conservation. If you manage recreation programs or facilities, skills need to include marketing and financial management as well as skills related to the recreation facility or program.

If it seems that management in the public sector is the most difficult of the three sectors, why would someone choose to do it? The answer is that it is just as rewarding as working for a nonprofit organization. Serving the public has its intrinsic rewards. There are also long-term financial rewards. Government service is one of the few professions where there are still **pension** programs available that provide a **defined annual income** no matter how long the manager lives after retirement. In the private and nonprofit sectors, defined annual incomes are becoming less common. In those sectors, retirement benefits are the amount of wealth that can be acquired during the individual's work life. Whatever you have in your 401k or other investments is what you have as a nest egg for the rest of your life. But for a government retiree, a defined lifetime annual benefit provides security for life.

SUMMARY

The leisure services environment comprises three sectors: commercial, nonprofit, and public. The public sector was the first, originating as municipal park systems in the mid-1800s. The nonprofit sector was created shortly after in response to the settlement needs of newly arriving immigrants, eventually adopting recreation programs into its mission. In the 1920s, when an American middle class emerged and it was clear that the public and nonprofit sectors would not be willing or able to meet their leisure needs, the private sector stepped in, creating leisure businesses.

Today, the three sectors of the leisure services industry coexist, with federal, state, and county governments focusing on parks and the conservation of natural habitats; local units of government providing park and recreation services; nonprofits providing facility or sport-based leisure services where governments are unwilling or unable to do so; and businesses identifying and fulfilling the leisure needs of the public in pursuit of the fees that customers are willing to pay. The three sectors can compete, such as for fitness customers, but mostly they don't compete because of their differing objectives.

The challenges of management in the three sectors have many similarities, but there are several unique financial management practices and political realities. Managers of for-profit leisure services need to focus on revenue generation through meeting customer needs. Nonprofit managers need to address a higher level of transparency and to raise funds. Public-sector managers exist in a totally transparent world where there are political consequences to their decisions. And no matter the sector, the prevailing condition of the local, state, and national economy can present both obstacles and opportunities for effective leisure services financial management.

Visit the Web Resource

For case studies, sample financial statements, key terms, and more, please visit the web resource at www.HumanKinetics.com/LeisureServicesFinancialManagement

chapter 2

Managing Resources

Learning Outcomes

After completing this chapter, students will be able to do the following:

- Explain the human factor in economics and differences between macroeconomics and microeconomics.
- Identify the economic theories of Adam Smith, Karl Marx, and John Maynard Keynes and how modern economic forces affect leisure services.
- Define the economic principles of supply and demand, product life cycle, marginal utility, and competition.
- Demonstrate an understanding of bonds as a method of borrowing money.
- Explain why leisure services managers need to know about banking, interest rates, and the bond industry.

To be successful managers, leisure services professionals need to be adept at managing resources within the prevailing economic environment. Those resources are money, goods and services, and people. A basic knowledge of economics is essential for many professions, including leisure services. Managers need to understand macro- and microeconomics and have a historical perspective of the social and political forces that have shaped the U.S. economy from colonial days to the present. Important economic concepts for leisure services financial management include supply and demand, product life cycle, marginal utility, and competition.

The first half of the chapter focuses on these four topics. The second half of the chapter focuses on financial principles related to borrowing money, interest rates, and the bond industry. This is a critical knowledge set for financial management of leisure services.

BASIC ECONOMICS

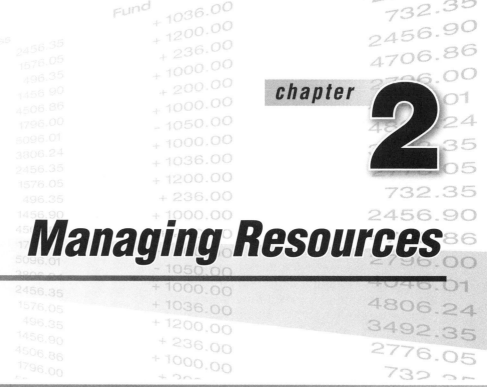

Economics is a social science studying how markets work, and a market is a segment of the economy where goods and services are exchanged. The study of markets includes the production, distribution, and consumption of goods and services. Economics also is a behavioral science, one dimension of which seeks to understand how human beings react to the availability of scarce resources and what they are willing to do to obtain those resources. **Social science** is the study of human society and includes the fields of sociology, anthropology, economics, psychology, political science, education, and history. **Behavioral science** is a subset of social sciences involving the study of actions and reactions of humans and animals.

Macroeconomics and Microeconomics

The study of large economies that exist at the world, national, state, and regional levels is the branch of economics called **macroeconomics**. It focuses on issues such as unemployment, business cycles, interest rates, finance, trade, currencies, output, and taxation policies. The goal of macroeconomics is making forecasts to shape economic policies at the national and international levels that will lead toward full employment and create national wealth.

The branch of economics focusing on the study of smaller economies, such as local or organizational markets, is **microeconomics**. It focuses on issues such as supply and demand so organizations can set prices for their products and services. Microeconomic analysis strives to understand market forces. This analysis gives organizations information about product life cycles so the organizations can survive and prosper over the long term.

The People Factor

Because both macro- and microeconomics involve people and because we can never be sure how people will act, economics is considered a soft science. **Soft sciences** are different from hard sciences such as chemistry, physics, or microbiology. **Hard sciences** begin with theories that can be tested as hypotheses. In hard sciences, if testing yields definitive findings, these findings may become laws, which are always true.

For example, take gravity, a physical law. When Isaac Newton saw that objects of a specified weight fell from a specific height at the same rate of speed, he theorized that there was a physical force called *gravity* that caused this phenomenon. When the hypothesis was tested in a laboratory setting by dropping an object from a specific height and measuring the speed, scientists proved Newton's theory and the law of gravity was thus identified.

Soft sciences, such as economics, are not like physics, where there are laws that are always true. In soft sciences, also known as social sciences, human beings are involved. Because human beings do not always act and react the same, understanding the impact of economics means understanding that when people change, economic systems change.

For instance, the expectation that human beings could be forced to work against their will became part of the Southern economic system in the United States before the Civil War. When that expectation changed, so did the economic system. That's why economies are constantly changing—human behavior and expectations drive economic changes.

Historical Perspectives

It is generally understood that the Greek philosophers Socrates, Plato, and Aristotle were the first **economists**. But the first economist who had a noticeable impact on the American economic system, and arguably leisure services financial management, was **Adam Smith**.

Adam Smith and Laissez-Faire

Living in Scotland during the 1700s, Smith observed that the wealth of nations was determined by their ability to improve their efficiency in producing the goods and services required to sustain themselves. If these nations could produce more than they needed, they could sell the excess goods and services to less efficient societies, thereby obtaining wealth. Smith believed that the markets should be left alone by governments as much as possible. Suggesting that government regulation would only constrict the private sector from growing and creating wealth, Smith's philosophy became part of the American capitalistic economic system, one of laissez-faire government regulation.

Laissez-faire economics is one of the guiding principles of capitalism, holding that economic systems should be free from government intervention and driven only by market forces. **Capitalism** is an economic system where individuals can accumulate wealth through private ownership of property and businesses, as opposed to **communism**, which abolishes private ownership in favor of a classless society.

The founding fathers of the United States obviously agreed with Smith's philosophy, because the system of government created by the Constitution imposes few government controls over the nation's capitalist system, with the exception of the monetary system and the management of trade between states and other nations. The Constitution also limits the taxation powers of the federal government. In other words, the federal government should stay out of the way of businesses.

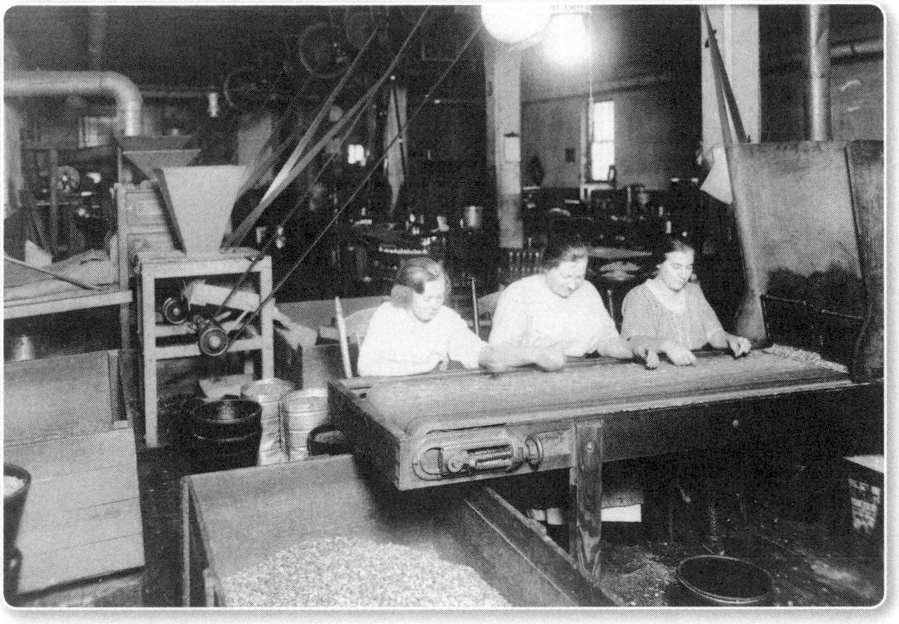

Courtesy of the Library of Congress

Thanks to factories made possible by the Industrial Revolution and laissez-faire policies against government regulation of business, the United States prospered by exporting goods to other countries.

It is commonly thought that the creation of the U.S. Constitution advanced individual rights; however, that's not entirely true. Slavery was accommodated as an economic system; women were not permitted full citizenship, including ownership of property; and even white men were not all equal under the Constitution. States had the right to determine voter eligibility, and most states only allowed landowners to vote. Because property taxes were the most unavoidable way to raise taxes, it seemed fair that only those people who paid taxes should have the right to vote. Those who did not pay could not vote, suggesting a rule of "No representation without taxation" rather than the reverse.

During the first century of the United States as a nation, there was virtually no regulation of business, just the way Adam Smith would have wanted it. In the late 1700s and early 1800s, many other developing nations began to embrace the U.S. economic model and followed suit. An **economic model** is a way of generalizing a complex economic concept or behavior expressed in the form of an equation, graph, or illustration for the purpose of predicting the future.

As can be imagined, with a labor force flowing into the United States from other countries, American businessmen had the upper hand. It was the Industrial Revolution that led to factories producing goods that were exported to the world. Adam Smith's vision had become a reality; the wealth of the United States was being created.

Karl Marx and Marxism

Other social scientists took notice of the negative benefits of industrialization. One of them was **Karl Marx**, a 19th-century German philosopher who became a political and economic revolutionary. Marx observed that, without any real power in the hands of workers, industrialists were able to pay workers low wages and force them to work long hours. According to Marx, the idea of workers having leisure time to enjoy life was being defeated by the greed of industrialists. The more hours industrialists could force laborers to work at low pay, the richer the industrialists got. The wealth of the nation and the benefits of leisure time went only to them. Marx's theory of power to the worker is known as **Marxism**, a political and economic system that advocates class struggle to create historical change and replaces capitalism with communism.

Although Marx should not be considered the founder of communism, he had an influence on its creation. He also was part of a growing number of voices advocating the unionization of workers, a way to shift power to working people so they could share in the wealth of their nation. During the late 19th century, unions and their ability to strike for higher wages had at least some support from the U.S. government. In addition, under President **Theodore Roosevelt**, the federal government attempted to break up monopolies that benefited the industrialists who came to be viewed as robber barons.

To constrain the supply of labor to these industrialists, in the early 1920s limitations were placed on immigration from other countries. As a result, wages increased, creating a middle class with leisure time. The YMCA saw it coming and adapted its organizational strategies. In addition, opportunists in the private sector started businesses to meet customers' leisure needs, namely the resort hotel business, which became more than just a vacation option for rich people.

John Maynard Keynes and Keynesian Economics

The **Great Depression** began in the 1930s, a time when even more government intervention became politically popular. With a 25 percent unemployment rate bringing **Franklin Delano Roosevelt** to the presidency, the political change brought a new economic philosophy as well. The second Roosevelt was a disciple of **John Maynard Keynes**, an economist who sought to improve on the economic theory of Adam Smith without going as far as Karl Marx. Keynes advocated a greater role for the federal government in managing the economy, and the Roosevelt administration agreed.

Playing a greater role in the economy, the federal government became a supporter of unionization, passing laws defending workers' rights to organize and strike. The government also believed its role in employment was more than sitting on the sidelines hoping the free market system would correct itself. The government could actually hire workers, which is what it did, creating jobs programs such as the Civilian Conservation Corps (CCC). The CCC built and improved state, federal, county, and municipal parks all over the country.

The government's response to the Great Depression is relevant to leisure services management and the topic of economics because it reveals a deeply rooted cultural value that embraces the **free enterprise system**, where anyone can own or operate a business with minimal government restrictions. Adam Smith's philosophy articulates those values, but Karl Marx's arguments against unregulated free enterprise are what led to John Maynard Keynes' modification of the role of the federal government in regulation. This modification created today's modern economic philosophy, known as **Keynesian economics**, which holds that some federal regulation is good.

However, the extent of the federal government's role in regulation is still unresolved. For the past 70 years, economists have sought a return to a less regulated economy. Political parties and candidates also have their own views, which become part of the national debate about how much regulation should be imposed on the private sector.

Impact of Modern Economic Forces on Leisure Services

The **Federal Reserve Board** is a seven-member board that oversees the U.S. banking industry and establishes monetary policy, namely interest rates and availability of credit. It also monitors the economic health of the country. In the 1990s, the board reduced interest rates, leading to an economic boom. From that point on, managing the money supply by raising and lowering interest rates has been one of the most important ways the federal government involves itself in managing the economy. High interest rates tend to slow down borrowing, which in turn slows demand for big-ticket items such as homes and automobiles. As the demand for homes and autos declines, employment in those industries and their related suppliers declines. With fewer people working, there is less purchasing power in the economy, and other sectors decline as well, especially those related to vacations and other leisure services. Decreasing interest rates is thought to have the reverse effect.

Managing the economy by raising and lowering interest rates is a simplistic theoretical construct. In reality, managing the economy is much more complicated. Under Keynesian economic theory, when the economy is weak, the federal government can and should do more. Just like in the 1930s, the government has a role in employing people. The federal government also has other tools that have a positive influence on the economy. It can pump money into the economy by increasing government spending on public works projects, such as the construction of highways, public buildings, and public recreation facilities. This means that periods of economic decline can actually be an opportunity for public leisure services agencies to expand, as they did during the Great Depression.

On the other hand, the public sector often sees a decline in tax revenues when there is high unemployment. When people don't work, they don't pay taxes. Reduced tax revenues during economic downturns are a reality for all governmental units, including the federal government. Lower income taxes put the national parks, forests, and recreation areas under financial stress. At the state level, reduced sales and income taxes put the state park system under financial pressure, and at the municipal level, declining sales and income taxes can lead to local leisure services agencies reducing their budgets. At the national level, when tax revenues decline during an economic downturn, the federal government is forced to engage in deficit spending to continue to operate and stimulate the economy. **Deficit spending** is defined as the government spending more than it has, financed by borrowing rather than taxation. But state and local governments do not have the option of deficit spending over the long run and are forced to balance their budgets, with leisure services often being the first to get cut.

© Andrew Kazmierski - Fotolia

Visiting a drive-through safari park is cheaper than taking a trip to Africa. In tough economic times, people spend less money on vacations and other leisure services.

As a leisure services manager, you need to understand how the economy is managed because the actions of the federal government affect all three sectors—private, nonprofit, and public—both directly and indirectly. When the government borrows too much money, it can limit the availability of capital and affect the ability of state and local governments to borrow money. It can dry up the availability of capital funding for leisure services in the private sector. It can also affect the public psychologically, which has political and economic consequences for leisure services as a whole.

In the spring of 2009, Congress considered an economic stimulus package that involved an increase of about $700 billion in national debt. One element of the package was improving the National Mall in Washington, DC, which is maintained by the NPS. Political opponents expressed outrage, claiming it was a luxury expenditure that had no place in a stimulus package. They obviously overlooked (or chose to ignore) that Franklin Roosevelt's **New Deal** of the 1930s, designed to promote economic recovery and social reform and reduce the effects of the Great Depression, had similar projects. The disagreement over the package caused enough political turmoil that the sponsors of the bill deleted the NPS funding for the mall.

Tough economic times can unleash powerful political forces that affect leisure services at the state level as well. During the recession of the 1970s, California voters passed **Proposition 13** in 1978, which severely reduced the property taxes that local governments could levy. During the campaign for Proposition 13, political supporters of lower taxes used park districts and municipal park and recreation departments as political symbols of why government spending had become a reason taxpayers should vote for the proposition. Proponents argued that basket-weaving classes offered at no fee by public leisure services were a wasteful use of taxpayer money. As a result of the passage of Proposition 13, all local units of government had their tax revenues reduced, not just those offering basket-weaving classes.

Economic booms and declines affect leisure businesses and nonprofit organizations even more than those in the public sector. Without the guaranteed sources of tax revenues provided to governmental agencies, businesses and nonprofits are totally dependent on the ability of their customers to pay fees for their services. During the 2009 economic recession, the total dollars spent on vacations and other commercial leisure services in the United States declined by the same rate as unemployment, about 10 percent. Nonprofit leisure services organizations saw declines not only in their revenues from activity fees but also in the amount of money they received from donors to make capital improvements. As a result, organizations could anticipate that capital improvements would also decline. The question is, how can understanding these economic conditions help leisure services managers cope with the effects on their businesses, nonprofit organizations, or governmental units?

Why You Need to Understand Economics

Leisure services managers need to understand economics because leisure services are such a large part of the American economy. Throughout U.S. history, leisure services managers have been able to develop services and financial resources that allowed their agencies to survive and prosper thanks to the ability to anticipate how changing social and economic behaviors would affect their agencies. As discussed earlier, the YMCA adapted to changes in U.S. society created by changing immigration patterns from 1850 to 1920. The YMCA is now a large national organization serving millions of people. Other organizations, such as Hull House, which spurred a national movement to address the social, economic, and recreational needs of working people, served an important purpose in their time but faded out as people became more self-reliant and other government and nonprofit agencies took over their responsibilities.

In many ways, understanding economics is all about understanding the present and anticipating changes in economic conditions in the future. Economists work to understand the present and predict the future the same way meteorologists predict the weather, by gathering data and building **models**. Models can be simple or complex formulas. Of late, models are created on computers and tested. Every large bank or investment company has macroeconomists working for them to build these models because correctly predicting the future can be very profitable.

Leisure services managers need a basic understanding of how the economy works because as the economy changes, so does the financial environment. Again, using the YMCA as an example, the initial dependence on contributions from

Jane Addams and Hull House

When Jane Addams, known for her influence in social work and the national playground movement, founded Hull House on Chicago's South Side in 1889, the house attracted many European immigrants, especially women. The objective of Hull House, as stated in its charter, was "to provide a center for a higher civic and social life; to institute and maintain educational and philanthropic enterprises, and to investigate and improve the conditions in the industrial districts of Chicago" (The Social Welfare History Project n.d., par. 1).

By 1911, Hull House had grown to 13 buildings. In 1912, the Hull House complex was completed with the addition of a summer camp, called the *Bowen Country Club,* which provided social, educational, and artistic programs. The Chicago Hull House spurred a national movement for helping the working poor, and by 1920, there were almost 500 similar settlement houses nationwide.

Hull House established Chicago's first public playground, bathhouse, and gymnasium in 1893, and Addams became a founding member of the Playground Association of America in 1906, which advocated for playgrounds nationwide. Addams fostered the play movement and the research and service fields of leisure, youth, and human services. Addams argued in *The Spirit of Youth and the City Streets* (1909) that play and recreation programs are needed because cities are destroying the spirit of youth.

According to the University of Illinois (2012), among Addams' civic activities, she was vice president of the Camp Fire Girls and a member of the executive board of the Playground Association of America. According to Linnea M. Anderson (2007), the association's first annual conference, called the *Play Congress,* was held in Chicago in 1907. The program clearly illustrated important themes of democracy, citizenship, and morality that continued to guide recreation through the mid-20th century. At this conference, Jane Addams spoke on public recreation and social morality. Unfortunately, in 2011 Hull House suspended operations due to lack of funding.

References

Addams, J. 1909. *The Spirit of Youth and the City Streets*. New York: Macmillan.

Anderson, L.M. 2007. "'The Playground of Today is the Republic of Tomorrow': Social Reform and Organized Recreation in the USA, 1890-1930s." www.infed.org/playwork/organized_recreation_and_playwork_1890-1930s.htm.

The Social Welfare History Project. n.d. "Hull House—circ. 1910." www.socialwelfarehistory.com/organizations/hull-house-circ-1910/.

University of Illinois at Chicago. 2012. "Jane Addams Hull-House Museum." www.uic.edu/uic/about/community/janeadams-hullhouse-museum.shtml.

churches and independent donors was part of the YMCA's financial environment when it was created. As immigrants' need for YMCA services declined, donors to the YMCA declined as well. They didn't see a reason for making donations when there was no one to serve. Foreseeing the changing environment, the YMCA found new financial resources that helped it survive and grow.

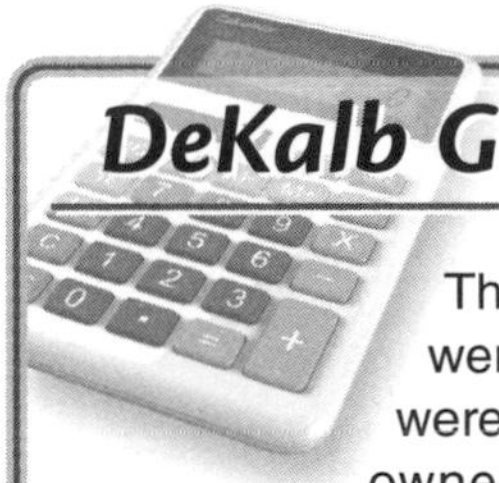

DeKalb Golf Courses

The earliest U.S. golf courses were built in the late 1800s and were almost exclusively privately owned. Today, there are about 25,000 golf courses, about half of which are publicly owned. Although most golf courses are still private ventures, it is not unusual for public agencies to acquire them during times of economic stress.

Buena Vista Golf Course, located on the north side of DeKalb, Illinois, was built in the early 1970s by a private developer to enhance the value of his single-family-home lots around the course. Buena Vista was then purchased by a charitable foundation, which donated it to the DeKalb Park District in 1979.

DeKalb was home to another privately owned golf course on the south side of town, the River Heights Golf Course. Once Buena Vista was acquired by the park district, River Heights was at a competitive disadvantage because Buena Vista had no bank loans to repay. Buena Vista could take the profits it would have spent to repay the bank loans and spend them on course improvements instead, which it did in the early 1980s. During the late 1970s and early 1980s, the United States experienced an economic recession. By 1985, the number of people who played golf had so diminished at River Heights that the course had become unprofitable to operate. The park district then purchased River Heights using tax money and expanded it to an 18-hole course.

Economic Principles

Economic principles are principles that early economists developed and that all economists agree upon. These principles are supply and demand, industry and product life cycles, marginal utility, and competition. They are assumptions about how markets work and form the basis of other economic assumptions.

Supply and Demand

Supply and demand governs all markets and is the most basic economic principle. If a product or service is in high demand but in low supply, buyers can expect it to be more expensive than if the supply matched the demand. And if the product or service is in great supply but the demand is low, buyers can expect the price to be lower than if the supply matched the demand.

The demand curve shows how that relationship exists in a two-dimensional matrix (figure 2.1). The assumption is that supply will always grow to meet demand, and the intersection of the demand curve with the quantity determines the price of the product or service, P1 and P2. Therefore, because demand is the most important element, it determines price. The graph shows that for two different demands and therefore two different points of intersection, there would be two different prices for the product, depending on the demand, at two different quantities, Q1 and Q2. Assuming demand increases or decreases at a given quantity, prices would increase or decrease accordingly.

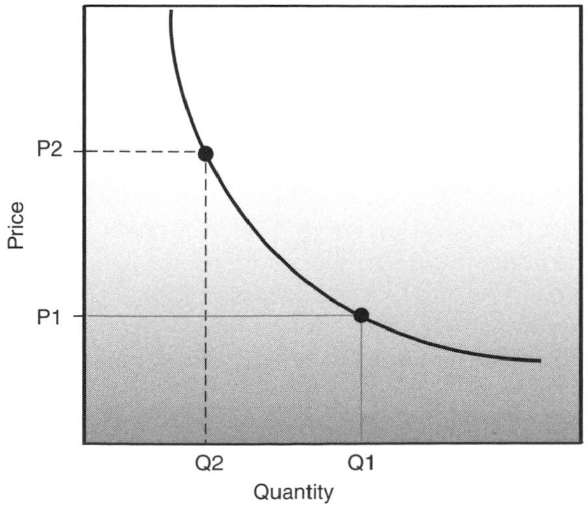

Figure 2.1 The demand for a product or service is the main factor in determining the price.
Adapted from http://en.wikipedia.org/wiki/File:Supply-and-demand.svg

The ability of businesses to predict demand for a product or service is key. Producing goods and services when demand does not exist will lower price below the cost of production. There are defunct silent-movie production companies that did not adapt by providing talkies. There are cellphone makers who did not adapt by making smartphones and now are about to become obsolete. There are textbook manufacturers who don't provide their material electronically. There are movie rental companies like Blockbuster that haven't adapted their services the way Redbox has. There are senior citizen centers that continue to provide potluck lunches and trips when a new generation of older Americans wants fitness and outdoor recreation programs. Not being able to meet demand soon enough can allow competitors to capture the market for demand of goods and services and seriously impair the ability of a business to be profitable.

The same is true for nonprofit organizations. Overestimating demand can allow overproduction of services to drive down prices of services, and underproduction allows other nonprofit organizations or businesses to meet customer needs first, capturing market share. Government organizations don't die as easily, but if they can't predict future demand for services, they can suffer negative financial and political consequences.

Industry or Product Life Cycle

To predict the demand for a leisure service, managers need to be familiar with the economic concept of product or industry life cycle. Leisure services go through the same life cycles that other products or services do. The cycle begins with a **market introduction stage**, where the product or service is new and unfamiliar to most potential customers (figure 2.2). At this point of the life cycle, costs to produce the good or service are high, demand is low, and customers have to be prompted to purchase it.

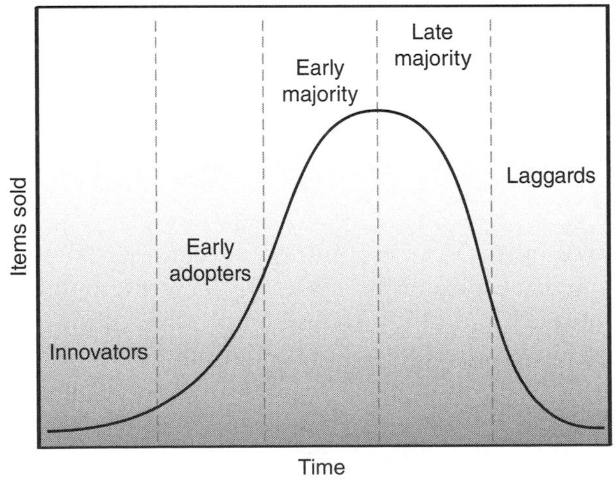

Figure 2.2 The industry or product life cycle, broken down by customer type. Innovators are the primary customers during the market introduction stage. The growth stage is when early adopters and the early majority become customers. The maturation stage is when the late majority makes up the customer base, and the saturation and decline stage sees the laggards finally become customers.
Adapted from http://en.wikipedia.org/wiki/File:DiffusionOfInnovation.png

During the second stage, known as the **growth stage**, producers can develop economies of scale, driving down production costs as demand increases. Competitors also become aware of the product and enter the market, further reducing prices. During this stage, the product or industry has gained acceptance and grows to reach its peak. During the **maturation stage**, the market for the product or service has peaked and prices are so low that some producers are no longer able to make a profit and thus they drop out of the market. During the **saturation and decline stage**, producers are struggling to survive; it doesn't seem that any of them are able to make a profit, and more producers go out of business.

The likelihood that businesses and nonprofit organizations will survive during the maturation and saturation and decline phases of product and service life cycles is often dependent on their abilities to find new markets for their products or services or new products and services to produce. Governments that subsidize their services with taxes can survive, but there can be political consequences associated with charging taxpayers for services they don't use. Municipal parks are a good example. Municipal parks supported by taxes may be in decline as U.S. society changes. With children staying indoors more and more, in the relatively near future it may be that municipal parks are not used extensively, raising the issue of whether municipal park and recreation agencies should continue to expand these services.

Marginal Utility

The idea that taxpayers may not value parks in the future is based on another economic principle, **marginal utility**. Marginal utility advanced after Keynesian economic theory was introduced. It holds that the use of a good or service is what determines its value, not the cost of labor to produce the good or service. The opposing view is the **labor theory of value**, offered by Adam Smith and supported by the Marxist school of economic theory, which suggests that labor costs are more relevant in estimating the cost of a good or service.

According to marginal utility, if a good or service has utility within the economy, it has value. If it does not have utility, its value should not be based on its cost. In other words, justifying the cost of providing parks that few people use is not a sound basis for defending the need for parks.

Providers of leisure services in the governmental sector should, therefore, identify the value to the community before deciding to expand their services.

Competition

Since the 1920s, when commercial enterprises began meeting the leisure needs of many Americans, **competition** for customers has changed the face of the industry. Competition occurs when two or more businesses, nonprofit organizations, governmental units, or any combination of the three attempt to sell their products or services to the same customers. Competition is the fiercest when product or industry life cycles are in their maturation or saturation and decline stages or when the marginal utility of a product or service is high.

Competition is generally held to be a good thing, benefiting customers with lower prices, better products or services, and greater availability and generally increasing marginal utility to customers. This is called **cooperative competition**. **Destructive competition** occurs when organizations seek to destroy each other so that the winner can take all by creating a monopoly. Typically, elements of cooperative and destructive competition exist in all arenas. Therefore, as a leisure services manager you need to understand not only how competition benefits the customer but also how your ability to address competition can lead to the success or demise of your organization.

Competition is a necessary element of a Keynesian economy. Marxists might disagree, focusing only on its destructive elements. But the Communist economic experiment, where everything is government owned and thus has no room for competition, has largely been judged a failure. Competition is a reality all over the world whether we like it or not. It is everywhere: in sports where championships and money are at stake, in politics where elections are at stake, and even in education where a limited number of scholarships outstrip the demand.

Competition involves individuals and organizations doing their best to win. In the case of leisure services, one way to win is to make money by providing services for fees or taxes. **Taxes** are required payments of money to government that are used to provide public goods and services for the benefit of the local community, state, or nation. Communities compete for tax-paying residents just as fitness centers compete for customers.

Competition is one aspect of designing a product or service to meet the needs of the customer. Often organizations face limitations on how well they can compete. Governmental units, for example, compete with each other in the provision of parks. Parks improve quality of life and play a role in attracting residents to a community. On the other hand, the tax base or availability of open space in a community can be a constraint in competing for residents. Access to capital can be a constraint for a private, for-profit fitness center, just as access to donations for capital construction can be a constraint for a nonprofit fitness center.

An organization must be realistic about its constraints and determine what it can and cannot do. Most organizations try to be competitive by doing a **SWOT analysis** of their organization first. *SWOT* stands for analyzing the **s**trengths and **w**eaknesses of an organization as well as the **o**pportunities and **t**hreats of the environment. If the organization's weakness is its tax base or access to capital, it needs to offset its weaknesses by focusing on its strengths, such as having employees who provide outstanding customer service. If the environment has the threat of macroeconomic conditions, such as slowing growth in the national economy, the (hopefully short-lived) lull provides an opportunity for the agency to focus on customer service training.

BASIC FINANCE

Understanding economics provides a foundation for understanding finance, but finance is a somewhat different discipline. **Finance** is the science of funds management, focusing on investments in the banking industry and other **financial markets**. Leisure services managers are intimately involved in banking and investments, so they need to understand the science of finance.

Banking Industry

Banks take your money and loan it to other people. For instance, a bank might pay you 1 percent annual interest on your savings account. If you deposited $10,000 in the account, you would have $10,100 in your account at the end of the year. The bank might also charge 7 percent interest on the car you bought. If the bank loaned you $10,000 for the car and you made no payments during the year, you would owe them $10,700 at the end of the year. (Of course, you would make payments during the year, so it wouldn't be quite that much, but you get the idea.) The bank makes $700 profit off your money.

If most people had $10,000, they would buy the car outright and save the $700. What happens more often is that people have less than the amount they need for a car or house. Most people take what little savings they have and put it in a savings account so they can earn some interest on their money, and they borrow the large amount for their house or car, paying interest on what they owe. The only way a bank can have enough money to make loans is to have a large number of small depositors, make a small number of loans to large borrowers, or get the money to make loans from the **Federal Reserve System**. The Federal Reserve, created by Congress in 1913, is the central banking system for the United States and is governed by a board that regulates interest rates and other monetary policies. All banks are members of the Federal Reserve, and the Federal Reserve supervises and regulates the banking industry.

Banks keep a small portion of their deposits as reserves so that if a few depositors need their money, they can access it immediately. In the 1930s, there was a rush on the banks. Everyone wanted their money back, but the banks did not have enough in reserve. As a result, the banking system collapsed, creating the Great Depression, where no one could borrow money and the economy was severely depressed. Since then, the banking industry has been rebuilt, with deposits federally insured up to $250,000, and banking has evolved into a complex maze of lending institutions.

Currently, banks exist as private businesses, incorporated by the states and regulated by the Federal Reserve and Federal Deposit Insurance Corporation (FDIC). The stockholders of banks still expect banks to make a profit and return that profit to stockholders through dividends or growth in the value of the stock. But banks have found new and creative ways to make a profit.

Leisure services managers work with banks and investors on many levels. For-profit and nonprofit leisure services deposit their funds in banks, using bank-operated checking accounts to disburse funds. They also borrow money from banks to create new **capital assets**, tangible properties such as land, buildings, and equipment that are intended to last a long time and generate more business. Public or tax-supported leisure services have bank checking accounts as well, but their loans are often in the form of **general obligation bonds**, also known as **tax-free municipal bonds**, on which the purchasing banks pay no income tax for interest earned. A general obligation bond is a common type of municipal bond that is repaid through tax revenue or fees. Municipal bonds are usually used to raise money for improvements in infrastructure or other aspects of the municipality or governmental unit.

As would be expected, leisure services managers try to minimize their capital costs by borrowing money when interest rates are low. However, capital costs tend to be the lowest when the Federal Reserve is trying to stimulate borrowing during economic downturns. During these times, construction is usually at a low point in the cycle, unemployment is high, and political forces advocate low taxes as another way of stimulating the economy.

Because commercial leisure services face reduced business during low periods in the economy, borrowing is more dependent on their revenue forecast than interest rates. For nonprofit organizations during economic downturns, donations are often down and belt-tightening, not borrowing, is on the horizon. Government tax sources can fluctuate as well when the economy is slow. As experienced during the economic slump starting in 2007, property values declined, lowering revenue from property taxes, and income tax and sales tax revenues dropped. And the electorate is

During economic downturns, leisure services managers might cut back on expenses such as groundskeeping in golf courses and parks.

rarely in a mood to allow state and local governments to increase taxes, even though the low cost of borrowing money would save taxpayers in the long run.

As mentioned, banks are businesses that collect money from depositors and loan it to borrowers, keeping the difference in interest rates between what they charge and earn. Wealthy people have always been too smart to let themselves be taken advantage of like that—otherwise they wouldn't be wealthy. When the banking industry was founded, wealthy people asked themselves, why should they allow banks to pay them a low interest rate for their deposits and charge borrowers a higher interest rate for loans? Wealthy people thought, why not cut out the middleman and make loans directly themselves? They also thought, why shouldn't they be able to sell those loans to other people who were willing to speculate on them? Thus **bonds** were created as certificates of loans that could be traded. Today, wealthy people are not the only ones who buy bonds. Bonds are available for everyone to purchase and are traded on markets in New York and other financial centers.

Bond Industry

What are bonds? They are loans in the form of a contract between the government or business and a bondholder that specify the interest rate and amount of the loan to be paid back over a specified length of time. "A bond is really not much more than an IOU with a serial number," said Russell Wild (2012) in a series titled *The Essentials of Investing in Stocks and Bonds*. Municipal or general obligation bonds are secured with the full faith and credit of taxpayers, meaning the government has a dedicated source of revenue to pay back the loans or pay off the bonds, usually through taxes but sometimes through fees.

Wild states: "A bond is always issued with a certain *face amount*, also called the *principal*. Most often, bonds are issued with face amounts of $1,000. If a corporation or government issues a $1,000 bond, paying 6 percent, that corporation or government promises to pay the bondholder $60 a year, or in most cases, $30 twice a year. Then, when the bond matures, the corporation or government gives the bondholder his or her $1,000 back." For municipal or general obligation bonds, the interest earned by investors is tax free, hence the term *tax-free municipal bonds*.

Bonds are usually purchased through a brokerage house or a bank, which in turn sells the bonds to investors for a fee that is included in the cost of the bonds. When governmental units need a bond issue, they often have to get approval from the electorate because it could mean a tax increase for property owners. Sometimes governmental units have bonding authority, so they do not need to get voter approval, but they must have board approval and time for discussion about the bond issue at a public meeting. Government units also get competitive quotes on interest rates from banks or brokerage houses to make sure they get the lowest interest rate possible.

The bond industry makes loans to businesses, nonprofit organizations, and governmental units. Wealthy people and institutions purchase the bonds that businesses, nonprofits, and governmental units sell. Investors who buy corporate bonds earn interest that is taxable, so that market is a little different from the municipal bond market. The interest earned by investors who purchase municipal bonds is not taxable, which causes the interest rates of municipal bonds to be lower. **Rate of return**, also called *return on investment*, is the percentage of money earned on the investment described in terms of how long it will take to recoup the investment.

Bonds are not to be confused with **equity** (stock). Equities are shares of ownership in the business that can be bought and sold by investors wishing to trade them for speculation. Bonds can be traded, too, but have specific conditions of repayment that equities typically don't have.

In addition to corporate and municipal bonds, the federal government sells Treasury bills, which pay interest that is *not* tax exempt. The federal government occasionally makes its T-bills tax exempt, such as is the case for the American Recovery and Reinvestment Act bonds sold in 2009. Municipal bonds are exempt from income tax at both the state and federal levels based on an 1895 Supreme Court ruling that the federal government has no authority to tax interest earned on municipal bonds. Investors look for guidance on the risk involved in purchasing municipal bonds. The most important way investors assess the risk of corporate bonds is through **bond ratings** by bond-rating agencies such as Moody's and Standard & Poor's (S&P).

Historically, municipal bonds have had lower **default rates** (i.e., the percentage of borrowers who are not able to repay the loans) compared with other types of bonds. Based on these rates, the **lending market** has to decide what level of risk it wants to assume and what interest rate it

Table 2.1 Cumulative Historic Default Rates

	MOODY'S (%)		S&P (%)	
Rating categories	Municipal	Corporate	Municipal	Corporate
Aaa/AAA	0.00	0.52	0.00	0.60
Aa/AA	0.06	0.52	0.00	1.50
A/A	0.03	1.29	0.23	2.91
Baa/BBB	0.13	4.64	0.32	10.29
Ba/BB	2.65	19.12	1.74	29.93
B/B	11.86	43.34	8.48	53.72
Caa-C/CCC-C	16.58	9.18	44.81	69.19

wants to charge for that risk. Table 2.1 shows the ratings and how they affect default rates.

Ratings are assessed by Moody's and S&P based on the probability that the borrowing business, nonprofit, or government organization will be able to repay the bondholders. The ability of businesses to repay is based on the current financial position of the business and the market forecast for its industry. The rating of nonprofits and governmental units is similar, with the financial position of the agency taken into consideration as well as the future outlook.

In assessing the risk of the business or agency, the skill of the management team is an important consideration, and it is becoming more important in the nonprofit and governmental sectors. Business schools teach that most of the variables affecting the success or failure of a business are within the control of management. Obviously, macroeconomic conditions are not, but the financial position of a company or organization is the result of management decisions. For instance, if a business or agency has taken on too many personnel, that can affect its profitability, as can a history of **leveraging assets**, which is borrowing money to create more total assets in order to generate more goods or services and thus more profit.

The financial condition of nonprofits is a function of the managers' business skills as well, especially as economic conditions force nonprofit organizations to shift from funding capital improvements with donations to funding them with loans or bonds. Likewise, sound financial skills are needed in the public sector, as evidenced by municipalities defaulting on their bond payments, such as New York City in the 1970s and several cities in Orange County, California, in the 1990s when they lost their investments.

Interest Rates

People and institutions have many options for investing their money. Many prefer their investments to be in cash in the event that investors need their money and want immediate access to it. Interest-bearing savings accounts and bonds provide relatively secure places to put money.

Interest is the cost that borrowers pay for the use of the lender's money. Think of interest as rent, except there are other considerations than just the cost of the rent. For businesses or individuals to be motivated to borrow money from a lender, they need to believe they will make more money than it will cost in interest.

Sometimes businesses borrow money to keep their heads above water in the short run rather than leverage their assets by purchasing more capital equipment or facilities to provide additional income. For lenders to be willing to loan money to borrowers who need the money just to stay afloat, lenders need to be sure the money will be repaid. Because there is a risk the money won't be repaid on time or at all, lenders usually charge higher interest rates than if the loan were made to leverage assets.

Throughout history, interest rates for low-risk borrowers have been set by governments and central banks. Interest rates are supposed to be driven by many factors in addition to the risk of repayment. One factor is the cost of money from the Federal Reserve. Another is the **time value of money**, which is the expected deterioration of the value of money over time due to **inflation**, which is the devaluation of currency. Thus, when the value of money declines, the value of goods and services purchased with a fixed amount of money also declines. Time value of money is a fundamental idea in finance—money now is worth more than money one will receive in the future. Because money can earn interest or be invested, it is worth more to an economic actor if it is available immediately (Farlex 2009). In short, the time value of money is the potential of money to deteriorate in value over time. Because of this potential, money that is available in the present is considered more valuable than the same amount in the future.

Inflation has the reverse effect on the time value of money. Because of the constant decline in the purchasing power of money, an uninvested dollar is worth more in the present than the same uninvested dollar will be in the future.

Whether banks charge interest on loans or pay interest to savings depositors, interest rates need to be considered. Nominal interest rates are the amount of interest payable in monetary terms. For instance, if a person deposited $10,000 in a savings account that paid 5 percent interest, at the end of the year that person would have earned $500 in interest.

Another category of interest is the real interest rate, which takes into consideration the inflation rate in the economy. If the **inflation rate**, the annual increase in the price of goods and services, were 3 percent, and the nominal interest rate were 5 percent, the real interest rate would be the 2 percent difference. However, if the interest rate were 1 percent and the inflation rate were 2.5 percent, both of which have been true for the past several years, the real interest rate would be a negative 1.5 percent. With the real interest rate being negative, investors are well advised to seek other investments for their money rather than savings accounts or bonds paying a lower rate of return than the inflation rate.

Typically, the riskier the investment, the higher the interest rate earned. If investors seek risk-free investments where there is practically no default risk, they can expect to receive lower interest rates for their investments. Although the concept of risk-free investments is purely theoretical, there are short-term bonds, such as U.S. Treasury bills, that would meet that standard.

Interest rates also have a dimension called **liquidity risk**. Defined as the ability of investors to take their money out of their investment at a moment's notice, liquidity risk considers the cost to the investor and how that affects the actual interest earned compared with the interest promised. In other words, there is usually a penalty for early withdrawal from the investment, be it a savings account or bond.

As investments earn interest, they are added to the principal, a process known as **compound interest**, which is interest calculated on the initial principal and the accumulated principal. For instance, for a savings account with $10,000 in its first year paying 3 percent interest, you would have $10,300 at the end of the year. With interest paid on the interest at 3 percent, at the end of the second year you would have $10,609. The additional $9 would be interest on the $300 earned during the first year. If the original $10,000 were left in the savings account for 25 years, the account would have $20,328.09, from that point on earning more money on the interest than the original deposit.

Considering inflation and the time value of money, there are formulas for calculating the effective interest rate of the investment. An example of a formula for calculating effective interest would be

$$A = P(1 + r)t,$$

where

P = principal amount (initial investment),

r = annual nominal interest rate (as a decimal),

t = number of years, and

A = amount over time t.

The model does not consider interest compounded more than annually, but there are more complicated models that can be used when that occurs.

Bonds do not pay compound interest; they pay a **coupon rate**. Bondholders receive the interest payment on the principal each year or every six months, depending on the payment schedule. Investors can do what they want with the interest payment, but they can't roll it into the principal. When bonds come due, the entire principal is repaid to the bondholder.

As a leisure services manager, you will be investing and borrowing money on a regular basis. Your understanding of finance allows you to weigh risk against return in investing. Your understanding of interest rates also allows you to minimize interest exposure in borrowing. How those lessons will be applied is discussed in future chapters.

SUMMARY

The fundamentals of business, no matter which sector, are the disciplines of economics and finance. Economics is based on theories and assumptions, with different schools of economics adhering to somewhat different beliefs, although all economists agree on certain assumptions. The most important assumption that serves as the foundation of economics is the principle of supply and demand, where it is assumed that as supply increases, prices drop, and as demand increases, prices increase. Other important principles of economics are the belief that competition leads to efficiencies and that consumers will purchase products and services only if they possess a marginal utility to the consumer.

Schools of economic thought have political implications. Democrats tend to favor a Keynesian view that governments can stimulate the economy by spending. Republicans tend to adhere to a more laissez-faire view that government should keep its hands out of the economy and let the market fix itself when there are economic downturns. The competing views affect the leisure services industry differently.

Finance is a knowledge set that considers the value of money, how time and inflation affect that value, and how the banking and bond industry rely on monetary supply and inflation rates to set interest rates. As a leisure services manager, you need to understand the field of finance so you can borrow money for business or agency expansion and pay it back without overburdening the financial stability of the organization.

Visit the Web Resource

For case studies, sample financial statements, key terms, and more, please visit the web resource at www.HumanKinetics.com/LeisureServicesFinancialManagement

chapter 3

The Art of Accountancy

Learning Outcomes

After completing this chapter, students will be able to do the following:

- Describe how and why accounting was created.
- Define accounting terms that leisure services managers need to know.
- Demonstrate manual posting of transactions.
- Describe the posting of transactions using computer software.
- Identify the ethical standards that guide accounting and reporting.
- Explain the complexities of leisure services accounting.

Most students of leisure services management look forward to studying accountancy about as much as they look forward to going to the dentist. Although both can be a little uncomfortable, the anticipation is usually worse than the actual event. And, similar to going to the dentist, modern techniques can make accounting a positive experience.

Accountancy is recording the acquisition of materials, keeping track of inventories, measuring output, analyzing the cost of goods sold, and managing the profitability of a company or agency. Practitioners of accountancy are known as **accountants**, and they oversee or participate in the maintenance of the financial reporting system of an entity. The day-to-day record keeping involved in this process is known as **bookkeeping**.

Transactions, which are exchanges of money, goods, or services or the transfer of funds into or out of an account, used to be recorded manually and chronologically in paper records called **journals** or **books**. Thanks to the advent of computer-based accounting, students can now focus on computer data entry, report generation and interpretation, and management of economic resources. However, small leisure services agencies may not have fully integrated computerized accounting systems, so an understanding of manual posting is still needed.

In spite of modern techniques, many leisure services managers are still unaware of what accounting is. This chapter discusses what accounting is, the language of accounting, and how accounting is done. The code of ethics that guides accountants in the posting of transactions and the presentation of reports also will be introduced.

In its discussion of transactional posting, the chapter also will demonstrate how transactions are posted manually. You need to understand how manual transactions are recorded if you are going to understand what is going on in the computer, and you also may encounter small agencies that still do some manual posting. After manual posting, this chapter introduces computer-based accounting, which makes the process of creating journals and **ledgers** infinitely easier than doing so manually, even if the process of interpreting reports is essentially the same.

Ledgers are the main accounting records of businesses and organizations. **Double-entry bookkeeping** refers to writing down transactions in chronological order in a journal and then posting the transactions to **accounts** in the ledger.

HISTORY OF ACCOUNTING

Accounting started as a relatively simple art, generally understood by most scholars to have begun in Asian and Middle Eastern countries some 7,000 years ago, when farmers and businesspeople relied on primitive bookkeeping to keep track of their livestock, crop production, inventories, and cash. Without a formal record-keeping process, business owners would have lost track of what resources they had or how much profit they stood to make, leading to counterproductive results.

Asian and Middle Eastern cultures were the first to use accounting because they were the first to be active in trading goods with other civilizations. According to Jared Diamond, a professor, scientist, and author who researched the relationship between geography and human society in his book *Guns, Germs, and Steel: The Fates of Human Societies* (1997), aboriginal tribes didn't trade very far outside their villages, but Asian and Middle Eastern cultures did for a number of reasons. They enjoyed goods made in other cultures, and they had beasts of burden that could carry the goods to faraway places, whereas sub-Saharan aborigines had no access to horses or camels, making transport impossible. Still another reason was that Asian and Middle Eastern cultures had written languages that could be recorded on stone tablets and eventually paper, a much better way of keeping records than verbal transmissions.

As trading in Asian and Middle Eastern cultures expanded, merchants developed double-entry bookkeeping as a method for writing down transactions, which are deals or business agreements involving an exchange or trade of goods or money. At the time, double-entry bookkeeping involved entering transactions in chronological order in one set of books and then posting the transactions to accounts in another. This was a much better management tool than trying to simply remember everything that happened.

As Mediterranean cultures grew and developed in ancient Greece and Rome, trade expanded and double-entry bookkeeping was refined. The focus became the reports that the ledgers generated and accounting became a more standardized process. Ancient records show the proficiency by which merchants and traders accounted for their goods and services, but a lot of the bookkeeping and accounting skills acquired in ancient times were lost when the Roman Empire fell into the Dark Ages.

© Super Stock/age fotostock

Before the computer age, bookkeepers and accountants kept track of company records manually, using adding machines and other equipment.

Who Created Modern Accounting?

Modern accounting can be traced to the work of an Italian monk, Fra Luca Bartolomeo de Pacioli, also called *Luca di Borgo* after his birthplace, Borgo Sansepolcro. He was also a mathematician, Franciscan friar, collaborator with Leonardo da Vinci, and seminal contributor to the field now known as accounting.

Pacioli was born in 1447 in Sansepolcro, where he received an abbaco education. This was education in the local tongue, rather than Latin, and focused on the knowledge required of merchants. Pacioli moved to Venice around 1464, where he continued his own education while working as a tutor to a merchant's three sons. It was during this time that he wrote his first book, a treatise on arithmetic for the boys he was tutoring. Between 1472 and 1475, he became a Franciscan friar.

Pacioli's 1494 publication described the double-entry system, which continues to be the fundamental structure for contemporary accounting systems. Early histories of business identify Pacioli as a valuable clergyman who not only helped his church but also developed a system whereby merchants would write down the dates and amounts of transactions in a journal and also record them in a ledger of accounts, keeping track of totals by transactional purpose or function.

As businesses became more complex, the need for more astute review and interpretation of financial information was met with the development of a new profession—public accounting. In the United States, public accounting began in the latter part of the 19th century. The first public accounting organization was established in 1887, and the first professional examination was administered in December 1896.

In the early days of the 20th century, numerous states established licensing requirements and began to administer examinations. During the first century of public accounting in the United States, the American Institute of Certified Public Accountants (AICPA) and its predecessor organizations provided strong leadership to meet the changing needs of business, nonprofit, and governmental entities.

References

Alegria, C. 2012. "Accounting." *eNotes.* Accessed January 29, 2012. www.enotes.com/accounting-reference/accounting-174096.

During the Dark Ages, feudal societies had less need for accounting because trading was much less of a factor in local economies.

After the Dark Ages in Europe ended with the Italian Renaissance, international trade reemerged and entrepreneurs rediscovered Middle Eastern bookkeeping. The accounting process was expanded when Luca Pacioli, the father of accounting, wrote the first accounting textbook in 1494. Pacioli wrote his text in response to the Renaissance trading systems, which required more capital than the one-owner businesses of ancient times. Accounting became a way for business partners to keep each other honest. At that time, the audience for accounting had grown to include investors and lenders.

Lenders became a primary audience as businesses began to borrow money to expand and leverage their assets, a concept discussed earlier. As local business systems grew to become macroeconomic systems, accounting provided an international language that everyone could understand. Accounting also became a way of measuring economic activity as well as keeping track of the microeconomic activity of a specific business.

Modern accounting became more complex as the British and American Industrial Revolutions of the 1700s and 1800s created large corporations. A massive amount of work was required to maintain records of company activities. Beginning in the late 1700s and continuing through today, companies employed whole departments of bookkeepers and accountants to record the acquisition of materials, keep track of inventories, measure output, analyze the cost of goods sold, and manage profitability.

As recently as 1950, many of these huge corporations maintained their records manually, a daunting task that buried them in paperwork. Most people are not aware that computers were primarily developed as accounting tools to maintain records electronically as opposed to writing down millions of corporate transactions, eliminating the need for paperwork but supplanting it with the task of maintaining the computer systems. At first, computers provided new challenges, causing many corporations to wonder if electronic accounting was truly an advancement in the field.

The refinement of reliable mainframe computers allowed large corporations to embrace computer-based accounting as the only way to manage their millions of transactions. And since the invention of the personal computer, even the smallest of companies performs accounting tasks using PCs. Accounting is no longer just bookkeeping; it is bookkeeping writ large.

ACCOUNTING

Leisure services managers across all three sectors need a command of accounting terms in order to communicate with their accountants, boards, and public. **Accounting** has been defined by the **American Institute of Certified Public Accountants (AICPA)** as "the art of recording, classifying, and summarizing in a significant manner and in terms of money, transactions, and events which are, in part at least, of financial character, and interpreting the results thereof" (Accountingexplanation.com 2011). That sounds complicated, but it's really not. There are **generally accepted accounting principles (GAAP)** that accountants follow, but by definition accounting is an art, not a science, and there are many ways of doing it.

As with any discipline, accounting has a language of its own. The words used in the language sometimes seem counterintuitive, but they are the terms with which managers must be familiar in order to be fluent in accounting. Learning the language of accounting is like learning any other language—it begins with the memorization of the most commonly used words.

You may be asking, "Why do leisure services managers need to understand the language of accounting when someone else will be doing the accounting for us?" The answer is that accountants work for and with leisure services managers, and if managers don't understand what their employees or colleagues are talking about, it becomes difficult to have any level of communication, let alone understand the most important element of management: managing the agency's money.

Expenses Versus Expenditures

All governmental units are considered **going concerns** because governmental units rarely go away, so **expenses** rarely comes up as a term in their context. Instead of expenses, governmental units have expenditures; whereas expenses are reductions in the equity of an entity, **expenditures** are the extinguishment of cash resources. Governmental units use **modified accrual accounting**, which is a type of accounting method where revenues are recognized in the period they are available and measurable, and expenditures are recorded in the period where the associated liability has occurred. **Liabilities** are loans or other short-term or long-term debts owed by the entity, individuals, or organizations.

Likewise, nonprofit organizations are almost always considered going concerns because their survival rates are much higher than businesses, although not as high as governmental units. Nonprofits, like governmental units, do not have owners. They exist as standalone entities, using much of the same accounting terminology as governmental units.

Equity Versus Fund Balances and Assets Versus Liabilities

The difference between equity and fund balances is important because governmental units and nonprofits don't have equity. *Equity* is the term used in business that refers to what is left over after the liabilities are subtracted from the **assets**, typically the value of the business to the owners. Assets are property, buildings, equipment, goodwill, or other measurable holdings of the entity. An **entity** is a legally recognized business, nonprofit organization, or governmental unit established to carry out specific purposes.

Getting back to the discussion of equity versus fund balances, no one person or group of people owns governmental units or nonprofits. Instead of equity, governmental units and nonprofits have fund balances on their balance sheets. A **balance sheet** is a report that provides a picture of the financial condition of an entity at any given point in time, including its assets, liabilities, and equity for a fund. A **fund** is a group of accounts within an entity for a specific purpose, such as the general fund or the recreation fund. A **fund balance**, like equity, is what's left over after liabilities are subtracted from assets, but it has nothing to do with measuring the net worth of the owner or owners.

Governmental units and nonprofits usually have multiple funds whereas business entities typically operate with one fund. That's because sources and uses of money must be separated in governmental accounting to maintain transparency, even though it leads to more complexity. Nonprofit organizations prefer to separate their money into operating funds and reserve funds. A **reserve fund** is an account set aside to meet unexpected costs in the future. It may be restricted to a certain purpose or used as a savings account for general future purposes.

We have seen how nonprofits use some of the same terminology as governmental units, but how is nonprofit accounting similar to business accounting? The answer is, nonprofits are similar to businesses in more ways than not. Nonprofits are supposed to use **full accrual accounting**, also known as *accrual-basis accounting*, just like businesses. In this accounting method, transactions are recorded as they are incurred, whether or not cash has been received or checks written. Both the nonprofit and business sectors also adhere to accounting rules prescribed by the **Financial Accounting Standards Board (FASB)**, which establishes rules that govern business accounting.

Depreciation

Full accrual accounting differs in several ways from the modified accrual accounting prescribed by the **Governmental Accounting Standards Board (GASB)**, which establishes rules that govern accounting practices of government agencies. One of the easiest differences to understand is that full accrual accounting depreciates or lowers the value of assets over time, whereas modified accrual accounting doesn't depreciate them during their useful life but extinguishes them when assets are taken off-line. **Depreciation** is the concept that some fixed assets, such as buildings and equipment, get used up and lose their value. A fixed asset is everything that depreciates (i.e., buildings, vehicles, equipment).

Accounting for depreciation can be confusing, but you need to understand it as a leisure services manager. Land never gets used up, so it doesn't depreciate. But buildings, vehicles, and equipment all have life expectancies. The more they are used, the less value they have. For businesses, depreciation is a deductible business expense. Businesses want to declare they are using up their extinguishable assets as fast as the IRS will permit them to. Nonprofits don't pay taxes unless they make a profit, so depreciation as a tax-deductible expense is an issue for them just as it is for businesses.

POSTING TRANSACTIONS

Posting transactions is the process of entering receipts, expenses, or expenditures in a journal and ledger. Journals are chronological records of the transaction number, amount, date, account, source, and any other important information. Posting this information is the first step in the process. Electronically, journals are drawn from consolidated databases sorted in the order of the date of the transaction. Ledgers have the same information but are sorted by the account number with total balances of the account shown.

Ethical standards are extremely important in accounting because accounting is partly a conceptual process. Inaccuracies in posting transactions can be unintentional or intentional. They usually occur when the person recording the transaction puts it in the wrong account or incorrectly describes the source of the money.

In double-entry bookkeeping, where a ledger and journal are maintained, the **general ledger**, sometimes called the *nominal ledger*, is the main accounting record of business. The book is the record of such items as current assets, fixed assets, liabilities, and revenues and expenses.

Each general ledger is divided into two sections. The left-hand side lists debit transactions and the right-hand side lists credit transactions, creating a *T* shape in each individual general ledger account, also known as a **T-account**.

Debits and **credits** are formal bookkeeping and accounting terms that refer to the most fundamental concepts in accounting, representing the two sides of each individual transaction recorded in any accounting system. A debit transaction indicates an asset or an expense transaction, whereas a credit indicates a transaction that will cause a liability or a gain. A debit transaction can also be used to reduce a credit balance or increase a debit balance. A credit transaction can be used to decrease a debit balance or increase a credit balance.

Figure 3.1 depicts a T-account in which debit and credit transactions would be recorded.

The general ledger is a collection of the account groups that supports the value of items shown in the major financial statements. It is built by posting transactions recorded in the sales daybook, purchases daybook, cash book, and general journal daybook. The general ledger can be supported by one or more subsidiary ledgers that provide details for accounts in the general ledger.

Debits	Credits

Figure 3.1 A depiction of a simple T-account without any account numbers or dates.

Journals are similar to the register in your checkbook where you record checks and deposits in chronological order. But ledgers are probably not records that you maintain for yourself, unless you own a business in your home or something similar. In setting up ledgers, the owner of the business, the bookkeeper, or the accountant decides how much detail the business needs to keep track of. They might decide to maintain a ledger account that keeps track of how much is spent for utilities, or they may want more detail, setting up several ledger accounts to keep track of water, sewer, electricity, and natural gas expenses separately. Either way, it's up to them.

If business owners didn't create ledger accounts, they would have to look through the journal and add up expenses every time they wanted to know how much they were spending on a commodity or service. Instead, they set up these accounts in the beginning and keep track of what they think they need to know as they go along. Government and nonprofit organizations are the same. What is amazing, though, is that governments and nonprofits have not been doing double-entry bookkeeping for very long—less than 100 years in most cases.

As mentioned, in double-entry bookkeeping, debits represent a depletion of the resources held by the entity, while credits represent an increase in resources. Think of debits as debts that are owed or that have been paid and credits as money that people have paid or that they owe you.

If you're still confused, let's take a moment to consider what has been discussed. If you write down your transactions in your checkbook, you should be fine with the concept of a journal. It's just the ledger that may have you baffled. Think of a ledger as a book where each page is where you keep track of a certain kind of expense. The purpose of this is to allow you to budget for next year's utilities based on what you spent this year. Figure 3.2 shows what a ledger might look like for the month of January for utility bills.

The ledger pages show that bills are recorded as debits when they come in. In short order, we'll show how it affects your overall net worth. But for now, the ledger pages also show that when the transaction is paid, there is an offsetting credit entry that causes the account balance to go back to zero when the bill is paid. There are no entries in your checkbook when the bills come in, only when they are paid. That's an example of **cash-basis accounting**, where only what is received or paid is recorded. However, if you record what you owe in your check register when you receive the bill and again in a ledger page as was just shown, that is an example of **accrual accounting**, where transactions are recorded as they are incurred, whether or not cash has been received or checks written.

Accrual accounting is more representative of what you owe because once a bill is received, it will inevitably get paid and you might as well count it. The same is true for money that is owed you. If you would apply accrual accounting to your **income**, which is money coming in, you'd find that you are owed pay from your employer even though you haven't been paid yet. In accrual accounting, you might as well count it now, when the amount is measurable and available for you to know.

Paper Accounting

Paper journal pages look like spreadsheets with columns for the fund, the activity, the date of the transaction, the debit or credit amount, the

Transaction number	Transaction description	Debit	Credit
11069	January electric bill	100	
12058	January electric bill payment		100
11091	January gas bill	100	
11101	January water bill	50	
12106	January water bill payment		50
11166	January cable bill	60	
12182	January gas bill payment		100

Figure 3.2 A T-account with transaction numbers, descriptions, and amounts.

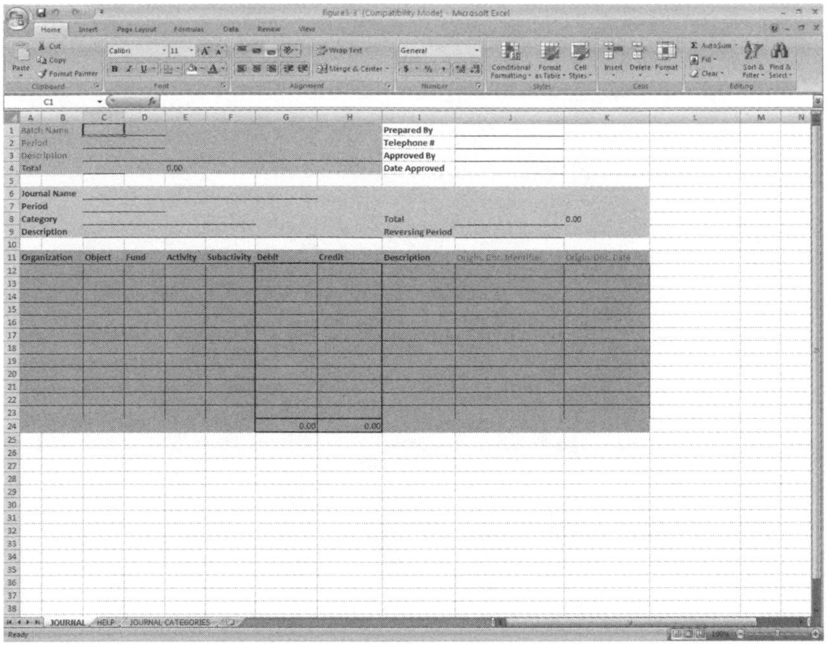

Figure 3.3 A journal page in a computer program as it appears on the screen.

check number, and the invoice number or receipt number. The accountant or bookkeeper decides what fund and activity account the transaction will be assigned to. Figure 3.3 shows an example of what a paper journal page might look like in an Excel spreadsheet.

Remember, on paper, journal entries are made before ledger entries are made. In fact, ledger entries are based on journal entries, but somewhat less information is on a ledger page. And the previous example in Excel has additional column categories that any entity may or may not use. Each entity has the ability to record the information that it wants, but all journals will at least have a column for the date of the transaction, the fund posted to, the activity within the fund, a description of what it is, whether it is a debit or credit, and the amount.

Paper systems allow activity accounts to be separated into their various funds using tabs to group them. Within those funds are ledger pages, which tend to be simpler than journal pages. The sample ledger page in figure 3.4 is still available in any office supply store and was used by everyone in the paper age of accounting.

The figure shows that there are columns for the date, a description of the transaction, and the amount of the debit or credit in columns on the right. The fund and activity numbers would be at the top of the page along with other descriptive information. The example shows that standard ledger pages are readily available, allowing owners and accountants to record any information that helps them track transactions and create reports that help them manage their business, nonprofit, or government entity.

At the bottom of a ledger page is a net total of debits and credits, arrived at by adding the dollar amount of the debit and credit transactions. This is a basic description of what is happening in ledger accounts, but in reality accounting is far more complex. Otherwise, there wouldn't be college curricula that have 60 or more credit hours in accounting courses.

So how does all of this tie into the concept of ethical behavior that was discussed earlier? As can be imagined, transactions, particularly cash revenues, can be entered incorrectly or fraudulently. Businesses, particularly those taking in a lot of cash, have been known to keep two sets of books: one that represents how much money the business has made and another that reports far less cash that can be used in income tax audits by the IRS to minimize the business' tax exposure. The classic example is Al Capone, who kept one set of books for his personal records and one that he used for income tax purposes (Linder 2011). Unfortunately for him, one of his lieutenants gave his personal books to IRS agents, which were used to prosecute him for tax fraud.

Stricter internal controls, credit card receipts, and computers have reduced the ability of businesses to misrepresent their revenues, but in some ways they have created a new set of ethical challenges, some of them larger than misrepresenting how much cash the business takes in.

Computer-Based Accounting

One of the obvious benefits of computer-based accounting is that the addition and updating of ledger account balance calculations are done much more quickly and accurately. Every time an entry is made in a computer-based system, the

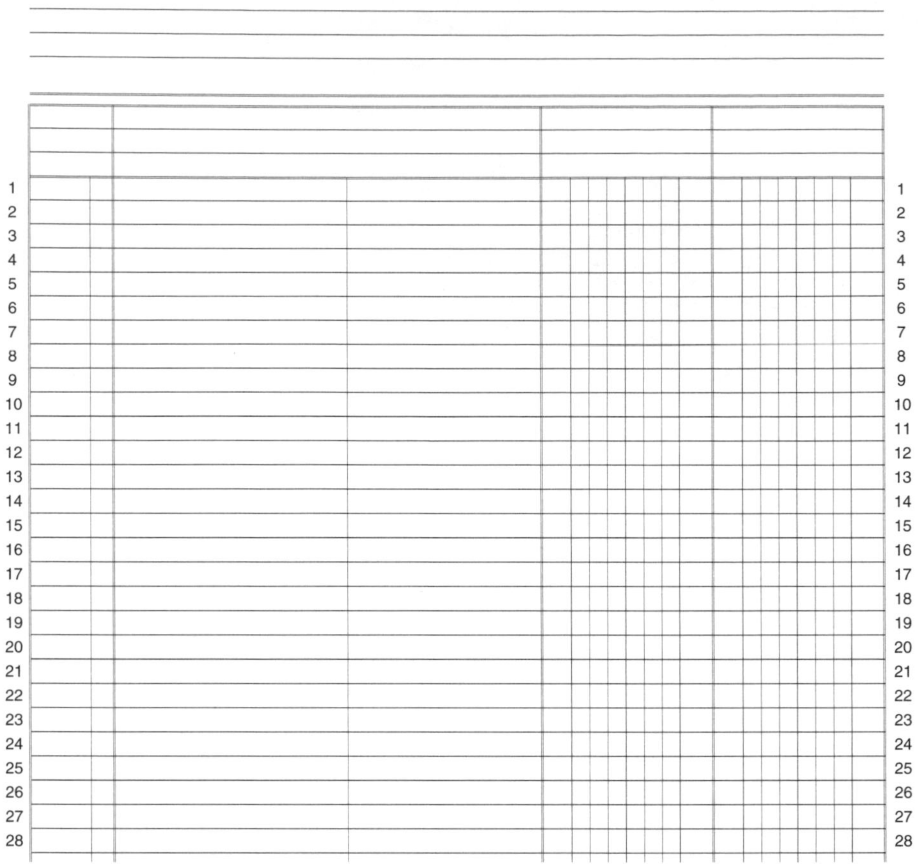

Figure 3.4 A paper version of a ledger page.

account balances are updated instantaneously. Computers can also generate reports with a fraction of the effort.

Computer-based accounting systems allow accounting to be done simultaneously with the collection of other data as well, including customer profiles. Computer-based accounting is more secure as well. Paper books of accounts can be stolen or destroyed relatively easily. Computer-based accounting allows for data to be backed up and for access to be limited by passwords. To prevent hacking, computer records can be encrypted, or coded in a format that only that computer or software program can translate back. Computer data can be archived and software programs are available to retrieve archival data and create comparative reports that help management analyze trends.

The difference between double-entry paper bookkeeping and computer-based accounting is that when transactions are entered into the computer system, they go into a large database that is similar to a journal but much more readily accessible. In computer-based accounting, one posting places the information everywhere it needs to be in one function.

The entry process is similar to entry in a paper system, except entries are done on a computer screen. The journals and ledgers can be reproduced on paper by printing spreadsheets that look similar to their paper cousins.

Another advantage of computer-based accounting systems is that entries can be made from remote locations in multiple batches. But the most important advantage of computer-based accounting is the immediacy of the reports that software programs generate. The generation and interpretation of computer-based reports are the main topics of subsequent chapters of this text.

CODES OF ETHICS AND CONDUCT

Codes of ethics and conduct have been adopted by a wide variety of professions and trades. Professionals frequently use their codes of ethics and conduct as proof that the services they provide are of high quality. Trades, such as electricians, carpenters, bricklayers, or ironworkers, not only let their work speak for itself but also have codes that prohibit them from producing poor work or looking the other way when their coworkers do (www.lrc.ky.gov/kar/815/035/080.htm).

Not lying, or honesty, is the most important ethical standard of all. It is never specifically mentioned in professional codes of ethics directly, but it is there nevertheless. Honesty is the basis for all ethical concepts. Honesty builds trust. It allows professions to assure new clients that their services will be of high quality and can be trusted.

Most professions adopt codes of ethics when they declare they are, in fact, a profession. That the profession will act in the best interest of the client is nearly always part of the codes. To prevent codes from being violated, professions have taken stronger action and adopted standards of behavior or codes of conduct that define what constitutes unethical behavior, requiring higher standards of professional honesty.

What makes codes of conduct complicated is that leisure professionals confront many of them. Leisure professionals in the public sector have their own codes of ethics and conduct, but so do the professionals they work with. The public sector is a veritable minefield of rules and guidelines.

For instance, professionals who work for **municipal park and recreation departments** work for city, village, and town managers and planning staff who adhere to the **International City/County Management Association (ICMA)** code of ethics. Leisure services managers who work for special-purpose districts, such as park districts, adhere to the **National Recreation and Park Association (NRPA)** code of ethics as well as state park and recreation association codes of ethics. A **special-purpose district** is a taxing unit created by legislation or voter approval for a special purpose such as parks and recreation.

Nonprofit organizations have standards of conduct as well. The Standards for Excellence Institute, an organization that develops ethical models for nonprofit organizations, allows nonprofits to have codes of ethics prescribed by their national organizations.

In the private sector, there are no umbrella organizations for business ethics. However, business codes of ethics or conduct are taught as courses in business schools, recommended alongside general guidelines by consultants, and adopted as corporate codes of ethics and conduct by individual companies.

The following discussion reviews important elements of codes of conduct. However, the code of conduct that leisure services managers must first understand is the code that accountants and **certified public accountants (CPAs)** in their agencies will feel a primary obligation to follow as part of their professional training.

After reviewing the code of conduct for accountants, general and specific codes of ethics and conduct for leisure professionals in the three sectors will be considered so that you can understand which are the most restrictive and other important considerations.

AICPA Code of Conduct

The AICPA is a professional accounting organization that has led the way in the transition to higher standards (AICPA 2012). The AICPA code of conduct is lengthy and specific in its pronouncements, providing a detailed pattern of behavior that would make most professions feel stifled. But because honesty and impartiality are so important to accounting, the profession believes that specific direction is required.

A good reason why the AICPA is so specific can be illustrated by the rapid demise of Arthur Andersen LLP, an accounting firm. In story after story in the media, a picture emerged of how the company pursued profits to the point of sacrificing its ethical standards of being an honest accounting firm. The company did this by cooperating with its corporate clients in misrepresenting corporate assets to investors. When this ethical lapse was revealed in 2002 during the collapse of the Enron Corporation, Arthur Andersen's complicity destroyed its reputation of ethical behavior and caused it to lose virtually all of its other corporate clients. The loss caused the collapse of the world's largest accounting firm in a few months.

The Andersen case is an example of why ethical conduct is so important to the AICPA specifically

Posting Transactions: An Ethical Dilemma

The ACME Team Building and Leadership Company, a small business in Oregon, applied for a $20,000 loan from a local bank to purchase the necessary equipment to continue its operations. One of the conditions of the loan was that ACME must use its monthly journal and ledger reports to prove that it generated enough revenues to pay back the loan, something that ACME's accountant Bob Clark was willing to do since revenues had been sufficient over the past two years.

However, due to a delay in state funding, one of ACME's clients, the local school district, did not have the funds available to pay for services ACME had delivered three months earlier. Knowing that the school district would probably pay but that the delay in payment made it look like ACME would not have sufficient revenues to repay the $20,000 loan, Clark had a dilemma. He had to decide if he would post the revenues as an account receivable at full value or if he should take into consideration that there was a chance the school district might not pay and discount the amount posted or not post it until he was sure.

Under pressure from ACME's owner, Clark decided to post the amount at full value even though he had read a newspaper article that said the school district would be delaying payment to some vendors for a year and would be discontinuing services with them in the future. The problem occurred when the bank officer handling ACME's loan application read the same newspaper article and questioned ACME's journal and ledger entries.

The bank officer not only rejected ACME's loan but made note of the transgression on ACME's credit report, making it difficult for the company to get a loan at another bank. Then the bank officer informed the AICPA of the ethical violation, causing Clark to lose his certification of public accountancy.

and to the accounting profession as a whole. Without absolute integrity, professional accounting has no meaning or value to business, nonprofit, and government entities. They might as well hire a person off the street to keep track of their money and audit their financial statements.

The following represents a small portion of the definition of integrity that the AICPA issues to its participating members, a code to which accountants are expected to adhere (American Institute of Certified Public Accountants n.d., section 54, article III.01):

> Integrity is an element of character fundamental to professional recognition. It is the quality from which the public trust derives and the benchmark against which a member must ultimately test all decisions.

Based on American Institute of Certified Public Accountants. Available: http://www.aicpa.org/About/FAQs/Pages/FAQs.aspx

Integrity requires a member to be, among other things, honest and candid within the constraints of client confidentiality. Service and the public trust should not be subordinated to personal gain and advantage. Integrity can accommodate the inadvertent error and the honest difference of opinion; it cannot accommodate deceit or subordination of principle.

Integrity is measured in terms of what is right and just. In the absence of specific rules, standards, or guidance or in the face of conflicting opinions, an AICPA member should test decisions and deeds by asking: "Am I doing what a person of integrity would do? Have I retained my integrity?" Integrity requires a member to observe both the form and the spirit of technical and ethical standards; circumvention of those standards constitutes subordination of judgment. Integrity also requires a member to observe the principles of objectivity, independence, and due care (AICPA 2012).

The code specifies that loyalty to the client shall not be subordinated to the public responsibility that accountants have to the general public, a directive other service providers and consultants are wise to embrace. Specific instructions on how these standards translate to ethical conduct are exemplified in additional AICPA pronouncements and are revealed by AICPA responses to hypothetical questions. In the case of business accounting, when a third party is seeking accounting information from a CPA about the business operations of a client, the following example illustrates the prescribed response the CPA should provide (American Institute of Certified Public Accountants n.d., section 391.1.002).

> *Question*—A member in public practice uses an entity that the member, individually or collectively with his or her firm or with members of his or her firm, does not control (as defined by generally accepted accounting principles) or an individual not employed by the member (a "third-party service provider") to assist the member in providing professional services (for example, bookkeeping, tax return preparation, consulting, or attest services, including related clerical and data entry functions) to clients or for providing administrative support services to the member (for example, record storage, software application hosting, or authorized e-file tax transmittal services). Does Rule 301, *Confidential Client Information* [American Institute of Certified Public Accountants n.d., section 301.01] require the member to obtain the client's consent before disclosing confidential client information to the third-party service provider?
>
> *Answer*—No. Rule 301 [American Institute of Certified Public Accountants n.d., section 301.01] is not intended to prohibit a member in public practice from disclosing confidential client information to a third-party service provider used by the member for purposes of providing professional services to clients or for administrative support purposes. However, before using such a service provider, the member should enter into a contractual agreement with the third-party service provider to maintain the confidentiality of the information and be reasonably assured that the third-party service provider has appropriate procedures in place to prevent the unauthorized release of confidential information to others. The nature and extent of procedures necessary to obtain reasonable assurance depends on the facts and circumstances, including the extent of publicly available information on the third-party service provider's controls and procedures to safeguard confidential client information.
>
> In the event the member does not enter into a confidentiality agreement with a third-party service provider, specific client consent should be obtained before the member discloses confidential client information to the third-party service provider.

Based on American Institute of Certified Public Accountants. Available: http://www.aicpa.org/About/FAQs/Pages/FAQs.aspx

This question and answer show that once a contractual relationship exists between an accountant and a client, specific rules of conduct must be followed.

This section of the AICPA code is part of a long list of ethical conduct guidelines to which accountants, particularly CPAs with auditing corporations, are expected to adhere. Responsibilities of accountants for nonprofit organizations are similar. But in the case of governmental units, the AICPA code states that the accountant's primary responsibility when reporting financial transactions is to the public rather than the governmental unit. In other words, transparency is the most important standard to which accountants working for government need to adhere.

Leisure services managers working in the public sector should take note. Accountants are never totally your employees. They have a responsibility to the public before they have a responsibility to you. Their job is not to keep the financial records of the government a secret. Accountants are responsible to report what the government is doing so the public will know how its tax money is being used.

Private-Sector Codes of Ethics and Conduct

Cynics have said that business ethics is an oxymoron. In other words, there are no ethical standards in business, just as there is no honor among thieves. However, we know this cynical view is not entirely correct because whole college courses are dedicated to business ethics, with case studies in these courses providing opportunities for students to apply ethical standards.

Business consultants provide templates for ethical standards of conduct for the private sector. Many of these standards are similar to personal ethical standards that individuals should maintain. Others are similar to the AICPA prescriptions for conduct. Generally, they fall into these categories:

1. Compliance with laws, rules, and regulations
2. Conflicts of interest
3. Insider trading

4. Corporate opportunities
5. Competition and fair dealing
6. Political contributions
7. Discrimination and harassment
8. Health and safety
9. Environment
10. Record keeping, financial controls, and disclosures
11. Confidentiality
12. Protection and proper use of company assets
13. Payments to government personnel
14. Trade issues
15. Waivers of the code of business conduct and ethics
16. Reporting any illegal or unethical behavior
17. Improper influence on conduct of **auditors**
18. Financial reporting
19. Compliance procedures
20. Annual acknowledgment

Courtesy of Grand Canyon NPS, photo by Michael Quinn

Ethical standards of conduct can involve environmental as well as economic issues. In June 2011, Secretary of the Interior Ken Salazar spoke in Grand Canyon National Park, advocating wise stewardship of the area's resources to protect tribal interests, drinking water supplies, and tourism.

These categories of conduct may seem to be randomly selected, but in the suggested codes, they are usually followed with a specific description of what is expected in terms of behavior. Similar to the AICPA code, questions are provided with categorical answers on what behavioral response is required. The website KnowledgeLeader (www.knowledgeleader.com) provides the previous list of categories of conduct and also is an example of online assistance that is provided to business managers to answer some of these questions.

Business codes of ethics tend to focus on ethical relationships with customers and employees, but they also consider relationships with suppliers and competitors. Honesty is at the heart of business codes of ethics for relationships with customers. However, in business, not always telling the truth to competitors is not a violation of ethical standards the way it is in other sectors. That is because the private sector is competitive. Not being fully transparent to a competitor gives the business competitive advantages. On the other hand, there is an assumption of fair play in business codes of conduct that restrict businesses from engaging in unfair advantages such as monopolistic practices. For example, as the owner of a private fitness center, you may have special talent as a negotiator and can get great discounts on equipment purchases. If a competitor asks you what you paid, you are under no ethical obligation to tell the truth.

Even then, codes of ethics are not enough to keep many businesses from going outside the lines of ethical behavior. Codes of ethics are harder to enforce in the private sector because businesses may remain secretive in their strategic operation, and it is often difficult for outsiders to see whether businesses are being unethical.

That's where the government comes in. As was discussed earlier, when businesses exploit their competitive advantages unfairly and to the detriment of their employees and customers, the government can step in by passing regulations that make businesses prove they are acting ethically. For example, in recent years the credit card industry has come under scrutiny for its consumer practices. In the United States, recent government regulations now prevent credit card companies from charging exorbitant interest on outstanding balances. The government stepped in and passed the Credit CARD Act, which went into effect in 2010. The new laws prevent retroactive increases in interest rates on existing card balances and require more time to pay monthly bills and greater advance notice of changes in credit card terms (Prater 2010).

Businesses do not always like it when government intervenes, invoking Adam Smith laissez-faire economics as an argument against government regulations. Sometimes businesses lobby for favorable regulations, and sometimes they donate to political candidates who support their positions. When businesses aren't able to influence the political process to get the regulations they want, sometimes they ignore those regulations and break the law, forcing regulating agencies and the courts to enforce the law.

All of this suggests that it may not be so cynical to say that business ethics is an oxymoron, but that would be an indictment of all the ethical businesses that exist today. The vast majority of businesses play by the rules.

Nonprofit-Sector Codes of Conduct

Nonprofit organizations come in many shapes and sizes, performing many types of services. National organizations have codes of ethics and conduct, but there is no one overarching code that applies to all of them. However, consultants for nonprofit organizations provide templates of guiding principles that are generic enough to apply to nonprofit organizations in general (Standards for Excellence Institute 2011), as represented by the following example of categories and their explanations.

1. Mission and program
2. Governing body
3. Conflict of interest
4. Human resources
5. Financial and legal
6. Openness
7. Fund-raising
8. Public affairs and public policy

Most national nonprofit organizations have their own codes of ethics or conduct that follow these categories. The themes of these codes focus on serving clients and doing some form of charitable work. The codes serve as a reminder to nonprofit organizations that they have a responsibility of service that goes beyond the personal interests of their employees.

Public-Sector Codes of Ethics

Codes of ethics in the public sector are much more complicated because of government taxation powers. In the United States, taxation is viewed as a necessary evil, yet there are differing views of the responsibility of public administrators to engage in the political arena.

Leisure services professionals in the public sector are expected to follow the code of ethics from one of the following professional organizations: the **American Society of Public Administration (ASPA)**, primarily for federal, state, and county agencies; ICMA, primarily for managers of municipal park and recreation departments; and NRPA, primarily for leisure services managers working for special districts.

Sometimes, state park and recreation associations have their own code of ethics, which can be a restatement of the NRPA code or an original code of their own. In other words, leisure professionals working for state or county agencies have to choose to follow the ASPA code, the NRPA code, or the code of their state association. Leisure professionals working for municipal park and recreation departments have to choose to follow the ICMA code, the NRPA code, or the code of their state association. As we will see, these codes can differ, posing ethical dilemmas for leisure professionals. However, when there are multiple codes to follow, a general rule of thumb and the safest approach is to follow the most stringent.

ASPA Code of Ethics

The ASPA code of ethics was developed in response to concerns raised by elected officials around the time of the Pendleton Civil Service Reform Act of 1883. The **Pendleton Act** was a Congressional action that essentially created the civil service system for the purpose of reforming government hiring practices and eliminating political patronage dating back to the 1820s.

In support of the Pendleton Act, in 1887 a Harvard University professor named Woodrow Wilson (who would be eventually elected U.S. president in 1912) wrote an article in *Political Science Quarterly* suggesting that there was a way to separate the process of making policy from the process of implementing policies. Calling it a **dichotomy of politics and administration**, Wilson argued that the field of public administration existed as a profession with a code of ethics whereby professional

Maintaining playground equipment is one way that managers of parks and recreation districts adhere to a code of ethics and promote public safety.

public administrators should be trained to efficiently implement policies without involvement in the political process (Wilson 1887).

The key to Wilson's argument was a code of ethics that would allow professional public administration while simultaneously keeping administrators from the political process that made policy decisions. Wilson argued that professional public administrators would create better governmental services than political patrons would because their code required them to focus on public needs.

ASPA was the first professional organization representing public administrators. One of its first acts was to adopt a code of ethics that focused on Wilson's suggestions. Leisure professionals who work in the public sector for federal, state, and county governments are expected to adhere to the same code of conduct as their bosses. Public administrators for federal, state, and county governments follow the ASPA code of ethics, which includes the following directives (American Society for Public Administration 2012):

I. Serve the Public Interest

Serve the public, beyond serving oneself.

II. Respect the Constitution and the Law

Respect, support, and study government constitutions and laws that define responsibilities of public agencies, employees, and all citizens.

III. Demonstrate Personal Integrity

Demonstrate the highest standards in all activities to inspire public confidence and trust in public service.

IV. Promote Ethical Organizations

Strengthen organizational capabilities to apply ethics, efficiency, and effectiveness in serving the public.

V. Strive for Professional Excellence

Strengthen individual capabilities and encourage the professional development of others.

What makes the ASPA code relevant to leisure services managers is that their ethical values focus on professional excellence but do not bar them from participation in the political process. In leisure services education, textbooks have argued that public administrators in leisure services need to take an active role in recommending policy decisions, and the role of the board is more to review them; "it is management, not the board, that conducts the affairs of the organization so that it becomes an effective, fiscally responsible organization" (van der Smissen, Moiseichik, Hartenburg, and Twardzik 2000, p. 32).

Part of the reason for this revolves around the political challenges facing leisure services agencies in competing with other government services for funding. Organizations such as NRPA host conferences in Washington, DC, each year dedicated to the purpose of leisure professionals lobbying their federally elected officials for funding. Although mayors and other elected officials of municipalities attend similar events, city managers have codes of conduct that oppose their participation in similar events.

ICMA Code of Ethics

As discussed in chapter 1, the leisure services profession was created when Frederick Law Olmsted was hired as the first superintendent of the Central Park Commission. During that period of American history, municipalities were run by political machines, with professional city management a rare occurrence. Most municipalities were run by elected officials, city staff members were political appointees, and corruption was rampant. In the early 1900s, though, suburban municipalities began to turn away from the political corruption of machine government, and professional city management became more prevalent, similar to the Central Park model.

One of the issues raised by opponents of professional administration of municipal government was that taking power from elected officials and giving it to professional administrators was antidemocratic. Opponents argued that no one elected public administrators. Why should they make policy decisions instead of the representatives of the people?

To appease the opponents and to foster professional administration of municipalities, the newly formed ICMA adopted a code of ethics that was designed to reassure the public and elected officials that the role of public administrators would be limited to the implementation of policy, not its creation. The code is simply as follows:

Tenet 1

Be dedicated to the concepts of effective and democratic local government by responsible elected officials and believe that professional general management is essential to the achievement of this objective.

Tenet 2

Affirm the dignity and worth of the services rendered by government and maintain a constructive, creative, and practical attitude toward local government affairs and a deep sense of social responsibility as a trusted public servant.

Tenet 3

Be dedicated to the highest ideals of honor and integrity in all public and personal relationships in order that the member may merit the respect and confidence of the elected officials, of other officials and employees, and of the public.

Tenet 4

Recognize that the chief function of local government at all times is to serve the best interests of all people.

Tenet 5

Submit policy proposals to elected officials; provide them with facts and advice on matters of policy as a basis for making decisions and setting community goals; and uphold and implement local government policies adopted by elected officials.

Tenet 6

Recognize that elected representatives of the people are entitled to the credit for the establishment of local government policies; responsibility for policy execution rests with the members.

Tenet 7

Refrain from all political activities which undermine public confidence in professional administrators. Refrain from participation in the election of the members of the employing legislative body.

Tenet 8

Make it a duty continually to improve the member's professional ability and to develop the competence of associates in the use of management techniques.

Tenet 9

Keep the community informed on local government affairs; encourage communication between the citizens and all local government officers; emphasize friendly and courteous service to the public; and seek to improve the quality and image of public service.

Tenet 10

Resist any encroachment on professional responsibilities, believing the member should be free to carry out official policies without interference, and handle each problem without discrimination on the basis of principle and justice.

Tenet 11

Handle all matters of personnel on the basis of merit so that fairness and impartiality govern a member's decisions, pertaining to appointments, pay adjustments, promotions, and discipline.

Tenet 12

Seek no favor; believe that personal aggrandizement or profit secured by confidential information or by misuse of public time is dishonest.

Reprinted, by permission, from International City/County Management Association, 2004, *ICMA code of ethics* (Washington, DC: ICMA). Available: www.icma.org/en/icma/code_of_ethics

The code suggests that public administrators remain in the background of government, similar to how umpires and referees are supposed to be invisible at sporting events. If they do their job right, the public will never notice them. Leisure professionals who work in municipal park and recreation departments are expected by their city managers to follow the ICMA code rather than the NRPA code. This puts park and recreation departments at a decided disadvantage in competing for funding with other city departments such as police and fire because the code says that public administrators of leisure services may not participate in the political process. Without the ability to lobby for their interests, few public administrators can argue that leisure services are as important as police and fire protection. More will be discussed in future chapters, but suffice it to say that the differences in professional values can cause friction between city managers and park and recreation managers.

Some leisure services managers in municipal settings choose to follow the less restrictive NRPA and state codes of conduct, but they may find themselves in professional jeopardy with their supervising public administrators who are trained to adhere to the ICMA code. The difference in values can cause ethical dilemmas. For instance, leisure services professionals may believe it is perfectly ethical to work with political candidates to achieve their goals whereas city managers do not. As previously mentioned, the NRPA sponsors a lobbying meeting in Washington, DC, every spring, a trip city managers usually are not willing to let their park and recreation department heads attend.

Fewer ethical dilemmas exist for leisure services professionals who work for special-purpose governmental units such as metropolitan authorities, forest preserve districts, or county or local park districts. Because these special-purpose governmental units provide only park and recreation services and generally don't hire managers trained in public administration, ethical dilemmas between competing codes of conduct are fewer.

DIMENSIONS OF COMPLEXITY IN LEISURE SERVICES ACCOUNTING

Accounting was originally developed primarily for businesses, but in modern times it has been applied to nonprofit organizations as well as government entities. Although the focus of this chapter has been an introduction and overview of accounting terms and codes of ethics that apply to all three sectors of leisure services, there are differences that bring a level of complexity to financial management in the leisure services industry. An overview of those differences follows, to be illustrated in more depth in the chapters that follow.

Financial accounting is a technique used to generate reports for investors, donors, the general public, and governmental units that tax businesses in the private sector, following rules established by the FASB. **Government accounting** is a technique used by governmental units that collect taxes and must remain transparent in the way they spend the public's tax money following GASB rules. CPAs are expected to understand both sets of rules, as are leisure services managers.

Nonprofit accounting is a hybrid of both financial and governmental accounting because nonprofit organizations are in a unique position. They don't pay taxes, but they don't collect them, either. As tax-exempt entities, nonprofit organizations must be transparent enough to show the state and federal agencies to which they must answer that they are staying true to their tax-exempt mission and reinvesting revenue over expenses back into the organization. To potential donors, they need to show they are worthy of being charitable recipients of donations.

But there is no board similar to the FASB or GASB that oversees nonprofit accounting. Nonprofit accounting generally follows FASB rules. Chapter 5 provides much detail on private-sector financial management and the FASB.

Businesses, governments, and nonprofits also use **management accounting** to generate reports, often not following GAAP. These reports may be on a cash basis so that leisure services managers can determine whether the revenues generated by their services are at least covering their costs. Management reports are not usually available to the public, lenders, investors, or donors in the private or nonprofit sectors, but via the **Freedom of Information Act (FOIA)**, they are available to the public in the governmental sector.

Because leisure services can be provided in any of the three sectors, managers not only must be aware of accounting principles for all three but also must be somewhat proficient in each technique. The differences between the three accounting systems are, again, the audiences. Governmental accounting systems must be detailed and transparent to satisfy a public that pays taxes to governmental units. Nonprofit accounting systems must be somewhat transparent to satisfy the IRS and state revenue services. But since no tax money is involved, nonprofit systems don't need to be as transparent as governmental units.

Private-sector accounting is done for shareholders, investors, and lenders so that corporate profits can be taxed. Businesses exist in a competitive market, so financial accounting allows commercial enterprises to conceal their trade secrets.

SUMMARY

With an understanding of the leisure services environment and basic economics, this chapter introduced the discipline of accountancy from a historical and ethical viewpoint. Comparisons can be made between leisure services codes of ethics and professional codes of conduct for business, nonprofit, and public administration. Leisure services financial management also is required to follow AICPA ethical standards.

Government accounting has many more dimensions than business and nonprofit accounting because of transparency. There is disagreement about what level of transparency should be provided because there is disagreement about what ethical standards public administrators must be held to. Leisure services managers feel less compelled to remain outside the political arena, particularly because some work for special-purpose governmental units. Others work for federal, state, and municipal governments, supervised by public administrators who adhere to the more restrictive codes of conduct of the ASPA and ICMA. Nevertheless, all leisure services managers, regardless of their sector, are obligated to follow the AICPA code of conduct that accountants follow when it comes to questions about the ethics of accounting for private, nonprofit, or public funds.

Finally, accounting is an ancient art, dating back to the dawn of civilization. Business accounting has provided the foundation for nonprofit and governmental accounting with terminology that is mostly common, but some differences exist. Accounting in the private sector primarily exists to help businesses make a profit by telling them what their costs are. In the nonprofit sector, accounting provides a basis for monitoring the provision of services, addressing client needs while informing the supervising governmental units that services are being delivered in a way that justifies their tax-exempt status.

Visit the Web Resource

For case studies, sample financial statements,
key terms, and more, please visit the web resource at
www.HumanKinetics.com/LeisureServicesFinancialManagement

chapter 4

The Private Sector

Learning Outcomes

After completing this chapter, students will be able to do the following:

- Understand why the private sector is so large.
- Identify how the private sector focuses on customer needs.
- Describe the process of making a profit.
- Explain the differences between debt and equity.
- Explain what happens when a business wants or needs to take on new owners.
- Learn what stockholders and boards are and how they influence a private company.

We now begin to delve deeper into the financial management of the three sectors, starting with the private sector, the largest of the three. Although a chapter is devoted to each sector, it should be clear by now that it's difficult to discuss one without the others. Much of the same skill sets and knowledge base apply to all, yet critical differences exist. Each sector has a unique set of techniques and thought processes, which will be explored in the next few chapters. The best way to explore these similarities and differences is through comparative analysis, so although this chapter is titled "The Private Sector," it includes comparisons with the other two sectors.

Governmental leisure services managers view money as a resource that gets spent. Expenditure accounting is a GASB concept implying the extinguishment of financial resources. Leisure services managers in the private sector view revenues as contributing to the equity of the company. Expense accounting is a concept from FASB that refers to the reduction in owners' equity. For nonprofit managers, money is a resource that is acquired through revenues and allows nonprofit organizations to do their work. There is no owners' equity on the balance sheet, but there are fund balances that need to be maintained. Nonprofit managers generally follow FASB regulations, but with GASB intentions.

Many politicians have said that governments, especially governments that provide leisure services, need to run more like businesses. But what does that mean? How would running a government like a business be better than running it like a government? Are the people who run businesses that much smarter than those who run governmental units? What do they know that people who run governmental units don't know?

To know if using a business model to run government is a good thing or not, let's start by answering the question, "How does business operate in the first place?"

HOW GREED AND POWER AFFECT BUSINESS MANAGEMENT

Greed is defined as "an excessive desire to acquire or possess more than what one needs or deserves, especially with respect to material wealth" (www.thefreedictionary.com/greed). This is the very definition of the desire to be rich. In other words, the desire to be rich is the desire to acquire more in material wealth than you need.

The Customer Difference

An urban legend says there are only three legal ways to get rich: Marry into a rich family, invest wisely, or start a business. There are other ways of getting rich, such as winning the lottery or discovering buried treasure, but the chances of those are statistically improbable. Nevertheless, marrying into money and investing wisely usually require having money in the first place, which leaves starting a business as the most viable option for getting rich.

Believe it or not, the reason most people go into business isn't to get rich. They go into business because they have a passion to do a certain kind of work (Allen 2006). Getting rich is a by-product of work done well, or rather, business done well. To people in leisure services, that concept should be understandable. We don't go into it for the money; we just love working in an environment where people are having fun. It follows that leisure services managers in the private sector go into business because they have a passion for adventure programming or running movie theaters, not to get rich.

Do politicians who say government ought to run like a business mean that people who run the government should get rich, just as the people who run businesses do? Probably not. Perhaps what those politicians mean is that government managers need to be passionate about what they do, particularly when it comes to focusing on customers.

In any industry, a business needs to focus on customer needs or it won't survive. Politicians would love for governments to cater to the public the way businesses cater to their customers, but that expectation misses an important difference between business and government. In a capitalistic system, where transactions are voluntary, buyers and sellers come together in a marketplace to do business. In government, taxpayers and governmental units come together at tax time, and there's nothing voluntary about it.

Maybe what politicians mean when they say government should run like a business is that it should try to focus on the customer even though many taxpayers are not happy they've been forced to pay taxes. The reason why businesses focus on customers is not because they're run by nicer people than governmental units are. It's because businesses want something from their customers: money. The government has already received what it wants—taxes—so instead, its job is to explain what it is doing with the taxes it has taken in.

Businesses get money in exchange for meeting customers' needs. After they pay the costs of meeting customer needs, businesses keep the leftover money for themselves as profits. Profits make the business owners rich.

By definition, nonprofit organizations can't do that. They can't make profits. They can only make enough money to cover their costs. If there is money left over after paying their costs, nonprofits can reinvest the extra money in capital expansion, but they can't keep it or give it to their owners. There are no real owners of nonprofits.

Governmental units are different in that they aren't even supposed to cover their true costs of providing services, largely because there is the assumption that some people can't afford to pay for government services, such as **indigent citizens**. Governmental units levy taxes to pay some of their operating costs. If there is money left over after paying the costs, governmental units are supposed to decrease their taxes or increase their services. But in no case is the governmental unit supposed to keep the extra money or give it to its owners. Similar to nonprofits, there are no real owners of governmental units.

For these reasons, some progressive economists believe that politicians are wrong. There is no practical way of running the government like a business or running a nonprofit, for that matter, like a business. Keeping the profits changes everything, because it is a powerful motivation in serving customer needs. Meeting customer needs becomes a way for businesses to acquire wealth

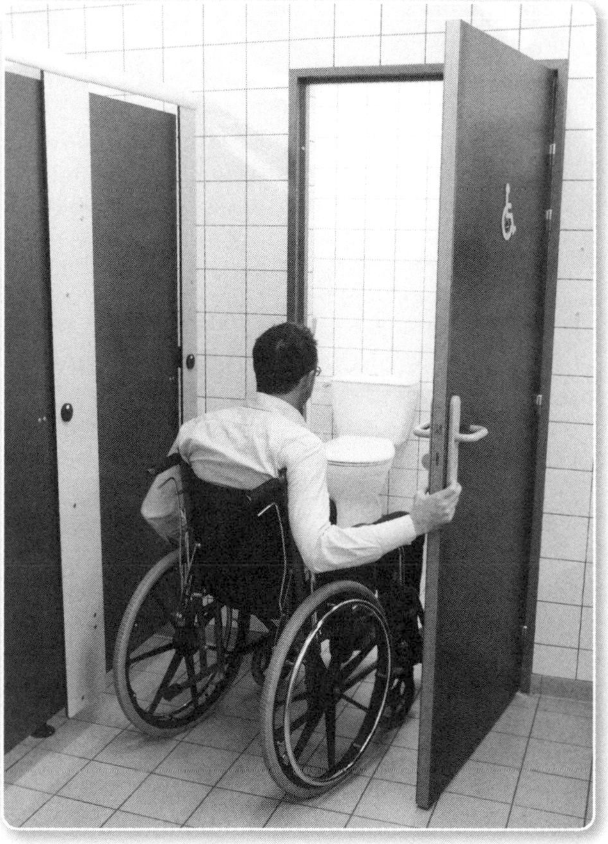
© Studio DER - Fotolia

To survive and thrive, any business must meet the needs of its customers, whether that means coffee, fitness classes, or special accommodations for those with disabilities.

from profits, wealth that can be kept by the owners or shared with the employees.

The pursuit of wealth is what makes so many people want to go into business, and it is what makes people in business work to meet customer needs. Governmental units and nonprofit organizations simply don't have profits as a motivational tool.

Greed

People outside business have called the pursuit of wealth *greed*. Greed is thought to be bad, one of the seven deadly sins. But many people in business disagree. Their point of view was expressed by the character Gordon Gekko in the movie *Wall Street*. In his famous speech to stockholders of the fictional Teldar Paper Corporation, Gekko observed that the company was being run more like a government bureaucracy than a business. He told stockholders they needed to hold management accountable for making a profit, not protecting their own jobs. He also told stockholders they needed to be greedy and allow him to take over the company for their own good (www.americanrhetoric.com/MovieSpeeches/moviespeechwallstreet.html):

> The point is, ladies and gentleman, that greed—for lack of a better word—is good.
>
> Greed is right.
>
> Greed works.
>
> Greed clarifies, cuts through, and captures the essence of the evolutionary spirit.
>
> Greed, in all of its forms—greed for life, for money, for love, knowledge—has marked the upward surge of mankind.
>
> And greed—you mark my words—will not only save Teldar Paper, but that other malfunctioning corporation called the USA.

The release of *Wall Street* in 1987 coincided with the business resurgence of the 1980s. This resurgence led to a movement where politicians suggested that business become the model of government, a model that was impractical but resonated with many people. Business came to stand for efficiency and effectiveness. The focus on customers caused this movement, and the byproduct of wealth creation fueled it.

SIZE OF THE PRIVATE SECTOR

The private sector is an example of a macroeconomic system, a large economy with influences on a national and global scale. All forms of exchanges occur in these national and world economies, including the private sector, where free enterprise takes place.

How big is the private sector? It's huge and getting bigger, especially with the decline of socialism in the Soviet Union, China, and some Pacific Rim countries. People in these societies have discovered that greed is good. They want more from life than what a managed socialistic economy was able to provide them. They want to live like Americans.

Nobody knows for sure how many companies exist in the world, or even in the United States, that are taking advantage of the free enterprise system. There are estimates, though, including one by Manta, a company that tracks other companies by websites. On April 3, 2012, the Manta website claimed to feature more than 89 million companies worldwide, including more than 29 million in the United States alone. It also recognizes more than 840,000 worldwide travel and leisure businesses (Manta 2012).

Manta sells access to websites by sorting them categorically by state, listing the number of corporations in each state (figure 4.1).

There are probably far more than 89 million companies worldwide and 29 million in the United States, because many of them don't have websites but are still doing business. Either way, the number is huge, employing a majority of the workforce. In the United States alone, more than 100 million people are employed in the private sector, compared with 21 million employed by governments and 10 million by nonprofit organizations.

Why is the private sector so large? One explanation is the dynamic of greed and power. The ability to make money can be a satisfying outcome of owning or operating a business. And the ability to live life on a high wire, meeting customer needs by providing a good or service that customers want, can be an exhilarating experience. But there are other reasons as well.

In countries that have not reached the economic ability to provide a safety net for their less fortunate citizens, starting a business is the only option for survival. In these nations, selling food at a market or scavenging for discarded items that can be resold are forms of businesses that people operate not because they are greedy or they desire power but because they must meet their basic needs to survive.

This book focuses on the leisure services industry in the United States, not leisure services in underdeveloped nations. The motivation of U.S. leisure services providers is not necessarily economic survival on the part of the owners. And although greed and power probably exist as motives somewhere in there, private-sector leisure services make up nearly 25 percent of all goods and services produced in the United States because of the abundance of customer needs that provide the opportunities to start businesses.

FOCUS ON CUSTOMER NEEDS

Leisure services, or any other services or goods provided by the private sector, exist first and foremost to meet customer needs. The vehicle for attaining revenues is the market that exists for whatever service or good you want to sell. It is not enough to just want to sell it.

Many university students decide to pursue a career in leisure services because they think it will be a fun profession. They are motivated by

Alabama	(424,622)
Alaska	(78,153)
Arizona	(523,023)
Arkansas	(264,944)
California	(3,331,655)
Colorado	(575,898)
Connecticut	(376,778)
Delaware	(88,843)
District of Columbia	(103,319)
Florida	(2,188,905)
Georgia	(977,140)
Hawaii	(109,667)
Idaho	(162,649)
Illinois	(1,090,587)
Indiana	(537,819)
Iowa	(323,910)
Kansas	(278,765)
Kentucky	(376,532)
Louisiana	(450,597)
Maine	(138,962)
Maryland	(549,840)
Massachusetts	(627,971)
Michigan	(921,232)
Minnesota	(545,664)
Mississippi	(265,823)
Missouri	(551,146)
Montana	(123,904)
Nebraska	(195,203)
Nevada	(228,869)
New Hampshire	(144,471)
New Jersey	(837,234)
New Mexico	(172,311)
New York	(1,744,782)
North Carolina	(865,006)
North Dakota	(86,684)
Ohio	(992,503)
Oklahoma	(337,667)
Oregon	(396,214)
Pennsylvania	(1,099,308)
Puerto Rico	(38,690)
Rhode Island	(93,966)
South Carolina	(400,038)
South Dakota	(95,893)
Tennessee	(571,436)
Texas	(2,361,249)
Utah	(250,300)
Vermont	(73,596)
Virgin Islands	(2,048)
Virginia	(717,559)
Washington	(667,232)
West Virginia	(137,517)
Wisconsin	(537,191)
Wyoming	(65,328)

Figure 4.1 Number of corporations by state.

the expression, "If you do work you love, you'll never work a day in your life." Leisure services sounds like something they could love. However, unless there are people out there who need leisure services, careers in the private, nonprofit, or government sectors are not likely.

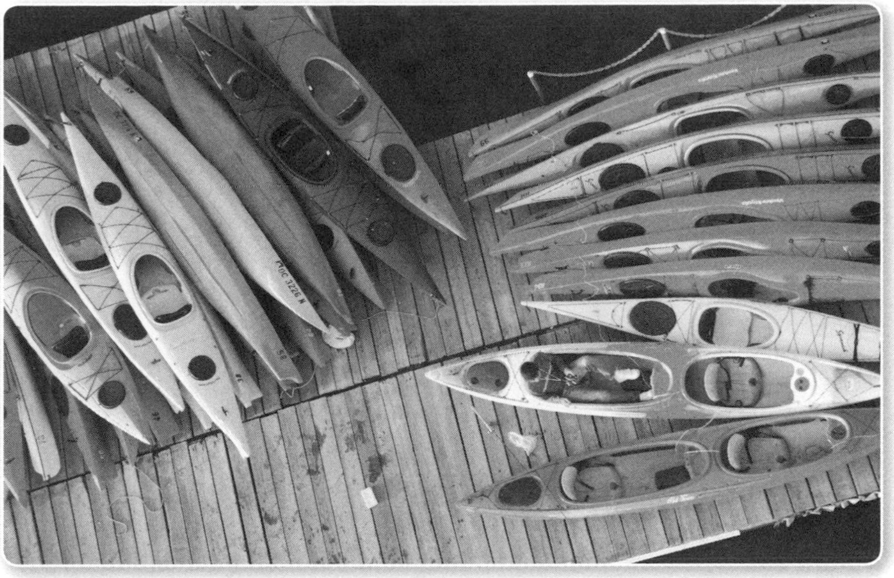

© kuosumo - Fotolia

A new business needs time to build up a customer base. How might the owner of a kayak rental shop promote her business and convince customers to try the service?

New Business Ventures

Entrepreneurs begin businesses without knowing if there are customer needs to be met. These entrepreneurs believe such needs exist, but they aren't entirely sure until they introduce the goods and services. For this reason, starting a new business venture is a riskier proposition than buying a business in a proven market. If an existing business is a going concern, it has already developed a customer base that has a demonstrated capacity of paying for its services. For new business ventures, though, particularly those in markets that are not yet developed, it is uncertain whether customer needs really exist.

The classic example in leisure services is golf. The invention of golf is in dispute. Some historians trace golf back to the Roman sport called *paganica*. In modern times, golf has evolved into a multibillion-dollar industry with 25,000 private and public golf courses in North America alone. But before 1900, golf courses were rare.

Initially, golf courses were built as recreational facilities for the affluent. In the late 19th century, only the affluent had time to enjoy the sport, because less affluent people were too busy working to support themselves and their families. But as North America developed a middle class that had time for leisure, the golf industry reached out to everyone, applying the same rationale to middle-class players that applied to the more affluent—that golf was a great way to relax and enjoy life while staying fit.

This history suggests that it was product development and innovation that ultimately led to the development of golf. The need was obvious to everyone; it just required inventors to figure out how to meet customers' needs. But that is not exactly the whole story. Even though many people believed they needed to play, there were cultural behaviors that caused the middle class to resist playing golf, believing it was the sport of the rich.

The point is that it was not the pursuit of immediate profits that caused the entrepreneurs of golf to seek markets for their products and services; it was their belief in the product itself and its ability to meet a human need and their determination to prove it to the world. After over 100 years of golf in North America, it has been accepted as a sport in which all classes can participate.

Many new ventures in leisure services follow a similar pattern as golf. The entrepreneur sees that a certain leisure service meets an obvious need. The first step is to develop the service itself and then to develop promotional techniques for educating potential customers to become consumers. Being a venture entrepreneur starts with a belief in the service and ends with convincing customers they need the service.

Because the transaction between provider and user is voluntary in the private sector, a fundamental mindset of the venture entrepreneur must be to focus on meeting customer needs and creating the want. But here's the irony of being a venture entrepreneur who believes in a product or service and makes the effort to convince the general public it needs that product: Once you convince people they need your product, competitors will enter the marketplace, and the competitive advantage that you enjoyed for a brief time will be lost. Convinced

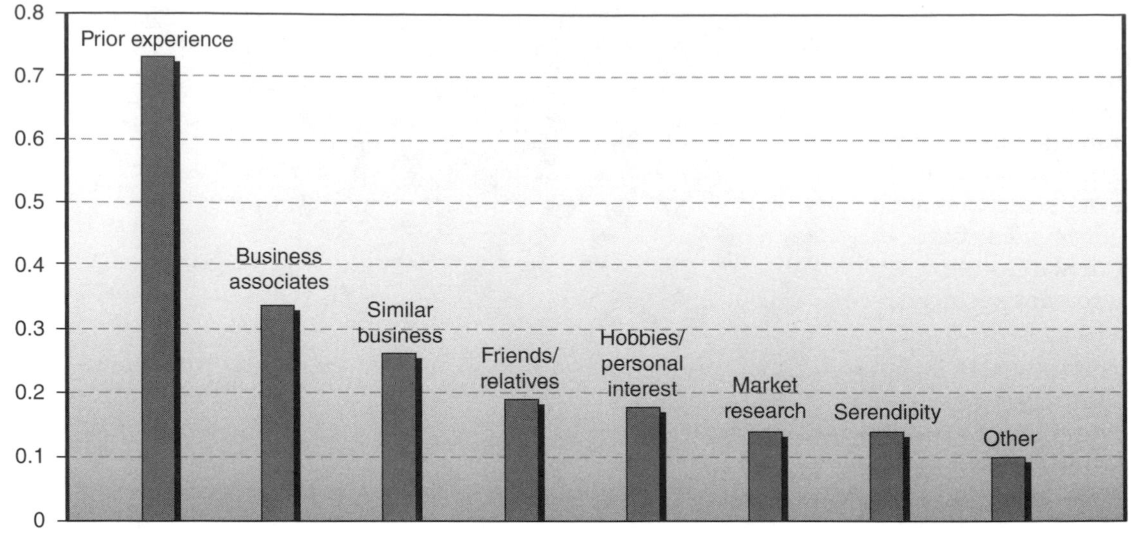

Figure 4.2 Sources of new business ideas.

that they need the product or service, consumers will not hesitate to buy a better or cheaper version somewhere else. Just think of how many golf courses are in North America alone.

According to G.E. Mills, a noted Canadian business environmentalist, 73 percent of new venture ideas originate from the entrepreneur's previous experience with the business, 33 percent come from business associates, 26 percent come from having experience in similar businesses, and 19 percent come from ideas provided by friends and relatives (Mills 1991) (figure 4.2).

But according to a recent study, "empirical results based on 303 responses received by mail survey of entrepreneurs in information technology consulting firms reveal clear differences between ideas and opportunities and further, that social networks are important at both the idea identification and opportunity recognition stages of the process" (Dess, Lumpkin, and Eisner 2011, p. 33). In other words, product and service ideas can come from anywhere. Leisure services entrepreneurs would be well advised to keep their eyes and ears open.

Existing Businesses

Successful businesses have already identified a need for their goods or services. To stay in business and defend against competition, they have to focus on how the business can *better* meet customer needs. In other words, they need to retain existing customers and convert potential customers to choose them over their competitors.

As mentioned before, creating and meeting customer needs is what differentiates the private sector from the public sector. Government services exist without competition, although, arguably, leisure services provided by governmental units often have competition from the private and nonprofit sectors. Nevertheless, the idea that governmental units should focus on members of the public as if they were customers of a business is not realistic. For most governmental services, there is no threat that they will lose their customers to competitors and, anyway, the public is forced to pay for the services.

Businesses existing in a competitive environment, as most of them do, also exist in a market that is growing, maturing, or declining, as discussed in chapter 2. The concept of competition, therefore, is that competing businesses vie for the attention and patronage of customers who have options of transacting with one business or another. If paying customers have other options, it would be smart for nonprofits and even governmental units to focus on customer needs.

Market Research

There are a number of ways to determine what people want and need so that a voluntary transaction can take place where customers pay for a leisure service through a business, nonprofit, or governmental unit that exists in a competitive environment. One way is to offer the product or service and see if anyone purchases it. That's what the vast majority of venture entrepreneurs do.

They believe their product or service is needed and they offer it. The offering is either successful or not, and the business either makes a go of it or doesn't.

Economists believe that the reason most businesses fail is because they do not have enough capital to sustain themselves for the first five years of the business. But that's not entirely true. Bill Gates didn't need five years worth of capital to survive. His idea of the Windows operating system was so good that Microsoft took off immediately.

Some businesses take off immediately, but most don't. According to the Small Business Administration (SBA n.d.), over 80 percent of all U.S. businesses fail in the first five years. If the government officials who work for the SBA are right, then how would they explain Microsoft, a company that started with virtually no venture capital? One possible explanation is that it was not the absence of capital but rather the presence of an excellent idea.

How does an entrepreneur know if a product or service meets people's needs in sufficient numbers for the business to take off, and when does the entrepreneur know that the mother lode has played itself out? There is only one way: unbiased market research. Performing market research can be as simple as the entrepreneur knowing the business or as complicated as hiring a consultant to build statistical models of market trends, performing consumer surveys, or test marketing a product in Peoria. The most important thing is that the research be unbiased.

Market research, feasibility analysis, and business plans are tools that venture entrepreneurs or, for that matter, established companies use to evaluate the potential for success that awaits them in the marketplace. Entrepreneurs purchasing existing companies outright or investing in the **stock** of existing companies would be well advised to perform some kind of market analysis before they spend their money. The landscape is riddled with the bankruptcies of those who don't.

MAKING A PROFIT

If profits are the retained earnings of businesses after expenses are paid, the question is, how do entrepreneurs make a profit? The simple answer is that they spend less than they receive in revenues. The more difficult question is, how does this occur? How does a business spend less than it takes in?

One way to spend is to begin with a plan called a **budget**. A budget is a prediction of how much money an entity will receive and how much it will spend over a given period of time. Typically, budgets are written each year, the beginning of which may or may not be January 1. Sometimes a budget year, commonly called a **fiscal year**, begins at a time when the business cycle for the entity logically begins or ends.

For the Walt Disney Company, the fiscal year begins on October 1 each year and ends on September 30. Many other leisure services corporations choose the same dates for the fiscal year because their busiest season is the summer, and by the end of September most of their revenues should be received and their bills paid. Using an October-to-September fiscal year allows the accounting system to match revenues and expenses, minimizing accruals.

Vetter Fairing Company

In the mid-1960s, a young entrepreneur, Craig Vetter, noticed that baby boomers were starting to ride motorcycles, particularly on long trips. With the construction of the interstate highway system and the infusion of larger and larger Japanese motorcycles that baby boomers were purchasing to ride on interstates, Vetter saw the need for a windshield system, or fairing, for these motorcycles that would protect riders from getting beaten up as they rode.

Starting the Vetter Fairing Company in his garage in Rantoul, Illinois, in 1966, Vetter built protective windshield systems with storage compartments as accessories. Within five years, the Vetter Fairing Company was making thousands of fairings a year at its factory complex west of Rantoul, filling a need that Japanese motorcycle manufacturers overlooked.

By 1978, motorcycle manufactures had begun making their own fairings for their larger models. Vetter saw the writing on the wall and sold his company to Bell-Riddell, Inc., a manufacturer of motorcycle and football helmets. With the decline in motorcycle riding in the early 1980s and the preference for American-made Harley-Davidsons over Japanese bikes, Vetter Fairing went bankrupt in 1983.

Within a business budget, the first issue is the **cost of goods sold**, which is the cost of producing the product or service considering its **direct costs**. For instance, suppose a person started a coffee shop called Coffee Café. If the average cost of a Coffee Café cup of coffee includes the cost of the cup, coffee, and condiments, the direct cost might be $1.00. If Coffee Café predicts it will sell 50,000 cups of coffee in a year, the predicted cost of goods sold is $50,000.

The next budget consideration is the **gross profit**, the difference between the total revenues of the product or service and the cost of goods sold. If the Coffee Café sold 50,000 cups of coffee at an average cost of $6.00 each, its total revenue would be $300,000, and its gross profits would be $250,000. Dividing gross profit ($250,000) by total revenue ($300,000) generates a percentage (84 percent) called the **gross profit margin**, which is pretty good since coffee stores usually sell more than coffee and have other gross profits in the mix. But let's assume that coffee is all the Coffee Café sells. If that awakens your sense of greed and makes you want to start a coffee shop of your own so you can keep 84 percent of the revenue that comes into the store, hold on a second. There are other costs to consider in a budget.

There is the labor to staff Coffee Café, rent or a mortgage to pay, utilities, cleaning supplies, the cost of furniture and equipment, and advertising. These are the **indirect costs** of doing business and must be subtracted from gross profits. Let's say these indirect costs of operating Coffee Café total an additional $200,000. Then the gross profit ($250,000) minus indirect costs ($200,000) would be a **net income** of $50,000. Dividing net income ($50,000) by total revenue ($300,000) generates a **net profit margin** of about 17 percent from the coffee product line.

If the owner of the fictitious Coffee Café sold only coffee, he would not have $50,000 at the end of the year, however. He would have to pay taxes on the profits. For the sake of argument, let's say that the owner is in a 35 percent tax bracket. His taxes on the net profits from the store would be $17,500, leaving $32,500 as the profit. Table 4.1 reflects the budget for the coffee shop.

Included in the budget is a column for the actual revenues and expenses. Assuming that only 80 percent of the total revenues are received, and considering that the direct expenses of coffee, cups, napkins, and condiments decrease accordingly, the Coffee Café is no longer profitable. Because the business is heavy on fixed and indirect costs of labor, rent, utilities, and other expenses, a 20 percent decline in predicted revenues changes everything.

That is why it is so important to accurately predict revenues for a business venture. Unfor-

Table 4.1 Coffee Café Budget

	Budget	Actual
REVENUES		
Latte—10,000 cups at $7.00 each	$70,000	$56,000
Domestic blend—20,000 cups at $5.00 each	100,000	80,000
Cappuccino—10,000 cups at $7.00 each	70,000	56,000
Flavored coffee—10,000 cups at $6.00 each	60,000	48,000
Total revenues	**$300,000**	**$240,000**
EXPENSES		
Labor—two people at $10/hour × 12 hours/day × 365 days	$87,600	$87,600
Rent—$8,000/month × 12 months	96,000	96,000
Utilities	9,000	9,000
Cleaning supplies	1,400	1,400
Furniture and equipment replacement and repairs	6,000	5,000
Marketing costs	1,000	1,000
Coffee, cups, napkins, and condiments	50,000	40,000
Total expenses	**$250,000**	**$240,000**
Net revenues	**$50,000**	**$0**

tunately, revenue prediction is not an easy task. Market research helps, but the basic product idea is the foundation. Without an idea that costs less to provide than the market will bear in price, there is no real opportunity to make a profit.

The points to remember are as follows: Profit margin is the difference between revenues received for the products or services and the cost of goods sold. Gross profits are a function of the total number of products or services sold as well. But net profits need to consider the indirect overhead costs that are part of running a business. This is a somewhat simplistic view of profitability, but a more detailed view will be presented as we continue.

© Monkey Business/fotolia.com

To start a business like the Coffee Café, an entrepreneur must have enough capital to cover startup costs, which might include the facility, supplies, equipment, furniture, staff salaries, and more.

DEBT VERSUS EQUITY

On a balance sheet, there are two terms that, when summed, equal the value of the total assets of the company: *debt* and *equity*. Liabilities include accounts payable and long- and short-term debt. Technically, accounts payable are short-term debts owed to other companies or individuals for products or services already purchased. That suggests that debt and equity equal total assets.

The assets of a company are what the company owns. The debt is what it owes to someone other than the owners, and the equity is the remaining value of the company that can be said to be the true worth of the company. When companies are bought and sold, it is the equity that should determine the sale price.

Debt

To get a business venture up and running, capital needs must be accommodated. **Capital needs** refers to the money needed to cover operations. In the Coffee Café example, capital needs might include furniture, equipment, and the down payment for purchasing the building. If the Coffee Café were a franchise, there would be a franchise fee to pay. If the building were rented, the first month's rent would need to be paid in advance. Suppliers would probably require supplies to be paid for with cash in advance, and there would be other startup costs associated with opening the store. To start the business, the entrepreneur would need to assemble enough capital to cover these costs.

To pay these costs, the venture entrepreneur probably would need to dedicate personal resources and might need to borrow money from someone else. That someone else might be a person, including relatives and friends, or a bank or other lending institution. Either way, some entity would need to be willing to share the risk with the new owner.

There are two directions the venture entrepreneur could go. He could seek partnerships with other entities, which means he would pursue the **sale of equity**, or co-ownership of the company. If the entrepreneur did not want any partners, he would pursue the **sale of debt**, which is not ownership of the company but rather a loan that would be paid back with interest.

Typically, banks do not prefer to purchase ownership in companies. They would rather loan money to individuals or businesses with the understanding that they will be repaid with interest. Discussions of the banking industry in chapter 2 illustrated how banks work to support businesses and individuals by paying interest to depositors and charging interest to borrowers. That's the business banks are in. They borrow money at a low interest rate and loan it at a higher rate. The difference is theirs to keep.

What needs to be included in this discussion is that banks are not interested (or shouldn't be interested) in taking unnecessary risks. If banks loan money to people or businesses who can't repay it, they not only lose the interest the borrower would pay back but also lose the principal.

Therefore, banks don't like to loan money to venture entrepreneurs. The proposition is too risky, especially if the entrepreneur has not done unbiased research to determine the odds of success. If more than 80 percent of businesses fail in their first five years, it's unlikely the bank will be repaid. There's no way banks could stay in business taking those kinds of risks.

That is why the capital and startup costs of new businesses are usually funded by the owner or the owner's family, called **equity contributions**. That is not to say that there are never other people willing to put up capital for new ventures. Sometimes there are, as in the case of Google. When Google went public, it had a track record of performance as a privately owned company. As a result, **venture capitalists** emerged to take risks that banks would not take, especially after the crash of the dot-com companies in 2000 (Beattie 2012). Venture capitalists were willing to do so because their mindset is similar to that of gamblers who play long odds for high payback. Venture capitalists are willing to take risks that banks and other lending institutions aren't willing to take. But even venture capitalists need favorable odds of success. It's just that every venture capitalist has a different idea of what favorable odds are.

Existing companies that do not want to borrow money from banks or sell stock to venture capitalists issue **corporate bonds**, which are a form of debt. Businesses who sell corporate bonds generally sell them to private investors rather than lending institutions. Corporate bonds are debt that pays a fixed interest rate to the holder, usually at a lower rate of interest than a bank loan, which is why banks are not interested in buying them.

For accounting purposes, bonds and bank loans go on the balance sheet as debt. Balance sheets were defined earlier as pictures of the financial position of a company at a given point in time. Balance sheets show that the assets of a company are equal to its liabilities and equity; in other words, that which the company *owns* is equal to what the company *owes*.

Equity

Equity is an accounting treatment of the source of what the company owes. Instead of owing debt to lenders, the company conceptually owes equity to the owners. When owners contribute money to the business, it is recorded on the balance sheet as owners' equity. There is no commitment to repay owners' equity. There is the belief on the part of the contributors of equity that the equity will grow as the business makes profits in future years, but there is no guarantee of profits.

Venture capitalists can purchase equity in a company when it is publicly sold, and it is the hope of private owners converting the company to a publicly owned business that venture capitalists will do just that. For established companies, stockholders buy and sell shares in corporate equity on stock exchanges. These publicly traded stocks are different, though, from ownership equity in privately owned companies. In the case of our hypothetical Coffee Café, only one person invested in the company: the owner. The balance sheet for Coffee Café (table 4.2) shows basic categories of assets, liabilities, and equity that would appear on the first day the business opened.

Assuming that Coffee Café's owner, the venture entrepreneur, put up all of the equity needed to start up the shop himself, the balance sheet on the first day would have no debt, just equity. There is a place for debt on the balance sheet, and, as will be discussed later, there are places for other categories of assets and liabilities that will be used as the balance sheet evolves over time.

Table 4.2 Coffee Café Balance Sheet (January 1, 2010)

Current assets	
Cash	$5,000
Inventories of supplies	10,000
Total current assets	$15,000
Fixed assets	
Furniture	$5,000
Equipment	20,000
Total fixed assets	$25,000
Total assets	**$40,000**
Liabilities	$0
Owner's equity	$40,000

The important consideration is that the accounting treatment of what has transpired before the opening of the new business is represented fairly. The venture entrepreneur took $40,000 of his own money, purchased supplies and equipment to make the coffee, bought furniture upon which customers would enjoy the coffee, and had $5,000 left over to pay some bills, hoping that customers would come into the store and provide revenue to keep the business operating. Debt is not yet an issue for the venture entrepreneur.

Existing businesses sometimes borrow money to leverage assets, using the value of their business assets to acquire more land, buildings, or equipment in order to produce or sell more products. If the company has had a good track record of making money, its debt will be considered a good risk, allowing the company to obtain a low interest rate on the loan. If the business has a less than stellar track record of making money, the interest rate for debt will be high.

On a balance sheet, debt is a liability, offsetting assets and ultimately reducing owners' equity. Interest is not recorded on the balance sheet; it is an expense. In our Coffee Café example, no interest is shown on the budget because the owner contributed all of the startup and initial capital costs. In the balance sheet for the business, which will be presented shortly, there will be.

But let's say that the owner of Coffee Cafe is six months into his new venture when a major piece of equipment breaks down, costing $10,000 to replace it. The owner has no money of his own to replace it but is able to convince a bank to loan him $10,000. Assuming that he still has $5,000 in cash and $10,000 in inventories, his balance sheet has changed as shown in table 4.3.

Table 4.3 Coffee Café Balance Sheet (July 1, 2010)

Current assets	
Cash	$5,000
Inventories of supplies	10,000
Total current assets	$15,000
Fixed assets	
Furniture	$5,000
Equipment	20,000
Total fixed assets	$25,000
Total assets	**$40,000**
Liabilities	$10,000
Owner's equity	$30,000

What has happened is that the transaction of borrowing money to replace the broken equipment is reflected on Coffee Café's balance sheet, showing that the owner lost $10,000 in equity and replaced it with $10,000 in debt. In other words, the owner lost $10,000 when the equipment failed and he had to borrow money to keep his business open. The good news is he is still the **sole proprietor** of the coffee shop, which means he is the only owner.

Being a sole proprietor is an attractive option to many businesspeople. Sole proprietors have complete control over all the operations of the business. They are the boss and can run the company any way they see fit. On the other hand, there is a downside. If the owner is ambitious and sees the opportunity to grow the company, let's say starting coffee shops in other locations, he will need money to do it. If the flagship Coffee Café is not yet profitable enough to finance expansion at other locations, he has two choices for leveraging his assets. He can borrow money from a bank, which has to be repaid with interest, or he can sell stock to investors, which provides them with ownership in the company.

TAKING ON NEW OWNERS

In order for a company to take on new owners, the new owners must be willing to buy into the equity side of the balance sheet. In other words, the new owners need to purchase a share of the equity from the current owners. That is precisely what happens among publicly traded companies. Corporate stock, which is equity in the company, is bought and sold at a market price.

Theoretically, the market price should be easy to determine. It should be the value of the equity on the balance sheet divided by the number of shares. But that would be too easy. In reality, other factors contribute to the value of the corporate stock that is traded on stock markets. One factor is how much revenue the company is expected to acquire in the future. That can be a function of the state of the economy, it can be related to new products in the pipeline, or it can be based on confidence in the management of the company.

Taking on new owners can be accomplished by individuals purchasing stock in stock markets, or it can be done by one company purchasing the stock of another. When the latter occurs, the purchasing company can pay for the equity of the purchased company using its stock, or it can borrow money to purchase the stock of the purchased company by going to banks and borrowing money, which, of course, adds debt to the purchasing company's balance sheet. Either way, equity ownership is a function of purchasing the equity of a company.

Equity Ownership

The disadvantage of borrowing money is that it creates an expense in the operating budget that may not be affordable. New coffee shops in new locations take time to generate the walk-in traffic necessary to increase revenue to cover the debt needed for expansion. Thus, borrowing money from a bank may not be feasible. The bank and the Coffee Café owner might not see it as a risk worth taking.

The other option is to sell stock in Coffee Café, Inc., a corporation created by the original owner. Venture capitalists might purchase stock in the company, showing a willingness to take on the risk that banks would not. Stockholders will not earn interest on this investment; instead they gamble that the stock will increase in value when the business is successful. For the Coffee Café owner, selling stock means there are no principal or interest payments to strain the budget.

The disadvantage of selling stock to new investors is that, with a share of ownership in the company, stockholders have a legal right to have a say in how the company is operated. When the Coffee Café owner incorporated his business, he filed a charter with his state government in which he agreed to the terms of how his company would be operated. Nearly all states require companies with stockholders to have annual meetings where management reports how and what it is doing to make a profit for the company.

The Pursuit of Profit

What makes starting a business so appealing to some people is that they are able to be their own bosses, they can set their own hours, and they can take the business in whatever direction they would like. And then there's the money. To some businesspeople, the money is secondary to the freedom of being their own boss, but to others, it is an important consideration.

One person who has learned the importance of making money in business is Tod Stanton, owner of Design Perspectives in Naperville, Illinois, a landscape design firm he started in 2004. (Tod was one of my graduate students in park and recreation administration at Aurora University.) Tod grew up in Ohio and decided to go to the University of Georgia to get a degree in landscape architecture. When he graduated, he was hired by a large landscape architecture company in Colorado that designed parks and playgrounds all over the United States. He then moved to a smaller firm in the Chicago area, but because of the turmoil in the industry in 2001, he decided to take a position as an in-house designer for the Naperville Park District, a public agency owning more than 140 parks.

During his career, Tod made a nice living as an employee for private firms and the park district, but he felt something was missing in his life. He was working hard for other people and he really wanted to work for himself. So in 2004, his wife secure in her job, he quit his job at the park district, bought $10,000 worth of computer hardware and software, and started his own landscape architecture firm. It was a risky move, but it paid off.

By 2011, Design Perspectives was a successful firm, earning about $400,000 in revenues each year. With that level of income, Tod could afford to own a new Escalade, buy his family a $500,000 house, take flying lessons, buy property for a summer home in Wisconsin, and travel to Eastern Europe and Haiti as a volunteer installing playgrounds for underprivileged children. As with friends of his who had started their own businesses, the extra income had become his motivator, not the autonomy of being his own boss. People get used to autonomy in the first two years of running a business, so it's what money can buy that often makes going to work every day worth it. Pursuit of profits was Tod's new boss, an extrinsic motivator that is not present in the public and nonprofit sectors.

Being motivated to run a business because you can become wealthy may seem unfair to people who are unable to do so. But it is the substance of the American Dream. To some people, being wealthy enough to have the finer things in life is what it's all about.

Ordinarily, annual stockholders meetings are formalities where, depending on the size of the company, not much happens. But for larger companies, votes may be taken on major issues that resulted from management decisions. In addition, the board of directors is elected at annual meetings. The board meets on a regular basis and has much more to say about how management runs the company than the stockholders do at their annual meeting.

For small companies such as Coffee Café, if owners choose to sell ownership in the company by issuing stock certificates at a specified sale price, company founders will be sure to retain a majority of shares for themselves. Because each share of ownership has one vote at the annual meeting, annual stockholder meetings and board meetings can be political events. Remember the earlier example from the movie *Wall Street*, in which Gordon Gekko was trying to oust the management of the Teldar Paper Corporation at its annual meeting? Gekko did not own enough shares of stock to control the vote. But by winning the support of other stockholders in the room, he got a majority of shareholders to vote in favor of making management changes.

Any politician who argues that government should be run like a business is missing the political dimension of how businesses are run. Any enlightened businessperson knows as much. Controlling a majority interest in a company means the person doing so has power. Our Coffee Café owner knows that, so when given the opportunity to sell stock to venture capitalists, he would make sure he retains 51 percent or more ownership. That way, at the annual meeting, there would be no Gordon Gekko to come forward and say that management should be replaced.

Boards of Directors

Corporate boards of directors are voted into office by shareholders. Sometimes, shareholders with large blocks of stock elect themselves to these boards. Other people are selected to serve on boards because of their business knowledge, political contacts, or the desire of the board to achieve diversity. For instance, Hillary Clinton was appointed to the board of Walmart because of her political contacts as well as to diversify the board (Barbaro 2007).

Corporations appoint board members who also serve on other boards and board members who are managers of other corporations in various industries. These are called **interlocking directorates**. This practice, though legal, raises questions about conflict of interest and the quality of decisions that board members may make on behalf of stockholders. It is difficult to provide evidence that interlocking directorates is harmful to stockholders, but there are plenty of examples of how corporate executives and board members are overcompensated for their services.

In our Coffee Café example, the fledgling company would not be in a position of dealing with interlocking directorates because, if the café sold up to 49 percent of its stock to outside investors, as a **private company**, two issues would prevent outsiders from getting on the board of directors. The Coffee Café owner could stipulate that the venture capitalists cannot resell stock to other individuals. Or, the terms could stipulate that the venture capitalists must sell the stock back to the owner if they decide they want out or he could allow them to sell it to someone he approved.

Politics of Business

To say that businesses operate strictly to serve customers is a myth. Just like the public sector, the needs of customers are often way down on the list of priorities. Whenever people are involved in anything, there will be greed and a struggle for power, resulting in politics. The customers' needs being paramount is probably more true when a business is small or starting up. What often happens to large companies is they evolve into bureaucratic cultures where the customer can become more of a nuisance than the reason the companies exist. But theoretically, businesses exist to meet their customers' needs.

Just because the business in question is within the leisure services industry is not sufficient to make an argument that people struggling for money and power will behave any better than people in other industries. A classic example of this is the service of Roy Disney, nephew of founder Walt Disney, who served on the Walt Disney Company board of directors for decades. Through his ownership of 16.2 million shares of Disney stock, worth $1.5 billion at the time of his death in 2009, Roy Disney was able to serve as an executive from 1956 to 1977 and then as a member of the board of directors for decades. As an active board member, Disney led coups to remove two CEOs of the Disney Corporation, Ron Miller and Michael Eisner, using the same techniques of mobilizing shareholders at the annual meeting to support his position of removing management.

Disney's tenure was highlighted by him bringing his experience as a corporate executive to the board of directors, which must have been a nightmare for management. Having a boss who has served in your position previously means that your decisions will always be compared with hers. This is similar to what happens in the public sector.

Corporate politics, being a struggle for control like any other political struggle, can involve efforts to remove the CEO or to influence the CEO's decisions, but more often than not, corporate board members are selected to protect the CEOs. As mentioned, some corporate board members are elected, but most are appointed, much the same as board members of nonprofit organizations. When a board seat is open, the remaining board members select the replacement.

Board members are generally selected because they will not rock the boat. Corporate board members are usually paid to attend meetings and review management decisions. Sometimes CEOs serve as board members themselves, and sometimes they are even the board chair. The next time you hear that someone is chairman of the board and CEO, it means he runs the business and is also chairman of the board that oversees him.

Maneuvering into positions is the art of politics—perhaps even the art of war, according to Sun Tzu, an ancient military general, strategist, and philosopher who believed that strategy trumped brute force and whose military strategies are considered metaphors for politics, corporate initiatives, and even relationships. Major corporations are much more about politics than our Coffee Café example. Coffee Café is a dictatorship. Unless the owner is forced to share power, he won't. Large corporations that have sought external funding from investors to get large investments in the first place are forced to be more democratic and, therefore, more political.

SUMMARY

If it seems that business is more efficient than government, one explanation may be that business is dependent on the financial support of customers. With customers holding the primary power over the business, business leaders are forced to focus on their need to make a profit.

Private entities begin, though, with ideas that originate from sources other than the customer. Often, venture entrepreneurs have ideas of their own about what goods or services they would like to provide. Original ideas need to be sold to customers because they've never thought of themselves as needing the product or service.

The process of turning an idea into a profit revolves around understanding the difference between the cost of providing a good or service and the revenues that can be generated from it. There are direct and indirect costs of doing business. Understanding the fragility of that relationship can help venture entrepreneurs understand the risk of failure.

All businesses need capital to get up and running. A basic challenge of starting a new business, therefore, is to determine the source of its startup capital. There really are only two choices, debt and equity. Debt is money that needs to be repaid with interest. Equity is ownership of the company that brings along with it a voice from the owner or owners about how the company should operate.

Ownership voice can manifest itself in various ways, depending on whether the company is privately owned or publicly owned. For privately owned companies, level of influence is determined by who has a majority ownership of company stock. Whoever owns a majority of company stock is the person or group of persons who makes the management decisions.

The same is true for **publicly held companies**. But since a larger group of people usually holds stock in a publicly traded company compared with a privately held company, the politics tend to increase accordingly. This is especially true because the accounting reports of publicly traded companies are made public.

Visit the Web Resource

For case studies, sample financial statements,
key terms, and more, please visit the web resource at
www.HumanKinetics.com/LeisureServicesFinancialManagement

chapter 5

Private-Sector Accounting

Learning Outcomes

After completing this chapter, students will be able to do the following:

- Define the function of the FASB.
- Identify basic financial accounting concepts.
- Describe some of the most important GAAP of business accounting.
- Determine how transparency for publicly traded companies works.
- Understand balance sheets and how they are used in financial reporting.
- Learn about income statements and their use in private-sector accounting.

As a leisure services professional, you need to know that when you manage the fun of other people, you must do so systematically and give the organization of financial systems top priority. The more organized an entity is about the way it handles its money, the more efficient it will be. And the more efficient an organization is, the more it can do, which is why it behooves leisure services professionals to understand financial management.

A basic tenet of the leisure services profession in all sectors is the business model that people will pay for services because leisure activities are worth the cost. This is why leisure services managers in the public and nonprofit sectors must understand financial management techniques used in the private sector. Many leisure services at the government level are operated as enterprises, using the same rules of accounting as the private sector. Swimming pools, golf courses, and recreation programs are operated as enterprises, just like Central Park and Disneyland.

As discussed in previous chapters, nonprofit leisure organizations, such as the YMCA, have been operated as enterprises since they stopped being totally charitable organizations. Nonprofit leisure providers charge fees for services, placing those monies into enterprise funds using FASB GAAP just as business and governments use enterprise funds. In the public and nonprofit sectors, an **enterprise fund** accounts for operations financed primarily through user charges or fees. With proper management, fees should be sufficient to make the enterprise self-sustaining, a private-sector concept embraced by the public and nonprofit sectors.

Therefore, no matter what sector you work in, you need the business mindset that leisure services can generate fees to pay operating costs. Having this mindset will help your agency or business provide more services than it ordinarily would.

ACCOUNTING STANDARDS

Following accounting standards is the first rule of financial management in the private sector. Accounting standards mean there is a correct way to do accounting, and anything short of those standards is the wrong way. Following standard accounting practices allows an organization to generate reports that show if the entity is making money or losing money. Obviously, organizations that lose money over the long term won't be around for long, and organizations that make money will.

Reports provide a clear and accurate picture of the financial conditions within an organization so that the manager can take appropriate action. Businesses don't have the safety net of taxes that governmental units do or the safety net of donations that nonprofit organizations do, so paying attention to the numbers is an essential survival skill for managers in the private sector.

Earlier you learned the ethical and legal reasons for adhering to accounting standards, largely to be fair to investors. Now let's focus on the accounting standards that allow leisure services managers in the private sector to determine if their companies are making a profit.

Financial Accounting Standards Board

As discussed in chapter 3, the FASB sets the standards for financial accounting for the private sector. It reviews and revises the reporting processes that businesses use so that their financial positions will be transparent to investors and so that business managers will know how their company is doing.

The FASB describes its mission on its website (www.fasb.org) as follows:

> The mission of the FASB is to establish and improve standards of financial accounting and reporting for the guidance and education of the public, including issuers, auditors, and users of financial information. [FASB's] financial reporting system is essential to the efficient functioning of the economy. That is because it is the means by which investors, creditors, and others receive the credible, transparent, and comparable financial information they rely on to make sound investment and credit decisions. Accounting standards are an important element of the financial reporting system because they govern the minimum required content of financial statements of U.S. public companies.

Consistent with that mission, the FASB maintains the *FASB Accounting Standards Codification* (Accounting Standards Codification), which represents the source of authoritative standards of accounting and reporting recognized by the FASB to be applied by nongovernmental entities. (Rules and interpretive releases of the SEC under federal securities laws are also sources of authoritative accounting principles for SEC registrants.)

To accomplish its mission, the FASB acts to:

- Improve the usefulness of financial reporting by focusing on the primary characteristics of relevance and reliability and on the qualities of comparability and consistency;
- Keep standards current to reflect changes in methods of doing business and changes in the economic environment;
- Consider promptly any significant areas of deficiency in financial reporting that might be addressed through the standard-setting process;
- Promote the international convergence of accounting standards concurrent with improving the quality of financial reporting; and
- Improve the common understanding of the nature and purposes of information contained in financial reports.

The FASB develops broad accounting concepts as well as standards for financial reporting. It also provides guidance on implementation of standards. Concepts are useful in guiding the Board in establishing standards and in providing a frame of reference, or conceptual framework, for resolving accounting issues. The framework will help to establish reasonable bounds for judgment in preparing financial information and to increase understanding of, and confidence in, financial information on the part of users of financial reports. It also will help the public to understand the nature and limitations of information supplied by financial reporting.

The Board's work on both concepts and standards is based on research aimed at gaining new insights and ideas. Research is conducted by the FASB staff and others, including foreign, national, and international accounting standard-setting bodies. The Board's activities are open to public participation and observation under the "due process" procedures established by the Board. The FASB actively solicits the views of its various constituencies on accounting issues.

The Board follows certain precepts in the conduct of its activities. They are:

- *To be objective in its decision making* and to ensure, insofar as possible, the neutrality of information resulting from its standards. To be neutral, information must report economic activity as faithfully as possible without coloring the image it communicates for the purpose of influencing behavior in any particular direction.
- *To weigh carefully the views of its constituents* in developing concepts and standards. However, the ultimate determinant of concepts and standards must be the Board's judgment, based on research, public input, and careful deliberation about the usefulness of the resulting information.
- *To promulgate standards only when the expected benefits exceed the perceived costs.* While reliable, quantitative cost–benefit calculations are seldom possible, the Board strives to determine that a proposed standard will meet a significant need and that the costs it imposes, compared with possible alternatives, are justified in relation to the overall benefits.
- *To bring about needed changes in ways that minimize disruption to the continuity of reporting practice.* Reasonable effective dates and transition provisions are established when new standards are introduced. The Board considers it desirable that change be evolutionary to the extent that it can be accommodated by the need for relevance, reliability, comparability, and consistency.
- *To review the effects of past decisions* and interpret, amend, or replace standards in a timely fashion when such action is indicated.

Adapted from Financial Accounting Standards Board.

The FASB is always changing the rules, though. Mostly it changes the rules because some corporate financial managers have tried to **game the system**,

As a business in the private sector, a marathon must accurately record revenues (such as registration fees paid by participants) and expenses (such as staff salaries and facility rentals).

which means manipulating the rules to achieve selfish ends. These unethical managers misrepresent the financial position of a company in order to make money for themselves. By overstating the assets of a company or understating its liabilities, financial managers can overstate the equity.

The FASB's job is to make sure this doesn't happen. The board makes the rules that say how assets and liabilities are supposed to be recorded. It also makes the rules that say how revenues and expenses should be recorded. Recording revenues and expenses is straightforward enough, but valuing assets and liabilities is more complicated.

How the FASB Helps Investors

Transparency is important not only to investors and stockholders but also to the managers of companies. In 2008 the United States experienced a banking crisis stemming from the need for banks to borrow money from the Federal Reserve to make loans because they couldn't always obtain enough money from depositors. To game the system, some banks sold the loans to other investors, other banks, and individuals. To prevent this from happening, the FASB required banks to fairly state their assets, including a representative presentation of the value of their assets, so that investors would not be purchasing **toxic assets**, a term used to suggest that the values of the loans were significantly lower than shown on their balance sheets.

The loan contract between the bank and the individual borrowing the money becomes an asset that can be bought and sold. Borrowers generally don't care who they repay the loan to; they just know they have to pay it. The bank knows there is a chance the borrower won't repay the loan. That means there is a risk of the bank losing money. Thus, many banks sell their loan contracts at a discount to investors who are willing to take the risk. A **loan contract** is the written agreement between the lender and borrower that spells out the terms of the loan. **Discounts** are decreases in the full value of principal and interest that the borrower would pay.

Banks have an expectation of the principal and interest that should be repaid overall. People or institutions purchasing loan contracts from banks also have expectations of the amount of principal and interest that should be repaid. If loan-contract investors didn't think more would be repaid than banks think would be repaid, they wouldn't buy loan contracts from banks. If banks didn't think less principal and interest would be repaid, they wouldn't sell loan contracts.

Here's where the FASB comes in: It sets the accounting rules of asset valuation. The FASB says banks can't misrepresent the value of the loan contracts by selling sell them to investors for more than they're worth. In other words, banks must put a fair value on the loan contracts. They must transparently represent their value by defining the risk of borrowers not repaying them.

Also, the FASB says that, while the bank owns the loan contracts, it can't misrepresent the contracts on its balance sheets as overvalued assets. To do so would unrealistically represent the corporate equity. As discussed earlier and will be discussed in more detail in this chapter, **stock price**, the market value of a share of common stock on any given day, tends to increase as owners' equity increases.

All of this may seem a little confusing, but it boils down to preventing financial manipulation for selfish ends. Remember our discussion in chapter 4 about greed? If corporate financial managers misrepresent their assets at higher values, they can sell those assets for more than they're worth, and stock prices can be higher than they should fairly be. There's a lot of money at stake. Financial managers who lie about their assets can make money doing so. The FASB's job is to make sure financial managers don't game the system, because the business code of ethics is simply not enough to guarantee this.

The FASB has recently developed rules that prevent banks from misrepresenting the value of their loan contracts as they did in the years leading up to the 2008 banking crisis. Banks must now show loan-contract investors their own expectation of loan repayment; in other words, banks must be more transparent in that regard.

Does that mean loans are valued fairly to investors? Not necessarily. There's a Latin phrase that governs sales: *caveat emptor*, translated to mean "buyer beware." Even with the FASB rules, buyers need to beware. It is always in sellers' interests to overstate the value of what they're selling, and it's always the responsibility of the buyer to beware. The FASB will never totally solve that problem, nor will government regulations. There's just too much money for sellers to make by figuring out a way around the rules.

How the FASB Helps Management

As stated earlier in this chapter, the financial reports that businesses generate should be transparent for management as well as investors. Some managers behave dishonestly, and investors need to be protected from them. But most private-sector managers behave ethically, because not only are they not big fans of prison food, but they are also basically honest people who want to be successful.

The FASB has specified that financial reports for businesses be straightforward and simple. These reports need to be consistent throughout the business sector so that anyone who has a basic understanding of accounting can understand any financial report, regardless of how large or small the company is. To the FASB, accounting standards mean that reports are standardized.

For instance, the fictitious Kids' Amusement Parks of America (KAPA) is an amusement park company with over 20,000 employees and billions of dollars in revenues and assets. For this example, it will be assumed that KAPA would use the same system of accounting and financial reporting that a mom-and-pop amusement park company would use. A person reading one would be able to read the other. The major difference would be the size of the numbers. A **mom-and-pop business** is a small business, usually owned by one or two people (i.e., husband and wife) with a small number of employees and relatively low volume of sales.

The **income statement** in table 5.1 shows the categories of revenues and expenses that any company would need to generate on at least an annual basis. The format of the report is fairly standard, but KAPA has chosen to show previous years' totals for the sake of transparency. Managers use these numbers to manage the company.

The Review of Accountancy Terminology section of this chapter (see page 70) defines and discusses some of the accounting terms that are necessary to understand the statement in table 5.1. The statement is presented now to show the format that any company would be required to use, a format that takes into account the transactions of a multibillion-dollar company for an entire year. The examples for a privately held company that will be shown later are somewhat simpler yet present the same concepts. The terminology used in smaller companies is the same, but certain categories may be left out because they don't apply.

Another report that the FASB requires businesses to generate using GAAP and accounting standards is the balance sheet. The balance sheet for KAPA (table 5.2) is also representative of what business managers and investors see.

Table 5.1 Kids' Amusement Parks of America Corporation Income Statement

	Dec 2012	Dec 2011	Dec 2010
Revenue	912.9	1,021.3	972.8
Cost of goods sold	502.3	505.7	513.2
Gross profit	410.6	515.6	459.5
Gross profit margin	45%	50.5%	47.2%
SG&A expense	196.9	214.3	244.4
Depreciation and amortization	145.9	139.6	138.8
Operating income	67.8	143.9	33.3
Operating margin	7.4%	14.1%	3.4%
Nonoperating income	(17.3)	92.3	(75.6)
Nonoperating expenses	(105.4)	(176.2)	—
Income before taxes	(203.0)	19.4	(237.9)
Income taxes	2.9	116.6	6.2
Net income after taxes	(205.9)	(97.3)	(244.1)
Continuing operations	(64.2)	(97.3)	(244.1)
Discontinued operations	11.8	(15.7)	(9.1)
Total operations	(52.3)	(113.0)	(253.2)
Total net income	(52.3)	(113.0)	(253.2)
Net profit margin	−5.7%	−11.1%	−26%
Diluted EPS (earnings per share) from total net income	(2.51)	(1.39)	(2.90)
Dividends per share	—	—	—

All amounts in millions of U.S. dollars except per-share amounts.

Table 5.2 Kids' Amusement Parks of America Corporation Balance Sheet

Assets	Dec 2012	Dec 2011	Dec 2010
CURRENT ASSETS			
Cash	164.8	210.3	28.4
Net receivables	19.9	20.1	26.5
Inventories	21.8	24.9	26.4
Other current assets	48.6	41.5	39.1
Total current assets	255.1	296.7	120.4
Net fixed assets	1,478.4	1,560.5	1,641.1
Other noncurrent assets	1,174.1	1,173.6	1,183.8
Total assets	**2,907.7**	**3,030.8**	**2,945.3**
Liabilities and shareholders' equity	**Dec 2012**	**Dec 2011**	**Dec 2010**
CURRENT LIABILITIES			
Accounts payable	25.3	25.1	42.7
Short-term debt	308.7	254.0	18.7
Other current liabilities	89.4	163.8	155.9
Total current liabilities	423.4	442.8	217.3
Long-term debt	829.5	2,112.3	2,239.1
Other noncurrent liabilities	2,238.9	919.6	741.5
Total liabilities	**3,491.8**	**3,474.7**	**3,197.9**
SHAREHOLDERS' EQUITY			
Preferred stock equity	0.0	0.0	—
Common stock equity	(584.2)	(443.8)	(252.6)
Total equity	**(584.2)**	**(443.8)**	**(252.6)**

All amounts in millions of U.S. dollars except per-share amounts.

A balance sheet for a small company will be presented later, with slightly less detail but in essentially the same format. Along the way, this chapter will return to discuss these reports and consider how they show the challenges that the management and shareholders of KAPA face.

GENERALLY ACCEPTED ACCOUNTING PRINCIPLES

Financial accounting information must be assembled and reported objectively. Investors and other third parties who rely on such information have a right to be assured that the data are free from bias and inconsistency, whether deliberate or not. As discussed in previous chapters, for this reason, financial accounting relies on certain standards or guides that are called *generally accepted accounting principles (GAAP)*.

According to a 2010 fact sheet of the Federal Accounting Standards Advisory Board (FASAB 2011),

> the term "generally accepted accounting principles" has a specific meaning for accountants and auditors. The Code of Professional Conduct of the American Institute of Certified Public Accounts (AICPA) prohibits members from expressing an opinion or stating affirmatively that financial statements or other financial data "present fairly . . . in conformity with generally accepted accounting principles," if such information contains any departures from accounting principles promulgated by a body designated by the AICPA Council to establish such principles.
>
> The AICPA Council designated FASAB as the body that establishes generally accepted accounting principles (GAAP) for federal

reporting entities. As such, the FASAB is responsible for identifying the "GAAP hierarchy" for federal reporting entities. The GAAP hierarchy consists of the sources of accounting principles used in the preparation of financial statements of federal reporting entities that are presented in conformity with GAAP and the framework for selecting those principles. The hierarchy lists the priority sequence of sources that an entity should look to for accounting and reporting guidance and is discussed in SFFAS 34, The Hierarchy of Generally Accepted Accounting Principles for Federal Entities, Including the Application of Standards Issued by the Financial Accounting Standards Board. The sources of accounting principles that are generally accepted are categorized in descending order of authority as follows:

a. Officially established accounting principles consist of FASAB Statements of Federal Financial Accounting Standards and Interpretations. FASAB Standards and Interpretations will be periodically incorporated in a publication by the FASAB.
b. FASAB technical bulletins and, if specifically made applicable to federal reporting entities by the AICPA and cleared by the FASAB, AICPA Industry Audit and Accounting Guides.
c. Technical releases of the Accounting and Auditing Policy Committee of the FASAB.
d. Implementation guides published by the FASAB staff, as well as practices that are widely recognized and prevalent in the federal government.

The FASAB recognizes that GAAP derive from tradition, such as the concept of matching. In any report of financial statements, the preparer or auditor must indicate to the reader whether or not the information contained within the statements complies with GAAP. The reports must recognize the following principles:

- **regularity**—Defined as conformity to enforced rules and laws.
- **consistency**—When a business has once fixed a method for the accounting treatment of an item, it will enter all similar items that follow in exactly the same way.
- **sincerity**—The accounting unit should reflect in good faith the reality of the company's financial status.
- **permanence of methods**—Allowing the coherence and comparison of the financial information published by the company.
- **noncompensation**—One should show the full details of the financial information and not seek to compensate a debt with an asset or a revenue with an expense.
- **prudence**—Showing the reality as it is; one should not try to make things look prettier than they are. For instance, a revenue should only be recorded when it is certain and a provision should be entered for an expense that is probable.
- **principle of continuity**—When stating financial information, one should assume that the business will not be interrupted. This principle mitigates the principle of prudence. For instance, assets are not to be accounted at their disposable value, but it is accepted that they are at their historical value.
- **periodicity**—Each accounting entry should be allocated to a given period and split accordingly if it covers several periods. A prepaid subscription or lease should be split to the entire time span and not counted for entirely on the date of the transaction.
- **full disclosure and materiality**—All information and values pertaining to the financial position of a business must be disclosed in the records.

These are some of the principles that guide the preparation of financial statements by company accountants and by the auditors who review the company's financial statements and express their opinions regarding the accuracy of those financial statements.

Why should leisure services financial managers understand these principles? Good question. As was discussed in chapter 3, professional ethical standards are at the heart of all that goes on in accounting. But more importantly, the principle of regularity says that laws must be followed, and adhering to all the other principles means the company's financial statements should be as transparent as humanly possible, both for management and investors.

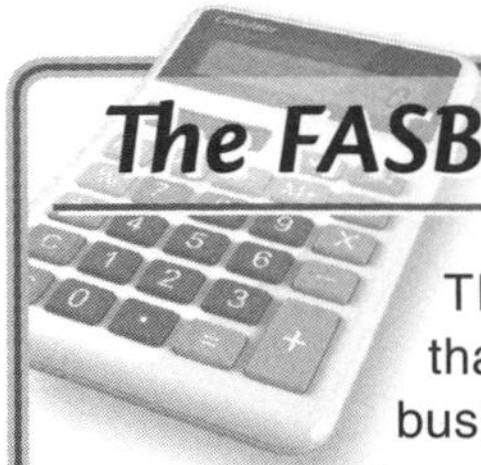

The FASB Is Not Always Perfect

The FASB is an organization that makes accounting rules for business, but it is not without its own challenges and controversies. A California-based technology company, Silicon Economics, Inc. (SEI), has been challenging an FASB financial accounting rule since 2006, but the controversy heated up in 2010, when SEI filed suit against the FASB in California, followed by more legal wrangling in 2011. In February 2011, SEI refiled the complaint in the U.S. District Court of Delaware, and in August of that year, the court ruled SEI did not have standing in the court, but it allowed SEI to file an amended complaint.

According to an SEI news release dated February 23, 2011, "The lawsuit concerns Silicon's *EarningsPower Accounting™ (EPA)*, a patented method developed by the company to improve the accuracy, validity, and usefulness of financial statements." This method, says the suit, is more accurate than fair value but has been squeezed out by the FASB's dominance. Since the FASB makes the rules for accounting, SEI asserts it needs to be compensated for the money it is losing or the rules need to be changed.

According to SEI, it had recommended EPA to the FASB in response to the regulator's open request back in July 2006 (No. 1260-001, July 6, 2006) for public comment on the objectives of financial accounting. The FASB then claimed that its website terms and conditions gave it ownership of the company's technology, though the company founder said there was no mention of these terms in the FASB's original invitation for comment.

SEI's legal counsel, Perry J. Narancic of Narancic & Katzman, P.C., Menlo Park, California, said in the February 23, 2011, news release that "FASB's unlawful attempt to appropriate SEI's intellectual property undermines innovation and competition, and harms the U.S. economy. SEI will defend its intellectual property vigorously."

In 2010, the California court ruled that it lacked jurisdiction, prompting SEI to file in Delaware. But in August, 2011, according to an article in *Law360,* U.S. District Judge Michael M. Baylson ruled that SEI "lacked standing and hadn't sufficiently pled its claims."

References

PR Newswire. 2010. "FASB Defendant in Suit Alleging Antitrust Violations and Patent Misappropriation." www.prnewswire.com/news-releases/fasb-defendant-in-suit-alleging-antitrust-violations-and-patent-misappropriation-92952429.html.

Silicon Economics, Inc. (SEI). 2011. "FASB Defendant in Suit Alleging Antitrust Violations and Patent Misappropriation." February 23. www.siliconeconomics.com/pdfs/NN_2011_02_23_SEI_Press_Release.pdf.

Uhlman, L. 2011. "FASB Dodges Accounting IP, Antitrust Suit." *Law360*, August 18. www.law360.com/articles/265865.

U.S. District Court, District of Delaware. 2012. "General Information." Accessed January 29, 2012. www.ded.uscourts.gov/CLKmain.htm.

ADVANCED FINANCIAL ACCOUNTING CONCEPTS

Basic accounting terms were introduced in chapter 3, but only in the sense of their definitions. In this chapter, those terms will be brought to life by considering how they affect the documents that accounting creates. Terms such as *balance sheet*, *income statement*, *gross profit*, *net income*, *assets*, *liabilities*, and *equity* will become more relevant as terms that appear in corporate accounting reports but also as terms used in the public and nonprofit sectors.

Review of Accountancy Terminology

The New York Society of CPAs maintains a website (www.nysscpa.org) with the definitions of hundreds of accounting terms that accountants and CPAs need to be familiar with in order to be fluent in the language of accounting. But our goal is not to be fluent; it is to be able to understand some of what accountants say.

To understand the language, let's start with business accounting terms that were previously presented. In alphabetical order, here are some basic business accounting terms that have already been introduced:

- **accountants**—People overseeing or participating in the maintenance of the financial reporting system of the entity.
- **accounting**—Defined by the AICPA as "the art of recording, classifying, and summarizing in a significant manner and in terms of money, transactions and events which are, in part at least, of financial character, and interpreting the results thereof."
- **accounts**—Places in an entity's books to where the entity records assets, liabilities, income, and expenses.
- **accrual accounting**—The business-type accounting method where transactions are recorded as they are incurred, whether or not cash has been received or checks written.
- **American Institute of Certified Public Accountants (AICPA)**—The professional organization of CPAs.
- **assets**—The property, buildings, equipment, goodwill, or other measurable holdings of the entity.
- **auditors**—CPAs who perform random checks of transactional entries and the resulting balances to determine if financial statements are fair representations of the financial positions of entities.
- **balance sheets**—Reports that provide a picture of the financial condition of an entity at any given point in time, including its assets, liabilities, and equity for a fund.
- **bookkeeping**—The formal record-keeping process to track expenses, income, and profits.
- **books**—Where accountants maintain the financial records of the entity. Books could be on paper or in electronic files.
- **cash-basis accounting**—The accounting method similar to what individuals do in their personal checkbooks, where only what is received or paid is recorded.
- **certified public accountants (CPAs)**—Professional accountants who have passed qualifying examinations demonstrating their knowledge in the field of accounting, allowing them to be auditors of other accountants.
- **credits**—Entries on the right side of double-entry bookkeeping accounts that represent the reduction of an asset or expense, or the addition of a liability or revenue.
- **debits**—Entries on the left side of double-entry bookkeeping accounts that represent the addition of an asset or expense, or the reduction of a liability or revenue.
- **depreciation**—The concept that some fixed assets, such as buildings and equipment, get used up.
- **double-entry bookkeeping**—The process of writing down transactions in chronological order in a journal and then posting the transactions to accounts in the ledger.
- **entities**—Accounting units.
- **equity**—What is left over after liabilities are subtracted from assets; typically the value of the entity to the owners.
- **expense**—Money leaving the entity for any purpose that decreases the entity's equity.
- **financial accounting**—The technique used for the generation of reports for investors, donors, the general public, and the governmental units that tax businesses in the private sector.
- **Financial Accounting Standards Board (FASB)**—Establishes rules that govern business accounting.
- **generally accepted accounting principles (GAAP)**—The rules by which transactions are recorded and reports are prepared, created by the FASB.
- **going concerns**—Entities that will likely be in existence within the next 12 months.
- **income**—Money coming into the entity from any source that increases the entity's equity.
- **income statements**—Reports that provide a picture of the income and expenses of an entity during a time period for a fund.
- **journals**—Books or electronic files that record transactions in chronological order.
- **ledgers**—Include the general ledger and the nominal ledger; the main accounting records of business that use double-entry bookkeeping where specific accounts are recorded.
- **leveraging assets**—Borrowing money, creating more total assets in order to generate

more goods or services and thus more profit.

- **liabilities**—Loans or other short-term or long-term debts owed by the entity to other individuals or organizations.
- **management accounting**—Used to generate cash-based expense and income reports so managers can determine whether the revenues generated by services are at least covering costs.
- **transactions**—Entries into accounts recording revenues and expenses.

Adapted from New York City Society of CPAs.

New Accounting Terms

You probably think you've learned enough accounting terms by this time. But there are a few more you should learn. These terms are all related to the discussion of the Kids' Amusement Parks of America Corporation balance sheet and income statement presented earlier and the ones that will be presented later in this chapter.

Balance Sheet Terms

If assets are measurable holdings of a company, including buildings, equipment, land, cash, inventories, and goodwill, the next level of the language of accounting is naming general subcategories. Really, there are only two: **current assets** and **noncurrent assets**, the latter of which are generally called **fixed assets**.

Current assets are those that would take the company a modest amount of time to convert to cash. Noncurrent or fixed assets are the value of the land, buildings, and equipment owned by the company.

Current assets include cash, short-term investments, net receivables, and inventories. **Short-term investments** are those that mature or expire in one year. **Net receivables** are payments owned to a business minus **bad debt**, or debt that the business knows won't be paid. **Inventory** refers to the supplies and materials a company has on hand to manufacture its products or provide its services.

Short-term investments are a little more complicated than other types of current assets. Short-term investments can be certificates of deposits, money markets, mutual funds, or even ownership of stocks of other companies. What makes these investments current assets is that they are convertible to cash in a relatively short time.

Accounts receivable are monies owed to the company by other companies or individuals who are customers. If the expectation is that the customers owing money to the company will pay their bills, the amount each customer owes is an account receivable. Of course, there is always the possibility that the customer who purchased the products or services on credit won't pay. The amount that isn't expected to be paid reduces the accounts payable total by that amount. The difference between what is owed and what is expected to be paid is considered bad debt.

Inventories are the supplies and materials a company has on hand to manufacture its products or provide its services. Ever since the 1980s, American companies have emulated Japanese companies in maintaining low levels of inventory as a method of avoiding inventory shrinkage or obsolescence, which tends to occur when large inventories are maintained. **Inventory shrinkage** is a reduction in the amount of inventory that is not easily explainable. The most common cause of shrinkage is probably theft. **Obsolescence** is when something becomes outdated or old-fashioned.

Companies also maintain low inventories because maintain-

© Fotolia.com

Bicycles are fixed assets owned by a business that hopes to make a profit from renting the bikes to the public.

ing high inventories consumes cash. But the real reason why inventories are considered to be current assets is because inventory can be returned to the supplier for immediate credit.

The category of fixed assets is a component of company worth. Fixed assets are the value of the land, buildings, and equipment owned by the company. Fixed assets are recorded at their original cost. Even though land and buildings tend to **appreciate** in value, meaning they become more costly to replace as the years pass, their value is not increased to reflect that appreciation. Instead, some fixed assets, such as buildings and equipment, are reduced in value as the years pass because it is assumed they will wear out. As will be considered later in this chapter, fixed assets have an expected life and a salvage value. The **expected life** is how long the asset will be useful; the **salvage value** is what it is worth at the end of its useful life. *Depreciation*, another important accounting concept, is decreasing the value of assets over time because of age, wear, or market conditions.

For instance, when it comes to the depreciation of equipment, the formula for calculating depreciation is to subtract the salvage value from its original cost and divide the remaining value by the number of years of expected life:

$$DV = \frac{OC - SV}{EL}.$$

where OC is the original cost of the equipment, SV is its salvage value, and EL is its expected life. That creates an annual **depreciation value**, which is subtracted from the original cost.

Sound complicated? An example will help explain the concept. Let's say a bicycle rental shop purchases a new bicycle that it will rent to people. If the original cost is $500 and its expected life is 5 years, where the bicycle will be worth $50, the annual depreciation of the bicycle is $500 – 50 / 5 = $90 per year. What is complicated is that for every piece of equipment and every building a company owns, an individual depreciation schedule needs to be maintained. If a company is large and owns a lot of things, that can be a daunting task.

Another issue to consider is that land is never depreciated because it is never used up, unlike buildings and equipment. Land is always there and never goes away. But its value is not increased either over time even though its value on the open market increases. As with all fixed assets, it is recorded on the balance sheet at cost.

To appropriately manage the finances of a private-sector leisure service, you also need to know the total value of all assets. **Total assets** are the sum of all subcategories of assets, representing the worth of the company. Because some fixed assets, such as buildings and land, may be worth far more than their original purchase price, the value of the total assets of the company may be an understatement of their market value.

The value of the company does take the value of the assets into consideration when a private company is sold or when the stock of a publicly traded company is valued on the open market. For instance, if the owner of the bicycle rental shop mentioned earlier decided to sell his company, its value would be the value of the depreciated equipment it owned. Likewise, when the market values the total stock shares of the Kids' Amusement Parks of America, it considers the value of the land and depreciated buildings and equipment owned by the amusement park company.

The balance sheet is so named because its two sides must be equal. Total assets, or what the company owns, need to equal what the company owes. On the opposite side of the balance sheet are terms you need know, including *current liabilities*, *long-term debt*, and *equity*. Equity has already been defined as what remains after all of the liabilities are taken into consideration.

Long-term debt is money owed that is paid back over a five-year period or longer. Corporate bonds were presented as one option and bank loans as another. The total principal that remains to be paid is recorded on the balance sheet, but the interest is not. As long-term debt principal is paid down, though, it is reduced on the balance sheet.

Current liabilities consist of money the company owes to individuals or entities that typically needs to be repaid in less than five years. Current liabilities can include short-term debt, usually in the form of bank loans, promissory notes, or lines of credit. **Promissory notes** are unsecured agreements between banks and companies, where companies receive a fixed amount of money and they agree to repay principal and interest at designated periods. **Lines of credit** are loans that are drawn as the company needs the money, with repayment dates depending on the amount used.

Another category of current liabilities is similar to accounts receivable. This category is called **accounts payable**. Since companies do business with each other for a number of reasons, they don't always pay for what they buy from each other, but they bill each other instead. If the term *accounts* *receivable* is what customers or other entities owe your company for what they purchased from you, then *accounts payable* refers to what you owe other individuals or entities for what you purchased from them.

Just as there is a summary term for assets, *total assets*, there is a summary term for all liabilities, *total liabilities*. **Total liabilities** are what the company must repay in the short or long term. Total liabilities rarely equal total assets, though. If total liabilities are worth less than total assets, there is corporate equity and the company has value. On the other hand, if total liabilities are worth more than total assets, then the balance sheet doesn't balance and the company is **bankrupt**.

Income Statement Terms

Income statement terms you need to know are those related to the Kids' Amusement Parks of America sample income statement (table 5.1). Similar to the terms introduced for balance sheets, once you become familiar with them, they can be applied anywhere.

Let's start at the top of the KAPA income statement. By now, everyone should understand what the term *revenues* means, but what is the *cost of goods sold*? Its definition is simple enough; it is the amount of money the company spent to buy raw materials and produce the product or service. In other words, the cost of goods sold only includes the direct costs of producing the product or service, not the indirect costs that include overhead or other expenses. Subtracting the cost of goods sold from the revenues creates the gross profit.

Gross profit margin is an important term to understand because it shows, without taking into consideration indirect costs such as overhead, how profitable it is to produce the product or service. The gross profit margin is calculated by dividing the dollar amount of the gross profit by the revenues, which produces a percentage. If the percentage is high, that's a good thing. If it's low, the business manager would wonder whether the company can cover its overhead, including the manager's salary.

The KAPA income statement uses the term *SG&A* to refer to **overhead expenses**, the indirect costs or fixed expenses of operating a business (i.e., those costs not directly related to the manufacturing of a product). Subtracting overhead from gross profits creates **operating income**, which takes into consideration how much money the company has made that year before it pays its income taxes at the end of the year.

The **operating margin** is calculated the same way the gross profit margin is calculated, by dividing the dollar amount of the operating income by the revenues, yielding a percentage. If that percentage is zero or a negative number, it can tell the manager whether the company's overhead is a concern.

Because it's impossible to understand every term simultaneously, we'll skip over **nonoperating income and expenses** except to say they are derived from sources of revenue outside the core business of the company. For instance, even though KAPA is in the amusement park business, it may have sources of revenue such as licensing fees for merchandise sold outside park operations that would fall in that category. But smaller companies usually do not have outside sources of revenue.

The important income statement terms remaining are **income before taxes**, **net income after taxes**, and *net profit margin*. In the case of smaller companies, if there are no nonoperating income or expenses, income before taxes would be the same as operating income. Income before taxes is how much money the company has made after all of its revenues and expenses have been considered.

Income after taxes is how much money is left after income taxes are paid to the IRS and to the revenue service of the state in which the business is incorporated. Net profit margin is calculated by dividing the dollar amount of net income after taxes by total revenues. This is the ultimate test of the profitability of a business. The percentage is an indication of whether investors should be in business at all or should have put their money in some other business or investment that would have provided a higher return.

As this chapter progresses, you will develop a better understanding of the balance sheet and income statement. Since businesses do not always make a profit, there needs to be a way of expressing when they don't. The standard practice for income statements is to show losses parenthetically. For balance sheets, the standard is similar. If a number is in a parentheses, that means it is a negative number. If it is not, it is a positive number.

A review of the KAPA income statement shows that the corporation has been losing money over the years. In December 2010, the company had a net income after taxes of $244.1 million; in December 2012, that net income had fallen to $205.9 million. A review of the balance sheet shows that, as a result, KAPA has become a company in which the owners have negative equity, at least on paper. Based on these financial statements, KAPA might

© tittletattle - Fotolia

Managing an amusement park isn't all fun and games if the business has a low net profit margin—the final word on whether money has been made or lost.

not be the best investment. Managing the company might be a challenge.

TRANSPARENCY

In its literal definition, *transparency* means that something can be seen through, as in the case of a window. As you should understand by now, for financial management, *transparency* means something can be clearly seen and identified. In the private sector, it means the company is not hiding its financial position from those who would be hurt by it being misrepresented. The earlier examples of the banking industry (chapter 2) and Enron (chapter 3) were situations where assets and liabilities were disguised, hurting buyers, investors, and company employees alike. The earlier example of the Kids' Amusement Parks of America is one where, even though the company is being managed honestly, it is in a precarious financial position.

In the case of Enron, as discussed in chapter 3, the Arthur Andersen accounting firm was accused of allowing Enron to misrepresent its assets, overstating the value of owners' equity. Stock prices increased, but when the scam was detected by investors, the jig was up. And it really didn't matter if Andersen was complicit or not; just the accusation of complicity was enough to sink the accounting firm. The Enron and Andersen example illustrates how difficult it is to run a company if you don't know what you're looking at on the balance sheet—that is, what the numbers mean and whether the numbers are fairly valued. Leisure services managers need to understand the structure and the meaning of these reports.

To understand the financial reports prepared for them, leisure services managers should assume that these reports fairly represent the company's financial position. To do so, they need to learn not only the language of accounting but also the rules of the game. The rules include how transactions (entries into accounts recording revenues and expenses) are recorded and more importantly, how the financial statements should be prepared.

Here's one more level of understanding you need about financial statements, particularly the concept of equity. Equity, the owners' financial stake in the company, is valued not just by the difference between assets and liabilities but also by the value of expected revenues. Stock prices fluctuate based on expected revenues. But equity on the balance sheet only changes based on actual revenues. Understanding the difference between what a stock ought to be worth and what the stock market thinks it's worth is the art of understanding that equity on the balance sheet is not the same as equity in the stock market.

An important consideration of transparency is that profits flow from the income statement to the balance sheet. Whatever is left after taxes can be spent at the discretion of the corporate board of directors. The board can declare dividends to stockholders or it can keep the profits for the company, building owners' equity on the balance sheet.

The reports, if prepared scrupulously, will show what happened and why it happened. They will show whether the company's cost of goods sold is too high or if it has too much overhead, which lets management know to make changes.

When compared with previous years, the income statement can show trends in sales of products or services, allowing management to take action in promoting them. Either way, transparency is important.

READING IMPORTANT FINANCIAL REPORTS

If the purpose of accounting is to generate fair and meaningful financial reports, what should leisure services managers be able to do with these reports? Is reading and understanding them enough? Evidently not, based on some of the discussions that have taken place thus far. The most important function of financial reports is to help management make decisions that improve the financial performance of the company.

Reading Balance Sheets

If it has not become apparent already, the most important report that a business needs to generate is its balance sheet. This report, often produced monthly, provides a picture of the financial health or condition of the business at a given point in time, showing its assets, liabilities, and equity.

Using a balance sheet as a picture of the financial health of a company is similar to using the medical chart that a hospital keeps for a patient. On the patient's chart, the hospital records the patient's vital signs, such as blood pressure and heart rate, and checking those vital signs at various points in time tells the doctor about changes in the patient's condition. If there are changes that warrant concern, the doctor knows something needs to be done to help the patient restore her vital signs.

Just like patient charts, balance sheets tell leisure services managers whether the patient is healthy. But in this case, the company is the patient. Instead of heart rate, the balance sheet shows the cash status of the company. Instead of blood pressure, corporate liabilities are shown. Managers can track changes in these vital signs over time and decide if anything needs to be done to restore the company to financial health.

Reading and understanding the balance sheet, therefore, is a critical financial management skill. The KAPA balance sheet presented in table 5.2 shows that the patient is ill: Revenues do not cover expenses. The owners' equity in the company is negative and getting worse each year. The patient appears to be dying.

What should the managers of KAPA be doing to save the patient? It is possible that nothing can be done. Perhaps the patient is just too old and its systems are no longer viable. Perhaps the market for the amusement park business is in decline due to changing population demographics in the United States, where the average age is increasing and the market for the product is becoming smaller and smaller. Maybe what KAPA needs is hospice care rather than a hospital.

Alternatively, maybe there is something management can do to prolong the life of the patient. Maybe going on a diet of expenses is a solution. Maybe cutting overhead will improve profitability. Maybe cutting the cost of goods sold will help. Maybe finding new markets for its product will help. Management has to decide: hospice or hospital. To make that decision, management needs more financial information—a deeper understanding of what is going on financially. Hopefully, by the end of this text, you will be able to interpret the financial reports that will help you make important financial decisions such as these.

Next, let's delve deeper into the balance sheet, because a solid understanding is essential for understanding other financial tools. Let's assume that a person named Sadie started her own privately owned leisure company providing amusement rides for children and families. Because she was proud of her own entrepreneurial spirit, she decided to call it Sadie's Amusement Park. Her park has lots of features to attract the public, including a merry-go-round, a Ferris wheel, a kid-sized train, games, and refreshments. The park is located in a community in southern California and is open all year long.

To start the company, Sadie borrowed $2 million from a local bank to purchase an existing amusement park that had gone out of business, using the park as collateral to secure the loan. Sadie also contributed $1,010,000 of her own money to get the company started. Initially, the balance sheet of Sadie's Amusement Park reflected the money that she and the bank invested in the company. On the last day of Sadie's first fiscal year, her balance sheet appeared as shown in table 5.3.

The balance sheet shows that, at the beginning of the fiscal year, Sadie's Amusement Park had different amounts in its assets and liabilities than it did at the end of the year. As discussed earlier, assets are what the company owns. Assets are divided into major categories, the first of which is current assets, meaning they are readily available. The current assets shown on the balance sheet are cash, receivables, and inventory.

Table 5.3 Sadie's Amusement Park Balance Sheet

	January 1, 2012	December 31, 2012
Current assets		
Cash	$5,000	$296,100
Accounts receivable	0	10,000
Inventories of supplies	5,000	50,000
Total current assets	10,000	356,100
Fixed assets		
Equipment	1,000,000	1,000,000
Less depreciation	0	100,000
Net	1,000,000	900,000
Buildings	1,000,000	1,000,000
Less depreciation	0	100,000
Net	1,000,000	900,000
Total fixed assets	2,000,000	1,800,000
Land	1,000,000	1,000,000
Total assets	**$3,010,000**	**$3,156,100**
Liabilities		
Accounts payable	$0	$20,000
Notes payable	0	0
Total current liabilities	0	20,000
Long-term debt		
Loans	2,000,000	2,000,000
Less payment of principal		200,000
Total long-term debt	2,000,000	1,800,000
Owners' equity	$1,010,000	$1,356,100
Total equity and liabilities	**$3,010,000**	**$3,176,100**

At the beginning of the fiscal year, the balance sheet shows that Sadie's Amusement Park has $5,000 in cash. Cash can be in a checking account or savings account. If it were invested in something less liquid, meaning it would take time to convert the investment to cash, the money would be recorded as an investment on the balance sheet but still considered a current asset.

Another asset category is receivables, or money owed to the company in the short term. At the beginning of the year, when the company first started, no one owed Sadie's Amusement Park anything, so there were no receivables to record.

But at the end of the fiscal year, let's say that a school visited Sadie's Amusement Park in December for a class trip and the school asked the park to bill it for the children's admissions so it could pay the bill later. If Sadie had a reasonable expectation that it would pay the bill, the amount it owed would be a receivable. On the balance sheet, $10,000 is shown under receivables, which are also considered current assets.

Another current asset type is inventories, which are supplies that were purchased and were being stored by the business at the time the balance sheet was prepared. Inventories are current assets if they can be returned for credit. In other words, if Sadie couldn't pay for the supplies in inventory, she might call the company she bought them from and return the supplies to them. The company would then reduce the amount owed in the payable category, which will be discussed later.

In Sadie's balance sheet, Sadie had $5,000 at the beginning of the year, which she needed in order to open for business. At the end of the year, inventories had increased to $50,000, which could be problematic if it is more than she needs to have on hand. Alternatively, $50,000 in inventories of concession supplies and gift-shop items doesn't seem to be a matter of concern.

A major category of assets on the balance sheet is fixed assets. As the Sadie's Amusement Park balance sheet shows, there are equipment and buildings, which are subcategories of fixed assets. Equipment is straightforward enough. It can come in the form of vehicles, office equipment, machines in the concession stand, or even the amusement park rides themselves. However, remember that equipment wears out, and GAAP determine that the wearing out of the equipment needs to be taken into consideration. This is done is through *depreciation*, a term introduced earlier.

Depreciation is the reduction of equipment value by a percentage, depending on its expected life. For instance, if a truck Sadie buys costs $30,000 and is expected to last five years and be worth $5,000 in salvage value at the end of that period, the truck will depreciate by $25,000 in value over its life. That means that if Sadie is following GAAP, she needs to reflect the reduction in the value of the truck by $5,000 at the end of each fiscal year.

Sadie needs to do that for all equipment, all of which has varying life expectancies. All of her equipment was worth $1 million at the beginning of the fiscal year and declined in value during the year for a total depreciation of $100,000, leaving a net of $900,000 in equipment value on her balance sheet.

Buildings are fixed assets as well and are depreciated, but usually over a longer period of time because of their expected life. Buildings usually can be expected to last 20 to 50 years, so it would seem that they depreciate less than equipment does. However, the FASB tends to change that, usually in response to IRS changes in the tax code.

In the case of Sadie's Amusement Park, the depreciation schedule for the buildings was over a 10-year period, mainly because she purchased the building and land from another owner, who operated the park for a number of years before Sadie bought it from him. The FASB and IRS have allowed Sadie to depreciate the buildings over a 10-year period because that's a reasonable life expectancy of the buildings based on their current age. As a result, under GAAP the $1 million in buildings at the beginning of the fiscal year is worth $900,000 after depreciation.

Land receives a different accounting treatment. It is not depreciated because it does not get used up. But even though it may actually appreciate in value, it is still recorded on the balance sheet at its original purchase price.

Whereas in the banking example, the assets considered were loan contracts, Sadie's Amusement Park assets are cash, inventories of supplies, furniture, equipment, buildings, and land. The company owns things that it needs to function as a business. Sadie's needs to create concession-stand products and machines in which to make the product. It needs equipment for rides, buildings to house mechanical equipment, furniture

Paying Attention to the Numbers

It is said that private-sector accounting is about as interesting as watching paint dry because it involves entering data onto paper or into a computer—to some a tedious task, and to others downright boring. But such was not the case for Josh Gardensmith, an accounting teacher in West Virginia.

Josh taught accounting at a community college for almost 20 years when he found his other passion, working at a resident adventure camp near Charleston in the summer. During his fifth summer at the camp, Josh was asked to help with the financial reports and soon discovered that the camp was in sad financial shape. One of the problems was that uncollected camper fees were routinely written off at over $30,000 each year. Another was that several vendors were allowed to restock camp supplies during the summer, resulting in large amounts of money tied up in food inventories.

Having found the problem, Josh went to the owner of the camp and let him in on the bad news. The owner was beside himself with anger and wanted to know who to blame. Josh told the owner that he should look in the mirror. Accounting was the owner's responsibility, and if the system broke down, it was the owner's responsibility to identify the problem and find a solution.

Unfortunately, the owner didn't like Josh's point of view. He became even angrier, telling Josh, if he was so smart, why didn't he buy the camp and run it himself? Having seen the potential for financial success by doing the accounting for the camp, Josh happily agreed to purchase it. During the winter of 2007, Josh bought the camp for $365,000, a bargain at the time.

With hard work and a focus on marketing, Josh decided to reposition the camp, making it smaller while increasing attendance fees. Josh believed that if his camp limited its size to 20 campers, he could improve its adventure focus by leading the trips himself, he could consolidate the housing and food service, and he could transport campers to and from the camp in his van at the beginning and end of sessions.

Today, Josh's camp is a modest financial success, operating at full capacity, charging $1,250 per camper per week. In his eight-week season, Josh generates $200,000 a summer. His camp is estimated to be worth twice as much as he paid for it because he understood its potential from an accounting standpoint and the original owner did not.

for customers to sit on, and a little cash to pay its bills in case there are not enough customers during slow periods.

The purpose of the balance sheet is to show the *proportion* of the various types of assets, liabilities, and equity. Proportion can make a big difference to companies depending on the industry they're in. Some industries require a lot of cash to do business, and some require more equipment. Leisure services usually need high proportions of land and buildings.

Take the cruising industry, where cruise lines are required to invest in billion-dollar ships. Their balance sheets are heavy in fixed assets. Their balance sheets are also heavy in liabilities, because companies need to borrow money from banks to build their ships.

Sadie's Amusement Park is in the amusement park industry. As with many sectors of the leisure services industry, it needs substantial fixed assets, such as land, buildings, equipment, and machines, but not many current assets. Therefore, Sadie's Amusement Park needs to have certain assets in the right proportions.

For instance, if Sadie's Amusement Park had a cash shortage, the company could be in trouble because it needs cash to pay its bills. If the inventories were too high, the company might have deprived itself of cash to purchase those inventories. Too much inventory and not enough cash can be bad.

The same is the case with equity and liabilities. If the company has too much debt, it might not be in a position to repay it, and it would therefore be a bad risk to loan it more money. If the company had too little equity, it would not be worth much to the owners or stockholders. Everything needs to be in proportion.

Understanding proportion leads to understanding why the balance sheet report is generated in the first place. Without it, management cannot take remedial action to correct financial problems, and investors or bankers can't determine whether they should put more capital into the company. **Remedial action** means fixing something that is not working. In the case of the patient's medical chart, when a doctor finds that some of the patient's vital signs are out of proportion, the remedial action is the doctor prescribing a medication to restore the vital signs to a better proportion. Similarly, if Sadie's vital sign of cash position is out of proportion, meaning the company doesn't have enough cash, Sadie can take a variety of remedial actions. She can borrow more money from a bank to get cash. She can put more of her money into the company as equity. Another option is to sell off the equipment to get some cash, but that's not a good idea if Sadie's Amusement Park plans to stay in business. A better remedial solution is to burn some inventory—in other words, to hold off buying supplies for a while in order to lower inventory levels. Doing so should increase cash without throwing liabilities and equity out of proportion on the balance sheet.

What proportion should cash and inventory be for Sadie's Amusement Park? It depends on how long Sadie can stay in business without enough customers coming to the amusement park. The answer that "it depends" is also a function of the industry of the company, the age of the company, the goals of the owners, and the projected sales revenues. It depends on all of those factors. It's complicated, but it is the job of the leisure services manager to know what proportions are appropriate. Sources within the accounting industry provide benchmarks that managers can use as guidelines.

Reading Income Statements

The question that balance sheets do not answer is why the balance sheet changed from the beginning of the fiscal year to the end of the fiscal year. The answer lies in the income statement.

Income statements have a specific order, a sequence of events that show how the company has been faring financially. These statements are designed to provide a different picture of the financial health of a business than balance sheets do. They show the revenues that the business generates and they subtract the direct costs of making the products (i.e., cost of goods sold), creating a gross profit margin.

The gross profit margin is an indicator of how profitable the making of a product or provision of a service is without taking into consideration the company's overhead and indirect expenses. Gross profit margins show the opportunity of the company to make a profit in the long run. But other considerations are important to consider first, such as overhead.

Overhead costs are the indirect costs required to keep the business going, such as the nonoperating expenses of repaying the loan Sadie needed in order to purchase the existing amusement park, loan interest, utilities, cleaning supplies, marketing costs, and equipment repair. Subtracting those costs from gross profits, as well as taking depreciation into consideration, creates income before taxes. Subtracting taxes from the income before taxes tells Sadie exactly how much money she made during her first year of operation.

Understanding these accounting terms allows us to understand Sadie's income statement (table 5.4).

Assuming preparers followed GAAP in producing the income statement, the report is a relatively straightforward presentation of how much money Sadie's Amusement Park made during the year. It shows that the total revenues are $2 million in admissions, fees, and charges.

The report shows that direct expenses, stated as the cost of goods sold, were composed of the labor and supplies necessary to operate the amusement park, totaling $1,270,600. Subtracting the cost of goods sold left $729,400 in gross profits. Dividing gross profit by the total revenue shows that the gross profit margin is 36.47 percent, which is substantial, considering the revenues generated.

Gross profit margins vary from industry to industry, particularly in the commercial recreation sector. In the hospitality industry, gross profit margins can be as high as 600 percent for beverage sales and as high as 200 percent for food sales. This is largely because the cost of labor and supplies to prepare food and beverages are low. In the athletic clothing industry, though, labor and materials to make the products can make the gross profit margin as low as 25 percent, because the cost of labor and materials is higher relative to the sale prices of the items.

For the amusement park industry, let's say that Sadie's Amusement Park is somewhere in the middle when it comes to its gross profit margin. The income statement shows that depreciation at the end of the year was $200,000 for buildings and equipment, and the indirect (overhead) costs, called *nonoperating expenses* on the report, were $75,400. This created income before taxes of $454,000 in profits. But, obviously, the company can't retain all that income because taxes need to be taken into consideration. Based on the corporate tax bracket for $454,000 in net operating income, Sadie's would pay 35 percent in income taxes to the IRS. The park would pay even more if it were in a state that taxed corporations, but let's assume it is not.

After federal income taxes, Sadie would be left with $295,100, which she can reinvest in the company, distribute as dividends to the shareholders (Sadie), or a combination of the two. As the balance sheet showed, Sadie chose to reinvest all of it in the company. Ordinarily, if the company decided to keep all of the net income after taxes, it would be reflected as an increase in cash as an asset and in owners' equity on the other side of the balance sheet to keep it in balance.

A couple of other changes in the balance sheet can be explained by the income statement. For instance, cash on the balance sheet increased by $291,100. That increase can be explained by depreciation on the income statement and

Table 5.4 Sadie's Amusement Park Income Statement (January 1, 2012-December 31, 2012)

Gross revenues	$2,000,000
Cost of goods sold	
Labor	870,600
Supplies	400,000
Total cost of goods sold	1,270,600
Gross profits	729,400
Gross profit margin	36.47%
Depreciation	
Equipment	100,000
Buildings	100,000
Total depreciation	200,000
Operating income	529,400
Operating margin	26.47%
Nonoperating expenses	
Interest	40,000
Utilities	9,000
Cleaning supplies	1,400
Marketing costs	10,000
Equipment repair and replacement	15,000
Total nonoperating expenses	**75,400**
Income before taxes	454,000
Income taxes (35%)	158,900
Total net income after taxes	295,100
Net profit margin	14.755%

balance sheet. Since depreciation is a noncash expense on the income statement but no cash was actually spent, Sadie's Amusement Park still has that money. Basically, the $200,000 from depreciation would be retained by the company to replace its buildings and equipment when they wear out.

On the balance sheet, owners' equity increases as the original loan to acquire the amusement park is paid down. Because balance sheets must balance, as debt decreases, owners' equity must increase. As considered earlier, the transactions from the income statement flow through to the balance sheet.

One obvious conclusion from the fictitious Sadie's Amusement Park balance sheet and income statement is that the company is doing a lot better than KAPA. Sadie's is profitable and KAPA is not. Sadie's is building owners' equity and KAPA is losing owners' equity. The reasons are transparent from the companies' income statements and balance sheets.

The Kids' Amusement Parks of America has a gross profit margin of about 45 percent, whereas Sadie's Amusement Park has a gross profit margin of just over 36 percent. That difference suggests that Sadie's has a higher cost of goods sold as a percentage of revenue than does KAPA. It would seem to indicate that KAPA has the competitive advantage because the direct costs of keeping its amusement park open are lower than Sadie's. On the other hand, as a proportion of revenues, KAPA has much higher overhead costs, which is why its operating margin is 7.4 percent compared with Sadie's 26.4 percent. A 7.4 percent operating margin doesn't leave much for KAPA to cover its massive losses between nonoperating revenue and expenses, something Sadie's is not required to do because it is a small private company that doesn't provide any services beyond the amusement park.

What should Sadie do to improve her business? Nothing is called for at the moment because the park's vital signs are good. On the other hand, what should the management of KAPA do to improve its apparently unhealthy financial position? One obvious solution would be to control overhead costs better. If that's not possible, perhaps they could do something about the company's nonoperating expenses. If that's not possible, they could try to increase revenues. And if that's not possible, a call to someone with a lot of money to buy them out might be in order.

SUMMARY

Managing the finances of leisure services in the private sector serves as a model for the public and nonprofit sectors. Private-sector management has the mindset that leisure services are valuable to people and something for which they are willing to pay fees. The question of how much people will pay was discussed in previous chapters as whatever the market will bear. What needs to be established is how revenues received from leisure services should be managed.

The FASB establishes reporting systems, and GAAP developed by the FASB dictate how balance sheets and income statements are to be prepared on an annual basis. The FASB is responsible not only for the GAAP to which business must adhere but also for the ethical standards that allow for transparency.

Publicly traded companies are required to make these reports public in order to protect investors, and privately held companies need to maintain these reports for their own purposes, to secure bank loans, and in case they ever want to sell the company. In addition, balance sheets and income statements are valuable management tools.

Balance sheets show the financial condition of a company at a given point in time. Income statements show why the corporate balance sheets change over time. Together, these reports show how the company is doing and indicate the strategies management might employ to make the company healthier.

Visit the Web Resource

For case studies, sample financial statements,
key terms, and more, please visit the web resource at
www.HumanKinetics.com/LeisureServicesFinancialManagement

chapter 6

Private-Sector Reporting and Analysis

Learning Outcomes

After completing this chapter, students will be able to do the following:

- Explain the facets of the budgeting process.
- Discuss what quarterly reports are and how management reviews budget details in order to manage a company.
- Determine how financial analysis is converted to management action.
- Identify formulas that business managers and investors use to diagnose the financial condition of companies.

By now it should be apparent that the amusement park industry may or may not be the segment of the private sector in which you'd want to start a business. With the fictional examples of the Kids' Amusement Parks of America Corporation and Sadie's Amusement Park, it is apparent that the amusement park industry could be a very profitable or unprofitable business. As with any leisure services venture, amusement parks are a risky business. They are risky because there is no guarantee that people will find amusement parks, well, amusing. Leisure businesses such as amusement parks also require large capital outlays to get a return on their investments.

That business in general is a **risky proposition** is also true. Any businesses requiring a large capital outlay are more risky than those not requiring one. But if a leisure services entrepreneur can be successful, there's a lot of money to be made. That's what a risky proposition means: You can make or lose a lot of money.

The question every investor or entrepreneur wants to know is how they can minimize their risk, maximize their probability of success, and make a lot of money. The answer is that investors need to learn how to take calculated risks. **Calculated risks** are risks that entrepreneurs take when they have an idea of what the probabilities of success are, or at least they think they know. If investors or entrepreneurs are correct in their assessment of risk, and the risk of losing money is high, then they avoid taking the risk. If the probability of making money is high, then they pursue the opportunity.

Thus, to make a profit on their investments, investors and entrepreneurs need to understand the risks. Their understanding can come from research or from experience. As earlier discussions have determined, a high percentage of entrepreneurs get into their industry because they are already familiar with it.

But not all investors are familiar with an industry before they invest in ownership of a company through purchase of its stock. To become familiar with the industry, they need to research it. Learning more is always advisable to minimize risk. Sometimes, investors have experience in an industry but could know that much more by doing a little research. That is what attorneys call **due diligence**—doing research to determine facts backed by evidence. Doing due diligence means attorneys have spent the time and effort to make sure they know what they are talking about. When attorneys make assertions, those assertions need to be backed up by evidence they are prepared to present. The same is true about investing in a company. Before investments are made, investors or entrepreneurs should do due diligence to determine the probability of making a profit.

This chapter focuses on ways entrepreneurs in leisure services can do their due diligence. Research is one approach. Understanding financial ratios is another. And application of the knowledge gained from this research is the most important part of the equation, because knowledge alone is insufficient without thoughtful application.

DUE DILIGENCE

Chapter 5 introduced two financial reports with which leisure services managers need to be familiar in order to assess the financial health of their companies: the balance sheet and the income statement. In chapter 5, a basic level of financial analysis was performed where the profitability of a company was measured in terms of three margins on the income statement: the gross profit margin, the operating margin, and the net profit margin. The financial condition of the company was assessed on the balance sheet only in terms of the availability of cash, and the value of the company was only considered in terms of owner equity.

These margins were useful in determining whether Sadie's Amusement Park was making a profit and in comparing the performance of the company against the average performance of other companies in the amusement park industry. Equity was presented as an important consideration in valuing companies. But there are other measures of corporate financial performance that are commonly considered in the business world, particularly by investors and industry analysts.

This chapter presents financial performance tools that leisure services managers can use to measure the performance of their businesses, nonprofit organizations, and governmental units. Some of the tools presented will not always be applicable to nonprofit organizations and governmental units. But most of them will be useful because they measure the financial health of the organization, and every organization needs to measure its financial health now and then.

First, however, a topic that was introduced earlier needs to be explored in greater detail. That topic—budgeting—applies to all three sectors of leisure services. Budgeting is a financial management technique that may seem obvious to many managers, but it is a technique that many managers are not very good at for a number of reasons. An important adage states, "There is no telling how many business failures could have been avoided had the person who started them put a pencil to paper first." In other words, most businesses fail because the people who started them had no idea how much money they would receive in revenue and how much they would need to cover expenses. Therefore, they had no way of knowing how much profit, if any, their business ventures would leave them with.

Had these failed entrepreneurs done minimal due diligence, they might have found that they were not likely to get the number of customers they needed to walk through their door. They might have also found that their operating and overhead costs would be prohibitively higher than their revenue would ever allow them to cover. In short, from the beginning, they would have realized that it would be unlikely that their business would ever make a profit.

So why don't entrepreneurs do their due diligence, especially since their success depends upon it? Doesn't it make sense for the owner of Coffee Café to put a pencil to paper to figure out how many customers buying how many cups of coffee at what prices are required to cover operating expenses, let alone make a profit? Likewise, doesn't it make sense for Sadie to figure out how many people spending how much money she needs each day to cover the amusement park's expenses?

There are two reasons entrepreneurs don't do their due diligence. One is that they don't know how to do it. They've never written a budget before. They don't know how to forecast revenues or predict expenses. They just don't know where to begin. For these people, this textbook is an important tool to help them understand how to do their due diligence.

But the other reason entrepreneurs don't do their due diligence is something with which this textbook can't help them. Many don't do their due diligence because they don't want to know if their business venture will be profitable. They might find out it won't be, and that news could deter them from starting it. And since they really, really, really want to start their business, they feel it's better if they don't know.

Many, if not most, leisure services professionals go into the field because they love the lifestyle. But if leisure services professionals want to stay in the business over the long run, they must develop a **business sense**—the ability to figure out how a product or service can make a profit.

This chapter shows leisure services professionals how to embrace tools that can give them a business sense and lead them to starting a successful business. If leisure services professionals don't learn how to use these tools, they may find themselves visiting amusement parks instead of running them.

BUDGETING

The word *budget* is derived from the French word *bougette*, meaning "purse." A purse is a place where a person puts money, making sure there is always something available. The accepted meaning of the term is that a budget is a plan for taking in revenue and expending it in such a way that there is always something available. In microeconomic terms, budgets organize spending for the fiscal year.

The purpose of budgeting is to construct a model of how a business might perform financially if certain strategies, events, and plans are carried out. The budget also allows the actual financial operation of a business to be measured against the forecast. Budgets do so by creating line items that explain revenue and expenses.

Corporate budgets are often compiled annually, but many companies prepare budgets for the next five years, revising their projections as economic conditions change. Typically, the finance department compiles the budget using computer software that allows hundreds or even thousands of people in various departments to participate in the budgeting process by submitting their expected revenues and expenses. If actual expenses and revenues come close to the budgeted amounts, the managers likely understand their business and have been successfully driving it in the intended direction. On the other hand, if the figures diverge widely from the budget, such as showing expenses way over budget or revenue way under budget, this sends a bad signal to investors, causing them to lose confidence in management.

Process and Purpose of Budgeting

The purpose of budgeting is to establish a plan that a businessperson can follow. Achieving goals usually works better with a plan, so having a budget usually leads to better outcomes than operating without one does. The budget process can be better understood by recognizing there are various types of budgets at the corporate level. They include the following:

- **operating budget**—A plan for the total revenues and expenses of the organization, typically on a department basis.
- **sales budget**—The sales budget is an estimate of future sales, often broken down into both units and dollars. It is used to create company sales goals.
- **production budget**—Product-oriented companies create a production budget, which estimates the number of units that must be manufactured to meet the sales goals. The production budget also estimates the various costs involved with manufacturing those units, including labor and material.
- **cash-flow budget**—Also called *cash budget*, the cash-flow budget is a prediction of future cash receipts and expenditures for a particular time period, usually in the short-term future. The cash-flow budget helps the business determine when income will be sufficient to cover expenses and when the company will need to seek outside financing.
- **marketing budget**—The marketing budget is an estimate of the funds needed for promotion, advertising, and public relations in order to market the product or service.
- **project budget**—The project budget is a prediction of the costs associated with a particular company project. These costs include labor, materials, and other related expenses. The project budget is often broken

down into specific tasks with task budgets assigned to each.

- **revenue budget**—The revenue budget consists of revenue receipts of the government and the expenditures met from these revenues. Tax revenues are made up of taxes and other duties that the government levies.
- **expenditure budget**—A budget type that includes spending data (Sullivan and Sheffrin 2003).

Most economists describe **budgeting as an art** rather than a science. A certain skill is required to do it, and the more experience managers have in writing budgets, the more accurate they become at predicting revenues and expenditures over time. With more experience also comes the ability to understand the variables that can affect the budget, such as macroeconomic conditions and industry life cycles.

Experienced managers also understand budgeting is a **political process**, defined as resolving important issues as a group through the use of influence. Getting issues resolved often means saying the right words at the right time. Understanding the political process in budgeting means knowing that corporate board members and CEOs like to hear rosy revenue and economic forecasts. Because investors are more likely to invest when financial forecasts are good, it means there is always pressure on managers to present budgets that show the company to be profitable at least in the long term, if not in the short term.

© iStockphoto/Catherine Yeulet

What are some questions a manager of a fitness center must answer in order to know whether the business will be profitable?

Traditional budget theory suggests that budgeting is incremental, meaning that projected revenues and expenses are generally based on historical data, particularly what occurred in the previous year, and are adjusted according to anticipated changes in the marketplace or economy. Typically, similar budget formats are used from year to year so that comparisons can be made. And it is typical that adjustments in line items within these budget formats are relatively small from year to year, though not always.

In the 1970s, a popular budgeting theory emerged, called **zero-based budgeting**. When zero-based budgeting is used, incremental changes in base line-item revenues and expenses are rejected. In zero-based budgeting, nothing is assumed. Every corporate department is required to prove that there is a reason every line item in the budget should exist and must show how it contributes to the bottom line of the company.

One of the consequences of zero-based budgeting is that it can lead to outsourcing departmental functions when it can be shown that it is more expensive to provide certain services than to hire someone else to do them. An unintended consequence of zero-based budgeting is that the process can be very destabilizing to a company. In addition, it is exhausting to do every year.

Incremental budgeting has advantages and disadvantages. One advantage of incremental budgeting is that financial change is gradual, which has the effect of stabilizing the company. On the other hand, a disadvantage is that there is less incentive to change expensive corporate practices or to introduce new ideas.

Because of the advantages and disadvantages of each budgeting approach, most companies use a combination of the two. When underperforming departments are identified, they may be subjected to a zero-based budgeting process. When highly performing departments are identified, they are allowed to continue to use incremental budgeting.

To determine if a department is performing well or poorly, **variance analysis** should take place during the fiscal year. Variance analysis is the line-item comparison of budgeted

Gaming the Corporate Budgeting Process

Corporate budgeting is often based on history. How much revenue a company has taken in during previous years and how much it has spent serve as a benchmark for future revenues and expenses. The process seems simple enough, but in business there are often complicating factors. One is that corporate managers are often rewarded with bonuses for exceeding their revenue estimates.

The natural inclination of managers might be to underestimate revenues so that they can exceed them. On the other hand, corporate stockholders benefit when revenue projections for the future are high, not low. High revenue projections indicate strength in the company and the belief that it will make more money next year than it is making this year. Corporate boards want their managers to estimate future revenues to be high, but corporate managers want to estimate future revenues to be low. As a result, there is a tension that occurs during the budgeting process.

According to Michael C. Jensen (2001), "Corporate budgeting is a joke, and everyone knows it." Jensen argues that corporate budgeting consumes inordinate amounts of management attention and numerous meetings, encouraging management staff to misestimate revenues and expenses.

Jensen presents two examples of corporate budgeting gone off the rails. One was an international heavy-equipment manufacturer whose managers were rewarded for achieving their sales goals by shipping unfinished products from their plant in England to a warehouse in the Netherlands for final assembly. By shipping the incomplete products, they were able to realize the sales before the end of the quarter and thus fulfill their budget goal and make their bonuses. Unfortunately, the higher cost of assembling the goods in the Netherlands required not only the rental of the warehouse but also additional labor, and it ended up reducing the company's overall profit. Upper management should have seen what was occurring, but since they were participating in the bonuses, they were not motivated to do so.

Jensen's other example involved a large beverage company. In this example, one of the regional sales managers would dramatically underpredict demand for the product during major holidays. He wanted to ensure he had a low revenue target that he would have no trouble exceeding. But his underestimations came with a price. The beverage company based its demand planning on his sales forecasts and constantly ran out of its product during the height of the holiday selling season. Again, upper management should have paid better attention to what was occurring, but they were sharing in the largesse of exceeding sales goals.

References

Jensen, M.C. 2001. "Corporate Budgeting Is Broken—Let's Fix It." *Harvard Business Review*, November. http://hbr.org/2001/11/corporate-budgeting-is-broken-lets-fix-it/ar/1.

revenues and expenses with actual revenues and expenses, where the analysis attempts to determine why there is a difference.

Variance analysis is where the rubber meets the road. It is the essence of how management comes to understand the financial position the company is in, how the company got there, and what management needs to do to make things better. Variance analysis is why financial reports are prepared and how management uses them to manage the company.

Forecasting Revenue

All budgeting begins with the process of forecasting revenues and expenses, regardless of whether the budgeting method is incremental or zero-based. **Forecasting** is not a mystical process but one that involves a little logic and experience, where a basic level of research is conducted and logical conclusions are drawn from that research. The kind of research that is needed to create reasonable forecasts is usually cheap and easy, nothing to be afraid of.

Forecasting revenue, particularly when the business has been in existence for a while, involves looking at historical revenue data, anticipating any economic trends that might positively or negatively influence the data, and determining where in the industry life cycle the business finds itself. Considering these effects means using business tools introduced in previous chapters.

Chapter 5 presented the income statement for the Kids' Amusement Parks of America (KAPA) Corporation with comparisons of the previous fiscal years. The historical data on the income statement showed that, in 2011, KAPA had increased its revenue from the 2010 level of $972.8 million to over $1 billion. But in 2012, total revenue fell to $912.9 million. Because these numbers are presented as total revenue, the information provided by the income statement does not show how budgeted revenue compared against the actual revenue. Therefore, it is not possible to determine if KAPA met its budget goals. But what is apparent from the historical data presented on the income statement is that it's a good thing that total revenue increased from 2010 to 2011, but it's a bad thing that revenue declined from 2011 to 2012.

As may be recalled from chapter 2, macroeconomics plays a role in the performance of every industry. For example, because the U.S. economy was growing between 2007 and 2008, an increase in total revenue for that fiscal year could be related to growth in the economy. Likewise, because the U.S. economy declined between 2008 and 2009, a decline in total revenue for that fiscal year could be a function of the decline in the economy. Other factors must be considered as well, such as industry growth trends. Growth in the amusement park industry could affect KAPA's growth in revenue just as growth in the economy might. Competition could affect total revenue as well. All of these could drive the total revenue of a company.

Since an understanding of historical data and macroeconomics is a good place to start and can provide a basis for predicting revenue for the next year, it's helpful to predict the economic forecast for the next year. This is not something leisure services managers necessarily need to do themselves. You don't need to become a macroeconomist. But you do need to develop a basic understanding of where to find reliable macroeconomic forecasts.

Many types of economists make economic forecasts. Each forecast has its value. But because they are all different, you need to determine which are the most important. Different forecasts make different assumptions in building their models. Business and economics models are simplified representations of a system or phenomenon that use a hypothesis to describe the system or explain the phenomenon, often mathematically. Models can be algebraic equations, called **regression models**. Regression models consider several variables to determine the relationship between a dependent variable and one or more independent variables. In this case the regression model predicts the independent variable of economic outcomes based on the dependent variable of gross domestic product or total employment, to name two.

These models are derived from data that economists collect and are based on assumptions that the economists make. Confusing, right? To minimize confusion, every corporate financial manager has a favorite economic forecaster to whom he likes to turn. These favorite forecasters may be people who share political views with the financial managers; after all, corporate financial managers and economists have political biases of their own based on their political views. These views affect the assumptions being made by economists when they build their models.

For instance, U.S. corporate financial managers of the Democratic persuasion may turn to Keynesian economists for their forecasts. Keynesian economists believe that economic stimulus packages, like the one passed by Congress in February of 2009, will increase economic growth. Because of the economic stimulus applied by Congress in 2009, Keynesian economic forecasts were a little rosier than others.

Financial managers of the Republican persuasion may turn to supply-side economists. Supply-siders believe that tax increases, like the one they feared would occur after the economic stimulus package of 2009, slow economic growth. Supply-sider economic forecasts were a little less rosy than others. Therefore, depending on assumptions, which are often based on political views, economic forecasts can vary greatly from forecaster to forecaster.

One way of minimizing forecasting bias is to consider all of the forecasts and average their predicted outcomes. A good website that digests multiple competing economic forecasts is Consensus Economics (www.consensuseconomics.com), which assembles a panel of economists who create a range of alternatives. The extremes of the range are not as important to consider as the middle. Within that range is the **mean**, the statistical average, or the **median**, the middle, either of which represents a much better estimate of the economic forecast than the extremes. It is the mean or median forecast that should be considered.

Here is how Consensus Economics interpreted the 2010 economy (www.consensuseconomics.com):

> Following a grim year where the United States experienced arguably its worst recession of the post-WW2 period, observers are now focusing on the long-awaited recovery. The pressing issue, however, is how strong—or weak—the revival will be. Judging by the chart (below [not pictured]), our US panel's confidence is somewhat skewed towards a positive surprise, with respondents assigning a 33 percent probability to growth exceeding 3.3 percent this year (the consensus averages 2.9 percent).

The forecast of 2.9 percent growth in the U.S. economy might cause a financial manager to conclude that this overall economic growth could lead to growth in travel and domestic tourism, ultimately affecting the revenue of KAPA in a positive way. The financial managers of KAPA or Sadie's Amusement Park might have been willing to project revenues as higher in 2012 than they were in 2011. The question is, how much higher?

Forecasting is an inexact science, which suggests that there are margins of error that can lead to predictions of profits or losses, depending on the model. This is particularly true when businesses have small profit margins. If the economic forecasts overstate economic growth, financial managers may assume that total revenue will be high. If managers then allow corporate expenses such as staff and inventory costs to go up, the company could lose money. The company might hire too many people and have too much inventory left over.

Conversely, if a manager believes that economic forecasts will be lower and cuts corporate expenses, the company may not be in a position to accommodate higher-than-expected business levels if they materialize. There are, therefore, opportunity costs associated with not being prepared to sell goods or services to customers. **Opportunity costs** are the costs of not being in a position to take advantage of a business opportunity. They are why it is better to be on target in forecasting revenue than not, especially if the revenue forecast affects production.

An example of being too conservative in predicting sales and opportunity costs is the automotive industry. When automobile manufacturers react to predictions of economic slowdown, they often shut down production and lay off workers. That is exactly what happened in the spring of 2009 after Congress enacted the Cash for Clunkers program, which provided federal vouchers of up to $4,500 for people to trade in their vehicles for new ones that got better mileage. When the economic stimulus package caused more automobiles to be sold in two months than automobile financial managers thought would occur, the industry experienced a shortage of inventory in certain models and had to gear up production in a hurry. That cost the companies overtime wages for their workers, increasing labor costs more than if they had maintained a steadier production schedule.

For a leisure services example, let's turn again to Sadie's Amusement Park. In chapter 5, the park's income statement showed gross revenues of $2 million for the fiscal year of January 1, 2012, through December 31, 2012 (see table 5.4). The question Sadie needs to answer: What is a reasonable amount of revenue to forecast for 2013? To determine her revenue forecast, she needs to consider her 2012 revenue and make a reasonable forecast based on macroeconomic forecasts from economists she trusts.

Considering Sadie's Amusement Park total revenue for 2012, let's say the economic forecast consensus for 2013 is that the economy will go into a slight recession, with the domestic product (GDP) declining by 2 percent. If gross revenue of Sadie's Amusement Park were only dependent on the GDP, she could forecast that amusement park revenue would decline by 2 percent for a gross revenue of $1,960,000.

Only considering one variable, in this case the GDP, is called **linear thinking**. It says that GDP is the only factor that affects total revenue, which is a simplistic way of viewing revenue generation. In reality, revenue generation is much more complicated; many variables affect it. Since it's impossible to consider all of them, Sadie's total revenue forecast needs to limit her analysis to the important ones.

The important variables always include **demographics**, the key attributes, characteristics, or statistics of a certain group or population—in this case, Sadie's customer base. How many potential customers live within driving range of visiting Sadie's Amusement Park, including their ages and ability to pay the admission price? A reasonable revenue forecast will take into consideration changes in demographics, such as growth, decline, or aging of the population.

Among other important variables to consider is competition. In the marketplace, competition can be direct or indirect. **Direct competition** is other amusement parks in the area. **Indirect competition** is more difficult to discern. It includes

Even if a business has no direct competition in the area, it faces indirect competition from alternative recreational services. On a hot summer day, people might visit a nearby water park rather than ride the attractions at Sadie's Amusement Park.

competition from recreational providers that are not amusement parks but still compete for the time and money of Sadie's Amusement Park patrons. Examples might include movie theaters, water parks, go-cart tracks, miniature golf courses, and so forth.

Another consideration in predicting Sadie's Amusement Park revenue is industry life cycle. Many products lose their allure in the marketplace—for example, VHS videotape machines gave way first to DVD players and then to streaming videos, CDs gave way to digital downloads, and so on. Eventually, products or services are replaced by others that meet the changing needs of the public. Where the industry is in the product life cycle can contribute to predictions of continued growth or decline for product or service demand.

For the sake of building a less linear model, let's assume that Sadie's Amusement Park is located in an ethnically diverse area with a higher-than-average household income. Let's also assume that the average age is younger than the national average, but the amusement park industry is past its peak in the industry life cycle.

Without the data to build a regression model, let's assume that Sadie's best estimate of her total revenue is based on a 2 percent decline in the U.S. GDP. Her park is in a growing, young, affluent area during a time when the amusement park industry is just past its prime. Based on her best estimates, Sadie forecasts the total revenue to be slightly higher in 2013 than it was in 2012, about $2,020,000, a 1 percent increase.

This reasonable forecast, although not the product of complicated data analysis, reflects a certain level of due diligence on Sadie's part. She has done her due diligence by making the total revenue forecast. There is no guarantee her economic and industry life cycle are spot on, but there is a better chance she is correct in her prediction than if her forecast were based only on her intuition.

Forecasting Expenses

Forecasting expenses is easier and less fraught with the peril of making large mistakes than is revenue prediction. Sadie has her own historical data from 2012 to use as a basis for predicting 2013 expenses, and expenses in general are influenced less by outside factors than are revenues. Management has more control over expenses, and that's a good thing. It would be nearly impossible to manage a business without the ability to exercise a certain amount of control over expenses.

Again, let's review the Sadie's Amusement Park income statement from chapter 5. The income statement for the 2012 fiscal year showed that labor cost $870,600 and supplies cost $400,000, so the cost of goods sold was $1,270,600. This was the direct cost of serving the park's customers.

Sadie can assume that these direct costs of doing business will increase if attendance at the park increases. Since she predicted attendance will increase slightly, it is fair to estimate that direct costs will increase proportionately. Since total revenue increased by 1 percent, it would be reasonable to predict that labor will increase to $879,306 and that supplies will increase to $404,000. Thus, the cost of goods sold can be predicted to be $1,283,306, a 1 percent total increase.

But Sadie has decided that her prediction of revenue growth is somewhat shaky. She believes the smartest way she can budget expenses for the 2013 fiscal year is to hold the line, budgeting expenses at exactly the same level they were in 2012. What Sadie has decided to do is to take a **conservative approach** on the expenses side. A conservative approach in budgeting means predicting that expenses and revenue will not increase.

As far as nonoperating expenses go, not all of them are within Sadie's control. Some indirect expenses might not increase while others will. Loan repayments will not increase due to the anticipated attendance increases at the park, nor will depreciation of buildings and equipment. But other nonoperating expenses, such as utilities, might increase due to additional attendance at the park, rate increases, or both.

On the other hand, nonoperating expenses such as utilities, cleaning supplies, marketing costs, and equipment maintenance are under the control of management. They are not required to be increased in the budget as expense items. For that matter, there are techniques for controlling the cost of goods sold, such as reducing labor costs or changing suppliers, that allow management to hold down increases in cost. But, the most reasonable way to approach direct costs is that they can be expected to increase as revenue increases.

The greatest challenge for management, though, is to hold down overhead costs. The previous comparison between KAPA and Sadie's Amusement Park showed that the differences in profitability were due not so much to differences in their gross income but to differences in their nonoperating expenses. Sadie's Amusement Park was profitable because it held down overhead expenses; KAPA was not profitable for the opposite reason.

With such a marginally small increase in total revenue, Sadie is wise to budget her expenses at exactly the same level as they came in during the 2012 fiscal year. This conservative approach should prevent her from spending money in anticipation of increased revenue, foreseeing the possibility that increased revenue may not materialize because her forecast was too rosy.

Line-Item Budgeting

Budgets are different from income statements in many ways. Income statements look backward, showing the profitability of the company when the fiscal year is complete. Budgets look forward, attempting to predict revenues and expenses with comparisons during the fiscal year, providing management with an opportunity to adjust spending before the business loses money. Therefore, budgets need to be more detailed than income statements, with specific line items for revenues and expenses rather than summaries. As has been said, the devil is in the details.

In chapter 4, the annual budget for Coffee Café was presented as a model for budgeting detail (see table 4.1). That budget was relatively simple because the nature of the business was relatively simple and the volume of business was relatively modest. Writing a budget for a business like Sadie's Amusement Park is more daunting because the business is more complex and the revenue is substantially higher.

As mentioned, Sadie's 2012 revenue and expense data are relevant in writing the 2013 fiscal year budget. The difficulty occurs when next year's budget needs to be written during the current fiscal year. That is why corporations often write budgets five years out, so they can make better use of **moving averages** to predict revenues and expenses, focusing on historical trends rather than economic modeling. Using moving averages makes these corporations less dependent on economic forecasts to predict revenue.

Moving averages are used in all sectors of financial management. They are created by summing the outcomes for a specific past number of years, with the result divided by the number of years. For instance, a three-year moving average of a person's salary is the sum of the past three years of salaries divided by three. The following year, the new salary is added to the average, but the first year is dropped; thus, the average moves.

But Sadie has only one year of historical data at the beginning of her fiscal year, making it impossible for her to predict revenue using moving averages. She can only use her first-year data to predict her second year. Therefore, her challenge is to write a realistic budget based on the one year of historical data she has, breaking that data into line items that reflect transactions within that year. **Line items** are individual listings in a budget for categories of expenses or revenues.

An issue that every leisure services manager confronts is also one that Sadie must determine in writing her budget: How much line-item detail should be included? Not nearly as much detail needs to be recorded on the revenue side, largely because revenue for the amusement park is derived from far fewer categories than expenses. But the amount of detail in the expense budget is a bigger consideration.

Because there are hundreds of expense types in any business, a manager should determine how many line items to include in the budget to guide management decisions. The optimal level lets managers make adjustments in spending when actual revenue is higher or lower than forecasted revenue. But too much detail can make the budgeting process cumbersome and budget reports too long to be easily interpreted.

The optimal level of detail is easier to understand when it is seen rather than described in writing. In the case of Sadie's Amusement Park, the income statement showed that the amusement park raised $2 million in revenue in 2012. Based on the macroeconomic forecast and other variables, the park was forecasted to receive $2,020,000 in 2013.

What the income statement doesn't show is from what categories the park raises this money. Sadie needs to know this because, as with any business of a similar size, her amusement park is a compilation of small businesses within a larger business. An amusement park sells rides, food, carnival games, and souvenirs, to name a few. The way to manage the larger business is to consider the smaller businesses within it as departments of Sadie's Amusement Park. The logical way of managing several smaller businesses within a larger business is to put a person in charge of each department and make that person responsible for its management.

The solution is for Sadie to build departmental budgets so she can observe how her smaller businesses are doing. That way, if one or more is not profitable, she can make adjustments in the operations of these smaller businesses without affecting the profitable departments. This approach applies the blended budget techniques of zero-based budgeting for unprofitable departments and incremental budgeting for profitable departments.

Large corporations do just that, although not only by department but also by company. Disney, for instance, has an amusement park company, a movie company, a product licensing company, and so forth. Each of these companies has its own income statement and balance sheet, and within each company are departments, which have line-item budgets. All of the department budgets are rolled into company budgets, and all of the company budgets are rolled into a corporate budget.

For Sadie's Amusement Park, a logical departmental structure is to design around the major sources of revenue: rides, food, carnival games, and souvenirs. Structuring departments around revenue sources allows Sadie to manage each of these smaller businesses within her larger business. Table 6.1 presents an example of the budget for rides, the largest department in terms of revenue.

In terms of gross profitability, the budget shows that amusement park rides derive revenue from two sources, daily admissions and season passes. This departmental structure is similar to how nonprofit and public entities structure their budgets.

Table 6.1 Amusement Park Rides Department (January 1, 2012-December 31, 2012)

REVENUES	
Daily admissions	$1,012,000
Season passes	200,000
Total revenues	**$1,212,000**
EXPENSES	
Department manager	$65,000
Employee wages	420,600
Supplies	210,000
Utilities	6,000
Cleaning supplies	1,000
Marketing costs	8,000
Equipment repair and replacement	10,000
Loan interest payment	30,000
Total expenses	**$750,600**
Department profit	**$461,400**

Nonprofit and public organizations usually have a departmental swimming pool or similar recreation facility budget that derives revenue from a few sources.

However, in Sadie's budget, the rides department expenses are more detailed. The manager's salary, although separated from other employees' wages, is still considered a cost of goods sold. The portion of supplies required to operate the rides is large at $210,000. Based on the budget expenses, the cost of goods sold for the rides departments is $695,600 ($65,000 + $420,600 + $210,400), and the gross departmental profit is $516,400 ($1,212,000 - $695,600). The gross profit margin is expected to be 42.6 percent ($516,400 / $1,212,000).

In the rides department, the budgeted nonoperating costs are the line items defined as utilities, cleaning supplies, marketing costs, and equipment replacement. Contribution to overhead is also a nonoperating cost, comprising the portion of the loan principle repayment fairly charged to the department.

One way of viewing the budget for the rides department is that the department is a **cash cow**, meaning it is a very profitable department to be milked for all it's worth. For the good of the organization, Sadie must make sure the department generates as much in profit as it can. Other departments may not carry their load in covering overhead, making it more important for the profitable departments to sustain themselves.

Table 6.2 Concessions Department (January 1, 2012-December 31, 2012)

REVENUES	
Food	$300,000
Beverages	100,000
Total revenues	**$400,000**
EXPENSES	
Department manager	$45,000
Employee wages	150,000
Supplies	100,000
Utilities	1,000
Cleaning supplies	200
Marketing costs	1,000
Equipment repair and replacement	5,000
Loan interest payment	5,000
Total expenses	**$307,200**
Department profit	**$92,800**

The concessions department is one of those departments that, although profitable, is not as profitable as the rides department. Table 6.2 shows how the budget for the concessions department might look.

In terms of gross profitability, it is clear that the concessions department is less profitable than the rides department. The cost of goods sold is $295,000 ($45,000 + $150,000 + 100,000), and the gross profits of the department are budgeted to be $105,000 ($400,000 - $295,000), putting the gross profit margin at 26.25 percent ($105,000 / $400,000), much lower than the rides department.

One reason the concessions department is less profitable than the rides department is because labor and supplies are higher costs in proportion to total revenue. The larger labor costs are associated with operating multiple concession stands throughout the park, increasing the cost of goods sold as a percentage of gross revenue. Nonoperating equipment replacement costs also are substantial for the machinery necessary to operate the concession stands. All of this combines to make concessions less profitable than rides.

Table 6.3 presents the budget for the carnival games department, which operates similar to a casino, where people pay to compete in games, and prizes are awarded to just enough winners to make people continue to want to play. In terms of gross profitability, the carnival games department is very profitable, with a cost of goods sold at $105,000 ($45,000 + $50,000 + $10,000), gross profits at $195,000 ($300,000 - $105,000), and a gross profit margin of 65 percent ($195,000 / $300,000). This suggests that the carnival games department is even more of a cash cow than the rides department.

The souvenir department, on the other hand, has some issues that require management attention. The department is not profitable at all, as shown in table 6.4. In fact, it is budgeted to operate at a loss, with the cost of goods sold at $175,000 ($45,000 + $50,000 + $80,000) and no gross profits or profit margin. When modest nonoperating costs are added, the department is downright unprofitable. This unprofitability raises questions:

- How can Sadie make the department profitable?
- Are there expenses, such as labor, that can be trimmed without affecting sales?
- How does the department contribute to the overall business of Sadie's Amusement Park?
- Without the souvenir department, how would the rest of the departments fare?

In the retail industry, supermarkets and department stores have **loss leaders**, which are products put on sale to bring customers into the store. These products are sometimes sold below cost. The strategy is that once customers are in the store, they buy other products that are profitable for the store to sell. Sadie's Amusement Park may

Table 6.3 Carnival Games Department (January 1, 2012-December 31, 2012)

REVENUES	
Games fees	$300,000
Total revenues	**$300,000**
EXPENSES	
Departmental manager	$45,000
Employees wages	50,000
Supplies	10,000
Utilities	1,000
Cleaning supplies	200
Marketing costs	0
Equipment repair and replacement	0
Loan interest payment	5,000
Total expenses	**$111,200**
Department profit	**$188,800**

Table 6.4 Souvenir Department (January 1, 2012-December 31, 2012)

REVENUES	
Souvenir sales	$108,000
Total revenues	**$108,000**
EXPENSES	
Departmental manager	$45,000
Employees wages	50,000
Supplies	80,000
Utilities	1,000
Cleaning supplies	200
Marketing costs	1,000
Equipment repair and replacement	0
Loan interest payment	0
Total expenses	**$177,200**
Department profit	**($69,200)**

be willing to lose money on the souvenir department if it brings people to the park for rides, concessions, and carnival games, all of which are profitable. But if other departments become less profitable, Sadie may need to revisit that decision.

As shown, managing line-item detail is the way to manage a company's department budgets. Managing the department budgets is the way to manage a company's income statement. And managing a company's income statement is the way to manage its balance sheet.

Managing the Budget

If the purpose of an operating budget is to provide a plan that leisure services managers can follow, how can the budget help managers follow the plan? As mentioned, the budget and actual reports are tools that management uses to manage expenses during the fiscal year. Since management has far less control over revenues than expenses, if Sadie expects to deliver the bottom line of her budget, she will need to monitor her revenues and adjust her expenses when possible. The **bottom line**, or the net income after taxes, is the most important number to a business. To make the bottom line, managers need to manage the numbers they have the power to manage and pay close attention to the rest.

Promotional techniques might help manage revenue. For example, advertising could be increased to bring in customers. But there is always the risk that advertising might not attract more people, leaving the business with increased advertising costs. Promotional discounts may help bring in customers, too, but there is always the possibility that most of the customers using the discounts would have visited the amusement park anyway. The promotional discount then ends up costing more money than it generated.

Likewise, there are expenses that management has absolutely no control over. The loan payment and interest on the loan are fixed indirect costs. Managers can turn off lights when their businesses are closed, and they can turn down air conditioning and heating, but they can't turn them off entirely. Broken equipment needs to be repaired regardless of revenue levels.

What managers can control are labor costs, to a degree; their inventories of supplies; and the purchase of new equipment, as long as the old equipment is still operational. And management can defer maintenance costs for a while, but not forever. All of these techniques for controlling expenses should be done in such a way as to not deter customers from doing business with the company, though.

To demonstrate choices a manager might make, let's consider the operating budget of Sadie's Amusement Park and the tradeoffs that come with managing that budget. Let's assume it is the second year of operation and that Sadie did a wonderful job accounting for her revenues and expenses in the first year. She did such a great job of recording her transactions in 2011 that on June 30, 2012, she knows on a department-by-department basis how much she received in revenues and spent in expenses on June 30, 2011, and can compare it with June 30, 2012.

Considering that the park is halfway through its fiscal year, Sadie's Amusement Park should have received half of its budgeted revenues and paid half of its budgeted expenses. On June 30, 2012, the second-quarter budget and actual report for the concessions department might appear as shown in table 6.5.

The budget and actual report shows that on June 30, 2012, the concessions department was well on its way to making the $200,000 in total revenues that had been budgeted for the entire 2012 year. However, it also shows that on June 30, 2012, the concessions department profits are only $3,980, not on track to make the $46,400 budgeted for the entire year.

Analysis of concessions department revenue shows that food and beverage revenues are both

Table 6.5 Concessions Department Second-Quarter Budget and Actual Report (January 1, 2012-December 31, 2012)

	Budget (6/30/2012)	Actual (6/30/2012)	Actual (6/30/2011)
	REVENUES		
Food	$150,000	$145,300	$152,000
Beverages	50,000	42,200	52,300
Total revenues	**$200,000**	**$187,500**	**$204,300**
	EXPENSES		
Department manager	$22,500	$22,500	$22,500
Employee wages	75,000	76,100	74,900
Supplies	50,000	79,500	49,300
Utilities	500	490	500
Cleaning supplies	100	80	90
Marketing costs	500	650	440
Equipment repair and replacement	2,500	1,700	2,900
Loan interest payment	2,500	2,500	2,500
Total expenses	**$153,600**	**$183,520**	**$153,130**
Department profit	**$46,400**	**$3,980**	**$51,170**

under budget, combining to make a $12,500 shortfall. On the expense side, employees' wages are only slightly over budget by $1,100, but supplies are over budget by $29,500. The cost of goods sold accounted for the majority of the difference in the profitability of the department.

The easiest way for Sadie to fix the lower profitability of the department is to slow down the purchase of supplies and burn through the inventory she has, converting it to cash as concession products are sold. But she might also want to get her labor costs back on track and try to increase sales by raising prices. Holding her concessions manager's feet to the fire might be one way of doing it, instructing that person to pay more attention to the budget and actual report each month and make particularly sure that supplies stay in line with the budgeted amount. Because the 2012 budget line items are based on the 2011 experience, it is difficult for the manager to avoid the blame.

The process of managing the finances of Sadie's Amusement Park is simple enough as long as Sadie keeps good accounting records that allow historical comparisons to be made with her budget and actual report and prepares reports that are accurate and timely. Managing the finances becomes a process of reading the reports and taking the appropriate action, something the department manager should have done already.

How often should the department manager read the budget and actual report? A good answer is that she can't read it often enough. If the report can be generated on a daily basis, that is all the better. But most accounting departments can't provide a report that often for a couple of reasons. One is that few computer-based accounting systems keep historical records on a daily basis. To do so requires transactions, such as payroll batches, to be run every day, and since payroll is usually done biweekly or bimonthly, daily budget and actual records do not accurately reflect payroll.

A better method is for businesses to create budget and actual reports on a monthly basis. This way, payroll comparisons are more closely aligned when comparing activity in various fiscal years, as are comparisons of supplies, utilities, marketing costs, equipment repairs, interest payments, and most other expense items. The same can be said for revenue, although in the case of Sadie's Amusement Park, daily admissions are pretty comparable.

FINANCIAL FORMULAS

Financial formulas may seem like a lot of algebra, but they are extremely useful for measuring the financial health of a company. Typically, these formulas consist of equations where one side of the equal sign is equivalent to the other, explaining relationships between variables. The variables begin as letters, where all of the variables on one side of the equation are known in order to calculate the other side of the equation, which is not known.

An example of a simple financial equation is that profits are equal to revenues minus expenses, expressed as $P = R - E$. Revenues and expenses are known, but profits are not known until expenses are subtracted from revenues. Most formulas are that simple once the numbers are known.

Purpose of Formulas

Budget and actual reports are tools for managing a company. In business, these reports are rarely made available to anyone outside the management team. Boards of directors don't even see them. For privately held companies like Sadie's Amusement Park, financial statements are not available to anyone other than potential buyers of the company. For publicly held companies, their corporate boards, potential investors, and the public only see quarterly income statements and balance sheets. Investors pay attention to what is going on within publicly traded companies by analyzing annual and quarterly income statements to determine if the company is healthy enough to invest in.

Let's revisit the hospital metaphor from chapter 5. Just as hospitals use tools and tests to keep track of patient health, the purpose of financial formulas is to measure the financial health of a company. Because financial health, like physical health, has many dimensions, there are many tests to measure these dimensions.

Before we look at the formulas themselves, you need to understand that privately held companies are best served by comparing themselves with other privately held companies of their size. However, the use of financial formulas in measuring the health of privately held companies is more difficult because the comparable companies are not required to divulge financial reports. Therefore, privately held companies can only compare themselves with publicly held companies that are required to be transparent to investors. And, of course, publicly held companies can use financial formulas to compare their financial formulas with the standards in their industries.

A number of financial formulas are used to measure the financial health of a company. These formulas create **financial ratios**. A ratio is a relative magnitude of two selected numerical values taken from the financial statements of a business. Often used in accounting, there are many standard ratios for evaluating the overall financial condition of a corporation or other organization.

Ratios can be expressed as a decimal value, such as 0.10, or as an equivalent percent value, such as 10 percent. Some ratios are quoted as percentages, especially ratios that are usually or always less than 1, such as **earnings yield**. An earnings yield ratio is the quotient of earnings per share of stock divided by the share price of that stock. Other ratios are decimal numbers, especially ratios that are usually more than 1, such as the **price–earnings (P/E) ratio**, which is the price of the stock divided by the earnings per share of stock. P/E ratios are part of the family known as *multiples*.

Given any ratio, an analyst can also calculate the **reciprocal** by reversing the two numbers, making the numerator the denominator and the denominator the numerator. The reciprocal expresses the same information but may be more understandable. For instance, the earnings yield can be compared with bond yields, whereas the P/E ratio cannot.

Here's an example. If the earnings are $5 per share for the year, then $100 / $5 = 20, which is the P/E. The P/E was arrived at by knowing that if a P/E ratio of a company's stock is 20, its rate of return is 5 percent. If the P/E of a stock is 40, its rate of return is 2.5 percent. The simplest way to calculate the rate of return of a stock if you know the P/E is to divide the P/E into 100. The easiest way to calculate the P/E of a stock if you know the rate of return is multiply the rate of return times 100. For instance, let's say a company's stock has a sale price of $100 per share, and the P/E is 30. The rate of return, then, is 100 divided by 30 or 3.33 percent.

Commonly Used Ratios

Many ratios are used in measuring the financial health of a company, but, as mentioned, some of these ratios only have meaning when they are compared with industry averages. Some have universal meaning, such as the P/E ratio, which measures the price of the stock against earnings per share. In the case of the P/E ratio, an investor wanting to invest in stock would compare companies across industries because, theoretically, investors don't care as much about the industry as they do about whether the stock is a good value.

The Visionary Who Started Disneyland

Walt Disney was a creative genius with an imagination to match. It's no exaggeration to say that his ingenuity sparked an entertainment and theme park industry that has touched billions of children and adults since his first cartoon release in 1923. The 1955 opening of Disneyland in Anaheim, California, marked a historical change in the amusement park experience that eventually became international in scope. According to the Disneyland Linkage (2012), in 2009 alone, accumulated attendance at Disney parks and resorts worldwide was more than 119 million.

Disney was born in Chicago in 1901. Soon after, his family moved to Marceline, Missouri, and then Kansas City, where he developed a love for nature and animals and a fascination with trains, all of which were the subjects of his passion for drawing.

In 1923, Walt and his brother Roy formed Walt Disney Studios. Walt thought that children would like to interact with the characters and devised the idea of a theme park where this could take place. They began thinking about their idea before World War II started, but plans had to be put on hold until after the war ended.

According to a history of Disneyland at DisneyDreamer.com (2007), "By 1953, Disney had stretched his personal resources to the limit. At that point, television, in the form of the American Broadcasting Co., came to the rescue. ABC had been after Disney to produce a weekly show for their struggling network. Disney agreed—in exchange for partial financing of his amusement park. Loans and an investment from the Santa Fe Railroad covered the rest, and with money secured, work began on Disneyland in earnest."

Construction began on July 21, 1954, and the theme park opened a year later. After several expansions, today Disneyland regularly draws huge crowds. The Walt Disney Company's corporate website provides a wealth of information about its business operations in its fact books and annual reports but does not report attendance data (http://corporate.disney.go.com/index.html). That is left for industry statisticians to glean from a variety of other sources, including the Themed Entertainment Association (TEA, www.teaconnect.org).

TEA released its 2010 Global Attractions Attendance Report in 2011 (TEA 2011). A June 2011 news release found on an unofficial Disney fan website provides insight into Disney attendance figures based on the TEA report: "Disney [do] not publish any attendance data, so these reports represent the industry's best estimates on the relative state of park attendance worldwide. The Magic Kingdom retains its top spot, with an estimated attendance of 16.972 million guests, a 1.5% decline from the previous year. Epcot saw a 1.5% decline with attendance of 10.825 million, with the Studios also seeing a decline of 1% at 9.602 million guests. Perhaps surprisingly, Disney's Animal Kingdom saw a rise in attendance of 1%, attracting an estimated 9.686 million guests. This is the first time that Disney's Animal Kingdom has surpassed Disney's Hollywood Studios in attendance estimates" (WDWmagic.com 2011).

Disneyland has the second highest attendance of any theme park in the world, second only to Disney World's Magic Kingdom in Orlando, Florida. Roy Disney lived to see the construction of Disney World and the growth of the Walt Disney Company to a Fortune 500 company, but Walt did not, dying in 1966 at age 65. Roy's son lived until 2009, overseeing the construction of Disney theme parks in Paris, Hong Kong, and Tokyo.

References

Crowe, T. 2007. "How Disneyland Got Started." http://ezinearticles.com/?How-Disneyland-Got-Started&id=652483.

Disney Dreamer. 2007. "Disneyland History." www.disney-dreamer.com/history/disneyland.htm.

Disneyland Linkage. 2012. "Yearly Attendance Figures of All Disney Theme Parks, 1991-2009." Accessed January 29, 2012. www.scottware.com.au/theme/feature/atend_disparks.htm#Yearly.

Disney Mouse Links. 2010. "History of Disneyland." www.disneymouselinks.com/disneylandhistory.aspx.

Themed Entertainment Association. 2011. "2010 Theme Index: The Global Attractions Attendance Report." www.themeit.com/etea/2010Report.pdf.

WDWmagic.com. 2011. "The Walt Disney Company News: Themed Entertainment Association 2010 Attendance Report Now Available." www.wdwmagic.com/Other/Walt-Disney-Company/News/17Jun2011-Themed-Entertainment-Association-2010-attendance-report-now-available.htm.

Ratios are categorized in terms of what condition of financial health they are intended to measure. An example is the **liquidity** of a company. **Liquidity ratios** measure the ability of a company to pay off its short-term debt obligations. This is done by comparing the company's most liquid assets (those that can be easily converted to cash) with its current liabilities.

Liquidity Ratios

Among the most commonly used liquidity ratios are the **current ratio**, **quick ratio**, and **cash ratio**. The liquidity ratios are expressed as formulas and are somewhat similar.

$$\text{Current ratio} = \frac{\text{Current assets}}{\text{Current liabilities}}.$$

$$\text{Quick ratio} = \frac{\text{Cash and equivalents + Short-term investments + Accounts receivable}}{\text{Current liabilities}}.$$

$$\text{Cash ratio} = \frac{\text{Cash + Cash equivalents + Invested funds}}{\text{Current liabilities}}.$$

As can be seen, all of the liquidity ratios have current liabilities as the denominator of the formula, but they have slightly different numerators. Sadie's Amusement Park could be compared with KAPA using the current ratio, but it can't be compared using the quick ratio or the cash ratio because it does not have short-term investments or invested funds of any kind, for that matter, whereas KAPA does. Calculating current ratios for Sadie's Amusement Park and KAPA yields the following results. (For the current ratio, the numerator and denominator come from the balance sheet.)

Sadie's Amusement Park current ratio as of December 31, 2012:

Current assets of $356,100 /
current liabilities of $20,000 = 17.8.

Kids' Amusement Parks of America Corporation current ratio as of December 2012:

Current assets of $255,100,000 /
current liabilities of $423,400,000 = .6025.

These calculations show that Sadie's can cover its current liabilities 17.8 times with its current assets, but KAPA can only cover 60 percent of its current liabilities with its current assets. The KAPA current ratio shows that if the company were called upon to pay off its current liabilities (which is unlikely), it would not have enough liquidity to do so. On the other hand, if Sadie's Amusement Park were called upon to pay off its current liabilities, it would be able to do so quite easily.

KAPA can be compared with any other publicly traded business and found to be marginally liquid. If Sadie's could be compared with other privately held businesses in its industry, which is unlikely, it would be found to be very liquid.

Liquidity is important because there are times when businesses need cash to pay their bills, pay off some of their short-term debt, or even pay off some of their long-term debt. It is nice to know a business is able to do that.

Profitability Ratios

The long-term profitability of a company is important to its long-term survivability. It is also an indicator to shareholders that the company will be able to pay dividends on its investments in company stock. In the case of the publicly traded KAPA Corporation, knowing profitability and how it compares with the amusement park industry and other companies in general is important. For the privately owned Sadie's Amusement Park, profitability is something that Sadie would like to know herself.

There are several ratios that measure the profitability of a company, but not all of them are important in comparing Sadie's Amusement Park with KAPA. A few of them have already been presented during income statement analysis, including the gross profit margin, operating margin, and net profit margin. Those don't need to be repeated. Two new ratios are not shown on the income statement because they are balance sheet numbers, which need to be introduced. They are the **return on assets** and the **return on equity**, expressed as the following formulas.

$$\text{Return on assets} = \frac{\text{Net income}}{\text{Average total assets}}.$$

$$\text{Return on equity} = \frac{\text{Net income}}{\text{Average shareholders' equity}}.$$

The return on assets divides the net income by the **average total assets**, and the return on equity divides net income by the **average shareholders' equity**. The term *average* refers to that which is present throughout the fiscal year, but for this analysis, because we can't really know what the averages are, we will use total assets and total equity at the end of the fiscal years.

Average total assets is a five-month average of a company's total assets. Average shareholders' equity is calculated by adding shareholders' equity at the beginning of a time period to the shareholders' equity at the end of that time period and averaging the total.

Calculating the return on assets and return on equity for Sadie's Amusement Park yields the following results. (They were not calculated for

KAPA because the company didn't have any net income, and showing a negative number might be confusing.)

Sadie's Amusement Park ratio on December 31, 2012:

Return on assets = net income of \$162,500 / average total assets of \$3,065,000 = 0.053.

Return on equity = net income of \$162,500 / average shareholders' equity of \$1,265,000 = 0.128.

The ratios show that the return on assets for Sadie's Amusement Park at the end of the 2012 fiscal year is 5.3 percent. To know if that is a good return on assets requires knowledge of the industry average. Suffice it to say that the amusement park industry requires a large amount of assets to operate. Financial analysts would conclude that 5.3 percent is generally good.

Understanding the return on equity does not necessarily require an understanding of the industry. In general, any business should return a reasonable amount of money to the owners, at least more than the investor could earn by putting the money in a savings account.

A return-on-equity ratio of 12.8 percent is considered very good. A 12.8 percent return on any investment is higher than what a savings account pays (i.e., typically 1 to 4 percent), meaning it was more profitable for Sadie to invest her money in an amusement park than in a savings account.

There are other categories of ratio analysis that investors and financial managers can perform, but the third category that is important for leisure services managers to know measures the ability of a company to pay its long-term and **short-term debt**. These are ratios obtained from numbers available on the balance sheet.

Debt Ratios

One of two ratios most commonly used in corporate financial analysis is the **debt ratio**, which compares total liabilities with total assets in order to see if debt is too high in relation to owner's equity. A high debt ratio indicates that the owners of the company are the lenders rather than the investors; in other words, they are the people who own the liabilities rather than the equity.

$$\text{Debt ratio} = \frac{\text{Total liabilities}}{\text{Total assets}}.$$

The other ratio is the **debt-to-equity ratio**. This ratio is calculated by dividing the total liabilities of a company by its shareholders' equity.

$$\text{Debt-to-equity ratio} = \frac{\text{Total liabilities}}{\text{Shareholders' equity}}.$$

Comparing Sadie's Amusement Park with KAPA is instructional (though perhaps painful to KAPA). Sadie's Amusement Park debt ratio on December 31, 2012:

Total liabilities of \$1,820,000 / total assets of \$3,065,000 = .594.

KAPA debt ratio on December 31, 2012:

Total liabilities of \$3,491,800,000 / total assets of \$2,907,000 = 1.201.

The lower a debt ratio is, the better. A debt ratio should be less than 1.0 to indicate more assets than debt. Sadie's Amusement Park has a debt ratio of .594, suggesting more in assets than in debt, which is a good thing.

If a person has more debt than assets, he is considered to be bankrupt, meaning that even if he liquidated everything he owned, he still could not pay off his debts. Such is the case for KAPA. A debt ratio of 1.201 suggests an inability to pay off its debt. However, KAPA may be bankrupt according to its debt ratio but not bankrupt in reality. That's because of an issue raised earlier during discussions about accrual accounting and how the value of

The carnival games at Sadie's Amusement Park are very profitable and contribute to the long-term survivability of the business.

assets is recorded at the time of purchase. It would be obvious to most lenders that the fixed assets of KAPA will be worth more on September 30, 2013, than they were at their time of purchase. The lenders would take some comfort in that knowledge, but only to a certain extent.

Because KAPA had a negative equity of $584.2 million, its debt-to-equity ratio is not meaningful; however, Sadie's Amusement Park's ratio is.

Sadie's Amusement Park debt-to-equity ratio on December 31, 2012:

Total liabilities of $1,820,000 /
shareholders' equity of $1,265,000 = 1.439.

An ideal debt-to-equity ratio is less than 1.0 because that means the owners have more invested in the company than the lenders do. However, Sadie's Amusement Park is a relatively new venture. New ventures tend to be somewhat debt heavy in the beginning, a condition that should reverse itself over time.

SUMMARY

Identifying how the budgeting process works in the private sector provides a basis for understanding budgeting in the government and nonprofit sectors. In all three sectors, budgeting is a planning process that puts the business or agency on the path to having some money left over at the end of the year.

Budgeting uses two major methodologies: incremental and zero-based. Incremental budgeting is the process of using historical revenue and expense data and revising them slightly. Zero-based budgeting is the process of starting from scratch with every department and justifying the existence of every line item.

Incremental budgeting is best applied to departments of businesses that are functioning well, making a profit. Zero-based budgeting is best applied to unprofitable departments where there might be better solutions to the status quo.

Forecasting revenues and expenses is required for either budget technique. Understanding macroeconomics can be an important skill in forecasting, but understanding other variables is important as well. Other variables include the life cycle of the industry, competition, and demographics.

Understanding quarterly income statements, balance sheet reports, and budget detail is essential for managing a leisure services business. Additionally, managers need the ability to convert financial analysis to management action.

One of the tools financial managers have is the budget and actual report, where budget and historical revenues and expenses are compared with actual revenues and expenses each month. From these reports, presented on a department-by-department basis, management action is sometimes required to correct financial problems as they become apparent.

Formulas that investors use to diagnose the overall financial health of a company are useful tools for financial managers as well. Knowing how these formulas are calculated and what they mean can help managers understand the financial condition of their business and whether outsiders would consider it a good investment. Though this is not always important to privately held companies, it is nearly always important to publicly traded companies.

Visit the Web Resource

For case studies, sample financial statements, key terms, and more, please visit the web resource at www.HumanKinetics.com/LeisureServicesFinancialManagement

chapter 7

The Nonprofit Sector

Learning Outcomes

After completing this chapter, students will be able to do the following:

- Use the IRS tax code to explain the three types of nonprofit leisure organizations.
- Compare and contrast the concept of making a profit in the three sectors using fitness center operations as an example.
- Differentiate between primary and secondary funding sources.
- Determine how fund-raising works in the nonprofit sector.
- Recognize the role of boards in the fund-raising and financial processes of nonprofit organizations.
- Explain the role of leisure services managers in the fund-raising process.

Nonprofit leisure services organizations can have different missions than governmental units while offering the same leisure services. For instance, whereas private health clubs have a mission of providing fitness services to people who are able to pay, YMCAs do so along with a mission of providing some charitable services to people able to pay and people not able to pay. Governments, on the other hand, sometimes have the mission of providing services for free to everyone.

To make the issue even more complicated, there are different types of nonprofit organizations, including those that operate for public benefit, those that operate for the benefit of members only, religious organizations, and educational organizations. All of these types are chartered as nonprofit corporations in their respective states, but the IRS views them differently in terms of their ability to accept charitable donations.

This chapter and the next contribute to a developing body of knowledge about nonprofit organizations that offer leisure services. This chapter explains how nonprofit leisure services financial management is similar to financial management in the other sectors and why it is unique. First, though, an understanding of the two types of nonprofit leisure services is needed.

NONCHARITABLE AND CHARITABLE NONPROFITS

The IRS tax code recognizes many types of nonprofit leisure services that are exempt from paying taxes. The first is social and recreation clubs, also known as mutual-benefit nonprofit organizations, which are exempt from paying taxes under section 501(c)(7) of the tax code, defined by the IRS as the following (Mancuso 2011):

> **Exempt Purposes—Internal Revenue Code Section 501(c)(7)**
>
> A social club must be organized for pleasure, recreation, and other similar purposes. A club will not be recognized as tax exempt if its charter, bylaws, or other governing instrument, or any written policy statement provides for discrimination against any person based on race, color, or religion. A club may, however, in good faith limit its membership to members of a particular religion in order to further the teachings or principles of that religion and not to exclude individuals of a particular race or color.

Whether an organization's purposes are consistent with tax exemption under section 501(c)(7) is generally determined based on its organizing documents. Examples of organizations that fall into this category include the following:

- College fraternities and sororities
- Country clubs
- Amateur hunting, fishing, tennis, swimming, and other sport clubs
- Dinner clubs that provide a meeting place, library, and dining room for members
- Variety clubs
- Hobby clubs
- Homeowners or community associations whose primary function is to own and maintain recreational areas and facilities

The other type of nonprofit leisure services organization that is exempt from paying taxes is charitable organizations, called *501(c)(3) organizations*, defined by the IRS as follows (Mancuso 2011):

> **Exempt Purposes—Internal Revenue Code Section 501(c)(3)**
>
> The exempt purposes set forth in section 501(c)(3) are charitable, religious, educational, scientific, literary, testing for public safety, fostering national or international amateur sports competition, and preventing cruelty to children or animals.

The term *charitable* is used in its generally accepted legal sense and includes relieving the poor, the distressed, or the underprivileged; advancing religion; advancing education or science; erecting or maintaining public buildings, monuments, or works; lessening the burdens of government; lessening neighborhood tensions; eliminating prejudice and discrimination; defending human and civil rights secured by law; and combating community deterioration and juvenile delinquency.

Obviously, the local Little League would not hire a leisure services professional to manage the organization, but Little League Baseball, Inc., which manages the Little League World Series, would. There are thousands of nonprofit international, national, and regional organizations that manage and coordinate recreational pursuits, from Little League to the Professional Golfers' Association of America (PGA) to the Olympics.

Nonprofit organizations that take in $25,000 or more in gross revenue annually must file an IRS Form 990 each year. Information on this form includes a list of board members, salary disclosure of the highest-paid employees, and other financial information. Completed forms are public documents and can be found through Internet searches, including GuideStar (www.guidestar.com). A website that offers instructions and education on becoming a nonprofit organization is the free legal information website at www.nolo.com. Forms and publications can be downloaded from the IRS at www.irs.gov/formspubs/index.html. The website of the National Center for Charitable Statistics (NCCS) is another online source (http://nccs.urban.org/).

The term *nonprofit* refers to the fact that the organization has no owner or stockholders who profit from its excess revenue. The IRS litmus test for bestowing tax-exempt status is whether the organization reinvests its revenue into the organization rather than giving it to owners or shareholders. In other words, nonprofits can make profit; however, a nonprofit that shows an excessive amount of excess revenue can be a red flag for the IRS to investigate further. According to NOLO Law for All (www.nolo.com), as long as the revenue is generated from purposes related to the organization's mission, tax exemption is allowed. But some revenue-generating activities could be viewed as unrelated to the organization's purpose, and unrelated business activities are taxable.

Challenges Facing Nonprofit Organizations

The Public Research Group (PRG) is a Chicago-based consulting company that helps start-up nonprofit organizations get started and identify the challenges they will face in the first year of their existence. Because nonprofit organizations can rarely afford consultants during their first year, PRG offers its services at no charge to build a relationship and the possibility of future work. PRG helps the organizations with problems such as fund-raising, community support, paperwork, accounting, and compliance.

Fund-raising: Nonprofits cannot exist without fund-raising, often referred to as *development*. An easy first step is to raise funds through memberships and user fees. Private foundations also can be a source of funding, so having someone on board to research these possibilities is helpful. Communication and storytelling also are essential to fund-raising. Ultimately, the best fund-raising results from cultivating one-on-one relationships and asking people for money in person. A wealth of information about fund-raising is available in articles on the GuideStar website (www2.guidestar.org/rxg/news/articles/index.aspx).

Community support: You can't raise funds without community support. Relationship building is essential and should start with the people in your organization, their contacts, and what they know about those contacts—information that should be added to a database or spreadsheet. Most nonprofits develop websites; produce newsletters, both print and electronic; and use social media to stay connected to their members and the community. They submit news releases with photos to the local papers about their members' accomplishments. Developing a logo and a catchy slogan also helps to communicate the organization's mission and connect with the community.

Paperwork: Nonprofits are required to apply for nonprofit status in their states and with the federal government, namely the IRS. In most cases, application forms are available online. But the paperwork must be exact, so professional help may be needed. It doesn't hurt for a start-up nonprofit to find a lawyer to help, especially one who supports the organization and will work for free.

Accounting: As with legal knowledge, it's always good to have someone in the start-up organization who has experience in accounting and bookkeeping. Nonprofits must keep good records and file reports as required by state and federal laws. Though the leaders of nonprofit organizations are not expected to be skilled in accounting, they are expected to be able to read and make sense of financial statements. Every nonprofit should have someone in their organization who can use basic bookkeeping software.

Compliance: Compliance involves filing the required state and federal reports, such as IRS Form 990. An organization that employs people and has complex fund-raising activities has more rules to follow. Complying with regulations becomes easier the longer an organization exists, but it requires computer expertise and appropriate software to generate reports.

PRG suggests that start-up nonprofit organizations purchase help books such as those published by Nolo out of Sacramento, California. These books provide step-by-step directions for creating a nonprofit organization as well as template documents where the blanks can be filled in and the documents submitted to the secretary of state and IRS for approval.

References

American City Bureau. 2012. "Small Town YMCA Executes 'Right' Steps for Campaign Success." Accessed January 28, 2012. www.acb-inc.com/acb-news-post-2/.

Mollsen, L.B. 2011. "Romancing Your Donors—Major Gifts Require Strong Relationship." www.acb-inc.com/wp-content/uploads/Romancing-Your-Donors-Major-Gifts-Require-Strong-Relationships.pdf.

Nonprofit Central. 2012. "The Top Five Problems Faced by Start-Up Nonprofits and How to Overcome Them." Accessed January 28, 2012. www.startnonprofitorganization.com/the-top-5-problems-faced-by-start-up-nonprofits-and-how-to-overcome-them.

In nonprofit financial management, it is important to never achieve a financial position where it looks like a business is being operated rather than an organization that is not attempting to make a profit. The IRS code requires that a substantial portion of the organization's activities must be related to charitable work for a 501(c)(3) status to be awarded, and for other 501(c) ratings to be maintained, only a small portion of the organization's activities can be related to profit generation.

Charitable nonprofit leisure services generate revenue through fund-raising. This can take the form of soliciting donations, charging membership or user fees, selling products or concessions, charging admission to events, and going after large corporate sponsors in exchange for advertising rights. One popular national PGA golf tournament was called the *Cialis Western Open*, for example, after its sponsor.

The YMCA and Boys and Girls Clubs have been mentioned before as examples of charitable nonprofit leisure services agencies. Other leisure services that fall into the charitable nonprofit category are non-government-operated museums, cultural centers, and historic sites and monuments, which are found in many communities and, of course, at the state and national levels.

NONPROFIT CHARITABLE STATUS

The IRS requires nonprofit charitable organizations to provide some, but not all, services to people with low incomes, putting the organizations in a position to enter into value-exchange relationships with paying clients while retaining their charitable status to provide free services to indigent people. What makes the job of nonprofit leisure services managers more difficult is that, with the ability to enter into value-exchange relationships with clients, they need to manage two relationships at the same time. Nonprofit managers need to manage their donor-exchange relationships by creating the dual identity that the nonprofit organization is self-supporting and yet is a needy charity that serves people who can't afford to pay. They also need to manage their value-exchange relationships with paying clients.

To manage this duality, organizations charge program fees for their services but waive the fees for low-income clients or provide scholarships for reduced fees. Providing too many scholarships can be an expensive proposition when the nonprofit organization needs to gather enough revenues to sustain operations. In cases where nonprofit organizations operate in economically depressed areas, they need external sources of funding, such as United Way or Community Chest. In places in the United States where United Way or Community Chest don't exist, nonprofit leisure organizations have developed their own donation-based funding sources to defray operating expenses.

Membership Model

One marketplace into which nonprofit leisure services organizations have ventured, although the private sector often objects, is the fitness center. Fees are generated through a **membership model**. YMCAs and many other nonprofit organizations have embraced the membership model for many years. The membership model is where people pay to join the organization and pay no additional fees for certain services.

What makes the model controversial is that public leisure services agencies that are developing membership models are competing directly with the private sector. Private businesses believe the other two sectors have unfair competitive advantages, including access to donations and public funding of capital costs.

The membership model was originally used in country clubs, tennis clubs, and similar activity-based nonprofit organizations. The model was based on new members being charged an upfront initiation fee and then flat-rate annual dues to continue membership. For private country clubs, the initiation fee bought a share of ownership into the club. Since shares were limited, the only way a new member could join was if an existing member left the club.

In the case of country clubs, annual membership fees usually covered the cost of members playing golf, using the pool, and playing tennis. Fees for purchasing food and drinks in the clubhouse were billed separately. Currently, some country clubs assess a minimum food and beverage charge to their members to encourage them to use the restaurant and bar. In many cases, those charges are automatically deducted from the members' checking accounts. In other cases, bills are sent out to members each month.

Based on the country-club model of memberships, YMCAs and other nonprofit organizations have developed a membership model where members pay for the privilege of using the fitness facility and swimming pool during certain hours. Members pay additional fees for instructional programs, day camps, racquetball courts, or other amenities. Nonmembers may register to use any of the YMCA's amenities or programs, but the rates are higher in order to encourage them to become members.

The YMCA model is different from the country-club model in that additional recreational services are paid in advance rather than billed to members after the fact. Table 7.1 shows an example of a fairly typical YMCA membership fee structure from the

Table 7.1 Membership Rates

Types	Joiner fee	Monthly fee
Family	$120.00	$75.00
Adult (19 yr+)	$120.00	$52.00
College (19-23 yr)	$35.00	$34.00
Youth (6-18 yr)	$67.00	$25.00

Heritage YMCA system in Naperville, Illinois. Membership fees for use of all three Heritage branches are the higher rates shown for each age group. The lower rates are for use of just one branch.

YMCAs, like country clubs, have been known to charge an initiation fee that is levied at the beginning of the membership period to discourage people from temporarily discontinuing their memberships during the summer months, when their use of the facility is less than it would be during the rest of the year. But the initiation fee does not buy equity in the Y, because it is a nonprofit organization where there is no stock. Theoretically, there is also no limit to the number of members, whereas in a country club, membership is limited to the number of equity shares available.

Memberships provide the **revenue engine** to sustain the YMCA's operating costs. Revenue engines are very profitable fee structures for programs that generate substantially more in revenues than it costs to provide the services. Nonprofit leisure services revenue engines are created when nonprofit organizations get into the marketplace for what were once privately offered recreational services.

Seeing no reason to charge less for recreational services than businesses do, nonprofit organizations charging the going rate for recreational services are able to generate the same profit margins as businesses. Since managers of nonprofit organizations have no obligation to return profits to shareholders, the excess revenue can be used to underwrite other programs or overhead not covered by program fees.

Other recreation programs within YMCAs and other nonprofit agencies may not be nearly as profitable, nor would they need to be. Fees for programs that are not revenue engines would only be expected to cover direct costs and rarely would contribute as much as membership fees do to the revenue streams of the agency.

It is important to understand the distinction between revenue engines and programs that are not revenue engines. The difference is that revenue engines are programs that are offered when nonprofit organizations venture into private-sector pricing and that are expected to be profitable. The programs that are not revenue engines are typically those that are left for the nonprofit and public sectors to provide. Yoga classes are a good example of programs that are not revenue engines. Years ago, there weren't many yoga classes in the private sector, but since the market for yoga participation has grown, the private sector now offers yoga.

Without a model for charging a higher going rate, managers of nonprofit and governmental leisure services agencies often choose to only cover their direct costs, something private-sector managers would not do. However, since the nonprofit and governmental leisure services agencies have already established the **price point** for yoga, and private providers would need to charge more to cover their indirect and overhead costs, private providers are boxed out of the market for yoga. They may offer yoga, but only as a loss leader. The price point is a point on a scale of possible prices at which something might be marketed, and a loss leader is a product sold at a loss to attract customers.

There are exceptions to this general rule, however. Some programs that are not usually revenue engines can still become business ventures. In many communities, the YMCA or park and recreation department's gymnastics or karate instructor may open a storefront business providing those services, charging more for lessons and hoping that their testimony of higher service levels will allow them to compete. Some of these businesses flourish and others don't.

In order to survive, every nonprofit agency needs to offer revenue-engine services that are profitable enough to cover overhead and administrative costs, because programs that are not revenue engines typically don't cover much more than direct costs. If nonprofit agencies aren't able to establish revenue engines, their only alternative is to seek donations or grants to defray operating costs.

Applying the example of the fitness center again, it is standard practice in the industry that fitness center membership charges are deducted electronically from members' checking accounts each month, providing a much more time-efficient and reliable revenue stream than billing members monthly. Members tend to keep their memberships even though they may not visit the fitness center frequently, because it takes time and trouble to cancel the membership.

Table 7.2 Membership Fees

Membership categories	Number of members @ rate per month	Total revenues
Family memberships	2,000 families @ $75/month × 12 months	$1,800,000
Adult memberships	3,000 adults @ $40/month × 12 months	$1,440,000
College memberships	300 students @ $30/month × 3 months	$27,000
Senior memberships	1,000 seniors @ $36/month × 12 months	$432,000
Corporate memberships	1,000 adults @ $36/month × 12 months	$432,000
Total membership revenues		**$4,131,000**

Table 7.2 provides an example of a membership scenario for a hypothetical YMCA that is a standalone agency without branches. The fees are calculated on an annual basis, with the understanding that the college membership program is designed to engage college students returning home for the summer.

The table shows the proportion of memberships at a suburban YMCA. The number of memberships by category is shown as what would typically be distributed across age groups. The table shows that the membership revenue streams generate over $4 million annually, which would cover most of the operating costs of a YMCA, but not the capital costs.

The program fees for other services would cover the direct costs of the programs. Donations would need to be generated for capital expansion. Putting membership revenues into perspective with the overall budget, table 7.3 represents a reasonable scenario for the YMCA in a simplistic summary.

The budget shows that memberships cover administration, facility maintenance, and staffing. Program fees cover program expenses and the annual fund-raiser covers scholarships for low-income members. The only problem with the budget is that it does not appear the YMCA would be providing 25 percent of its services to low-income people. This problem could be overcome with the argument that $60,000 in direct scholarships was provided. In its defense, the YMCA could say that 25 percent of its clients were provided program fee discounts in addition to those who were provided outright scholarships.

Table 7.3 Membership Revenues Placed Into Perspective With the Overall Budget

REVENUES	
Memberships	$4,131,000
Program fees	1,260,000
Annual fund-raiser	60,000
Total revenues	**$5,451,000**
EXPENSES	
Administration	$1,231,000
Facility maintenance	1,000,000
Facility staffing	1,900,000
Program expenses	1,260,000
Scholarships	60,000
Total expenses	**$5,451,000**

Management of Memberships

In nonprofit membership management, there is an old saying: It's cheaper and easier to keep an existing member than to find a new one. The concept of keeping existing members was learned from the private sector. Marketing courses teach that advertising is primarily aimed at existing customers, building customer loyalty for the same reason—it's cheaper and easier to keep existing customers than find new ones.

Since keeping existing memberships is important for nonprofit leisure services organizations, it is not unusual for nonprofits to have full-time people on staff whose jobs are to keep in contact with members and make sure they are using the benefits of their memberships. Membership directors track membership usage, e-mailing and calling those who haven't used their memberships for a while, because they know that the people who don't use their memberships are the most likely to discontinue them.

That is not to say that membership managers don't seek new members. They do. Finding new members sometimes requires what many nonprofit organizations call **missionary work**, which is converting people to the idea before converting them to the specific institution. Fitness centers may convert people to being fitness participants by offering a free monthly membership but find that some of these converts ultimately join other fitness centers because they are cheaper or more convenient. The problem with missionary work is that it is time consuming, it is fraught with failure, and sometimes people buy into the idea but go to a different institution instead of to the one that sold them on the idea.

The art of being a membership director is building relationships with the members. Membership directors believe it is important to build personal relationships with members because it is the feeling of being welcomed to the agency that keeps many members coming back, even though it might be cheaper for them to purchase daily admissions than to purchase a membership. Staff attention to customers also is important, which is why membership managers get involved with staff training and customer service.

The membership manager's message to the staff during customer service training is that it is every staff member's responsibility to retain customers. Part of the membership director's job is to make sure everyone keeps their eye on the ball when it comes to customer service.

One of the ways the membership director measures staff performance in the aiding of membership retention is through periodic surveys of members to determine their levels of satisfaction. Conducting surveys is called **cross-sectional research**, where increases and decreases in member satisfaction can be measured. If these surveys are repeated at various intervals in time, comparisons between the data can be made, making the research longitudinal. **Longitudinal research** tracks trends and changes in participation and behavior.

Membership directors also develop relationships with members by staying in regular contact with them, encouraging them to use the agency's services. Membership directors know that if members actually use the services, it is unlikely they will resign their memberships.

Another way to build relationships with members is to offer them special programs, personal services, or discounts. Many nonprofit leisure agencies offer bonus bucks, which are basically play money that members can only spend at the agency for goods or services if they refer new members. Special events or programs for members only are other features that membership directors can offer in order to boost member retention.

The previous revenue scenarios show that there is too much money on the line for nonprofit leisure agencies to not be constantly focusing on membership retention. Membership development is, therefore, an extremely important component of the membership model of revenue generation. Nonprofit agencies that are in economically depressed areas or can't manage their membership retention become much more dependent on external funding sources.

Other Revenue Engines

A number of revenue engines are available to nonprofit leisure services agencies. They include day care, early childhood development programs, before- and after-school programs, and fitness centers. As mentioned, what distinguishes revenue engines from non-revenue-engine programs is the willingness on the part of customers to pay substantially more than the service costs the nonprofit agency to provide. In other words, the customers don't put pressure on nonprofit organizations to lower their revenue-engine fees much below what the private sector charges, because customers expect to pay that much.

For instance, parents are used to paying a lot of money for day care, early childhood programs, and before- and after-school programs, so nonprofits that offer those services do not need to drastically undercut private-sector prices. Doing so would defeat the purpose of getting into the day-care business, which is to generate excess revenues. It would also place nonprofit organizations in a position of being accused of using their tax advantages to outcompete private businesses, which is not why the IRS gave them tax advantages in the first place. Their purpose is to do charitable work, not to compete with the private sector. Therefore, the safest strategy is for nonprofit organizations to charge the same prices for their day-care services as business providers charge.

Program fees can generate substantial revenues if their price points are both competitive and substantial. Two revenue engines that many nonprofit leisure agencies operate are early childhood development programs, including day care and birthday parties, and summer day-camp programs for school-aged children. These programs charge fees that parents are used to paying, generating revenue that is substantially more than their operating costs.

Because nonprofit leisure organizations rely on program fees to pay the majority of their operating costs, they must set the fees high enough to accomplish that goal. But in economically depressed areas where program fees cannot be charged for indigent clients, program revenues often fall short of covering costs. External sources of funding, such as donations, might defray operating costs, but economically disadvantaged areas usually aren't in a position to raise large amounts in donations, either. In this way, leisure agencies that exist in economically depressed areas are truly charitable organizations.

There are models for dealing with economic disadvantages. An example is the YMCA of Metro Chicago, which has branches in the city and suburbs. Several of the YMCA city branches do not generate enough fee revenues to sustain their operations. To cover their costs, the suburban YMCA branches that generate excess revenues are required to share those revenues with the city branches. The separately chartered YMCAs in the suburban areas that are not part of the YMCA of Metro Chicago are not required to share their revenues because they are completely different nonprofit corporations. That may be one of the reasons they chartered themselves independently in the first place.

© James Steidl – Fotolia

The Boy Scouts and Girl Scouts are two well-known nonprofit leisure services organizations that raise funds in part by asking for donations.

FUND-RAISING AND DONATIONS

Fund-raising is the process of soliciting and gathering monetary contributions or donations of nonmonetary resources. Nonprofit and governmental agencies request donations or grants from individuals, businesses, charitable foundations, or governmental agencies.

A number of techniques are used to raise funds. One technique is **primary fund-raising**, where organizations conduct their own campaigns, competing for donations against each other. Another technique is **secondary fund-raising**, where another nonprofit organization, such as United Way, Community Chest, or Community Foundation, takes on the role of centralized fund-raising to avoid competition for donations to support community services. These services often include nonprofit leisure services organizations, such as the local Little League, YMCA, Boys and Girls Club, Girl Scouts, and Boy Scouts. However, as state and federal funding for social services has dried up, the need for United Way dollars far exceeds what's available. Thus, when United Way prioritizes community needs, leisure services are often the first to be cut back. When money is tight, the rationale is that nonprofit leisure services have more options for raising revenue than social services do.

As a side note, although *fund-raising* typically refers to efforts to gather money for nonprofit organizations, it is sometimes used to refer to the identification and solicitation of investors or other sources of capital for profitable enterprises. The latter definition will not be used in this textbook. In this context, fund-raising is for nonprofit organizations.

Primary Funding

Primary funding can take place in a number of ways. Nonprofit agencies can have annual fund-raising events to defray operating costs, they can have capital campaigns to defray capital costs, or they can build endowment funds that cover one or both. Building an **endowment fund** is the ultimate goal of most nonprofit organizations because it provides security for the future. Endowment funds are typically groups of investments that provide a fairly steady stream of dividends to the nonprofit organization, smoothing out the effects of donations that rise and fall as the economy rises and falls. Nonprofit organizations, such as educational institutions, can use the dividends from endowment funds for operating costs or scholarships or can draw down the funds for capital projects.

Another goal of primary fund-raising was described earlier: to raise money for specific capital projects. In many cases, fund-raising efforts are built around naming rights, where donors are encouraged to contribute to a project so it can be named after them or another member of their family.

A capital campaign is typically a major effort on the part of a nonprofit organization to get the community engaged in making large and small donations to build a facility that can be sold to donors as something that will improve the quality of life. Campaigns of this scale can be handled in-house by a staff member designated to coordinate efforts, or they can be run by a committee of the board of directors, typically with the help of a **fund-raising consultant**, a company hired to oversee the fund-raising effort but not raise funds itself. Donors rarely give money to consultants. The role of the consultant is to tell the organization how it should solicit funds using techniques that any development director would use.

Development Directors

For nonprofit organizations, it's everyone's job to raise funds, just as membership retention is everyone's job. But like managing memberships, proper management of fund-raising is best done with a fund-raising manager, or **development director**, a full-time employee who has the responsibility of cultivating (developing) prospective donors and harvesting their donations.

Development directors are much sought after. They can work for many agencies over their careers and often bring with them a group of donors who are more loyal to them than to the agency itself. Development directors can also be totally new to the profession and learn as they go, cultivating a group of donors who are loyal to the agency. And they can be everything in between the two extremes.

Donor cultivation, or relationship building, is the foundation on which most fund-raising takes place. Most development strategies divide donors into categories based on annual gifts. For instance, major donors are those who give at the highest level of the fund-raising scale and midlevel donors are in the middle. More sophisticated strategies use tools to overlay demographic and other market segmentation data against a database of donors in order to more precisely customize communication and more effectively target resources.

Donor relations and stewardship professionals support fund-raisers by recognizing and thanking donors in a way that cultivates future giving to nonprofit organizations. These donors come from a **donor base**, typically a group of people within a community who are regular contributors to community charities and nonprofit organizations.

Donor lists are tools that are available to nearly every nonprofit organization. These are lists of names, addresses, telephone numbers, and e-mail addresses of people who have been donors to some charity in the past and have the financial capability to be donors in the future. The lists represent a good starting place for soliciting donations, the alternative being missionary work.

As described earlier, missionary work involves convincing people who have never given to a charity that making a donation is a satisfying act. The problem with missionary work is that, after spending the time and effort trying to convince donors that giving is a good idea, they might ultimately reject the idea or donate to another charity. For these reasons, many fund-raising campaigns would rather start with a list of people who believe in the concept of donating and only need to be convinced that the cause is worthwhile. Using a donor list as a starting place, all that remains is to build a relationship with the donor.

Relationship Building

There is an art to fund-raising, and there are some commonly held beliefs about it among development professionals. But everyone knows that relationships are the key to success. Development directors know that donors don't just donate money to their favorite organizations; they donate money to their friends. The art of soliciting donations is the art of making friends. Although that may sound somewhat devious, it isn't. Making friends is a good thing, and in the case of fund-raising, the richer they are, the better.

One of the commonly held beliefs is that the art of relationship building is one where development managers must have a certain level of restraint in their temptation to ask donors to write checks. The restraint is adhered to by using the **rule of ten**, which says that when building a relationship with a potential large donor, the development manager should never bring up money until she has had at least 10 meetings with that person.

The first meetings should be social in nature. The development person should not even mention the nonprofit organization initially so as to avoid scaring off the potential donor. The ideal is that the donor initiates the idea of a donation. If that doesn't happen, then there is a point at which the development director pops the question. But that should be down the road, after 10 meetings or so.

The rule of ten would suggest that it takes a long time and a lot of effort to cultivate relationships, which it does. But doing so is worth it, particularly if the donation itself has the potential to be large. Obviously, if the donation does not have that potential, it is less likely that a large amount of time will be spent on the donor.

Because development managers spend so much time developing relationships with potential donors and because these relationships tend to be strong bonds of friendship, when development managers leave one agency and go to another, the donors often go with them. Donors going to other agencies is a good thing for the development manager because it makes the manager more marketable, but it is a bad thing for the agencies because donor loyalty is more a function of personal loyalty to the manager than loyalty to the agency. But that's the way many people view the world—personal relationships are extremely important.

Fund-Raising Consultants

Fund-raising consultants, such as Blackbaud Internet Solutions, which is a leading provider of YMCA fund-raising campaign consulting, usually provide consultation within a specialized portion of the nonprofit sector. The main reason smaller nonprofit organizations bring in fund-raising consultants is to reassure the board and staff that a licensed pilot is flying the plane. Inexperienced boards and staffs need that type of reassurance. Larger nonprofit organizations bring in fund-raising consultants to pull together all of the agency resources for the effort. Larger nonprofit organizations have the muscle to run their own campaigns but need a trainer to help them do heavy lifting.

Fund-raising consultants provide a variety of services that allow nonprofit leisure services organizations to have successful campaigns. One of the tools consultants bring with them is software packages that help the agency handle the complexities of donor management. Fund-raising consultants also provide a formula for success. The formula usually involves identifying one large donor to provide up to half of the campaign's financial goal. In addition, fund-raising consultants teach clients how to ask people for money and how to build relationships.

Fund-raising consultants can be expensive, commanding as much as 10 percent of the total goal of the campaign. Some work for flat rates, though, often as little as $30,000 to coordinate the campaign effort. However, if a nonprofit organization has a lofty financial goal and the fund-raising consultant is working for a percentage of the total, the consultant will be highly motivated to make sure as much money is raised as possible. Of course, there are no hard and fast rules about fees, and they vary depending on the size of the campaign.

Secondary Funding

Many nonprofit leisure services organizations pay for operating, overhead, and administrative expenses through secondary funding. Secondary funding comes in many forms, including charitable-foundation donations, United Way or Community Chest fund-raising campaigns, or the solicitation of donations from private benefactors.

Secondary funding from foundations as a source of revenue is not usually used to defer operating expenses. Charitable foundations may provide money for capital projects through grants for specific projects. On occasion, foundations may provide short-term operating grants to introduce new programs or support existing ones, with the long-term expectation that the agency will assume future operating costs. But as a revenue source to defer ongoing operating costs, foundations are not the answer.

Community-wide fund-raising campaigns, such as the United Way or Community Chest, were at one time sources of revenue upon which many local nonprofit organizations could depend. Between the 1950s and 1980s, these fund-raising campaigns raised much of the revenue needed to support local YMCAs and youth baseball and softball programs, and on occasion they contributed to local Boy Scout and Girl Scout troops.

During those four decades, as much as 50 percent of the operating budgets for local nonprofit leisure services organizations were contributed from United Way and Community Chest campaigns. But two things occurred to change their level of support. First, publicity showing national United Way officials living the high life, drawing large salaries and flying in personal jets around the country, made donors skeptical that their donations were being used as intended. Second, the creation of local community foundations provided alternatives for donations.

The problem with local community foundations is that, as mentioned, their donations are more often to defer capital costs than operating costs. This leaves nonprofit organizations with the problem of how to fund operating costs, which leads back to the solution of revenue engines as alternative sources of funding.

The public sculpture *Cloud Gate* (also known as "The Bean") draws visitors to Chicago's Millennium Park, a popular tourist attraction that was funded in part by contributions from private donors.

Nonprofit organizations have come to realize that support from United Way or Community Chest will only supply a small portion of their operating budget. The responsibility for fund-raising falls upon the organization's own efforts. And with every nonprofit organization doing its own fund-raising, they often find that fund-raising is as competitive as the private sector itself.

BOARDS OF DIRECTORS

By state law, nonprofit organizations are entities because they have boards of directors. Unlike board members in the private sector, nonprofit board members receive no compensation. The boards are responsible for the overall financial health of the organization, for staffing, and for all matters related to operations and fund-raising. Nonprofit organization boards have fiduciary duty or responsibility to their organizations and the states in which they are chartered. **Fiduciary** refers to the legal or ethical relationship of confidence or trust between two or more parties, usually related to the management of money or property. Boards never have fiduciary responsibility to stockholders because there aren't any, and they don't have fiduciary responsibility to the general public because they are not taxing bodies.

Many large nonprofit organizations have boards that operate the same as corporate boards, meeting occasionally and leaving it up to the manager to run the organization. Other large nonprofit boards function like state legislatures, meeting all the time and attempting to make every decision they can. An example of a nonprofit board operating like a corporate board is a local youth baseball board that meets monthly and oversees the operations, often micromanaging what the volunteers do. The earlier example of the YMCA of Metro Chicago is similar to the latter description, where the board of a large organization delegates daily operations to staff while the board focuses on sweeping policy issues.

Most small nonprofit organizations or organizations functioning in suburban areas comprise at least 10 board members. Many have over 20, and some have as many as 60. Suburban and small nonprofit organizations have large boards because they believe they need a broad base of representation in the community and because the more people are on the board, the more likely it is that the nonprofit organization will have successful fund-raising campaigns.

Most board members of small nonprofit organizations believe they have been appointed to their positions because they are prominent members of the community who can bring a fresh point of view to the agency. But in reality, most were appointed to their boards for one reason and one reason only: fund-raising.

The boards of smaller nonprofit organizations are not necessarily in place to run the overall organization. The professionally trained chief executive and staff do that. In this case, the board members' job should be to think of ways to raise funds, and in many cases they are expected to be donors themselves.

For small nonprofit organizations, which make up most of the 1.8 million nonprofit organizations in existence, the boards serve as staff as well as fund-raisers. For larger entities that employ staff, board members are selected because they are donors or can solicit donations. Board members may have served on support or other fund-raising committees of their nonprofit organizations, or they might have been large one-time donors themselves. Either way, the board members of smaller nonprofit organizations are there to raise funds.

This is the point of view of the professional CEOs of nonprofit leisure organizations interviewed for this textbook. But these same professionals attest that once people are appointed to nonprofit boards, the last thing they want to do is raise funds. The first thing they want to do is to drive the train, telling the nonprofit manager how to do her job and telling her that she should really do the fund-raising as well.

Working with nonprofit boards can be challenging for nonprofit managers, with the care and feeding of board members consuming as much as 80 percent of their time. With 20 or more board members, the time it takes for nonprofit managers to keep them all informed can be daunting. As mentioned, larger nonprofit organization boards are policy-making bodies that meet regularly and act upon the recommendations of the manager. The boards of larger nonprofit organizations are typically smaller than suburban or small nonprofit organizations, with 5 to 11 board members a common number. Having smaller boards for larger organizations makes sense. Larger boards would make the nonprofit manager's job harder, not easier, and there is less need for boards of larger organizations to raise funds because the organization has professional staff for that purpose.

ROLE OF THE NONPROFIT MANAGER IN FUND-RAISING

Theoretically, the role of the nonprofit manager in fund-raising for large and small agencies should be relatively minimal. Larger nonprofit institutions should have staff members to oversee fund-raising, and smaller nonprofit organizations should have board committees who oversee fund-raising. But theory is often not the same as reality.

Nonprofit leisure services managers attest that most of the fund-raising, particularly for capital campaigns, falls on them. Since most board members dislike fund-raising themselves, they prefer

Creating BikeAssist.org

In 2011, a California entrepreneur in San Diego County named Daniel Powell, an avid bicyclist, thought there was a need for roadside bicycle assistance, similar to what AAA and automobile insurance companies provide for cars and motorcycles. Willing to spend some of his own money to see if the San Diego County public agreed, Powell hired Impact Planning (IP) to do a study.

The study, completed in June 2011, showed that a higher-than-national-average number of San Diego households owned bicycles, that a substantial portion of them owned bicycles worth more than $2,500, and that the households who rode expensive bicycles saw the need for roadside assistance. In addition, households headed by single mothers saw the need for bicycle safety training for their children, and a majority of county residents saw the need to promote bicycle path construction and the expansion of bicycle lanes along busy streets.

With this information, Powell hired a web designer to create a website in advance of creating a nonprofit organization. IP applied for articles of nonprofit incorporation from the State of California. With those in hand in November 2011, IP applied for an Employer Identification Number (EIN) with the IRS and became a nonprofit entity in the eyes of the state and federal government.

An important part of the process was selecting the name for the organization, BikeAssist.org, the same name as the URL for the website. Incorporating as a nonprofit organization with the state and federal IRS made sure that no other entity could exist with the same name. Corporate and nonprofit names are important to organizations because they describe the product or services offered.

The next step was creating a board of directors. Under the IRS tax code, there are different classifications for nonprofits. Receiving donations that are tax deductible for the donors requires designation as a 501(c)(3) organization. To receive this designation from the IRS, the board of directors of BikeAssist.org adopted bylaws consistent with 501(c)(3) status as a public-benefit corporation.

Like many other nonprofits, BikeAssist.org is currently struggling to get up and running.

telling the manager how to do it. And for large nonprofit organizations, the fund-raising staff members need a face for the fund-raising efforts. They need people like Bill and Melinda Gates, who were the face of the statue of their foundation that helps save children's lives in sub-Saharan Africa. They need someone to be one voice for the nonprofit organization, someone donors can identify with the organization.

What this testimony suggests is that nonprofit leisure services managers must be willing to raise funds. It won't be their only duty, but raising revenues is elemental to the management of the nonprofit organization.

Fund-raising is difficult for a number of reasons. One is that asking people for money is similar to being a salesperson. There is a lot of rejection, which is hard on the ego. Developing relationships with donors is time consuming and gets in the way of overseeing agency operations.

The worst problem reported by nonprofit leisure services managers is that everyone on the board and staff expects each fund-raising campaign and, for that matter, the total revenue generation of the agency to be higher than the previous year. This expectation is because operating costs increase each year. Salaries are expected to increase. Utilities increase. Just about everything costs more as the years go on, including construction costs.

The expectation that internal funding sources from memberships and fee revenues will increase may not materialize. And increasing external capital donations in a world where more and more charities have their hands out also may not materialize. Therefore, the greatest challenge that nonprofit managers face is making ends meet, which can stress anyone out.

Exceptions certainly exist, but they are few and far between. Most managers of nonprofit leisure services organizations reported that delivering services in a world with a growing number of people needing help and a shrinking number of people willing to contribute provides many challenges. Most of these retired professionals also reported that they loved the profession, though, and wouldn't trade their experience for anything. They reported that overcoming obstacles is one of the greatest satisfactions in life. It's just nice to know what those obstacles are going to be so we can be prepared for them. That's part of the reason for this textbook—to identify the obstacles that need to be overcome.

FINANCIAL CHALLENGES

Funding sources for nonprofit organizations are voluntary, where people are encouraged to donate in order to see their money do good work. This is called the **donation exchange**, where people give money and receive a good feeling in return. The donation exchange is different from the **value exchange** in business, where people trade their money for a product or service that has value, and it is different from the **taxation exchange** in government, where people pay taxes and in return receive services that they may or may not use. The donation exchange is a concept that is unique to charitable nonprofit financial management.

In governmental financial management, where taxes are required from taxpayers, governmental organizations focus on conserving their scarce tax resources so they don't burn through them before achieving their objectives of providing a base level of governmental services. Since taxes are a given, governmental financial managers work on conserving resources rather than acquiring them.

Resources of nonprofit organizations are scarce as well, but in a different way. Many nonprofit organizations started out as charitable agencies providing services that governmental units were not willing to levy taxes to provide. These nonprofit organizations initially lived from hand to mouth, waiting for donations to arrive, and were conscious not to waste them. As a result, nonprofit organizations are very focused on their expenses.

On the revenue side, since nonprofit organizations solicit donations, they have an intense revenue focus that governmental units don't have but businesses do. Soliciting donations is closer to what businesses do, where transactions are voluntary. Winning donors over to the donation exchange is a sales skill, similar to winning customers over to the value exchange, causing nonprofit revenue generation to be similar to that in business.

However, the donation exchange, while similar to the value exchange, is also different. Motivating people to accept good feelings in return for their money is a little trickier than asking them to receive a valuable product or service. It's almost like being a cult leader who convinces people that if they give their money to the cult, great rewards will be waiting for them in the afterlife, while in reality the leader wants to spend their money now.

Altruism, the unselfish concern for the welfare of others, is the lifeblood of nonprofit organizations that serve a charitable function. Nonprofit leisure services agencies rely on the generosity of their donors by creating the charitable feeling that donors are helping people play who can't afford to pay for it themselves. It may not be that easy of a case to make, though. Donors may not always see why they would need to donate their money to an agency that helps people play.

If one of the challenges of leisure services managers in the nonprofit sector is to create a willingness among donors to contribute money to a nonprofit leisure agency to help people play, another challenge is how the managers can make their agencies seem charitable and self-supporting at the same time. One way is for managers to make a case that there is a motivation on the part of donors to contribute because play has a therapeutic value unto itself. As the saying goes, keeping kids off the streets keeps them out of mischief. Thus, play itself has a value to society—helping people who wouldn't ordinarily be able to pay for leisure services is helping society. Another selling point might be the appeal of helping children and adults live healthier lifestyles.

The distinction of keeping kids off the streets to keep them out of mischief had a lot more resonance with donors in the time of George Williams, who founded the YMCA in 1844, than it does now. Nonprofit agencies now sponsor "leave no child inside" programs to get them out of their latchkey environments and into play. Childhood obesity is a problem that leisure services managers are challenged to solve, and they promote the message that charitable donations to agencies can help address this problem.

Boys and Girls Clubs, Girl Scouts, Boy Scouts, YMCAs, and YWCAs, to name a few, are examples of charitable nonprofit leisure services organizations that have successfully asked donors to contribute money so that low-income and middle-class children can play. Within the missions of these agencies are dimensions of **social engineering**, the process of manipulating the way people behave in order to bring about positive change. Donors who want to help others are told that helping people play helps society.

These views are presented from hours of interviews with retired nonprofit managers and their years of experiences in the field. In a series of interviews conducted with six retired YMCA executives during the summer of 2009, their financial challenges were considered. The retired directors suggested that, as far as fund-raising was concerned, motivating donors was one of the primary responsibilities they faced. These professionals were successful because they believed in leisure services and could make the case that leisure services are vital to the quality of life in a community.

Nonprofits Need to Make Money

Students often ask, if for-profit business organizations exist to make a profit, why are nonprofit organizations specifically required to avoid making a profit? The answer is, of course nonprofits are not specifically required to avoid making a profit. They are just required to not distribute profits to owners (because there are none) or employees. Nonprofits can compensate employees for their work, but they can't overcompensate them. First and foremost, nonprofit organizations exist to provide services. They do so with the understanding that any profit goes back into the agency to support the services.

Some nonprofit organizations are so efficient at producing services and their services are in such demand that they earn a lot more money than they can spend on their operating costs. Since nonprofits are chartered by state governments with the understanding that they can't distribute profits to owners or stockholders, the challenge of these profitable nonprofit organizations is to figure out creative ways of spending the extra money to maintain their nonprofit status. Spending excess money usually is done by making capital improvements.

But it would be unfair to say that most nonprofit organizations are swimming in excess revenues. Most nonprofit organizations would be pleased to have such problems. Of the 1.8 million nonprofit organizations that exist in the United States, most are not as efficient or as profitable as they would like to be. Most nonprofit organizations don't have an overwhelming demand for their services and, as a result, most have a problem making enough money to survive (Powell and Steinberg 2006).

These two financial conditions, making extra money and not making extra money, cause nonprofits to differ greatly from each other. The ones that make money are more similar to businesses, marketing their products and seeking well-heeled clients. The ones that don't make money are more similar to governments, providing services to people who might be needy.

The nonprofit organizations that generate enough revenue to exceed their operating costs are different from businesses, though. Using fitness centers as an example, nonprofit fitness centers compared with for-profit fitness centers compared with government-run fitness centers provide a relatively clear example of the differences among the three sectors.

Fitness Center Example

Fitness centers are operated in the private, nonprofit, and public sectors, often so similarly that customers themselves are not sure in which sector they are. For this reason, fitness centers in the three sectors provide a good platform for describing how they can be operated differently in financial terms but appear to be similar in operational terms.

Nonprofit Versus For Profit

For-profit fitness centers, such as the large national Bally Total Fitness, can be privately held or publicly traded corporations. Managers of fitness centers answer to stockholders, since the primary purpose of these corporations is to make profits so stockholders' equity shares will increase in value. Dividends to stockholders can be paid at the rate that shareholders are earning on their shares, or they can also be distributed, an expectation of **return on stockholders' investments**. Return on stockholders' investments, also called *return on equity*, is the rate stockholders earn, determined by dividing shareholders' equity into net income.

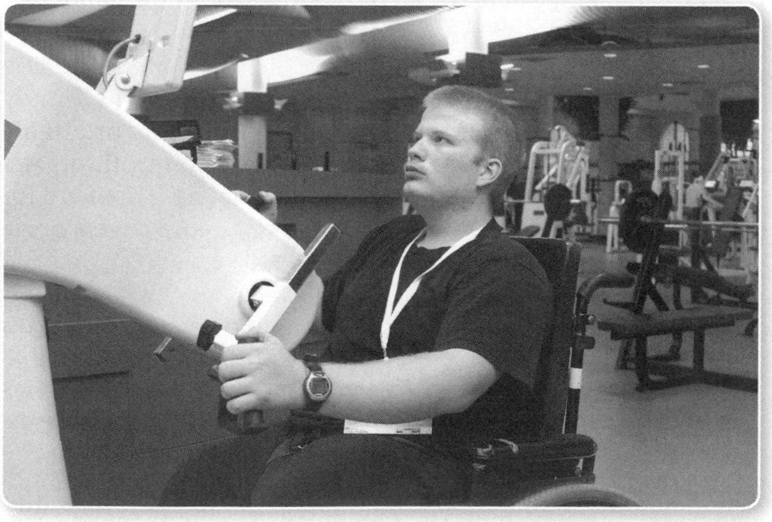
© Realistic Reflections/Getty Images

Regardless of sector, a successful fitness center caters to the needs of its customers, including people with disabilities who need specialized equipment.

The management decisions that occur in for-profit fitness centers are made with profitability in mind. Any capital purchases need to consider the return on the investment that the center and, therefore, the stockholders, will receive. That is not to say that all capital equipment decisions are made with profits in mind, but it is a major consideration.

Managing a for-profit fitness center can mean capital decisions are not always about purchasing the newest or most modern fitness equipment, particularly during years when the health club industry is experiencing economic flatness and when the equipment won't pay for itself in the long run. If purchasing the equipment will cause profits to decline, stockholders will think the decision is not in their best interest.

Nonprofit fitness centers like the HealthBridge system, on the other hand, are part of nonprofit hospitals. Hospitals often build fitness centers to provide cardiac rehabilitation and then expand the centers beyond that mission. A good example is the fitness center in Huntley, Illinois, that provides cardiac rehab but also indoor and outdoor recreational swimming as well as other recreation programs. These nonprofit fitness centers do not answer to stockholders, and they have a unique focus. Since they have no stockholders, management's responsibility is primarily to the state within which the center is chartered and to the federal government, which regulates the center. Nonprofit fitness centers have no stock, and there are no dividends returned to investors. Any money left over from operations can remain on the balance sheet as cash and fund balances as long as the state or federal government allows it. Fund balances are the net worth of a fund, measured by total assets minus total liabilities. If the state or federal government determines that a fitness center falls outside of the tax-exempt purpose of the hospital, the hospital might be required to pay income tax on the excess revenue from the fitness center.

Therefore, managers of nonprofit fitness centers are vigilant about not acquiring an excessively high amount of cash. They are under obligation to do something with the cash so as not to lose their nonprofit tax status. It is rare that nonprofit fitness centers lose their nonprofit status. There are a few examples of agencies that have lost their status, but mostly the threat of losing it is sufficient to prevent nonprofit fitness centers from making a profit.

This simplistic view of managing for-profit and nonprofit fitness centers is not to diminish the fitness services that the various sectors provide. Rather, it is to point out that for-profit businesses can make profits and distribute them to owners and employees whereas nonprofit organizations cannot. This discussion considers that nonprofit financial managers operate under different constraints than for-profit managers do. Managing a Bally Total Fitness Center is different from managing a HealthBridge Fitness Center when it comes to managing the money.

Nonprofit Versus Government

Using the fitness center example as a measure of comparison, nonprofit and for-profit fitness centers differ from government-operated centers in that nonprofit and for-profit centers have substantial revenue streams that are not necessarily available to fitness centers that are government owned and operated. This is largely for political reasons—since governments tax their citizens, elected officials are less willing to charge the public high fees for services.

Government-run fitness centers, such as those operated by local park and recreation departments of municipalities, primarily exist to provide fitness services to senior citizens or other residents who are not willing or able to pay for-profit or nonprofit fitness center fees. Government fitness center usage can be free for residents or at very low fees. The revenues these fitness centers generate are constrained by the tax revenues they receive from their governmental owners.

As a result, the fitness center services that governmental units provide may be severely limited, and new fitness equipment can only be purchased when there is money to do so, which is far less often than for nonprofit or for-profit fitness centers. That is not to say that government-run fitness centers do not get money from certain clients, however. They do, such as in partnerships with hospitals offering SilverSneakers, a national program that encourages older adults to live active and healthy lifestyles (www.silversneakers.com). SilverSneakers is a preventative health care program that is funded by insurance benefits that pay daily admission fees. The health care insurers encourage fitness center usage by paying for it.

Fitness center users who can afford to pay have a choice of where they want to go for services. First, they can go to for-profit fitness centers, knowing that profitability is important to the business investors and thus the fitness center may not purchase the newest fitness equipment and a certain percentage of their fees will be going toward corporate profits. Second, users can go to nonprofit fitness centers, knowing that, if the fitness center has excess revenues, it may have purchased the newest fitness equipment just to expend that excess revenue, and that the nonprofit fitness center may be overcharging paying clients because they have a certain responsibility to serve low-income clients. Third, these customers can go to government-run fitness centers that are financially constrained because of their reliance on tax revenues and their focus on low-income clients. The question is, where would a person who can afford to pay for fitness services go?

Different financial management skills are required to manage fitness centers in each of the three sectors. The focus on managing a for-profit fitness center would be on marketing the center to paying clients and containing costs in order to generate profits. The focus on managing a nonprofit fitness center would be on marketing to paying clients while balancing revenue generation with service to low-income clients in order to avoid making a profit or to spend any profits made. And the focus on managing a government fitness center would be on expenditure containment and on interaction with the political environment that provides the tax money to pay for fitness center services.

SUMMARY

Managing a leisure services organization in the nonprofit environment is different from managing one in the public or private sectors. Nonprofit leisure services managers face special challenges that include covering revenue shortages caused by their mission. When there are revenue shortages, managers need to find other sources of revenues.

One source of revenue is the development of revenue engines, which cover most of the indirect overhead and facility operating costs. Developing revenue engines involves venturing into the private sector, competing directly against private companies in terms of price and service.

Another source of revenue is primary fund-raising. Fund-raising campaigns can be set up to defer operating costs. Many, though, are capital campaigns that are efforts to make brick-and-mortar improvements to the agency that donors can see.

An important element of fund-raising is developing relationships with donors. Within the profession of development directors, it is thought that doing missionary work with potential donors who have never donated to charities is less effective than building relationships with people who have donated before. Donors who have previously donated are available on donor lists.

The role of board members in nonprofit leisure organizations varies. For larger and urban institutions, the boards are smaller and more policy oriented. For smaller and suburban agencies, the boards are larger and more fund-raising oriented.

Regardless of the size of the agency, leisure services managers play a substantial role in fund-raising. For larger agencies, the managers are expected to be the face of the fund-raising campaign. For smaller agencies, the managers are expected to develop relationships directly with the donors.

Visit the Web Resource

For case studies, sample financial statements, key terms, and more, please visit the web resource at www.HumanKinetics.com/LeisureServicesFinancialManagement

chapter 8

Nonprofit Accounting and Reporting

Learning Outcomes

After completing this chapter, students will be able to do the following:

- Recognize how funds are segregated in nonprofit entities and how segregation affects nonprofit accounting.
- Specify how reporting requirements lead to a heightened level of transparency for nonprofit entities.
- Determine the budgeting process and cycles for nonprofit agencies and how they relate to cash-flow management.
- Present balance sheets and income statements as they appear in nonprofit accounting.
- Identify the various federal and state reporting requirements with which nonprofit entities must comply.

Leisure services financial management is an important topic for leisure services professionals, particularly at the nonprofit level. With a succession of economic recessions, nonprofit leisure services have been receiving lower and lower levels of donation funding, forcing nonprofit managers to become better at revenue generation while maintaining their focus on the missions of their organizations.

With the very survival of the nonprofit leisure services organization dependent upon the financial management skills of the administrator and staff, it is essential that administrators be able to design financial statements that provide a clear understanding of the financial condition of the agency and that the staff understand how to live within their means. The recurring theme of this textbook is that leisure services financial management takes place in the for-profit, nonprofit, and public sectors, and for leisure services managers to be employable in all three sectors, they need to speak the various dialects of the language of accounting and financial management. This chapter introduces one of those dialects, that of nonprofit financial reporting.

This chapter discusses how charitable contributions mixed with revenue-engine and program revenues are recorded and reported. The chapter also considers how the nonprofit budget process works using these multiple sources of revenues. Additionally, it considers how the accounting process affects the budgeting process within the context of requirements imposed by the FASB and of reporting responsibilities to state departments of revenue and the IRS.

Most financial management textbooks that teach nonprofit accounting combine the topic of nonprofit financial accounting with government accounting. This book does not; instead, it treats nonprofit accounting and financial management as separate disciplines with important similarities but even more important differences. The important similarities that nonprofit organizations share with governmental units include the fact that both types are primarily service organizations, not profit-making entities. In addition, nonprofit organizations account for their financial resources in funds, just as governmental units do, and each fund is its own accounting entity.

Nonprofits are watched by states and federal departments of revenue far more than local governments are watched. The oversight provided by states and the federal government also differs. Nonprofits need to be transparent to show that they are reinvesting profits back into the organization and not avoiding paying taxes so that their boards or managers can enrich themselves. Governments need to be transparent to show taxpayers that they are using their tax money wisely.

FUND SEGREGATION

Under the FASB, nonprofit leisure services organizations are required to segregate their revenue and expenses into separate funds. Funds are entities, defined as different accounting units within the organization. The FASB requires at least three categories of these entities: unrestricted funds, temporarily restricted funds, and endowment funds.

Unrestricted funds are typically used for operating purposes. **Unrestricted funds** are the repositories of **mission program** revenues, revenue-engine program memberships and fees, and unrestricted donations. Mission programs are programs operated as part of the mission of the leisure services organization. If a children's discovery museum had the core mission of presenting displays that were both fun and instructional, its mission program revenues would include minimal daily admissions to the museum from schools and youth groups. The revenue engine might include annual memberships from adults who benefited from activities aimed at them. And the museum would accept donations from people who had no intention of using the museum but wanted to help the museum continue to serve children.

Temporarily restricted funds are a second group of funds required by the FASB. These funds often are used to accept donations for capital projects. They can be groups of accounts that accept donations that are specifically earmarked for capital projects and cannot be used for any other purpose. These account groups usually contain individual funds that are named specifically for the project for which the donations are intended.

In our example of the children's discovery museum, the group of temporarily restricted funds could include a fund to build a wing onto the museum for an interactive space-shuttle flight simulator that children's groups and schools would visit to learn about space travel. Donors to the space-shuttle wing would be assured that their donations could not be used for any other purpose by depositing and reporting donations within the temporarily restricted fund group. The IRS and the state overseeing the nonprofit children's museum would also be assured by the transparency of not comingling donation money with operating money. It would be easy to see that donations intended for construction were not used to cover operating costs.

Endowment funds, which are permanently restricted for such things as scholarships or capital projects, represent money invested to generate dividends and interest that then become income for operating or capital purposes. Generally, endowment funds are created to help support the mission programs of the organization by underwriting lost revenues for undercharging for mission program services.

In the example of the children's discovery museum, let's assume admission fees for mission programs are minimal and do not cover the cost of staffing and maintaining the museum. The museum's development department would create an endowment fund to cover these costs and would seek donations specifically for this fund. Because it is an endowment fund, donors would know that their contributions are being invested over the long term and that once the principal reaches a certain amount, interest will be earned annually **in perpetuity** (for life) to cover the costs of mission programs.

Accounting for these three categories of program funds makes balance sheets for nonprofit leisure organizations more complicated compared with for-profit leisure organizations, which have only one fund. With three separate categories and the possibility of having multiple funds within a category, leisure services managers are required to keep track of multiple funds, generating reports that are similar to balance sheets and income statements for each fund. In addition, each fund should have its own budget.

Financial Statements

The proper FASB accounting term for balance sheets in nonprofit accounting is the **statement of financial position**. The financial condition of the nonprofit organization is reflected in the statement of financial position, just as the financial condition of a for-profit business is reflected in its balance sheet. Each fund is considered an entity by the FASB, tantamount to being a separate individual with separate reasons to exist within the larger organization, although they aren't actually separate.

Instead of having an equity category, which in business accounting is the difference between assets and liabilities, statements of financial position reflect no ownership value because there are no owners of nonprofits. Instead, there is a category on the statement of financial position similar to the corporate equity category of **net assets**. Similar to equity, the net assets reflect the difference between assets and liabilities.

And similar to equity on balance sheets, net assets can be positive when assets are greater than liabilities or negative when liabilities are greater than assets. But net assets are not owned by anyone. They are simply the difference between total assets and total liabilities, a reflection of the retained value of the fund. The cumulative sum of all funds would reflect the retained value of the organization.

Under FASB accounting rules, statements of financial position are created using full accrual accounting, where assets and liabilities are recorded when they are available and measurable. Two categories for assets include current assets and pledges receivable. Current assets consist of cash and investments. **Pledges receivable** are similar to accounts receivable. They are donation commitments made to the nonprofit organization that have not been received yet. Pledges receivable are also considered current assets.

A statement of financial position for a nonprofit children's discovery museum (table 8.1) shows how similar it is to a business balance sheet.

Table 8.1 Children's Discovery Museum of Recreation: Combined Statement of Financial Position as of December 31, 2011

ASSETS	
Current assets	
Cash and cash equivalents	$680,000
Short-term investments	1,400,000
Accounts receivable	
Clients	450,000
Pledges	3,250,000
Noncurrent assets	
Long-term investments	10,150,000
Land, buildings, and equipment	9,000,000
Less depreciation	(2,000,000)
Total assets	**$22,930,000**
LIABILITIES	
Current liabilities	
Accounts payable	$250,000
Accrued expenses	750,000
Short-term debt	500,000
Noncurrent liabilities	
Long-term debt	1,000,000
Total liabilities	**$2,500,000**
Net assets	
Unrestricted	$8,880,000
Temporarily restricted	1,400,000
Permanently restricted	10,150,000
Total net assets	**$20,430,000**

The statement of financial position for the Children's Discovery Museum of Recreation shows that all of the assets, liabilities, and total net assets are combined into one businesslike statement that looks similar to a balance sheet. The difference is that each category has its own separate statement of financial position, and each of the funds within those categories has its own as well. Table 8.2 shows the individual balance sheets for each of the fund accounting groups.

Separating the Children's Discovery Museum of Recreation statement of financial position into separate balance sheet group totals shows how transparent it is to have unrestricted, temporarily restricted, and permanently restricted account groups. It is clear that the unrestricted fund shows the financial condition of the museum operations. The temporarily restricted fund shows how much

Table 8.2 Children's Discovery Museum of Recreation: Statement of Financial Position by Fund Group as of December 31, 2011

	Unrestricted	Temporarily restricted	Permanently restricted	Total
ASSETS				
Current assets				
Cash and cash equivalents	$680,000			$680,000
Short-term investments	400,000	$1,000,000		1,400,000
Accounts receivable				
Client groups	450,000			450,000
Pledges		400,000	$2,850,000	3,250,000
Noncurrent assets				
Long-term investments	2,850,000		7,300,000	10,150,000
Land, buildings, and equipment	9,000,000			9,000,000
Less depreciation	(2,000,000)			(2,000,000)
Total assets	**11,380,000**	**1,400,000**	**10,150,000**	**22,930,000**
LIABILITIES				
Current liabilities				
Accounts payable	250,000			250,000
Accrued expenses	750,000			750,000
Short-term debt	500,000			500,000
Noncurrent liabilities				
Long-term debt	1,000,000			1,000,000
Total liabilities	**2,500,000**	**0**	**0**	**2,500,000**
Total net assets	**$8,880,000**	**$1,400,000**	**$10,150,000**	**$20,430,000**

money has been raised for the space-shuttle wing, and the restricted endowment fund group shows how much money is available to support operations of the museum if needed.

The various fund groups are how nonprofit leisure organizations reflect their financial positions differently than their for-profit counterparts. The report also shows how the assets and liabilities of nonprofits consist of investments rather than fixed assets or current assets and liabilities.

The statement of financial position shows that the museum has higher amounts of cash and investments in proportion to fixed assets for individual fund groups than a business would be expected to have on its balance sheet. That is because restricted funds, typically endowment funds and temporarily restricted funds, are primarily maintained as short- and long-term investments that generate dividends and interest.

Most businesses invest their money in fixed assets to leverage their revenues. Nonprofit organizations need an investment strategy that will generate dividends and interest to help pay for operating costs. In this way, the organization will not be dependent on secondary donations or have to live hand to mouth from its own fundraising efforts.

Since permanently restricted funds may be retained in perpetuity and are not a reflection that the nonprofit organization is profitable, the segregation of permanently restricted funds from unrestricted funds is important to the state and federal revenue services that have oversight over nonprofits. Most permanently restricted funds are endowment funds. Interest income in these funds can be reinvested in the fund or dispersed to unrestricted operating funds while keeping the principal of the endowment fund intact. Segregation of the funds provides the transparency required for government oversight.

Statements of Activities

Each entity within a nonprofit leisure services organization is required to generate an annual financial report that is similar to an income statement. The FASB term for income statements in nonprofit accounting is the **statement of activities**. This statement tells how each of the funds changed its financial position over the year and what revenues and expenses caused those changes, as exemplified in the following table, which uses round numbers for ease of interpretation. The statement of activities is similar to the income statement used in business accounting. It is intended to show how cash flowed through the entity and how much cash is left over at the end of the fiscal year.

The statement of activities for the children's museum (table 8.3) shows the financial activities that took place during the fiscal year by fund. Separating the financial activities into the funds shows how the financial activities are separate and that cash is being used appropriately.

For instance, the statement shows the revenue streams from admissions and patron donations in the unrestricted operating fund. It also shows $250,000 in investment proceeds transferred from the endowment fund to cover a $250,000 shortfall in revenue in the unrestricted operating fund, bringing losses back to zero.

The statement of activities for the permanently restricted endowment fund shows that $250,000 was received from **investment proceeds** (earnings or dividends from preferred stocks), which would be paid to the fund in cash, and $400,000 was received from **investment appreciation**, which is the increased value of the investment **portfolio** for the endowment fund. The portfolio is the record showing all the investments by name, including stocks, bonds, and mutual funds, that are bought and sold on behalf of a business or nonprofit agency.

Investment proceeds can be transferred without restriction to the unrestricted fund in order to underwrite the unrestricted fund losses. But

Table 8.3 Children's Discovery Museum of Recreation: Statement of Activities for the Year Ending December 31, 2011

	Unrestricted	Temporarily restricted	Permanently restricted	Total
SUPPORT AND REVENUES				
Admissions	$400,000			$400,000
Concessions	100,000			100,000
Memberships	300,000			300,000
Investment proceeds			$250,000	250,000
Investment appreciation			400,000	400,000
Auxiliary revenue	100,000			100,000
Unrestricted contributions	200,000			200,000
Restricted contributions		$1,000,000		1,000,000
Total	**1,100,000**	**1,000,000**	**400,000**	**2,750,000**
EXPENSES				
Program				
Curator and exhibits	1,000,000			1,000,000
Education	100,000			100,000
Support services				
Fund-raising		50,000		50,000
Administration	250,000			250,000
Total	**1,350,000**	**50,000**		**1,650,000**
Excess (deficiency) of support	(250,000)	950,000	400,000	1,100,000
Resources released from restrictions	250,000			250,000
Net (decrease) in fund balances	0	950,000	400,000	1,350,000
Net assets beginning of period	8,880,000	450,000	9,750,000	19,080,000
Total net assets at end of period	**$8,880,000**	**$1,400,000**	**$10,150,000**	**$20,430,000**

if part of the portfolio would have to be sold off, then those funds could not be accessed; doing so would violate the restricted definition of the fund. If this seems a little confusing, let's see if we can make it clearer.

If you had an unrestricted fund holding corporate stock with a dividend reinvestment arrangement, when the stock declares a dividend, the dividends would automatically be used to purchase more stock. The only way you could get that dividend out of the stock would be to sell it. But selling stock in the fund would not be legal because it would be impossible to know which stock was being sold, the original stock in the fund or the dividend-purchased stock. On the other hand, if you had a corporate bond that paid cash dividends, you would have cash you could transfer. You would not be touching the principal.

The museum's statement of activities for the temporarily restricted fund shows that during the fiscal year, $1 million was raised in contributions to fund the construction of the space-shuttle wing. The fund-raising cost was $50,000, which was the cost of bringing in a consulting firm to assist in the effort. That meant that the net gain to the fund was $950,000.

At the bottom of the statement of activities for the individual fund groups are two lines. The net assets at the beginning of the fiscal year show how they existed at the beginning of the year, and the total net assets at the end of the fiscal year show how the net assets ended. The report shows that the unrestricted fund stayed the same. The temporarily restricted fund grew by $950,000 to $1.4 million, and the permanently restricted endowment fund grew by $400,000 to $10.15 million.

The statement of activities provides a summary that can be used to assist in the preparation of the various fund budgets for the museum. But it is not a budgetary management tool. As in the business sector, the best way to manage the cash flow of nonprofit leisure organizations is not by waiting for the statement of activities to be reported at the end of the fiscal year. By that time, it is too late to manage anything. The best way is to create an operating budget with line items that can be compared with actual revenues and expenses in the line-item categories. That process is the essence of financial management.

The statement of activities can also be used as a report to show the state department of revenue and the IRS that the Children's Discovery Museum of Recreation is playing by the rules. The report shows that the museum is not making a profit and its fund-raising efforts and endowment fund are within the letter and spirit of the law.

FUNDAMENTALS OF NONPROFIT BUDGETING

Back in the day when YMCAs, Boys Clubs, Girl Scouts, and a few other charitable nonprofit leisure organizations received a good amount of financial support from United Way and Community Chest, these nonprofit organizations usually had only one fund to manage. That fund, today called the *operating fund*, received the revenues from fund-raising and fees and distributed the money.

The reason for just having one fund was that United Way and Community Chest preferred to receive a relatively simple budget from the agencies when they made their annual requests. The United Way or Community Chest board would review the budgets of the YMCA, Boys Club, Girl Scouts, and social services agencies and then determine how much money it would seek in its annual fund-raising campaign.

Fund-Raising Revenues

As United Way became more about providing funds for in-demand social services, funding for youth leisure services began to decline. During the heyday of United Way, there was a prohibition against individual agency fund-raising so as not to diminish the United Way campaign. But as it became clear that the burden of fund-raising would fall on the agencies themselves, the prohibition was removed. Today, United Way and Community Chest funds primarily go to social services. Some funding still exists for youth leisure services, though, such as soccer and YMCA memberships in the form of money to underwrite scholarships for children who otherwise could not afford to participate.

With the decline in United Way funding, one of the first changes made by boards of directors of nonprofit leisure services agencies was to develop alternative sources of revenues. As chapter 7 described, in many cases board members would rather set policy than raise funds. One policy they set was a focus on revenue generation, rather than fund-raising, to defray operating expenses while still focusing on the agency mission.

The budgeting process for nonprofit leisure services is both technical and political. The technical aspects involve following accounting

© Pavel Losevsky - Fotolia

A children's museum with a core mission of presenting fun and instructional displays would count daily admission fees from schools and youth groups among its mission program revenues.

standards once budgets are adopted for the various funds. Politics come in when board members have their own ideas about the direction the agency should take and how the money should be raised.

Leisure services managers are ethically bound to make it clear to the board of directors that political concerns must never get in the way of technical concerns, such as adherence to the FASB guidelines or IRS codes. Another responsibility is to make sure political concerns never get in the way of managing the overall financial health of the agency.

Applying fund-raising principles to our example of the Children's Discovery Museum of Recreation, the museum raised $200,000 in contributions for the unrestricted fund and $1 million in contributions for the temporarily restricted fund to build the space-shuttle wing. The unrestricted contributions could have been United Way or Community Chest donations, but they were not. Instead, they resulted from an annual fund-raising effort of soliciting members to contribute tax-deductible donations in addition to their membership fees. To encourage the extra donations, the membership director of the museum might have offered social events that charged extra fees.

The capital campaign for the space-shuttle wing was conducted by a professional consultant who targeted donors to make large contributions. As a large nonprofit organization, hiring a consultant allowed the board of directors to oversee the effort rather than getting directly involved.

Program Revenues

Whereas fund-raising is partially the responsibility of the board of directors and partially the responsibility of designated staff members, managing program revenues is exclusively the responsibility of the staff. Because revenue-engine and mission program revenues are the major sources of funds, predicting the amount that each will generate is crucial for the financial health of the nonprofit leisure services organization. This is not difficult if the prediction process is a function of historical data. Therefore, keeping historical program revenue data is essential.

In the example of the Children's Discovery Museum of Recreation, admissions and memberships are the program revenues. The number of line items the museum financial manager uses in the budget is a function of how that information might be used to make management decisions.

For instance, if it's important to track admissions by days of the week, a line item for daily revenues for each day is useful. That way, the budget can be used much the same way an admissions report is used to manage staffing levels of the facility based on attendance. The same budgetary line-item process can be developed for the concessions line items under program revenues. Revenue for concession stands could be separated into line items to see which are the most profitable. Staffing levels and their associated costs could be managed by identifying revenue streams and assigning more people to the concession stands that are expected to be busy and fewer people to the concession stands that aren't.

Budget line items for program revenue, therefore, become a management tool for making decisions. The budget is different in that way from the statement of activities introduced earlier. The statement of activities shows the net effect of decisions that occurred during the fiscal year. Program budgets are the tool that makes those numbers come out good instead of bad.

Cash-Flow Management

Cash flows are the movement of money within an entity, in this case, the individual fund entities of nonprofit organizations. The two types of cash flows are **inflows and outflows**, money moving in and out. Cash flows are conceptual in that inflows are derived from revenue streams created by revenue and nonrevenue engines, and outflows are created by expenses.

The timing of inflows and outflows is important to a nonprofit agency that doesn't carry large balances in its funds. In the old days, leisure agencies were not permitted to carry large balances by the United Way or Community Chest because having a large fund balance was a sign it didn't need fundraising assistance.

Because of low fund balances and the resulting low cash reserves, leisure services agencies tended to run short on cash until they received their first advance from United Way or Community Chest. With lower levels of funding coming from these organizations, nonprofit leisure agencies are now permitted to carry larger fund balances in their operating funds. Cash-flow management becomes more about making sure that membership fees are received in a timely manner than waiting for the United Way or Community Chest check.

From a technical point of view, cash-flow management begins with making sure FASB guidelines are followed. The "FASB is concerned with how entities report their overall financial position and operating results, not with the specific funds they maintain" or dollar amounts in those funds (Granof and Wardlow 2003, p. 297). This makes nonprofit leisure organizations similar to businesses. The FASB position suggests that nonprofit organizations maintain a number of entities in a businesslike way, but not that they act like businesses entirely.

This would suggest that the essence of managing funds in a businesslike way is measuring the cash flows of each fund. But in the end, the FASB has little concern for whether the nonprofit entity is profitable; it is more concerned that the reports are accurate and follow GAAP.

In addition to operating activities, cash flows are budgeted for investing activities and financing activities, the two financial activities upon which nonprofit organizations focus. Pledges and contributions are activities that take place within certain funds, and exchange transactions are activities that take place in other funds. Depending on the nonprofit organization, these cash-flow activities are managed in segregated funds, each with its own budgeted revenues and expenses.

If cash-flow management is the essence of financial management in the nonprofit sector, the challenge that most nonprofit organizations face, particularly the smaller ones, is to make sure that the outflows do not exceed the inflows. For larger organizations, the challenge is to make sure there is not a huge amount of surplus revenues caused by excessive inflows.

FASB standards are important in terms of their effect on the preparation of financial statements, budgeting, and financial management. The most important FASB topic discussed in this chapter is how nonprofit leisure services managers use their understanding of nonprofit financial management to advance the mission of the organization. In nonprofit management, the ability to manage cash flow is a tool that nonprofit managers use to accomplish good things.

One budgeting issue related to nonprofit financial management in leisure services that other nonprofits may not confront is cash-flow timing. Nonprofit organizations that carry large fund balances, much of it in the form of cash on their balance sheets, have a large enough cushion to pay their bills at the beginning of the fiscal year. But consider a local youth baseball nonprofit organization as an example. It needs to order equipment and uniforms for the players before the season begins. To do so, the program needs to have cash available to pay the sporting goods store shortly after the equipment and uniforms arrive.

If the youth baseball organization has a relatively low cash balance at the end of the season, it needs to make sure registration for the next season takes place far enough in advance to have the cash on hand to pay for equipment and uniforms when they are delivered. That is what cash-flow management means to a small nonprofit leisure services organization.

For larger nonprofit leisure services organizations, cash management becomes an issue if they don't have enough cash to pay bills at the beginning of the fiscal year. More often than not, cash-flow management is an issue during capital projects, which provide two cash-flow management challenges. The first is when a capital campaign falls short of raising enough money to complete the project. That happened to the Geneva Lakes Family YMCA in Wisconsin in 2001. During the capital campaign for a new swimming pool, the

The manager of a small youth baseball organization must ensure that the group has enough cash on hand to pay for equipment and uniforms at the beginning of the new season.

YMCA raised $750,000 of the $1 million it needed for the project. When it seemed probable that the final goal would not be achieved, the YMCA had to decide what to do with the money it had raised: Either return it to donors or build the addition using the $750,000 and borrowing the other $250,000. It chose to borrow the balance.

The other cash-flow challenge the YMCA faced was collecting the original $750,000 from the pledges it had received. Some of the pledges were slow coming in while the project was under construction. Since the YMCA did not have the cash on hand in other funds to loan to the capital project, it had to borrow more money via a bridge loan to pay the contractor until the donations were paid. A **bridge loan** is a short-term loan used until permanent financing is secured or the obligation is met.

Cash-flow issues can exist for medium and large nonprofit leisure services agencies in their operating budgets as well. Many large agencies live hand to mouth when it comes to cash flow. Larger metropolitan YMCAs, which share funding with their suburban branches, have cash-flow problems from time to time. The solution that many nonprofit leisure agencies adopt is to acquire fund balances and cash during their fat years that will get them through their leaner years. But if there are no fat years, the only other solution is to go out of business, so it is essential for nonprofit leisure organizations to create appropriate fund balances.

Politics of Budgeting

Budgeting isn't as simple as forecasting the revenues and expenses the organization will receive and spend. In reality, budgeting is a political process, and a budget is a political document. Although nonprofits seem to be businesslike organizations, their nature of existence is political. In chapter 7, we considered how large nonprofit organizations have small boards of directors that primarily exist to set policies, and small nonprofit organizations have larger boards whose purpose is to raise funds (though they'd rather set policy, too).

Any organization with a board of directors will have a political dimension. The very act of appointing members to the board is a political act. Determining which board members will be the most influential in making policy decisions is a political process involving alliances and power plays. The influence of the executive director and staff over the policy decisions of the board is a political dimension.

Who gets what, when, and how is the essence of the political process, and the annual budget has the greatest influence on how this plays out. It's not a secret; board members and staff know it. Decisions about whether additional staff are to be hired or cut, new facilities are going to be built, or new programs are going to be offered are made during the adoption of the budget. Therefore, getting something in the budget is just as political now as it was in the old days when nonprofit leisure services organizations took turns presenting their budgets to United Way or Community Chest, competing with each other for funding. The difference is that the competition is now an internal one for scarce financial resources.

Political dimensions to the budgeting process are everywhere. Leisure services managers gain greater control of the political process by using a methodology that enhances their power and control. Earlier, zero-based budgeting was discussed as a budgeting methodology of the 1970s, where nothing was assumed and every line item needed to be justified. Such a system is possible with an autocratic business management environment, where the boss asks each department to justify its expenses. But zero-based budgeting doesn't work very well in the nonprofit environment. There might be a board of directors of more than 20 people who review the budget first. How would the board, or even one of its subcommittees, choose the winners and losers without major political struggles?

Therefore, the budgeting process that works best to control the political machinations of nonprofit organizations is incremental budgeting, where last year's budget is amended, not completely rewritten. And, as the saying goes, if executive directors write the first draft of the budget, they will probably get 80 percent of what they want.

Budgeting Process

Unlike businesses, nonprofit organizations are governed by their budgets, not by the marketplace, although nonprofits are certainly influenced by the marketplace. For nonprofits and businesses both, publishing an annual report is important. Whereas businesses create annual reports for their stockholders, nonprofits create them for their donors and the community at large as a tool for fund-raising and documenting executive performance. Annual reports also are an important historical document. Government leisure services agencies typically do not publish annual reports.

For a nonprofit organization, the budget is the culmination of a political process that reflects most of the organization's important decisions (Granof and Wardlow 2003). Ideally, the budget is a plan that identifies the financial resources required to achieve programming objectives and how to assemble the resources. It also considers the likelihood that the resources will materialize. Thus, a process needs to be in place to accomplish these goals. Once constructed, this process assists staff and board members in managing the organization both programmatically and financially throughout the year.

As mentioned, whoever controls the process controls 80 percent (or more) of the outcome. Formalizing the process and adhering to it each year give the staff more control over the budgetary outcomes. Nonprofit organizations are not governmental units. Board members are not elected by the public and there is no need to adhere to democratic principles. Similar to business leisure services managers, nonprofit leisure services managers need the opportunity to manage. Board members do not always understand that, but managers do.

That is not to say the board is the enemy of management—an adversary sometimes, yes, but an enemy, no. To minimize the adversarial relationship between the board and staff, it is advisable to maintain a level of participation to keep everyone engaged. Treating board members as rubber stamps for managers' financial decision making won't make board members happy, especially if managers expect the board to go out and raise funds. Establishing a schedule of key action and decision points in the process is an important method of participatory budgeting. Doing so allows adequate time for information gathering by the staff and decision making by the board. The most important elements of the process are time for gathering and reviewing information and target dates for making decisions.

How long the process should take and who should be involved depends on the management style and complexity of the organization. Typically the budgeting process should begin about four or five months before the end of the fiscal year to ensure the budget is approved by the board before the start of the new fiscal year. Some organizations start the process six months or more before the new fiscal year begins, and some start even earlier.

The process begins with assembling historical data. The most useful financial data that can be assembled by staff and presented to the board are historical data from the previous three fiscal years, especially if the budgeting process is incremental. Historical financial data provide a basis for how cash flows occurred in the past and how they are anticipated to occur in the future. Three years of historical data help smooth fluctuations in economic conditions.

Identifying a Process

In terms of identifying a process, the Nonprofits Assistance Fund (NAF) (www.nonprofitsassistancefund.org) is a consulting firm that works with nonprofit organizations to add rationality to the budgeting process. NAF helps nonprofit organizations by prescribing a budgeting process that board members can understand and that addresses staff members' concerns. The step-by-step process (NAF 2006) is relatively simple:

Step 1: Plan the process

- Identify who will coordinate the budgeting process and which staff, board members, and committees need to be involved.
- Agree upon key definitions, assumptions, and document formats.
- Set timelines and key deadlines.
- Determine and schedule any training or key meetings.

Step 2: Communicate about the process

- Clearly communicate responsibilities, expectations, and deadlines to everyone involved.
- Explain and distribute forms and assumptions.

Step 3: Set the program goals

- Determine program goals and objectives.
- Project staffing requirements and salary and benefit assumptions based on program goals.
- Get board agreement on goals and assumptions.

Step 4: Gather information

- Research and gather information about income and expenses based on program goals and assumptions.
- Construct budget details by program.
- Communicate regularly to avoid duplication of effort and to share information and assumptions.

Step 5: Compile and revise the information

- Have one person compile all information, review it for consistency, and redistribute to everyone involved.
- Leave plenty of time for review and revisions.

Step 6: Have a committee review the first draft

- Have the finance committee and other appropriate staff and board committees review a budget draft and key assumptions.
- Be sure to allow enough time between committee meetings and the final approval deadline to address questions and recommendations and make revisions.

Step 7: Spend time on the final approval

- Distribute information to the board before the board meeting, including budget draft, program goals, and other supporting information.
- Have program and development committees make an informative presentation to the board based on the opportunities, challenges, and resources behind the budget numbers.
- Have the finance committee or treasurer present the budget proposal to the board.

Step 8: Implementation and management

- Communicate budget, program goals, and timelines for the next year to staff.
- Review actual income and expenses compared with the budget on a monthly basis.
- Update and revise the budget as there are changes during the year. Depending on the significance of changes, the board may need to approve revisions.

This process allows board and staff members to understand in advance what their roles will be. The process can be changed, but only before it begins and only with the approval of all parties concerned. Otherwise the process could be the subject of debate during the time when the budget itself should be the primary matter of consideration.

Budget Preparation Schedule

With the process adopted, a timeline for the budget preparation schedule should be established based on the start date of the fiscal year. Assuming the fiscal year begins January 1, the milestones for the schedule might begin as early as July or August, similar to the following schedule (NAF 2006).

July and August—step 1: Planning begins when the executive director meets with the financial staff and the finance committee to plan the budgeting process and set timelines. The chief financial officer begins gathering historical data from the previous three fiscal years, and the budget worksheet and template formats are updated.

September—step 2: The executive director communicates about the process at a staff meeting, assigning responsibilities and setting deadlines to all participants. At the September monthly meeting, a report is given to the board about the process, timelines, and assumptions.

September—step 3: The board assigns the budget committee the responsibility to review the organization's strategic goals and identify priorities. The staff meets within programs and departments to brainstorm and plan programming goals for next year.

September and October—step 4: The staff department managers draft program or department budgets based on plans and assumptions. The executive director reviews these drafts, providing department heads the opportunity to make changes.

November—step 5: The board's budget committee reviews amended drafts with the executive director and department managers, providing the department managers time to make any changes. Then, a budget draft is sent to the entire board of directors for review.

December—step 6: The budget committee reviews changes from the board of directors. If the committee agrees with the changes, it is appropriate to incorporate them into the final budget draft. If the committee does not agree with the changes, the board is informed. Either way, the board receives the final draft for approval.

The 2011 Ardmore United Way Campaign

As discussed in this chapter, United Way has been a frequent source of funding for charitable leisure services organizations. Such is the case in Ardmore, Oklahoma. In September 2011, United Way of South Central Oklahoma in Ardmore announced a fund-raising goal of more than $800,000 to support 33 agencies. All 33 organizations set up booths at the Mountain View Mall to showcase their services and the importance of United Way funding for their operations. An article in the local news detailed the event (Shanahan 2011), demonstrating United Way's role as a newsmaker and its importance in the community.

United Ways across the country support social and leisure services that are important to a community's quality of life. The Ardmore United Way's website (www.uwsco.org) provides a list of allocations for 2011, including these that are related to leisure services organizations (United Way of Central Oklahoma 2012):

Big Brothers Big Sisters of Oklahoma, OKC Office	$162,000
Boy Scouts of America, Last Frontier Council	$497,814
Boys & Girls Club of Oklahoma County, Inc.	$160,000
Camp Fire USA, Heart of Oklahoma Council	$249,317
Coffee Creek Riding Center for the Handicapped	$102,847
Girl Scouts—Western Oklahoma	$296,589
Tinker AFB Youth Center	$20,933
YMCA of Greater Oklahoma City	$180,000
YWCA Oklahoma City	$680,895

In the newspaper article, the campaign chairman explains the beauty of United Way: "Your dollar goes further when you donate to United Way because you're funding several agencies, and maybe even a service you might need one day."

In January 2012, the Ardmore United Way website wrapped up the campaign with this message: "This year's goal of $800,000 was exceeded by $75,699 for a total of $875,699. Thanks to our many donors, division leaders, volunteers, individual and business supporters and everyone that donated. What generous communities we live and work in! These funds will help 33 partner agencies provide services to those in need in our five county area! THANK YOU! THANK YOU!"

References

Shanahan, K. 2011. "United Way Kicks Off Fundraising Campaign in Ardmore." *KXII News*, Sept. 13. www.kxii.com/home/headlines/United_Way_kicks_off_their_fundraising_campaign__129699273.html.

United Way of Central Oklahoma. 2012. "Agency Allocations: 2011-2012 United Way Community Investment Funding." www.unitedwayokc.org/partner-agencies/agency-allocations.

December—step 7: The board of directors votes on the final budget draft. If the budget passes, it is adopted for the new fiscal year. If the budget is rejected, it is sent back to the budget committee for revision, with the understanding that the fiscal year will begin without an adopted budget.

January—step 8: If the budget is adopted at the December board meeting, the executive director hosts a meeting with department managers to discuss the budget, program goals, and timelines for the new fiscal year.

The schedule allows staff to develop the first two budget drafts based on historical information from the finance department. The historical information is provided to the budget committee along with the staff's second draft, which supports staff recommendations.

The process meets the goal of maintaining the proper balance of power between the board of directors and staff. The board has the ability to make last-minute changes, and ultimately it has the power of final approval, which is democratic. The process blocks the board from micromanaging, which would be entirely possible without such a process.

Using Budgets to Make Decisions

As mentioned, when nonprofit organizations create budgets, there should be an appropriate number of line items to suit their budget management needs. In the case of the Children's Discovery Museum of Recreation used as an example earlier in this chapter, managers would want to see line-item breakdowns of revenue sources at the end of each month.

For instance, assuming the fiscal year begins on January 1, the museum managers should review a monthly report on front-desk admissions. Comparing January admission revenues from the current fiscal year with admission revenues from the previous January allows financial managers to see if they are ahead of the previous year or behind and if the museum is on track to make its total admission revenue budget.

The revenue budget for the Children's Discovery Museum (table 8.4) is straightforward enough, simpler than most nonprofit leisure services organizations that provide an array of recreation programs or fitness memberships. Similar to other nonprofit leisure organizations, the museum budget uses numbers derived from the previous year's actual experience. Revenues are presented by source, not according to any departmental considerations, with the exception of concessions. Otherwise, revenues are expected to support expenses.

Table 8.4 Children's Discovery Museum of Recreation: Revenue Budget for the Year Ending December 31, 2012

PROGRAM REVENUES	
Daily admissions	
Monday	$40,000
Tuesday	50,000
Wednesday	45,000
Thursday	45,000
Friday	50,000
Saturday	75,000
Sunday	65,000
Schools	50,000
Concessions	
Restaurant revenues	220,000
Gift-shop revenues	110,000
Memberships	
Individuals	
300 @ $500	150,000
Corporate	
100 @ $1,500	150,000
Auxiliary club revenue	
Annual art fair	70,000
Garage sale	40,000
Contributions	
Annual fund-raising campaign	210,000
Endowment fund	
Transfer	56,000
Total all revenue sources	**$1,370,000**

The revenue budget shows that daily admissions are forecasted as totals by day and that school group admissions to the museum are forecasted separately. The revenue budget shows that concessions are separated by function, with restaurant and gift-shop gross revenues shown. On the statement of activities, net concessions revenues are shown as prescribed by the FASB. Budgets need to take into consideration gross revenues and expenses, though, in order to get there, cost of goods sold must be subtracted from gross revenues.

The budget process described earlier in this chapter is one where department heads negotiate what financial resources they need to function.

Departmental budgets have line items that are sufficiently descriptive to help the board committee understand whether they are padded or not. **Padding the budget** is the practice of department heads asking for more money than they need so that they will have wiggle room within their budget to meet any unanticipated needs.

The expense budget total for the Children's Discovery Museum of Recreation (table 8.5) shows expenses would have exceeded revenues if not for money transferred from the permanently restricted endowment fund. The expense budget for the 2012 fiscal year is built upon the expenses from the 2011 fiscal year, reducing curator and exhibits department expenses from $1 million in the 2011 fiscal year to an anticipated $956,000 in the 2012 fiscal year. This reduction moves the budget toward being balanced, but it does not get the job done.

One option for balancing operating expenses with revenues is to reduce artifact purchases and construction of displays by the curator and exhibits department. On the other hand, the curator could argue that cutting down on displays would have a spiraling effect on the museum's core business. Budget-balancing zealots might make the argument that cutting down on the exhibits would save money, but this could be counterbalanced with arguments that new displays keep the museum fresh and give people a reason to return. Without new displays, attendance would decline; admission revenues, memberships, and donations would decline; and in the end more money would be lost than saved.

Since the exhibits and displays are the core business of the museum, the person in charge of that department would have a disproportionate amount of power in the organization. Curators are the superstars of museums. The reputation of the museum is often that of the curator. It's possible to nibble away at the margins to reduce his budget, but too much nibbling could cause the curator to seek employment elsewhere. And he would be correct; cutting down on exhibits and displays would likely cost more than it would save.

Table 8.5 Children's Discovery Museum of Recreation: Expense Budget for the Year Ending December 31, 2012

ADMINISTRATION	
Salaries	$200,000
Pension contribution	20,000
FICA (employment tax)	14,000
Conferences and training	3,000
Office supplies	5,000
Office equipment	5,000
Utilities	3,000
Total	**250,000**
CURATOR AND EXHIBITS	
Salaries	150,000
Pension contribution	15,000
FICA	11,000
Museum staff wages	450,000
Exhibit displays	80,000
Artifact purchases	250,000
Total	**956,000**
RESTAURANT	
Wages	60,000
Retirement and FICA	12,000
Food	78,000
Supplies	10,000
Utilities	10,000
Total	**170,000**
GIFT SHOP	
Wages	15,000
FICA	1,000
Gifts	40,000
Utilities	4,000
Total	**60,000**
Total all departments	**$1,436,000**

Using Budget and Actual Reports to Manage

Budget and actual reports are financial management tools that track the revenues and expenses of nonprofit leisure services organizations. The reports may be produced as frequently as the agency's software permits, usually upon demand. The reports show the line-item budgeted amounts for revenues and expenses and the actual amounts of revenues and expenses to date. They may include data showing the amount of revenues and expenses for the month, comparing them with the revenues and expenses of the previous year. Typically, there are separate pages sorting line items by department.

The budget and actual report for the museum's restaurant department (table 8.6) illustrates

Table 8.6 Children's Discovery Museum of Recreation: Budget and Actual Report for June 30, 2012

RESTAURANT DEPARTMENT						
	Budget	Actual	Variance	June 2012	June 2011	Variance
Food	$190,000	$90,000	–$100,000	$16,500	$15,000	$1,500
Beverages	30,000	15,500	–14,500	3,000	2,500	500
Total	**220,000**	**105,500**	**–114,500**	**19,500**	**17,500**	**2,000**
Wages	60,000	31,000	–29,000	5,200	5,000	200
Retirement and FICA (employment tax)	12,000	5,100	–6,900	1,200	1,100	100
Food	78,000	39,000	–39,000	7,000	6,500	500
Supplies	10,000	5,500	–4,500	1,100	800	300
Utilities	10,000	4,500	–5,500	900	1,100	–200
Total	**$170,000**	**$85,100**	**–$84,900**	**$15,400**	**$14,500**	**$900**

how the report provides information to manage the department. The total budgeted revenues of $220,000 were separated into two categories, food and beverage, but the expense items were provided at the same level of detail as the budget.

The year-to-date total actual revenues show that, at the midpoint of the fiscal year, the restaurant department is less than halfway to its goal of generating $220,000 in food and beverage revenues, but it is slightly more than halfway to spending its budgeted goal of $170,000 in expenses. However, revenues for the month of June 2012 were higher than for the same month in the previous fiscal year at $19,500 compared with $17,500. Expenses for the month of June 2012 were higher as well compared with June 2011, but not as much.

The management response to the budget and actual report for the restaurant department might be cautious. With the first five months of the fiscal year showing lower revenues and higher expenses than anticipated, the traditional management response would be to cut costs. But with the month of June performing somewhat better than anticipated, management might want to wait another month to see if improved business at the restaurant is a trend or an aberration.

The key to managing a nonprofit leisure services organization is to pay attention to the budget and actual reports. Many nonprofits generate these reports on a weekly basis because they need to know where they stand financially so they can make adjustments in spending if revenues are down. This typically occurs at weekly senior staff meetings where reports are shared so key staff can see where adjustments need to be made.

However, when the nonprofit organization has a history of budget and actual reports showing net revenues exceeding budget projections, staff meetings are less frequent and reports are not shared so that staff members don't think there is money they can spend. It's human nature to share financial pain and hoard pleasure, but many nonprofit organizations report that it's how the process works.

FEDERAL REPORTING

Although states charter nonprofit organizations, they usually defer to the federal IRS to supervise them. Part of the reason is that the IRS has a policing force of agents with worldwide reach. They are vigilant to make sure that nonprofit organizations are not established as tax-avoidance vehicles, where nonprofit executives pay themselves exorbitant salaries to launder money.

As discussed previously, the IRS issues 501(c) status to nonprofit organizations. The oversight that 501(c) reporting provides is usually sufficient to satisfy states that the nonprofit organization is not a sham, but leisure services can be delivered by nonprofit organizations other than 501(c)(3)s.

Reporting to the IRS

Each year many nonprofit organizations must file Form 990, Return of Organization Exempt From Income Tax, with the IRS. (If the nonprofit is a charitable organization, it must file a second form and consider a number of state requirements.)

© PhotoDisc

Regularly comparing a restaurant's budget report with its actual report will help a manager track revenues and expenses to determine the financial health of the organization.

Form 990 provides annual financial information that the IRS uses to determine if the organization is worthy of tax exemption. Organizations with annual gross revenues between $25,000 and $500,000 and total assets less than $2.5 million file Form 990-EZ. Organizations with gross receipts of under $25,000 in a year are not required to file Form 990.

Once Form 990 is filed with the IRS, it becomes public information that can be requested under the Freedom of Information Act (FOIA), although the IRS rarely requires such requests. The IRS will send members of the public requesting the 990 filings to the nonprofit organizations themselves. Federal public inspection regulations state that a nonprofit organization must provide copies of its three most recent Form 990s to anyone who requests them, whether in person or by mail, fax, or e-mail. Additionally, requests may be made via the IRS using Form 4506. Copies of 990 reports also can often be found online at sites such as the Foundation Center's 990 Finder (http://foundationcenter.org/findfunders/990finder/), GuideStar (www.guidestar.org), and the NCCS website (http://nccs.urban.org/).

Form 990 is also used by other government agencies to prevent organizations from abusing their tax-exempt status. For instance, in June 2007, the IRS released a new Form 990 that requires significant disclosures on governance and boards of directors. These new disclosures were required for all nonprofit filers for the 2009 tax year, with more significant reporting requirements for nonprofits with over $1 million in revenues or $2.5 million in assets. In addition, certain nonprofit organizations have more comprehensive reporting requirements, such as hospitals (i.e., Schedule H).

Form 990 disclosures do not require but strongly encourage nonprofit boards to adopt a variety of policies regarding governance practices. These suggestions go beyond requirements for nonprofits to adopt whistleblower and document-retention policies.

The IRS has indicated it will use Form 990 as an enforcement tool, particularly regarding executive compensation. For example, nonprofits that adopt specific procedures regarding executive compensation are offered safe harbor from excessive compensation rules under Internal Revenue Code section 4958 and Treasury Regulation section 53.4958-6.

Legal Responsibilities of Nonprofit Organizations to States

Each state has slightly different requirements for filing as a nonprofit corporation. The goal of the state is typically to offer nonprofit status only to organizations that have a legitimate charitable purpose. Organizations should begin with a mission statement that briefly describes their purpose, such as, "Our mission is to provide recreational services for low-income members of the community."

Most states require an established board of directors. Five board members are usually recommended, and at least three board members are required—president, secretary, and treasurer. The real paperwork begins when the organization writes bylaws to govern how the board functions.

Losing Nonprofit Status

In 2011, when the IRS purged more than 275,000 charities from its ranks, 3,700 agencies in Eugene, Oregon, were among those affected, according to an article by Diane Dietz (2011) in the *Register-Guard*. The Foundation Group, a Tennessee consulting firm to nonprofits (McRay 2011), cited the ramifications of this massive national revocation of 501(c) status. Donations would no longer be tax deductible, a for-profit corporate tax return might be due, and the organizations could be found liable for sales and property taxes, payroll and unemployment taxes, and workers' compensation.

In Eugene, although most of the revoked charitable organizations no longer existed, in some cases it wasn't the greater organization itself but just a project or subsidiary that was no longer active. Other organizations were in the process of coming to an end or were too small to be required to file with the IRS.

According to the *Register-Guard*, an example was the compost tea organization, an organization that had been struggling for several years. The newspaper quoted Michael Alms, who has been paying to keep the group's website up so the domain name *CompostTea.org* would not be lost: "Three years ago, it was a vital agency with members from the academic, agricultural and manufacturing sectors. Since then, the organization has run out of energy. It was a great thing. It's just that everybody went away, and nobody wanted to support it anymore" (Dietz 2011).

The IRS said it had been granting extensions and reminders for three years, trying to inform groups that the deadline for a new filing requirement was coming. Previously, nonprofit agencies that took in less than $25,000 weren't required to file tax returns. Congress changed that law in 2006. Most nonprofits must now file every three years or be automatically purged from the tax-exempt rolls.

Failure to file is part of the problem, but the main issue is that some nonprofit agencies go through a life cycle similar to private-sector companies. There is a need for the service initially and a group of people who enthusiastically support providing it. As other agencies fulfill that need, sometimes the nonprofit is simply outcompeted. In other cases, the people who started the organizations simply drift away. And in still others, the need for the services goes away. All three occurrences cause some nonprofit organizations to dissolve or lose their status.

References

Dietz, D. 2011. "Hundreds Fall From Nonprofit Rolls." *Register-Guard*, June 11. http://special.registerguard.com/web/newslocalnews/26371594-41/nonprofit-irs-status-groups-lost.html.csp.

GuideStar. 2011. "How Automatic Revocation of Tax-Exempt Status Could Affect You as a GuideStar Customer." www2.guidestar.org/rxa/news/articles/2011/revocations-and-guidestar-customers.aspx.

McRay, G. 2011. "275,000 Nonprofits Lose Tax Exempt Status." *Foundation Group*, June 9. www.501c3.org/blog/275000-nonprofits-lose-tax-exempt-status-2/.

There are annual paperwork requirements that the board is legally obligated to oversee, such as the following:

1. Filing Form 990 with the IRS each year if the organization has more than $25,000 a year in financial activity (purely religious organizations are exempt)
2. Completing an audit if total organizational revenue exceeds $350,000 in a year; file with the charities division of the state attorney general's office
3. Reporting changes of name and address or amendments to the organization's articles of incorporation to the secretary of state and paying the fee for such changes
4. Making Forms 990 and 1023 available to the public
5. Reporting any unrelated business income to the state department of revenue and the IRS and sending tax payments if applicable
6. Withholding taxes from employees and sending withholding payments to the IRS and state department of revenue
7. Complying with laws that affect all employers, including ADA, OSHA, FLSA, FICA, COBRA, Family Medical Leave Act, and unemployment insurance requirements
8. Reporting any lobbying activities on Form 990 and registering as a lobbyist if required by the state

9. Giving receipts to donors for contributions above $250
10. Collecting sales tax on items sold by the organization, unless it is selling tickets to performances as a performing arts organization
11. If the organization owns real property, paying property taxes or obtaining an exemption from the county where the property is located
12. If the organization sends bulk mail, paying regular bulk mail rate or obtaining a nonprofit bulk mail permit from the local post office
13. Complying with the terms of donations; promises made to donors are legally binding and funds given for specific projects or programs need to be kept separate
14. Making sure any professional fund-raisers register with the state attorney general's office or charities division; filing a copy of the contract
15. Recording minutes of board and annual meetings, preferably electronically so others can examine (but may wish to restrict viewing)

States basically mimic the federal government in their interpretation of what constitutes a charitable organization, but they have requirements of their own to consider. For instance, the real estate holdings owned by nonprofit organizations could be required to pay state, county, and local property taxes unless the nonprofit organization files for an exemption, which most states permit.

Since states charter nonprofit corporations before they ever file tax returns with the IRS, it is the state's responsibility to supervise the activities of the board of directors to make sure the nonprofit is fulfilling its stated mission. Submitting articles of incorporation, making minutes from board meetings available to the public, and filing tax returns with the supervising state are part of that oversight. But mostly the state and federal government expect transparency levels to be high.

With tax returns and board minutes available to the public, the expectation by states and the federal government is that the public and the media will pay attention to what nonprofit organizations are doing. But the reality is, with 1.8 million nonprofit organizations in the United States and more being created every day, the level of oversight by the public and media is pretty thin. Paying attention to the financial reporting process to the states and federal government is the best way that nonprofit managers can stay out of trouble and fulfill their missions. And for nonprofit leisure services organizations, fulfilling their mission means that recreational services continue to flow while the organization remains financially viable.

SUMMARY

Nonprofit leisure services organizations face unique financial challenges compared with the private and public sectors. The language of accounting is also somewhat different than in the other sectors, with the reporting process a blend of business and governmental accounting. The financial reports in which leisure services managers need to be fluent are the statement of financial position, the statement of activities, and the monthly budget and actual report.

Statements of financial position are pictures of the nonprofit organization at a given point in time, and statements of activities are reports describing how the agency's financial position changed over the year. The budget and actual report is a tool that nonprofit financial managers should use to manage the financial condition of the organization.

State and federal governments require a level of transparency from nonprofit organizations. This includes the responsibilities of nonprofits to report their board activities, comply with federal and state laws, and file tax returns justifying their nonprofit status. Federal oversight of nonprofit organizations is primarily provided by the IRS, which is concerned with making sure that the nonprofit organization is not a vehicle for tax avoidance.

Visit the Web Resource

For case studies, sample financial statements,
key terms, and more, please visit the web resource at
www.HumanKinetics.com/LeisureServicesFinancialManagement

chapter 9

The Government Sector

Learning Outcomes

After completing this chapter, students will be able to do the following:

- Compare the financial structures of federal agency financial management with those of state and local governments.
- Identify the similarities and differences among federal, state, and local government leisure services agencies.
- Describe the various structures of local government.
- Explain how taxation works at the local level and how it relates to political culture.
- Differentiate between the levels of autonomy that exist at the local level and how they affect the finances of local governments.
- Reproduce the budgeting process and cycles for governmental agencies, and understand how they relate to the political process.

Chris Rock, a modern-day American comedian, said "You don't pay taxes—they take taxes" (ThinkExist.com 2012). Will Rogers, an American humorist from the 1930s, said, "I don't make jokes. I just watch the government and report the facts" (The Quotations Page 2012). Many Americans really do see the government as a robber or a joke. Of course, democratic governance has its advantages and disadvantages. Among the advantages is that taxation is supposed to occur with the consent of the governed. Among the disadvantages is that there are so many governmental units in the United States, it's difficult for the average American to keep track of the governance to which she is consenting.

The United States was founded on the principle that there will be no taxation without representation. Other political milestones of that concept include the 15th Amendment, which extends suffrage to freed slaves but not women, and the 16th Amendment, which allows the federal government to collect income taxes from all working people. That made women officially taxpayers, and seven years later, with the adoption of the 19th Amendment, women were extended the vote. The final expansion of voting rights occurred in 1971, when it was recognized that people 18 years of age and over are also taxpayers and the 26th Amendment lowered the voting age of all men and women to 18.

As more and more people received the right to vote, you might think there was more participation in governance. Because more and more people had the right to know what the government was doing with their tax money, you might think elected officials had to be more accountable about how they were spending it. But, sadly, such has not been the case. Although the electorate has grown, accountability has not.

Part of the reason is that, as the country has grown, over 87,000 units of government (otherwise defined as a public entity supported by property) have been created nationwide. Americans may live in one country and one state, but usually they live in more than one local governmental jurisdiction. Whether a person lives in a city, village, or township, he lives in a county, to which he pays taxes. Everyone has to live in a school district, another governmental unit to which he pays taxes. Urban dwellers often live in fire protection districts, library districts, and even park districts, to which they pay taxes. Who among us has time to pay attention to all of these governmental units and their taxation policies, elections, and so on? Political scientists argue that we all should, but it's a daunting task and most of us simply tune them out.

In previous chapters you learned about the role of the GASB in designing government financial reporting. The GASB designs these reports knowing that most taxpayers don't have the time, interest, or expertise to understand how to read them. But the GASB knows the media do, and the media are the real audience of those reports. The GASB can't review the financial statements of all 87,000 governmental units on a regular basis, but they have designed a financial reporting system with a level of standardization that allows media outlets to understand them.

Leisure services managers working in the public sector need to know they are being watched by the media, just as every other governmental unit is being watched. Even though the electorate may not pay attention to what leisure services units are doing, there are plenty of opportunities for the media to read government financial statements and report their findings to the public.

Knowing that the media are watching encourages people working for government leisure services agencies to take financial reporting seriously. There are criminal consequences for public officials mishandling public money, which should help government leisure services managers understand they are answerable to the GASB, the public, and the media. Missteps can land leisure services managers in jail, costing them their freedom, fortunes, and the very existence of their governmental units.

This chapter covers the governmental financial reporting process, transparency, and the consequences of messing up government financial reports. You'll learn about not only accounting standards and laws that apply to government financial accounting and reporting but also the political consequences of the process. Such consequences are far greater than the consequences in the private and nonprofit sectors and include being embarrassed publicly, getting fired, losing elections, and squandering scarce taxpayer resources. There are plenty of experts, such as lawyers and accountants, who can tell public-sector leisure services managers how to stay within the GASB regulations and the law. There are plenty of elected officials who know how to get themselves reelected. But there are far fewer people to tell public-sector leisure services managers how to spend tax money wisely so the public gets something of value in return. As this chapter will consider, it's one thing to account for money accurately, obeying the law as you go, and it's another thing to spend it wisely.

FEDERAL GOVERNMENT

When the U.S. Constitution was written in 1787, the authors were attempting to create a strong national government in order to provide a unified monetary and banking system, consolidate debt accumulated from the Revolutionary War, manage a strong national defense system, and coordinate international trade between the states. The remaining governing responsibilities were retained by the states, including the right to allow slavery, to charter local governments, and to create criminal and civil laws. The Constitution severely limited the role of the national government.

That changed over the years, especially during and after the Civil War in the 1860s, when the federal government assumed a greater role. Since that time, the debate about limits of federal governance and its interference with the role of the states continues to take place. A significant issue today is federal mandates that states and local governments are required to pay for, just as voting rights was an issue in the 1950s and 1960s. To the states, it may seem that the federal government always wins such controversies regarding the extension of federal authority, but state and local governments still retain a large amount of authority, particularly in the provision of leisure services.

Federalism

To understand how government leisure service agencies operate, you need to understand the concept of federalism. Federalism can occur in layers, where the national government provides some services, the state others, and local units of government others. That concept is called **layer-cake federalism**. An example of layer-cake federalism is recreation programs such as athletics or instructional programs. The federal government provides virtually none of these programs. Federal agencies provide recreation areas to host recreational activities, but these sites largely provide passive recreation. States also tend to stay away from offering active recreation programs, leaving the activities under the domain of county and local leisure services providers.

The other concept is **marble-cake federalism**, where national, state, and local agencies provide similar services. Similar to a marble cake, for example, providing public parks for mostly passive recreation and conservation is a blend of the three levels of government. There are national parks, state parks, and county parks.

Layer-cake federalism is the concept that governmental services are the exclusive domain of one level or another. Marble-cake federalism is the concept that all levels of government choose, or feel they are forced, to provide the same services, often in competition with each other. Understanding how each level of federalism—national, state, and local governments—functions financially is one goal of this chapter. Another goal is for you to understand that managing money in public-sector leisure services can be very different from managing money in the private or nonprofit sectors. There are different accounting systems and different levels of transparency.

Government Accounting and Financial Standards

Government accounting and financial standards are recent phenomena. The federal government did not have a budget until the 1920s and has yet to establish a modified accrual accounting system that takes into consideration future commitments such as Social Security. State and local governments did not have direction from the GASB until the 1970s, with most local governments still not completely adhering to GASB guidelines.

This chapter takes a look at accounting at the federal, state, and local levels. Of the three, the local level is where most leisure services professionals work in the government sector. That's why this chapter dedicates more attention to the local level than the federal and state levels. Another reason is that the local level is where leisure services professionals have the most authority to make financial decisions, since federal and state governments are more in the hands of elected officials.

Yosemite National Park in California, with its large areas of protected wilderness, is a popular tourist destination and an example of marble-cake federalism—state and local governments also provide public parks.

Accounting at the Federal Level

Governmental accounting at the federal level is all about the appropriation budget. *Appropriations* are budgeted amounts of money that a governmental unit intends to spend. Federal accounting focuses more on spending money than on raising revenue. The premise for this statement is that the federal government controls the money supply. If the federal government spends too much and runs out of revenue, it can borrow or print more money. Revenues are not all that relevant. From the viewpoint of federal agencies, such as the NPS, the budgetary process is about gaining approval for expenditures. It is the job of Congress to worry about where the money will come from to cover those expenditures, something Congress does not do nearly as well as authorizing expenditures.

This chapter does not consider the accounting and financial standards of the federal government because, as some people would argue, there aren't any. The U.S. government is not required to follow GAAP as prescribed by the GASB, but states and local governments are. That is not to say that the federal government doesn't try to follow accounting principles, however. The Federal Accounting Standards Advisory Board (FASAB) is the agency that advises the federal government about accounting principles. The board has the specific mission to

> promulgate federal accounting standards after considering the financial and budgetary information needs of citizens, congressional oversight groups, executive agencies, and the needs of other users of federal financial information. Accounting and financial reporting standards are essential for public accountability and for an efficient and effective functioning of our democratic system of government. Thus, federal accounting standards and financial reporting play a major role in fulfilling the government's duty to be publicly accountable and can be used to assess (1) the government's accountability and its efficiency and effectiveness, and (2) the economic, political, and social consequences of the allocation and various uses of federal resources. (FASAB 2008)

The problem is that because the FASAB is advisory, Congress and the Department of the Treasury are under no legal obligation to follow its recommendations. And the board cannot force the Treasury Department or Congress to follow GAAP, so as a result, the U.S. government does not account for all of its revenues and expenditures on an accrual or modified accrual basis.

That's not to say that the federal government doesn't accrue some expenditures. For some items, such as accounts receivable and payable, it does. But the U.S. government does not accrue its debt. If it did, the national debt would be over $50 trillion, considering what it owes in unfunded Social Security benefits. Reporting the national debt at a lower level would not be permitted in modified accrual accounting under GAAP. By not following GAAP, the federal government is not being as transparent as it should be, but who is going to force it to be transparent?

A logical answer is the media, but sometimes financial management at the federal level befuddles even them, and the stories are not as interesting as when someone messes up managing the money in local government. But the stories at the national level still get reported. Truth in Government describes itself as "a non-profit organization dedicated to revealing what Congress has kept hidden for many decades: how much money it really spends and how much money all of us taxpayers really owe" (www.truthingovernment.org). The underlying premise in its many articles is that the U.S. government is kind of using cash-basis accounting—*kind of* meaning that its financial position is like your checkbook balance, not accurately reporting your financial position. For instance, in 2011, commitments to pay Social Security benefits to people currently working combined with those receiving benefits were estimated to be in excess of $56 trillion. On a cash basis, the national debt then was reported by the federal government to be under $16 trillion, $40 trillion less.

There is no real reason Congress and the Treasury Department should change the way they account for money. Doing so would be political suicide. That's why Congress and the Treasury Department feel they have no choice but to continue on the way they have for over two centuries, focusing on expenditures and hoping the revenues will be there someday to pay the bills.

Because leisure services financial management at the federal level exists in an accounting and political system that defines how federal leisure agencies budget for and operate their departments, managing the expenditures in the budget is what they need to focus on. Federal leisure services professionals, such as those managing the national park, recreation, and forest systems, know they have far less power than their counterparts at the local level to influence policies that generate revenue; at the federal level, this power is in the hands of Congress. Federal leisure services managers can only manage the expenditure budgets that Congress provides.

Managing the expenditures of federal leisure services agencies is much like managing expenses for private businesses and nonprofit organizations. The budget and actual report is the best tool for keeping expenditures within their budgeted

Flood Planning and Recovery

In 2011, the Bismarck (North Dakota) Park District experienced severe flood damage, something many municipal parks and agencies throughout the country also experience. This happens because many parks are built on floodplains, a better place for a park or golf course than for homes.

According to a September 1, 2011, article in the *Bismarck Tribune*, the park district's capital budget had to be reevaluated in light of damage done to the parks during the flood. The executive park and recreation director determined that the focus of the 2012 budget would be recovery first rather than planning upgrades for facilities. He proposed nearly $15.1 million in spending, $327,000 lower than in 2011, because the park district was no longer managing the Bismarck Community Bowl and because the Prairie Rose State Games had been canceled.

The park district finance director determined that $4.07 million in property taxes would be levied. The tax levy for Social Security, construction, pension, and special assessments funds would be $4 million. "Taxes make up 40 percent of the district's general fund income. About 9 percent comes from state aid revenue and 51 percent is taken from park fees/contracts," the article said. The finance director reported that a home valued at $150,000 would pay $265 for park district's tax share, about $3 more than 2011.

According to the article, flood damage in the park district could exceed $2 million. The park district set aside $325,000 for its share of a local match for flood recovery projects from the Federal Emergency Management Agency (FEMA) instead of pursuing a low-interest loan from the state. The park district planned on paying the upfront cost of repairs reserves, park improvement funds, and building funds. Eventually, FEMA would repay the district for its flood recovery efforts.

Park district floodplain property damaged by the flood included a golf course, parks, playgrounds, parking lots, boat ramps, and a volleyball court. Trees also were damaged and needed to be replaced. Many park projects were going to be put on hold for flood repairs, but dirt work would be done on two ball fields near the golf dome. Trail work would be completed at the Tom O'Leary Golf Course and the new ball fields encircled with the help of grants. Other properties would be repaired as funds become available. But one thing was clear: The 2011 flood would not be the last the park district would need to confront. Planning for future recoveries needed to be a component part of the Bismarck Park District budgeting process.

References

Eckroth, L. 2011. "Park District Doesn't Expect Flood Damage to Hurt Budget." *Bismarck Tribune*, Sept. 1. http://bismarcktribune.com/news/local/park-district-doesn-t-expect-flood-damage-to-hurt-budget/article_2bd7ff1a-d4e5-11e0-94ee-001cc4c03286.html#ixzz1h097s9xy.

line-item amounts. Unlike private businesses and nonprofit organizations, however, governmental units pay virtually no attention to the revenues. If revenues do not materialize, that's a problem for Congress to handle. Congress will need to authorize additional borrowing or the Treasury will need to create more money to meet their obligations of providing revenues to federal agencies, but the agencies themselves are not expected to cut their expenditures.

Not being motivated to cut expenditures when revenues do not materialize is a big difference between federal agencies and private and nonprofit agencies—and local governmental agencies, for that matter. Managing only the expenditure side of the budget causes federal leisure services managers to ask for more financial resources than they need so that they have money on hand in case of emergencies. Inflating budget expenditure requests is only human nature, as is spending all of the given resources so that the manager's budget request for the following year isn't cut.

Budgeting at the Federal Level

Since 1994, the U.S. federal government has increased the national debt substantially, an estimated $1.3 trillion in 2011 alone. Although there would not seem to be a lot of budgeting taking place, Congress does require federal agencies to submit budget expenditure requests each year. The NPS website describes the budgeting process for federal leisure services agencies as follows (NPS 2012):

> The National Park Service (NPS), like most Federal bureaus, by law, submits a budget request to Congress for each fiscal year. The NPS submits its budget proposal in a publication called *Budget Justifications*, which includes a summary of bureau accomplishments for the current year and funding requests for the next year. The NPS *Budget Justifications* book is organized by appropriation including Operation of the National Park System, National Recreation and Preservation, Historic Preservation Fund, Construction and Major Maintenance, and Land Acquisition and State Assistance. It also includes budget information for each of the units and programs of the NPS. The NPS is part of the Department of the Interior (DOI). Each bureau in DOI has a separate *Budget Justifications* submission. In DOI circles, the *Budget Justifications* book is commonly referred to as the Greenbook.

The *Budget Justifications* publication explains why the budget appropriation was requested by the NPS. The publication is available to the media and is scrutinized by senators and representatives who review the budget. The compelling nature of the justifications is part of the strength of the budget request, but the political influence that the department wields is equally as important.

As can be imagined, with an exploding federal deficit and many federal agencies competing for funds, the budget process is extremely political. Most federal agencies make their appeals to Congress, rallying their lobbyists and interest groups on the side of the agency. Since budgeting is an ongoing process, federal agencies such as NPS find it politically effective to form permanent alliances among their departmental staff, interest groups, and key Congresspersons (e.g., committee chairpersons that shepherd the budget through to the floor of the House and Senate). The political term for this type of alliance is **iron triangles**.

The triangles are iron because they are such strong alliances. They are triangles because they involve three groups: interest groups, elected officials, and bureaucrats. Each of the parties is trying to achieve its own goals. Interest groups want their interests promoted, elected officials want to get reelected, and bureaucrats want their budget requests approved. Communication is multidirectional, as is support.

The iron-triangle relationship model at the federal level is a model that works at the state and local levels as well, particularly during the budget process. Federal budgeting is largely incremental, just as it is at the state and local levels, where the goal is to make sure the previous year's budget is not reduced and is, if possible, increased at the margins. The system works when the budgetary focus is on expenditures with little accountability of leisure services professionals to achieve revenue goals.

At the federal level, the iron triangle is made possible by the lower accounting standards of the financial system. Were Congress to fully comprehend the financial position it is in, with at least $50 trillion in debt reported in financial statements for everyone to see, it might be inclined to ignore iron-triangle relationships that cause entitlements and increase federal agency budgets, driving the debt higher. But with a political process in place and not much motivation to balance the federal budget in an environment where the government can always print or borrow more money, financial reporting according to GAAP is unlikely for now.

An important point for federal leisure services professionals to understand is why the federal government is not better at budgeting than it is. The federal government didn't even create a budget until 1920, and Congress has adopted a balanced budget only 10 times since then. Politics being what they are, it is doubtful that Congress will adopt a balanced budget in the foreseeable future.

In response to the economic downturn that began in 2007, there has been much speculation among political leaders, economists, and the media about whether the U.S. government can grow itself out of its national debt, which reached new heights during the administrations of George W. Bush and Barack Obama. At the time of this writing, the accumulated national debt amounted to more than $15.37 trillion, approximately $49,104 for every man, woman, and child living in the United States (www.usdebtclock.org).

There are only three ways to control per-capita debt: The government can dramatically cut spending, it can substantially raise taxes, or inflation of the dollar can minimize the value of the national debt. All of these would be detrimental to the average citizen. Taking $49,104 from each person would cause a great deal of pain and would be nearly impossible politically. Inflation would make the cost of goods and services more expensive, and it is unlikely that earnings would keep pace.

This leaves cutting government spending as the only practical solution. Assuming that Congress had the political will to cut spending, it is likely that federal leisure services agencies would be hurt as much as any other sector. Cutting funding to the NPS, USFS, national recreation areas, national wildlife refuges, and national conservation areas would severely curtail the ability to protect federal land and resources. One solution being tried by Washington State is pay-as-you-go fees charged to those who use the public areas ("Washington state parks to charge fees starting Friday" 2011). This revenue source could change the financial management dynamic of federal leisure services agencies.

The good news is that paying fees for leisure services is not a new concept. Private, nonprofit, and many local governmental agencies have been charging fees from the beginning. But charging pay-as-you-go fees is new to federal leisure agencies. They would need to adjust their budgeting process, pay attention to revenues, and manage their expenses, something local governmental agencies have been doing for decades.

STATE GOVERNMENT

Accounting and financial management at the state level are similar and yet different from the federal level. One similarity they share is the political process of budget adoption. Departmental budgets are negotiated, interest groups are involved, and iron triangles exist. Revenues are rarely matched with expenditures, and departments try to spend every penny of their line items so that their budgets won't be reduced the following year.

An important difference in accounting and financial management at the state level is the fact that states can't print more money. They can borrow it, but with limits. States can borrow money to fund capital projects or to cover shortfalls in their operating budget, which is tantamount to the federal government increasing the national debt to augment its operating budget.

Political culture plays a large role in the financial condition of a state. Fiscally conservative states like Texas, that have proportionately less land in public ownership for leisure services such as state parks and conservation areas, tend to have the lowest tax rates and be in the best financial positions. States such as New Jersey, which has had a more liberal political culture, have higher taxes and are in worse financial positions, particularly in terms of their per-capita debt ratios (Robyn and Prante 2011).

State financial positions are often reflected in **statements of net assets**, which are similar to balance sheets for businesses. The difference between assets and liabilities on a balance sheet is a reflection of the wealth of a company. The difference between assets and liabilities on a statement of net assets is a reflection of the wealth of a state. Statements of net assets are also used in financial management of local public-sector leisure services and will be discussed in this context later in the chapter.

Table 9.1 shows the net assets of the 50 states from their statements of net assets for the fiscal year 2010.

Some states have large amounts of net assets and others have negative net assets. An explanation for the wide range could be political culture. Daniel Elazar, a political scientist and founder and director of the Center for the Study of Federalism at the University of Philadelphia, described political cultures in states as taking three basic forms: traditionalistic, moralistic, and individualistic (Riley 2012).

Traditionalistic cultures are found in states that have values, beliefs, and traditions that generally cause states to not want to change. Therefore, individuals and groups that have been in power tend to stay in power. Elazar showed that many Southern states are traditionalistic.

Moralistic cultures are found in states that have values, beliefs, and traditions that generally cause states to want to do the right thing for everyone, whether they are a special interest or not. Moralistic states try to minimize the influence of interest groups. Among the dominant moralistic states, according to Elazar, are Minnesota, Wisconsin, Michigan, Maine, Oregon, Utah, and Colorado.

Individualistic cultures are those that tend to accommodate interest groups. The values, beliefs, and traditions of individualistic states are such that it is every man for himself, and it would be irrational for anyone to act otherwise. Dominant states in this category include Illinois, Indiana, Ohio, Pennsylvania, and New York.

Table 9.1 shows that every state is different in the amount of wealth that it carries on its statement of net assets. The states with the highest net assets are usually Southern and Western states with predominantly traditionalistic political cultures. States with the lowest or negative net assets tend to be the ones with predominantly individualistic political cultures. And states in the middle appear to be the ones with predominantly moralistic political cultures. The table suggests that political culture does make a difference.

State accounting techniques are supposed to follow GAAP as prescribed by the GASB, but they have been accused of avoiding GAAP in their financial reporting. States manage state employee

Table 9.1 State Comparison of Net Assets of Governmental Activities for FY10

State	Net assets (in billions)	State	Net assets (in billions)
Alabama	$22.1	Montana	$6.4
Alaska	$49.9	Nebraska	$10.4
Arizona	$16.1	Nevada	$4.0
Arkansas	$11.5	New Hampshire	$2.0
California	$5.4	New Jersey	–$21.5
Colorado	$15.5	New Mexico	$12.1
Connecticut	–$9.6	New York	$30.9
Delaware	$2.2	North Carolina	$28.8
Florida	$47.1	North Dakota	$4.4
Georgia	$13.9	Ohio	$18.6
Hawaii	*	Oklahoma	$12.6
Iowa	$7.6	Oregon	$10.1
Idaho	$7.1	Pennsylvania	$23.2
Illinois	–$29.9	Rhode Island	$0.84
Indiana	$17.6	South Carolina	$13.4
Kansas	$9.8	South Dakota	$4.1
Kentucky	$14.8	Tennessee	*
Louisiana	$18.5	Texas	$95.9
Maine	$3.8	Utah	$14.3
Maryland	$9.4	Vermont	$1.2
Massachusetts	–$12.2	Virginia	$16.1
Michigan	$14.0	Washington	$23.9
Minnesota	$9.9	West Virginia	$10.1
Mississippi	$11.2	Wisconsin	$5.7
Missouri	$28.5	Wyoming	$10.3

*Data for Hawaii and Tennessee were not available as of June 30, 2010.

Source: Compiled by Illinois Auditor General's Office from Comprehensive Annual Financial Reports (CAFR) for each state. www.auditor.illinois.gov/Audit-Reports/Comptroller-Internal-Controls-and-Compliance.asp

Reprinted from Governmental Accounting Standards Board.

and local teacher retirement programs, and some of them manage municipal employee retirement programs. Because accruing pension commitments would show how much debt they really have, most states don't provide balance sheets that accrue these pension commitments. If they did, it would be difficult for them to approve spending of any kind.

The tenuous financial position of some states can be demonstrated in their net assets. New Jersey and Illinois are two states that have experienced financial problems during the past decade, largely due to their pension fund obligations. These states owe so much money in unfunded pensions to retired teachers and state and local employees that their statements of assets show large negative net assets. Unfortunately, New Jersey and Illinois are not alone in their financial plight.

In spite of the inability of states to print money, the budgeting process at the state level is similar to the process at the federal level. Similar to Congress, state legislatures have the power to appropriate money for state departments to spend. State departments make budget expenditure requests using whatever political leverage they have to get their requests funded, including iron triangles at the state level.

It is no wonder that California and Illinois, two states where interest groups have been effective in getting what they want, are in the direst financial shape of all states in the country. The iron triangle has caused financial chaos. California and Illinois are in dire financial shape because their pension commitments have caused their financial positions to acquire about as much debt as lenders will allow. And even though they don't produce GASB-prescribed balance sheets and income statements, their financial inability to acquire more debt can't be disguised much longer.

This leads us to the politics of why unhealthy finances are not good for state leisure services. When states are unable to borrow more money, they are forced to cut back on expenditures. When this happens, as it already has in Illinois, the first place legislatures look to cut is leisure services, especially if funding for leisure services comes from the state's general funds.

That happened in Illinois, where state parks were closed because of budget shortfalls during the summer of 2008, and in Minnesota, where state parks were closed over the July 4 weekend in 2010. To the fiscal conservatives who take their state's financial crisis as an opportunity to cut what they believe is unnecessary spending, leisure services are a luxury that the state can't afford. They see the crisis as an opportunity to advance their **public choice** political model, positing that some services should not be provided by government. If the public really wants these services, such as parks and recreation, the public should pay fees for them. The government should not charge taxes to provide them.

Leisure services are funded through state budgets as departments in the general fund. **General funds** are groups of accounts, usually segregated by state departments, where the funding comes from a multitude of revenue sources. If the revenue sources are not dedicated to leisure services by law or preferably the state's constitutional provisions, legislatures are free to spend the general fund as they see fit. This leads to state departments competing for their budget requests, much as they do at the federal level but with the ultimate consequence that there will be winners and losers, particularly if the state can't borrow more money to make sure there aren't any losers.

The process of financial management for state leisure agencies is a lot easier if there is a **dedicated tax source** of revenues. A dedicated tax source is property, sales, excise, or other taxes that can only be spent for a sole purpose, like park and recreation services. For instance, in some states, a portion of the state sales tax is dedicated to the state park system. In those states, there is no competition with other departments for funding. Whatever is derived from a dedicated portion of sales tax is what the state park system receives. As can be imagined, that dramatically changes the budgeting process.

With a dedicated source of tax revenue, the budgeting process is similar to the private and nonprofit sectors. Forecasting tax revenue needs to be done first. Once the dedicated tax revenue is predicted, the expenditure side of the budget is developed. Then the task of the leisure services financial manager is to seek approval from the state legislature to spend the forecasted revenue, with the understanding that if the revenue doesn't materialize, expenditures need to be reduced. And if the dedicated tax revenue exceeds expectations, an amendatory appropriation needs to be approved by the legislature.

State leisure services agencies play the political game with legislatures by making sure all of the dedicated tax revenue gets spent. Otherwise, there is always the chance that the unspent money will be given to another department. The best way to make sure that doesn't happen is for state department heads to overestimate the dedicated revenue within their budget and underestimate other revenue. That way, if extra money comes in from the dedicated tax portion of the revenue budget, it will get spent.

But in an environment where fiscal conditions or fiscal conservatives threaten general fund support of leisure services, spending excess revenue is not as much of an issue as how to get funding in the first place. The alternative of fees and charges is one option, although it is unlikely that state park systems will ever be funded on a pay-as-you-go basis.

LOCAL GOVERNMENT

Local governments are under the jurisdiction of the states that created them. Every state is entitled to its own unique means of managing the local governments it charters, including providing direction about how local governments will account for their revenues and expenditures. In addition, each state has its own political culture, creating local government structures that fit with the state's overarching cultures.

At the local level, governments follow the guidelines of states, sometimes adopting prescribed budgetary processes and sometimes following the GASB. Leisure services departments of general purpose governments can have different budgeting processes than leisure services special districts. It all depends on the level of supervision state governments choose to exercise.

Local governmental units offer active recreation services such as swimming lessons, which typically aren't provided at the state or federal level.

Accounting for Local Governments

Federal and state leisure services agencies are supposed to have different missions than local leisure services agencies, but this is not always the case. Marble-cake federalism would argue that national parks serve some of the same clientele as state parks. Such an argument was repeatedly refuted by John Muir, the Scottish-born American naturalist, who said the purpose of national parks is to capture the spiritual quality of nature (McNamara 2012). State parks do some of that, but it can be argued that state parks primarily exist as camping, hunting, and fishing sites.

Leisure governmental units at the local level have been known to provide natural habitats for passive recreation, but mostly they are designed to house athletic fields, playgrounds, tennis courts, swimming pools, and other active recreation amenities. From a financial position, passive recreation is generally provided for no fees, but active recreation services can charge fees.

With their differing missions, the financial management of leisure services agencies at the local level is very different from the financial management of federal and state agencies. Federal and state leisure services agencies have primarily expenditure budgets, with or without dedicated revenue sources. Leisure government agencies at the local level typically provide parks for free. But with the ability to charge fees for recreation services, the financial challenges are more similar to nonprofit and business entities than federal and state agencies.

Unlike federal and state governments, local governmental units typically do not account for their money on a cash basis. For local governments who follow the GASB and adhere to GAAP, even if they account for their money on a cash basis, they need to provide certain accrued financial statements to meet the requirements imposed on them by their states. Local governmental units must provide financial reports similar to business balance sheets or nonprofit statements of financial position. As introduced earlier in this chapter, these reports are called *statements of net assets*.

Statements of net assets contain similar categories in slightly different terminologies than business and nonprofit balance sheets and statements of financial position. There are current assets and current and long-term liabilities, just like on business balance sheets. As with nonprofit statements of financial position, the difference between total assets and total liabilities is called *fund balance*, not *equity*, the business term. And similar to nonprofit accounting, within the governmental agency there can be several entities, each with its own fund, whereas in business accounting, the company is the entity that comprises one fund.

The business accounting report called the *income statement*, where each entity has a report that tells the accounting story of what activities changed on the balance sheet from the beginning of the year to the end, is called the *statement of activities*. This statement includes revenues, expenses, and changes in fund balances.

There are differences in the way that states require their local governments to account for their transactions. Some states, such as Illinois, allow local governments to create their own **line-item accounts** in an order that best serves the missions of their agencies. Other states have more specific requirements, such as Indiana, which requires that transactions be recorded following the standards of the Indiana State Board of Accounts (SBOA), whose mission is stated here (2012b):

> As an agency of the executive branch, the State Board of Accounts audits the financial statements of all governmental units within the state, including cities, towns, utilities, schools, counties, license branches, state agencies, hospitals, libraries, townships, and state colleges and universities. The agency, as a part of the audit process, renders opinions on the fairness of presentation of the various units' financial statements in accordance with the same professional auditing standards required of all independent audit organizations. Investigatory audits are performed to reveal fraud or noncompliance with local, state, and federal statutes.

Through the SBOA, Indiana has a system where the state itself audits the financial statements of its local governmental units. To make that task easier for the auditing teams that visit each local governmental unit about every two years, the SBOA requires that line-item accounts adhere to standardized descriptions and transactional entry practices. That way, no matter where a team of auditors is working, they don't have to figure out the system of the local governmental unit. The one-size-fits-all accounting process eliminates major differences in local systems.

Illinois, on the other hand, allows its local governments to design their own line-item accounting descriptions and transactional entry practices. There is no Illinois state board of accounts to audit local governments, mainly because, with nearly 7,000 local governments, it would be a daunting task. Indiana has fewer than 3,000 (Dye 2000), permitting the state to keep closer tabs on them. Because of the number of local governments it has to oversee, Illinois allows local governmental units to hire their own auditing firms, typically serving the local governmental unit for a number of years and becoming familiar with its accounting system.

States such as Illinois are more concerned with their local units of government following GAAP than they are with finding fraud or noncompliance. The Indiana model of financial reporting shows that some states don't trust local government to report their financial positions fairly, and the Illinois model shows that some states do.

State boards of accounts are not to be confused with **state boards of accountancy**, which are nonprofit agencies independent of state government or are departments of state government that exist to fulfill a mission similar to that of the board in Washington. The mission of the Washington State Board of Accountancy (2012) is to promote the dependability of information that is used for guidance in financial transactions, accounting, or assessing the status or performance of commercial and noncommercial enterprises, whether public, private, or governmental, and to protect the public interest.

State boards of accountancy are largely advisory and generally have no legal power to force compliance. Left to their own devices, most state governments follow the mandates of their constitutions in financial matters, but some do not. For instance, there are states whose constitutions mandate the percentages of support for primary and secondary education for which the state is required to provide. In several states, those percentages are ignored by the legislature because the state simply does not have the funds to provide that support.

Structures of Local Government

The total number of people working at the various levels of government is an indication of the amount of services provided at each level. According to the Bureau of Labor Statistics, there are about 1.9 million federal employees, not including military personnel. Comparatively, there are about 5 million employees working for the 50 states and 12.5 million people employed by the 87,000 units of local governments (www.bls.gov). Of those nearly 20 million governmental employees, it is estimated that slightly less than 5 percent work for leisure services agencies (i.e., slightly fewer than 1 million leisure services employees) at all levels of government.

Leisure services providers at the local level of government exist in two general forms. The local providers are either departments of larger general-purpose governmental units, such as park and recreation departments of counties, cities, villages, towns, or townships, or they are special-purpose governmental units, such as park, recreation, conservation, or forest preserve districts. These two structures create two completely different challenges when it comes to leisure services accounting and financial management, especially with respect to the revenue side of the equation. One challenge is the autonomy (or lack thereof) to raise tax revenue, and the other is the ability to use fees as a revenue source. Autonomy can be provided through the legal authority of special districts and municipal departments to raise tax and fee revenues, and it can also be provided by the delegation of authority from elected to appointed officials.

Tax Revenues

States can create their own rules for tax revenue generation and can share some of those with local governments or not. States can also permit local governments to levy limited or unlimited taxes, depending on if the local government is subject to home rule or Dillon's rule. **Home rule** means a local government can levy whatever taxes it wants except for those that the state limits or prohibits. **Dillon's rule** means a local government can only levy what taxes the state permits and nothing else.

Home rule and Dillon's rule may not seem that different, but they are. Imagine your parents went out of town for a week. Under home rule, their instructions to you could be, "Use your own judgment, but don't have any parties." Under Dillon's rule, their instructions to you would be more along the lines of, "Call us every night and don't do anything that we don't approve first."

In some states, such as Alabama, general-purpose municipalities are not permitted a dedicated tax for leisure services. Park and recreation department budgets are part of the general fund, competing for financial resources against other municipal departments, such as police and fire protection. The source of revenues for the general fund for states that have no dedicated park and recreation tax can include sales taxes, general property taxes, utility taxes, and revenue sharing from the state, including motor fuel taxes, income taxes, and sales taxes.

In states such as Wisconsin, school districts are permitted to levy dedicated property taxes for recreation services, with no cap on how much they can levy. This tax allows school districts to operate recreation departments as part of school services. Initially operating continuing and adult education programs, today Wisconsin school districts provide a diverse array of recreation services that include athletics, swimming, and early childhood development programs. There are 22 Wisconsin school districts that levy recreation taxes, but there are also park and recreation departments of municipalities that occasionally coexist in communities with school recreation departments.

In some states, such as Indiana, school districts are not permitted to levy a dedicated park and recreation property tax, but general-purpose municipalities are. Park and recreation taxes in these states can be deposited in the general fund of the municipality or can be accounted for in separate funds. The municipalities are restricted by state law from using the park and recreation tax for any other purpose, dampening the need for park and recreation departments to compete with other departments for financial resources for operations. But there is still some level of competition for financial resources for capital improvement.

In other states, such as Missouri, municipal park and recreation departments have dedicated sales taxes that can only be used for parks and recreation. This money can be accounted for within the general fund or in separate funds. By referendum, residents can allow sales taxes to be dedicated to park and recreation operations or capital improvements. The dedicated sales taxes mean that there is little competition with city departments for funding.

In still other states, such as North Dakota and Illinois, special-purpose governmental units, called *park districts*, can be created by a **referendum**, giving voters the authority to levy various types of property taxes to support park and recreation services. These special-purpose districts are not affiliated in any way with municipalities, so there is no competition with other governmental services for operating or **capital resources**. But there are usually limits on the ability of special districts to tax, often calling for referenda before taxes can be raised. In some communities in Illinois, park and recreation departments coexist with park districts.

The challenge for leisure services professionals is to understand that each state has its own political philosophy of how leisure services should be funded. Moralistic states, such as Wisconsin, believe that cooperation is important, not competition. Because school districts can levy a recreation tax, existing school buildings can be used during off times. This is the lighted schoolhouse concept, which originated in the 1940s.

Individualistic states, such as Illinois, believe that cooperation is not as important. Municipalities, school districts, and park districts can exist as separate entities, allowing them to focus on their missions and to have their own taxing authority to fund those missions. There are more governmental

Winning the NRPA Gold Medal Award

To many leisure services professionals serving in the public sector, the pinnacle for their agency is winning the Gold Medal Award for Excellence in Park and Recreation Management presented at the NRPA conference each year in partnership with the American Academy for Park and Recreation Administration. In October 2010, the NRPA presented the Gold Medal Award to the Lee's Summit (MO) Parks and Recreation Department. Other finalist agencies serving populations of 50,001 to 100,000 were the Waukesha Parks, Recreation, and Forestry Department (Wisconsin), the Schaumburg Park District (Illinois), and the Temple Parks and Leisure Services (Texas).

Lee's Summit is the third Missouri agency to receive the national award since it began in 1966. Finalists are judged on long-range planning, resource management, volunteerism, environmental stewardship, program development, professional development, and agency recognition. Lee's Summit Parks and Recreation was recognized for using in-house resources to stretch dollars, allowing for quick response to rapid growth; the development of Legacy Park, which houses 39 athletic fields, a large community center, a park construction and operations center, 5.2 miles (8.4 km) of multiuse trail, an inclusive playground, shelters, and an 18-hole disc golf course; and effective use of citizen-based groups and task forces to create facilities, parks, and programs.

To Tom Lovell, Lee's Summit Parks and Recreation administrator, the Gold Medal Award was more than affirmation that the community supports the park and recreation services provided by its municipality. It was also affirmation that Lovell has been an excellent administrator. After all, the full name of the award is the Gold Medal Award in Parks and Recreation *Management*, the last word of which is often left out of news releases. Lovell's 32 years as administrator of the department, spent managing the budget and staff, passing referenda to build facilities, and engaging the community, is much of the reason why the agency won the award. The Gold Medal Award recognizes excellence in park and recreation management, and a major component of that management success is understanding and overseeing sound financial practices.

References

Lee's Summit Parks and Recreation. 2011. "Lee's Summit Wins Highest National Award for Parks and Recreation." http://cityofls.net/Parks/Parks-and-Trails/Parks-Progress/articleType/ArticleView/articleId/1133/lees-summit-wins-highest-national-award-for-parks-recreation.aspx.

units under such a system, but that is the price of each unit focusing on its own mission.

In traditionalistic states such as Alabama, the political culture of maintaining the current balance of power suggests that park and recreation services are not a recent phenomenon. They see no reason to give school districts or municipalities more power by providing them with dedicated property taxes. The traditionalistic culture goes hand in glove with a fiscally conservative political culture. Fiscally conservative traditionalistic states tend to have municipal park and recreation departments. Allowing special districts would upset the status quo.

In Illinois, there are more than 300 park districts and 125 municipal park and recreation departments. In North Dakota there are about 250 park districts. These park districts have an array of property taxes they can levy, which will be considered in chapter 11. Municipal park and recreation departments in these states have the option of levying their own dedicated property taxes.

In Illinois, where park districts are created by referenda, municipalities have the choice of supporting the creation of a separate taxing district or creating a park and recreation department. Municipal park and recreation departments exist next to communities that have created park districts. Inevitably, the park and recreation department will be compared with the park district. If municipalities shortchange their park and recreation departments, voters always have the option of creating a park district, which many have done.

California is another state that has created a park district system that provides an alternative to municipal park and recreation departments. California tends to create these districts as regional agencies, providing services to multiple communities through a dedicated property tax. These districts can also be coterminous with the boundaries of a municipality, standalone entities, or in coexistence with municipal departments.

States that permit the creation of park districts for delivering leisure services tend to provide more services to the public compared with states that do not (Flickinger and Murphy 2004). Studies have shown that, although municipal park and recreation departments may provide as high of service levels as park districts, states that allow voters to create park districts have more agencies (Dye 2000).

The Dakotas are a case in point. North Dakota allows park districts and has 250 of them, most of them in small rural communities because that's how North Dakota is populated. South Dakota, which does not permit the creation of park districts, has fewer than 40 municipal park and recreation departments, even though its population is greater than that of North Dakota.

In states that permit voters to decide how they want leisure services provided, voters are willing to tax themselves for the services. In states where it is left up to the city council to decide if they want publicly provided leisure services, funding for leisure services may crowd out funding for police, fire, or other municipal services. Thus, city councils are less likely to establish park and recreation departments, and when they do create a municipal department, they tend to fund them at lower levels than park districts (Emanuelson 2007b).

Fee Revenues

Regardless of whether publicly funded leisure services at the local level are delivered by county park departments, county forest preserve districts, municipal park and recreation departments, or park districts, their financial statements are required to follow the GASB accounting principles in financial reporting. However, the financial statements all look different from each other.

Formats vary for two reasons: States permit different sources of tax revenue, and elected officials have different policy preferences for overseeing the operations of leisure services agencies. Some local leisure services agencies are designed to generate program and facility revenue in addition to tax revenue. Others are designed to generate minimal program fee revenue, making the agency largely supported by taxes.

An example of an agency supporting itself almost entirely from tax revenue is a county park department. Many counties, such as Rock County in Wisconsin, provide county park services but no accompanying recreation services. These park systems offer parks and practically nothing else. The systems are almost entirely supported by taxes, and their budgets look like miniature versions of the national park or the state park system. Other counties, such as Milwaukee County in Wisconsin, provide not only parks but also an array of services that include facility rentals, golf courses, marinas, and swimming pools, all of which generate substantial user fees. Systems such as those in Milwaukee County and Rock County have financial statements that look very different from each other, and for that matter, they have very different budget processes.

A West Virginia study on political autonomy identified a range of political autonomies that were held by municipal park and recreation departments (Anderson 1986). The study showed that if the boards and administrators of the park and recreation departments had high levels of **autonomy** (i.e., the ability to act on their own without seeking approval from a city manager or city council, for example), they tended to use that autonomy aggressively to charge program and facility fees. If they had low levels of autonomy, the city councils tended to suppress program fees because they thought it would be politically popular to do so.

An intuitive hypothesis might be that leisure services delivery systems in traditionalistic political environments are either uniformly low or uniformly high. The West Virginia study shows, though, that even within a statewide traditionalistic delivery system, there can be differences in levels of autonomy and therefore differences in how revenues are generated. Those differences manifest themselves in different financial reporting systems.

In moralistic systems such as Wisconsin, there can be similar differences in levels of autonomy as well. In Wisconsin, there are municipalities that provide autonomy to their park and recreation departments by segregating the department's financial resources into various funds. This segregation of funds partitions the money of the park and recreation department from the money of other municipal departments. But individualistic states such as Illinois have uniformly higher levels of autonomy that permit local governments to set their own fees for services and create their own accounting systems to manage their revenues (Emanuelson 2007a).

When the park and recreation department raises revenues through fees, if there is a fund balance at the end of the year, it stays with the park and recreation fund. For the communities that operate the park and recreation department from the general fund, any fund balance at the end of the year stays in the general fund and can be used for purposes other than leisure services. This suggests that the construction of financial statements makes a difference at the local level. Such is not the case at the national and state levels, where there is no point to maintaining separate funds for leisure services. Leisure services at the federal and state levels are largely tax supported, and financial management is a process of expending the resources provided by the legislative bodies. Financial management in local government leisure services is a very different animal.

The form of financial reports depends on whether municipalities segregate or do not segregate their leisure services. Associated politics of budgeting can differ as well, if segregation of the finances of the park and recreation department is accompanied by an increase in board and administrative autonomy to set user fee policy.

Special districts have far fewer autonomy differences because park and forest preserve districts are already autonomous governmental units. The issue is whether the elected board allows the administrator and staff to set fees or whether that policy-making authority is retained by the board.

Budgeting Process at the Local Level

Budgeting at the local level varies depending upon the structure of government as well as the level of autonomy of a leisure services agency. Special-purpose leisure services districts in individualistic states typically have their own dedicated taxing authority, only limiting their budget authority by the amount of resources available to them. Leisure services agencies that are departments within general-purpose governments can have different budgeting processes with different levels of autonomy.

The availability of financial resources for leisure services agencies within municipal and county governments that have home rule authority is less of an issue because the elected officials that ultimately approve the budget can theoretically tax the citizens of the community at whatever level the elected officials choose. But in reality, there are political consequences that serve as de facto political boundaries to overtaxing community residents.

Leisure Services Departments of General-Purpose Governments

The budgeting process for park departments of counties, particularly ones that generate little in user charges, is one where the county council decides what it can afford to spend on parks from the general fund. The city council or county board adopts a resolution in each budget cycle regarding how much the park department is allowed to spend, and that spending level depends on the political influence exerted to increase or decrease the park department budget.

The budget process for county or municipal departments that generate substantial user fees has a somewhat different dynamic. For departments that generate substantial user fees, the budget process includes discussions about the level of user fees that should be charged and whether those fees should offset taxes that can go to support services provided by departments that cannot generate fees as readily, such as the public works, police, or fire departments.

Politics enter the budgeting process in two ways. The first is through opportunities for the public to complain about taxes and fees. The second is that elected officials making the tax and fee decisions need to stand for reelection if they expect to continue to serve. These political dynamics are unique to governmental units. Unlike nonprofit organizations and businesses, where boards are self-appointed and board meetings are not public, the opportunity for the public to apply pressure to public boards changes everything.

For instance, when it comes to user charges, when businesses and nonprofit organizations determine the charges, the main consideration is what the market will bear. If business or nonprofit organizations set their fees too high, customers won't pay, and the organizations will have to shut their doors due to lack of revenue. In government, the fees that the elected boards are willing to charge for leisure services, or for any governmental service for that matter, could be perfectly reasonable. The market could bear the user charges, but people who simply don't want to pay those charges could apply political pressure on the elected officials to charge less. With the desire to be popular or to avoid the pain of political conflict, elected officials often charge less for fees than the market will bear because the real criteria is that user fees are set at what the political process will bear.

Political negotiation for user fees is an ongoing process. Elected county, city, village, and township councils may retain the responsibility of setting user charges for leisure services, or they may delegate that responsibility to the advisory boards and administrators (Anderson 1986). It just depends on the political culture of the community.

The issue of whether the state within which the local government resides allows for a dedicated property or sales tax is another issue that affects the budgeting process of leisure services departments. In states such as Wisconsin, which have no dedicated property tax at the municipal level and where the municipalities rely on substantial revenue sharing from the state, every budget cycle for leisure services departments is an adventure. Because revenue sharing is dependent upon the economy, when state revenues are lower than the previous year, there is not as much revenue to share with municipalities. During those years, municipalities need to cut their overall budgets, and one of the first places they look to cut is leisure services.

For states such as Indiana, which have dedicated park and recreation property taxes, their budgeting process is less adventurous. Since the dedicated property tax revenues cannot be used for purposes other than leisure services, there is less opportunity for the park and recreation budget to be cut. And since property tax revenues are relatively stable, funding of leisure services is stable.

In states such as Missouri, where there is a dedicated sales tax supporting leisure services, the budgeting process of municipal park and recreation departments is less stable than in states where municipalities can levy dedicated property taxes, but it is not as unstable as in states where there is no dedicated property tax. The reason the budgeting process for departments with dedicated sales taxes is more of a challenge is that sales tax revenues fluctuate with the economy.

Role of the Leisure Services Board

Just as the 50 states provide local governments with various abilities to provide leisure services by taxing their residents, the states provide municipal department oversight boards with various levels of authority. In Indiana, where there is a dedicated property tax for leisure services, the appointed board that oversees the park and recreation department has a great deal of authority over the operations of the department. In Wisconsin, where there is no dedicated property for leisure services, the appointed board is strictly advisory.

Although a lot of things in government don't make sense, it does make sense that Indiana permits more oversight by the appointed board and less by the elected city council. Because there is a dedicated tax, elected officials have less discretion in the budgeting process, and they don't need oversight. In Wisconsin, it makes sense that the appointed board is advisory because, without a dedicated property tax rate, the elected officials must decide how leisure services are funded. Since user fees

© Photodisc/Getty Images

Many factors, such as political influence, sales and property taxes, and revenue sharing, can determine whether funding for leisure services is stable or unpredictable. A tour guide's salary might be cut if revenues decline.

affect the allocation of county or municipality taxes, in Wisconsin the elected officials set the user fees. In Indiana, where there is a dedicated leisure services tax, the appointed board sets user fees.

The same is true in states such as Missouri, where there are dedicated sales taxes. In these states, the appointed boards overseeing the leisure services departments have more oversight responsibilities, as they should. As sales tax revenues fluctuate, the appointed board needs the authority to make budget adjustments.

The role of leisure services managers also varies during the budgeting process, depending on the level of authority of the appointed board. In states where leisure services departments are overseen by strictly advisory boards, typically the manager shares the budget with the advisory board but negotiates it with the city or county administrator and the elected officials' budgeting committee. In states where the appointed oversight board has more authority, the manager negotiates the budget with the appointed board and then shares it with the city or county administrator and the elected officials' budgeting committee.

The authority of the appointed board overseeing the leisure services department makes all the difference. The more authority it has, the more the elected officials rely on it to set budget policy. But legally, the elected officials have the power to approve or disapprove the decisions that the oversight board makes. In every state, the power to tax can only be decided by elected officials or the people themselves.

The politics of each municipality determine the extent of the budgeting process for a leisure services department depending on whether or not elected officials want a high degree of formality. The following is a suggested process and timeline for advancing the budget process to a January 1 start date.

September—step 1: The city manager tells the department managers to begin the budgeting process, setting deadlines for all participants.

September—step 2: The city council announces that the budget committee has the responsibility to review the departmental budgets as they become available.

October—step 3: The department managers draft program or department budgets based on plans and assumptions. The city manager reviews these drafts, providing department heads with the opportunity to make changes.

November—step 4: The budget committee of the board reviews amended drafts with the city manager and department managers, giving the department managers time to make any changes. Then, a budget draft is sent to the entire city council for review.

December—step 5: Changes from the city council are reviewed by the budget committee. If the committee agrees with the changes, it incorporates them into the final draft of the budget. If the committee does not agree with the changes, the city council is informed. Either way, the council is sent the final draft for approval.

December—step 6: The city council votes on the final budget. If the budget passes, it is adopted for the new fiscal year. If the budget is rejected, it is sent back to the budget committee for revision, with the understanding that the fiscal year will begin without an adopted budget.

The process is similar to that of nonprofit organizations but at a slightly lower level of review than nonprofit organizations would undertake. This is largely because nonprofit organizations are less sure of their revenue streams than are general-purpose governmental units. Another difference is that general-purpose governmental units tend to include a certain level of **slack**, or padding, in their budgets in order to build fund balances, which helps the financial managers sleep better at night. Padding the budget means budgeting expenditures higher than the financial manager thinks they will actually be. When expenditures do not get spent at the level they are budgeted, the surpluses create budget slack.

Budgeting Process of Leisure Services Districts

Special districts that provide leisure services are similar to special districts that provide other services, such as school districts or fire protection districts, in the way they levy taxes, charge fees, and budget for their expenditures. Their boards are elected, they have taxing authority allowed by the state, and they have a level of responsibility to be transparent to the public.

Leisure services districts are permitted to levy an array of property taxes, including a tax to maintain parks, another to provide recreation services, and still others for employee retirement, for liability insurance, and even for auditing their financial records. Leisure services districts, such as those in the Illinois park district system, are created by referenda, which authorize the districts to collect one or several of these taxes. If a district wants to expand its taxing authority, it can do so only by voter approval.

Because the boards are elected by the voters, there is no need for park district managers to go to a higher level for budget authorization. The process typically begins with the authorization of the annual **tax levy**, or the amount of taxes to be collected or raised. Every state that has leisure services districts has a slightly different timeline for levy authorization, but most of them are between December 1 and January 31 each year.

The levy is stated in an ordinance, or law, that leisure services district boards must approve, telling the county tax collector or treasurer the total amount of property taxes to collect from homeowners and businesses. Once approved, the levy ordinance goes to the county treasurer or collector, who issues property tax bills to be paid the following spring. The money is forwarded to the district from the county once it has been collected.

The levy process usually precedes the budget process, but not always. In some states, the beginning of the fiscal year is prescribed by state statute. The fiscal year is the period in which an organization determines its financial condition, which may or may not be the same as the calendar year. Some states require their special districts to begin their fiscal years on January 1, to parallel the federal income tax year. Some states require May 1, so the fiscal year of the leisure services district begins about at the time when property tax receipts are available to be forwarded from the county. Other states allow leisure services districts to set their own fiscal years.

The determination of fiscal year starting and ending dates affects the accounting process in two ways. Regardless of whether an agency is accruing its receipts and expenditures under the GASB standards, the availability and measurability of receipts and expenditures are an issue. If a leisure services special district takes in golf, swimming, and summer athletic revenues in May, it might be better to begin the fiscal year sooner rather than later. On a cash basis, it is easier to match revenues with expenditures because revenues and expenditures will show up in financial reports at the same time. On an accrual basis, it's just easier not to have to accrue as many transactions.

The difference between special districts and municipal leisure services departments is that municipalities are less likely to consider just user fees from leisure services in setting their start and end dates for the fiscal year. Water and sewer fees generate much more revenue than do leisure services fees. In addition, municipalities need to consider the receipt of revenue sharing from state government. Special districts receive far less.

As was the case for the nonprofit budget period, special districts and general-purpose governments need time, sometimes called *lead time*, to gather data and prepare the budget. Assuming a leisure services district has a fiscal year of May 1, the following represents a process and timeline for presenting, reviewing, and approving the operating budget of a leisure services governmental unit.

January—step 1: Planning begins with the executive director meeting with the operating managers to assign responsibilities and timelines for departmental budget submissions.

February—step 2: The executive director reviews the budget submissions, makes adjustments, and delivers them to the elected board.

March—step 3: The board reviews that budget and submits changes to the executive director.

April—step 4: The board approves the final budget.

The process is simpler than the municipal process because there is less to decide. Leisure services districts have less competition between departments for financial resources than do general-purpose governments. Leisure services district managers have more autonomy than do leisure services department heads of municipalities, and elected leisure district board members have more authority to set fees than even the most autonomous appointed municipal leisure services board. In addition, budgeting is incremental, which means budgets are not written from scratch each year but represent amended versions of the budget from the previous year, as discussed in chapter 6. What has not been considered is that incremental budgeting is one of the greatest challenges to improving government leisure services that local leisure services professionals face.

Incremental budgeting says that the budget will only be changed around the margins; nothing big or new can be expected this year or next year. In traditionalistic and moralistic political cultures, incremental budgeting provides the excuse that proponents of the public choice model need in order to stifle funding for public leisure services. In traditionalistic states, where the status quo is king, the argument is that this is no time to change, no matter if the leisure services agency wants to increase taxes or fees. In moralistic states, the argument is that it would be unfair to others to change.

Only in individualistic states, where it is every person for herself, do publicly provided leisure services have opportunities to grow and catch up to other governmental services in terms of their funding and, ultimately, their importance. It is no coincidence that a relative handful of states including Illinois, Colorado, and California, all of which have leisure services districts, have won over half of the Gold Medal Awards for Excellence in Park and Recreation Management.

It takes more than money to be a good manager, but the ability to use money wisely often sets the good manager apart from the mediocre one. Political autonomy helps provide that money, and political culture provides the autonomy.

SUMMARY

There are profound differences in the accounting and financial management of federal, state, and local government agencies that provide leisure services. Federal leisure agencies are subject to the appropriation and expenditure process, with a focus on expenditures rather than revenues. The political challenge is to gain political advantage in budget appropriations, and one way to do that is by making use of iron triangles of alliances among elected officials, bureaucrats, and interest groups.

The financial processes of state leisure services agencies are similar to those at the federal level, except less money is at stake and the state cannot print its own money supply. In addition, there is the challenge that states have specific political cultures, some of which are friendlier to publicly provided leisure services than others.

Financial management of leisure services at the local level is much more complex because an element of revenue management is present. But again, the political culture of the state becomes an issue because local governments are the creation of state legislatures.

In some states, dedicated property and sales taxes are made available to general-purpose leisure services departments. In others, special districts are permitted by referenda. In states that permit the creation of these leisure services districts, there are more agencies and higher service levels.

Visit the Web Resource

For case studies, sample financial statements, key terms, and more, please visit the web resource at www.HumanKinetics.com/LeisureServicesFinancialManagement

chapter 10

Government-Sector Accounting

Learning Outcomes

After completing this chapter, students will be able to do the following:

- Recognize GASB financial reporting.
- Describe how GASB fund accounting is different than FASB accounting.
- Read and understand comprehensive annual financial reports (CAFRs) produced by local governments.
- Determine how the CAFR can be utilized by leisure services financial managers.
- Identify how budget and actual reports help leisure services financial managers control costs and manage revenues.

A challenge of working in the public sector is the public scrutiny of how taxpayer dollars are spent. Sometimes decisions generate a lot of heat, depending on whom you please and whom you upset. Survival can be the name of the game in the public sector. The easiest way to survive is to be a good manager, providing a high level of services at a reasonable cost to your constituents.

An important measure of success for a public leisure services manager is the ability to keep track of the public's money and make decisions that have a positive impact on the bottom line. Remember, the ability to deliver great park and recreational services to the public can only be accomplished when finances are in order.

The skills necessary for keeping track of the public's money are relatively basic. You need to understand how to read financial statements, what they mean, and what actions to take when you find a problem. That's the purpose of this chapter: to teach future leisure services managers how to keep track of public money.

THE GASB AND THE FASB

Understanding that governments follow different accounting principles than those that guide business and nonprofit organizations is a first step to becoming a good leisure services manager. Grasping the evolution of how this came to be can provide a basis for understanding why the accounting principles that guide government accounting are a moving picture rather than a still photograph.

It's not just a matter of learning the principles in this textbook—it's recognizing that government accounting will continue to change in response to the public's need to know and that financial managers in the public sector must stay current with those changes. The boards setting standards will continue to seek ways of making governmental accounting and financial management more transparent. As mentioned previously, these boards are the Governmental Accounting Standards Board (GASB) and the Financial Accounting Standards Board (FASB).

The Difference Between the FASB and the GASB

There was not always a standardized method of governmental accounting, nor was there always a standardized method of business accounting. In the beginning, oversight of business accounting was a disjointed process. It became more formalized during the economic boom of the 1920s, the stock market crash of 1929, and the Great Depression that followed. Because of the economic trauma of the Great Depression, by the mid-1930s, both the financial community and the federal government had responded to the obvious need for uniform accounting standards, particularly for the financial statements of publicly traded corporations.

Recognizing that it was important to create a standardized set of accounting principles to help investors understand the risks before they invested in a company, the AICPA Committee on Accounting Procedure assumed the role of setting financial accounting standards in 1939. For the subsequent 30 years, accounting principles were defined and refined by the AICPA.

In 1971, a special AICPA committee was created to review the process of setting business accounting principles. The committee suggested that the AICPA turn over the role of setting accounting standards to an autonomous body. In 1973, the FASB was established within the AICPA. The FASB was ultimately incorporated as a nonprofit organization, independent from the AICPA.

Through the Securities and Exchange Commission (SEC), the federal government ratified the role of the FASB in promulgating financial accounting and reporting principles, standards, and practices. From that point on, the FASB became the final authority for business and nonprofit accounting standards.

During the first 10 years of the FASB, it became apparent that many of the principles that applied to business accounting could not be applied to governmental accounting, and thus a similar standards board for governmental units was needed. In 1984, the GASB was established to develop a standardized reporting model to address problems that arose during the evolution of fund-based accounting in the 1920s. As discussed in earlier chapters, this period was considered the reform era of government.

Government fund accounting was a direct result of earlier budgeting efforts to segregate tax and fee receipts, deriving from the preeminence of the budget. The GASB was created because the constituents of state and local governments wanted assurances that spending would not exceed the authorized amounts. The GASB was established following the principle that "the accounting system and resulting financial reports must be designed to provide that information" (Granof and Wardlow 2003, p. 10).

The FASB and GASB have continued to define and refine accounting standards since their inceptions. Whereas the GASB is the primary overseer of accounting principles for state and local governments, the FASB continues to oversee certain aspects of governmental financial management. One aspect is the oversight of government enterprises, also known as **proprietary funds**. Proprietary funds are very much like business funds using FASB accounting guidelines.

As state and local governments have evolved, elected officials have come to recognize that certain services need taxpayer support, but others can sustain themselves with **program fees**. Municipal water systems are an example of enterprises supported by program fees. Most municipalities charge a fair price for providing water to their residents, which covers the operating costs of providing the water as well as the capital costs of providing the infrastructure.

A city water system, then, is much like a business in that it is possible to cover direct and indirect costs with revenues, even though most people would consider a city water system to be a monopoly that doesn't compete in the marketplace the way businesses do. Nevertheless, because a city water system is similar to a business, the GASB has decided that FASB

If a park district cultural center charges fees to cover the costs of art supplies (among other expenses), the organization must follow FASB accounting standards.

accounting principles should be applied to the presentation of financial reports. As a result, state and local governments that have fee-supported enterprises use both GASB and FASB accounting standards in the preparation of their annual financial reports. Leisure services provided by state and local governments can also use both sets of standards.

For instance, government-operated water parks, golf courses, fitness centers, tennis and racquetball facilities, or any other type of facility charging fees that cover the direct and indirect cost of providing those services use FASB accounting standards. The same leisure services governmental units may operate public parks, senior centers, or recreation facilities that do not charge any fees for services, relying on taxpayer support. The accounting for these services follows GASB standards.

The FASB accounting standards have already been presented in this textbook, as have the financial reports that are generated. This chapter focuses on the GASB standards and how they apply to leisure services financial management at the local level. Most of the examples are derived from county and local governmental units because there is opportunity at the local level to manage these financial reports that does not exist at the state or federal level.

GASB Objectives

Under the accounting standards for financial accounting as prescribed by the FASB, revenues have become a measure of how the business entity is meeting a social need. Under the GASB, that relationship does not exist because the relationship is not transactional. The **matching concept**, the idea that the expenses of a business must be matched with its revenues, is not the case for governmental units. Taxes may support part or all of certain governmental services. To meet certain social needs, governmental units may provide services with or without corresponding fees, changing the purpose of GASB financial reports compared with FASB reports.

The difference between the missions of the FASB and GASB is the difference between the purposes of the entities for which they prescribe accounting standards. The FASB prescribes accounting standards for entities that provide services for which people are willing and able to pay. The GASB prescribes accounting standards for entities that provide services for which people may not be willing and able to pay.

One of the other differences between the GASB and the FASB is their objectives. GASB reporting has the goal of accountability that the FASB does not have. Businesses are accountable to their stockholders and potential stockholders, whereas governmental units are accountable to their constituents.

Citizens have the right to know that financial reports should provide information to determine if the governmental unit has revenues sufficient to pay for the services it provides, a concept called **interperiod equity**. Citizens have the right to know if the financial resources gathered by the governmental unit were used in accordance with the governmental unit's budget, a concept called **budgetary and fiscal compliance**. And citizens have the right to know the **service efforts, costs, and accomplishments** of the governmental unit.

On the other hand, FASB accounting and financial reporting goals are to inform investors of the level of risk their investments will incur. The goals of both the GASB and the FASB are that governmental financial reports should assist citizens in evaluating the overall operating results of the governmental unit for the fiscal year and tell the public whether the governmental unit is able to meet its financial obligations as they come due.

GASB and FASB Standards

The fact that leisure services use both FASB and GASB accounting standards is a function of how diverse leisure services are and how some leisure services can be provided exclusively for fees and others cannot. Local government leisure agencies provide some recreational services that are totally tax supported, such as the provision of parks and open space. Other recreational services are partially tax and partially fee supported, such as programs for senior citizens and special populations, and still other facilities are totally fee supported, such as golf courses and swimming pools.

Services that are entirely tax supported adhere to modified accrual accounting under the watchful eye of the GASB. Modified accrual accounting is different from cash accounting and similar to full accrual accounting. Cash accounting only records transactions where money has actually been received or disbursed. Full accrual accounting records transactions that are available and measurable. Modified accrual accounting records transactions that are available and measurable, but it does not depreciate fixed assets, recording them in different funds.

Full accrual accounting is used by local government leisure services when the facilities or services are supposed to be self-sustaining. Golf

Cutting the Park and Recreation Budget

In 2011, the City of Roseville, California, like many other local governmental units, experienced stagnant economic conditions that suppressed tax revenues. Drops in development-related impact fees and property and sales taxes required the city to make a series of thoughtful cuts to balance the budget. As often occurs, the park and recreation department was the first place city officials looked to make cuts and seek additional sources of revenue. The city officials eliminated or reduced some programs and services, including the following:

- Reduced $900,000 in expenditures for materials, supplies, travel, and unfunded vacant positions
- Eliminated services that did not meet the criteria for being a core service
- Reduced overall program expenditures
- Reduced agency operating hours to make better use of staff time
- Eliminated some highly subsidized programs
- Reduced overall staffing levels
- Reduced or deferred maintenance of parks and facilities
- Increased program fees by an average of 5 percent
- Added revenue-generating programs where demand was present

Through its website, the park and recreation department informed the public that the programs to be eliminated or cut included the bookmobile, sport center café, synchronized swim teams, soccer and softball concessions, and more. Other programs that were eliminated were those that could not pay their direct operating costs, including all ski trips, a football tournament, adult baseball, dive-in movies, basketball and swimming programs, and more.

Many public leisure services providers have been forced to cut park and recreation services, taking a more businesslike approach by focusing on increasing their revenues and eliminating unaffordable expenses. In the case of Roseville, the agencies are forced to go on without providing the previous high level of services. But in other cases, budget cutbacks permit these public leisure services agencies to take a fresh look at their missions, determine where they would like to go in the future, and set a course in that direction. Some agencies do so even before they are forced to.

References

City of Roseville. 2012. "Parks & Recreation Budget: Planning for Uncertain Economic Times." Accessed January 29, 2012. www.roseville.ca.us/parks/contact_us/budget.asp.

courses should generate enough money to support their operating costs and overhead. If not, and a leisure services agency is willing to use tax money to underwrite the operations of the golf course, the leaders of the agency likely do not have the political will to charge a **fair price** for the service.

Economically, not charging a fair price for golf means the governmental leisure services agency will use tax money to underwrite the costs of the services, providing a competitive advantage against privately owned golf courses, which obviously cannot underwrite their costs with tax money. Politically, underwriting golf services with tax money puts the local government leisure services agency in the position of being criticized for misusing tax money to put a taxpaying golf course out of business.

For economic and political reasons, most publicly owned golf courses are run as **enterprises** and use FASB accounting methods. This means that the playing field is level. The public entity has made a decision to play fair with the privately owned golf courses against which it competes. For a public agency to run a golf course as an enterprise, it must segregate revenues and expenses into a separate fund, called an *enterprise fund* or *proprietary fund*, and apply FASB accounting principles to it, including depreciation of fixed assets. That financial structure forces the public leisure services agency to charge a fair price for golf services.

When there is no urgency to charge a price for leisure services that cover operating and overhead costs, or when there simply is little opportunity to do so, the GASB accounting principles apply. In the case of park services, it would be difficult for a municipal or county agency to charge admission to all of its park facilities. And if it did, the fees might discourage people from using the facilities. That's why it has become a tradition in this and other countries that parks are generally entirely tax supported.

It is possible (and desirable) to charge some fees for leisure services but not enough to cover all of the overhead costs. For instance, local governmental senior citizen programs often provide trips to points of interest, such as theaters or casinos. Seniors are usually required to pay a fee to go on the trip, which covers the bus cost, the wages of the trip supervisor, and admissions. But the trip fees rarely cover the share cost of the administrator, office help, infrastructure, or any other overhead costs required to put the trip together.

FASB objectives applied to local government enterprise funds are similar to GASB objectives for local governments, including the goal of providing useful information to stakeholders to determine the financial condition of the entity (Granof and Wardlow 2003). Because local governmental agencies use both full and modified accrual accounting, leisure services managers need to be familiar with both.

The methods have begun to merge of late. For example, GASB Statement 34, adopted in June of 1999, recommends that local governments provide financial reports that are more businesslike in their presentation, and it requires local governments to provide unified statements of net assets that are similar to FASB corporate balance sheets.

ANNUAL FINANCIAL REPORTS

Annual financial reports are the cornerstone of financial reporting under GASB accounting principles. State governments require local governments to provide annual financial reports with a number of statements within them that achieve the GASB goals presented earlier in this chapter. Among these reports are the statements of net assets, statements of activities, balance sheets, and **statements of revenues, expenditures, and changes in fund balance**.

The GASB requires that each of these financial statements be presented using modified accrual and full accrual accounting, depending on whether the fund is a governmental unit or an enterprise. The GASB typically does not review the financial reports of the 87,000 local governmental units, though. That responsibility falls on the state government that created the local unit of government. Each state discharges its responsibilities differently.

Comprehensive Annual Financial Reports

The GASB requires at least an **annual financial report (AFR)** but prefers a **comprehensive annual financial report (CAFR)** at the end of the fiscal year of a local governmental unit. The distinction between an AFR and a CAFR is that a CAFR is accounting done by the book and an AFR is accounting with a few things left out. It is easier to understand the difference by understanding a CAFR first.

A CAFR is a report that comprises three chapters: introduction, financial, and statistical. The first is the introductory chapter, which contains a **letter of transmittal**, essentially a document from the chief administrative and chief financial officers of the governmental unit summarizing what the unit did during the fiscal year. Most letters are several pages long, making it impractical to reproduce them here. But if there is no letter of transmittal in the financial report, it cannot be called *comprehensive*. It is an AFR rather than a CAFR.

The other elements of the introductory chapter of a CAFR are a listing of the elected and appointed officials of the governmental unit, the **organizational chart** of governmental departments, and a copy of the Certificate of Achievement for Excellence in Financial Reporting for the previous fiscal year issued by the Government Finance Officers Association (GFOA), if the governmental unit was awarded such an honor.

The organizational chart is a straightforward concept. It is a picture of the hierarchy of the organization, including the lines of authority and responsibility. The organizational chart for the fictional City of Fiesta, New Jersey (figure 10.1), was presented in its 2012 CAFR and shows that the city operates a park and recreation department, which has four divisions: recreation, park maintenance, special events, and shade-tree services.

Following the organizational chart is the list of elected officials. The list does not show appointed park and recreation board members, or any other commission, for that matter; it just includes the

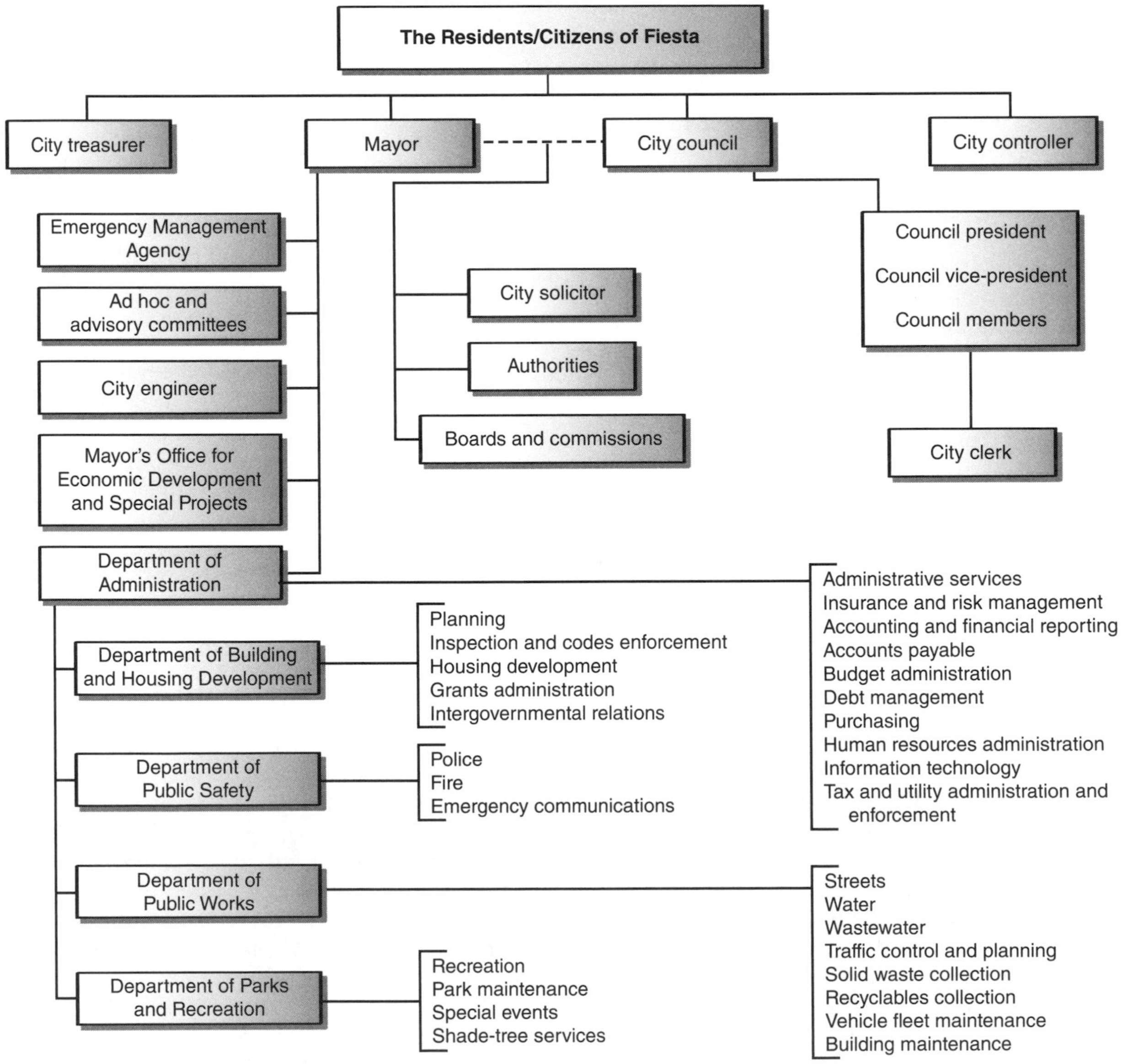

Figure 10.1 The organizational chart of the City of Fiesta, New Jersey.

mayor, city council treasurer, and comptroller. The choice of whether to include appointed officials is entirely up to the governmental unit. Since most local governments want to keep the list to one page of the introductory section, larger governments do not include appointed officials, but small governments often do.

Fiesta received a Certificate of Achievement for Excellence in Financial Reporting for the previous fiscal year. More and more local governments are receiving these certificates, showing that compliance with GASB accounting principles is becoming more widely accepted. When they do receive one, they proudly display it in the introductory section of their CAFR. Figure 10.2 shows the certificate awarded to the City of Harrisburg, Pennsylvania, for the 2007 fiscal year.

The second section of a CAFR is the financial section. Leisure services managers must have the ability to read these financial reports. A basic level of understanding is the ability to differentiate between CAFRs and AFRs.

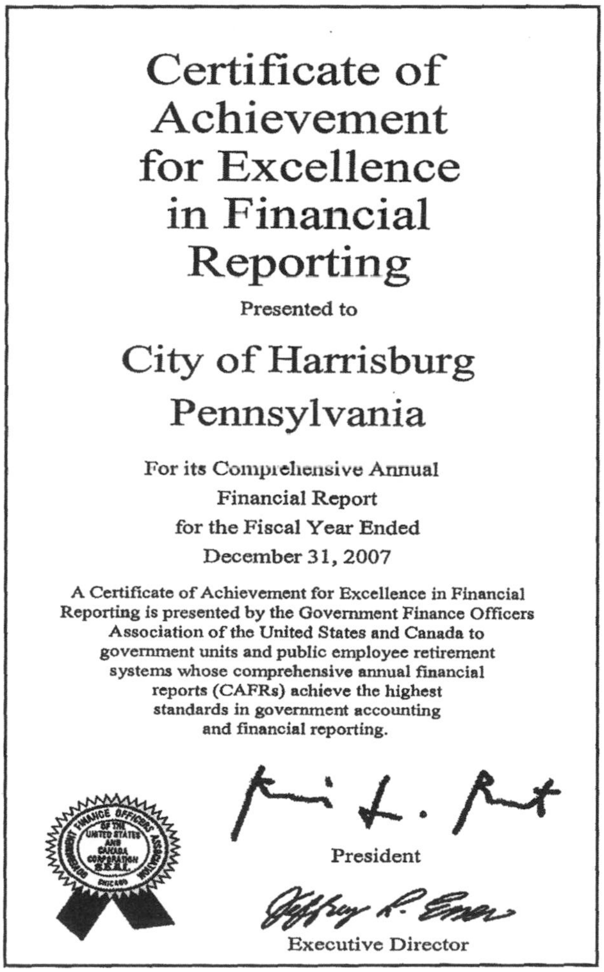

Certificate of Achievement for Excellence in Financial Reporting

Presented to

City of Harrisburg Pennsylvania

For its Comprehensive Annual Financial Report for the Fiscal Year Ended December 31, 2007

A Certificate of Achievement for Excellence in Financial Reporting is presented by the Government Finance Officers Association of the United States and Canada to government units and public employee retirement systems whose comprehensive annual financial reports (CAFRs) achieve the highest standards in government accounting and financial reporting.

President

Executive Director

Figure 10.2 The Certificate of Achievement for Excellence in Financial Reporting that Harrisburg, Pennsylvania, received for the 2007 fiscal year.
Reprinted, by permission, from City of Harrisburg, PA.

For a financial report to be a CAFR, not an AFR, it must contain the specified reports in its financial section that the GASB requires. Before presenting these reports, the GASB requires a letter be presented from the firm that audited the financial report. The letter from the auditor must say that the governmental unit followed GAAP and that the report is a fair representation of the financial position and activities that occurred during the fiscal year, preferably without any reservations.

If the auditor expresses minor reservations, she will usually accompany that statement with another that says the reservations do not impede the financial reports contained in the CAFR from being fair representations of the financial position of the governmental unit. If there are serious reservations, though, the auditor must state them or be in violation of her own code of ethics. Minor reservations might include headings on financial reports. Serious reservations might include major misstatements of financial positions.

The letter from the auditor of the City of Harrisburg, Pennsylvania (2008), shows that the auditing firm gave the city a clean bill of health in the presentation of its financial statements: "In our opinion, based on our audit and the report of other auditors, the financial statements . . . present fairly, in all material respects, the respective financial position of the governmental activities, the business-type activities, the aggregate discretely presented component units, each major fund, and the aggregate remaining fund information of the City . . . in conformity with accounting principles generally accepted in the United States of America" (p. 30). The letter also shows the auditors to be candid in their pronouncements, particularly regarding which financial entities within the municipality they did not audit.

Statements of Net Assets

The first financial report to be presented in the financial section of the CAFR is always the statement of net assets, which shows the overall financial condition of the governmental unit in a businesslike presentation. The statement of net assets has been added to the CAFR since GASB Statement 34 determined that every CAFR was required to contain one. Fiesta's 2012 statement is presented from its CAFR.

The elements of the statement of net assets are similar to those of a balance sheet in business accounting. On the asset side, they include cash, investments, receivables, capital assets, and deferred charges. On the liability side, they include accounts payable, long-term liabilities, and deferred revenue. The net remaining is the difference between total assets and total liabilities.

The statement of net assets is presented in two ways. One is the statement of net assets for governmental activities and the other is for business-type activities. What services local governments finance through each type is up to them; leisure services can be in both. But when comingled with other departments, it's difficult to know the financial condition of leisure services agencies. The solution would be for municipalities to create separate funds for leisure services. Some municipalities do, but most don't.

There are government structures, such as special districts, that only provide parks and recreation, but such is not the case for Fiesta, where park and recreation services are buried in the financial statements, as supported by the statement of net assets (table 10.1) and the balance sheet.

Statements of net assets are combined reports that apply business accounting principles to governmental accounting. Similar to a business balance sheet, the categories of assets and liabilities include totals that can be seen on a balance sheet. But statements of net assets are recent phenomena, resulting from GASB Statement 34.

One reason the GASB requires statements of net assets is because private-sector lending institutions that purchased debt from governmental units

Table 10.1 City of Fiesta, New Jersey, Statement of Net Assets (December 31, 2012)

	PRIMARY GOVERNMENT				
	Governmental activities	Business-type activities	Total	Component units	Total
	ASSETS				
Cash and cash equivalents	$10,270,721	$4,610,640	$14,881,361	$10,418,620	$25,299,981
Investments, at fair value	4,386,405	1,543,559	5,929,964	—	5,929,964
Receivables, net of allowance for uncollectible accounts					
Taxes	6,766,244	—	6,766,244	—	6,766,244
Accounts	235,408	3,184,573	3,419,981	5,594,556	9,014,537
Loans	6,805,595	—	6,805,595	—	6,805,595
Other	185,234	—	185,234	21,800	207,034
Internal balances	(477,222)	477,222	—	—	—
Due from component unit	822,037	243,159	1,065,196	—	1,065,196
Due from primary government	—	—	—	2,340,676	2,340,676
Assets held for sale	1,727,384	—	1,727,384	—	1,727,384
Other assets	147,526	920,968	1,068,494	166,238	1,234,732
Restricted assets					
Cash and cash equivalents	1,298,399	2,159	1,300,558	—	1,300,558
Cash with fiscal agents	—	—	—	4,171,731	4,171,731
Investments, at fair value	3,664,822	10,213,205	13,878,027	84,425,578	98,303,605
Litigation settlement receivable	—	—	—	5,415,000	5,415,000
Accrued interest receivable	—	—	—	21,509	21,509
Future lease rentals receivable from primary government	—	—	—	4,830,416	4,830,416
Capital assets, not being depreciated	25,307,096	9,068,508	34,375,604	19,934,361	54,309,965
Capital assets, less accumulated depreciation and amortization	88,607,388	37,438,666	126,046,054	231,931,455	357,977,509
Equitable ownership interest	—	—	—	14,000,500	14,000,500
Deferred charges, net of accumulated amortization	—	—	—	21,524,841	21,524,841
Total assets	**$149,747,037**	**$67,702,659**	**$217,449,696**	**$404,797,281**	**$622,246,977**

	PRIMARY GOVERNMENT				
	Governmental activities	Business-type activities	Total	Component units	Total
		LIABILITIES			
Accounts payable and other current liabilities	$2,372,069	$261,140	$2,633,209	$1,819,549	$4,452,758
Matured bond coupons	20,097	—	20,097	—	20,097
Accrued liabilities	3,030,681	173,511	3,204,192	—	3,204,192
Due to primary government	—	—	—	923,074	923,074
Due to component unit	387,667	2,095,131	2,482,798	—	2,482,798
Unearned revenue	14,049,484	—	14,049,484	643,096	14,692,580
Liabilities payable from restricted assets	—	—	—	16,120,474	16,120,474
Noncurrent liabilities					
Due within one year	13,819,576	3,558,461	17,378,037	12,424,977	29,803,014
Due in more than one year	105,244,439	12,955,387	118,199,826	552,883,259	671,083,085
Other postemployment benefits	12,697,698	605,472	13,303,170	—	13,303,170
Deferred revenue	—	—	—	5,763,821	5,763,821
Accrued landfill closure and postclosure liability	—	—	—	2,270,163	2,270,163
Total liabilities	**$151,621,711**	**$19,649,102**	**$171,270,813**	**$592,848,413**	**$764,119,226**
		NET ASSETS			
Invested in capital assets, net of related debt	$30,518,850	$34,753,854	$65,272,704	($163,625,152)	($98,352,448)
Restricted for:					
Highways and streets	203,308	—	203,308	—	203,308
Culture and recreation	861,055	—	861,055	—	861,055
Debt service	—	658,397	658,397	16,579,776	17,238,173
Capital projects	—	6,386,545	6,386,545	3,895,146	10,281,691
Guarantee agreement	—	—	—	295,358	295,358
Water operations	—	—	—	4,091,374	4,091,374
Other	65,658	—	65,658	—	65,658
Unrestricted	(33,523,545)	6,254,761	(27,268,784)	(49,287,634)	(76,556,418)
Total net assets	**($1,874,674)**	**$48,053,557**	**$46,178,883**	**($188,051,132)**	**($141,872,249)**

The accompanying notes are an integral part of these financial statements.

had trouble reading CAFRs and understanding the level of risk they would incur in lending money to the government agency. The statement of net assets tells private-sector financial analysts what they need to know.

Balance Sheets

Before statements of net assets were required of governmental units, the GASB required balance sheet summaries that complied with GASB transparency guidelines. The problem was, balance sheet reports told the public what it needed to know, but they did not tell lenders what they needed to know; hence, GASB Statement 34. So as not to deprive the public of the level of transparency it deserves, the GASB continues to require balance sheets to be presented in CAFRs, such as the example from Fiesta's CAFR (table 10.2).

The balance sheet may seem a bit confusing at first or even redundant with the statement of net assets, but it's not. To show the differences, another CAFR needs to be presented, the reconciliation report (table 10.3). The reconciliation report shows that the statement of net assets includes a number of items that were not included on the balance sheet. Among them are items that are included on business balance sheets, such as depreciated fixed assets, accrued debt, and accrued employee benefits. The result is that by

Table 10.2 City of Fiesta, New Jersey, Balance Sheet—Governmental Funds (December 31, 2012)

	General	Grant programs	Debt service	Capital projects	Other governmental funds	Total governmental funds
ASSETS						
Cash and cash equivalents	$4,669,898	$4,749,623	$173,811	$337,299	$340,090	$10,270,721
Investments, at fair value	3,064,865	440,498	357	4,655	876,000	4,386,405
Receivables, net of allowance for uncollectible accounts						
Taxes	6,724,157	—	—	42,087	—	6,766,244
Accounts receivable	235,408	—	—	—	—	235,408
Loans receivable	2,943,994	3,811,201	—	50,400	—	6,805,595
Other receivable	68,835	—	—	116,399	—	185,234
Due from other funds	1,570,801	685,564	—	185,998	—	2,442,363
Advances and amounts due from component units	21,854	—	—	800,183	—	822,037
Other assets	75,791	—	—	5,068	—	80,859
Restricted assets						
Cash and cash equivalents	65,658	—	—	1,232,741	—	1,298,399
Investments, at fair value	3,664,822	—	—	—	—	3,664,822
Total assets	**$23,106,113**	**$9,686,886**	**$174,168**	**$2,774,830**	**$1,216,090**	**$36,958,087**
LIABILITIES AND FUND BALANCES						
Liabilities						
Accounts payable	$750,668	$1,456,026	$—	$512	$164,863	$2,372,069
Accrued liabilities	1,445,487	17,035	—	—	—	1,462,522
Vested compensated absences	189,337	—	—	—	—	189,337
Matured bond coupons payable	—	—	20,097	—	—	20,097
Due to other funds	1,150,564	429,599	—	606,475	732,947	2,919,585
Advances and amounts due to component units	387,667	—	—	—	—	387,667
Deferred revenue	5,588,403	7,784,226	—	—	—	13,372,629
Total liabilities	**9,512,126**	**9,686,886**	**20,097**	**606,987**	**897,810**	**20,723,906**
Fund balances						
Reserved						
Encumbrances	2,688,134	—	—	61,493	—	2,749,627
Debt service	—	—	154,071	—	—	154,071
Capital projects	7,737,852	—	—	—	—	7,737,852
Workers' compensation	151,650	—	—	—	—	151,650
Revolving loan program	2,796,229	—	—	—	—	2,796,229
Unreserved, reported in						
General fund	220,122	—	—	—	—	220,122
Capital projects fund	—	—	—	2,106,350	—	2,106,350
Special revenue funds	—	—	—	—	318,280	318,280
Total fund balances	**13,593,987**	**—**	**154,071**	**2,167,843**	**318,280**	**16,234,181**
Total liabilities and fund balances	**$23,106,113**	**$9,686,886**	**$174,168**	**$2,774,830**	**$1,216,090**	**$36,958,087**

Table 10.3 City of Fiesta, New Jersey, Reconciliation of the Balance Sheet to the Statement of Net Assets (December 31, 2012)

Fund balances—total governmental funds		$16,234,181
Amounts reported for governmental activities in the statement of net assets are different because of the following.		
Capital assets used in governmental activities are not financial resources and, therefore, are not reported in the governmental funds.		
Governmental capital assets	230,387,474	
Less accumulated depreciation	(116,472,990)	113,914,484
Artifacts held for sale by the city are not financial resources and, therefore, are not reported in the governmental funds.		1,727,384
Other assets are not available to pay for current-period expenditures and, therefore, are deferred in the funds.		5,413,493
Guarantee and swap fees and bond issuance costs are deferred and amortized over the life of the guarantee, swap, or bond period but are available to pay current-period expenditures and, therefore, are not reported in the funds.		(6,023,681)
Long-term liabilities, including bonds payable, are not due and payable in the current period and, therefore, are not reported in the funds.		
Workers' compensation	(3,599,404)	
Bonds payable	(47,331,645)	
Notes payable	(50,013,240)	
Capital leases payable	(9,043,850)	
Compensated absences	(8,886,539)	
Other postemployment benefits	(12,697,698)	
Accrued interest payable	(1,568,159)	(153,140,535)
Net assets of governmental activities		($1,874,674)

The accompanying notes are an integral part of these financial statements.

showing these deductions from the fund balance of $16,234,181 on the balance sheet, a lender (and the public) can see that a better representation of financial condition of the City of Fiesta is that it has a negative fund balance of $1,874,674.

A question that comes to mind is why does the CAFR show the balance sheet report at all? A good answer is transparency. A statement of net assets is a summary report about the financial condition of the governmental unit without much additional detail. For a governmental unit to be transparent about its financial condition, a greater level of detail is needed than the statement of net assets provides. The balance sheet report provides more detail.

The question of how much detail a CAFR should show is probably a matter of opinion. Some citizens may not be interested in much detail at all. For them, the statement of net assets will suffice. For other citizens, the detail provided in the balance sheet report may satisfy them. Knowing the fund balance of each category may suffice. But for other citizens, more detail may be important, which is why the GASB has required that CAFRs have additional reports, such as the financial condition of the nongovernmental proprietary funds.

Statements of Activities

Statements of activities are similar to business income statements. The purpose of statements of activities is to show, in a summarized format, the financial activities that caused changes in the statement of net assets. Again, Fiesta is used as a model (table 10.4).

The statement of activities shows the program revenues that were received from governmental and business-type activities but not tax revenues. The report shows that program revenues fell short of covering expenses by over $44 million, largely because the $35 million cost of providing public safety (police and fire protection) had no

Table 10.4 City of Fiesta, New Jersey, Statement of Activities (Year Ended December 31, 2012)

					NET (EXPENSE) REVENUE AND CHANGES IN NET ASSETS				
		PROGRAM REVENUES			PRIMARY GOVERNMENT				
Functions/ programs	**Expenses**	**Charges for services**	**Operating grants and contributions**	**Capital grants and contributions**	**Governmental activities**	**Business-type activities**	**Total**	**Component units**	**Total**
Primary government									
Governmental activities									
General government	$11,227,267	$14,879,393	$134,317	$1,136,239	$4,922,682	$—	$4,922,682	$—	$4,922,682
Building and housing development	6,074,003	2,214,519	3,561,177	—	(298,307)	—	(298,307)	—	(298,307)
Public safety	43,249,161	4,215,536	2,619,985	990,925	(35,422,715)	—	(35,422,715)	—	(35,422,715)
Public works	9,439,071	2,375,503	963,451	—	(6,100,117)	—	(6,100,117)	—	(6,100,117)
Parks and recreation	4,797,981	175,629	2,108,139	36,114	(2,478,099)	—	(2,478,099)	—	(2,478,099)
Incinerator	—	714,171	—	—	714,171	—	714,171	—	714,171
Tourism	280,072	—	—	—	(280,072)	—	(280,072)	—	(280,072)
Interest on long-term debt	5,859,272	—	—	—	(5,859,272)	—	(5,859,272)	—	(5,859,272)
Total governmental activities	80,926,827	24,574,751	9,387,069	2,163,278	(44,801,729)	—	(44,801,729)	—	(44,801,729)
Business-type activities									
Sewer	15,093,480	15,054,421	—	1,025,582	—	986,523	986,523	—	986,523
Sanitation	3,380,182	4,204,769	137,294	—	—	961,881	961,881	—	961,881
Fiesta Falcons baseball team	677,038	715,113	—	—	—	38,075	38,075	—	38,075
Total business-type activities	19,150,700	19,974,303	137,294	1,025,582	—	1,986,479	1,986,479	—	1,986,479
Total primary government	100,077,527	44,549,054	9,524,363	3,188,860	(44,801,729)	1,986,479	(42,815,250)	—	(42,815,250)
Component units									
Fiesta Authority	65,884,629	41,127,328	—	—	—	—	—	(24,757,301)	(24,757,301)
Fiesta Parking Authority	17,769,855	12,967,547	—	—	—	—	—	(4,802,308)	(4,802,308)
Coordinated Parking Fund	7,809,802	8,229,232	—	—	—	—	—	419,430	419,430
Redevelopment Authority	5,029,764	1,528,759	304,897	250,907	—	—	—	(2,945,201)	(2,945,201)
Total component units	96,494,050	63,852,866	304,897	250,907	—	—	—	(32,085,380)	(32,085,380)
		General revenues							
		Property taxes			15,879,973	—	15,879,973	—	15,879,973
		Real estate transfer taxes			1,044,116	—	1,044,116	—	1,044,116
		Local services taxes			1,950,258	—	1,950,258	—	1,950,258
		Occupational privilege taxes			85	—	85	—	85

					NET (EXPENSE) REVENUE AND CHANGES IN NET ASSETS				
		PROGRAM REVENUES			PRIMARY GOVERNMENT				
Functions/ programs	Expenses	Charges for services	Operating grants and contributions	Capital grants and contributions	Governmental activities	Business-type activities	Total	Component units	Total
		Earned income taxes			3,810,889	—	3,810,889	—	3,810,889
		Business privilege taxes			3,980,739	—	3,980,739	—	3,980,739
		Franchise taxes			510,448	—	510,448	—	510,448
		Public utility realty taxes			36,288	—	36,288	—	36,288
		Payments in lieu of taxes			429,151	—	429,151	—	429,151
		Grants and contributions not restricted to specific functions			7,340,486	—	7,340,486	—	7,340,486
		Other income			—	—	—	942,855	942,855
		Unrestricted investment earnings			477,404	215,292	692,696	3,204,369	3,897,065
		Extraordinary item			—	—	—	3,580,909	3,580,909
		Transfers—internal activities			(349,699)	349,699	—	—	—
		Total general revenues, transfers, and extraordinary item			35,110,138	564,991	35,675,129	7,728,133	43,403,262
		Change in net assets			(9,691,591)	2,551,470	(7,140,121)	(24,357,247)	(31,497,368)
		Net assets—January 1, 2012			7,816,917	45,502,087	53,319,004	(163,693,885)	(110,374,881)
		Net assets—December 31, 2012			(1,874,674)	48,053,557	46,178,883	(188,051,132)	(141,872,249)

The accompanying notes are an integral part of these financial statements.

accompanying revenue source, suggesting that taxes would need to be that source.

The statement of activities shows that business-type activities (sewer, sanitation, and the baseball team) covered their costs. Important to leisure services financial analysis is that the park and recreation service expenditures of $4,797,981 were only offset by $175,629 in program revenues, implying that the difference needed to be made up from other sources.

Statements of Revenues, Expenditures, and Changes in Fund Balance

Just as the statement of activities shows the financial activities that changed the fund balance in the statement of net assets from one year to the next, the statement of revenues, expenditures, and changes in fund balance describes how balance sheet fund balances changed from one year to the next.

The difference between the statement of net assets and the balance sheet is the categories of assets and liabilities that are included in the report. The same difference exists between the statement of net assets and the statement of revenues, expenditures, and changes in fund balance. Some categories, such as fixed assets, are included on the statement of net assets but not on the balance sheet. Therefore, changes in fixed-asset valuation and depreciation are presented on the statements of activities but not on the statement of revenues, expenditures, and changes in fund balance.

If it sounds a little complicated, it's another example of how the GASB believes that, for governmental units to provide relatively transparent CAFRs, there needs to be a sufficient level of detail. Table 10.5 is taken from the Fiesta CAFR for the 2012 fiscal year.

The statement presents a slightly different picture of what financial activities occurred during the 2012 fiscal year compared to the previous fiscal year. For the parks and recreation department, which is listed as only a line item under expenditures, the report shows that $3,931,704 was expended during the fiscal year, of which $205,836 was spent on grant programs. The report also does not show any accompanying program revenue attributed to the parks and recreation department because it lumps all department

Table 10.5 City of Fiesta, New Jersey, Statement of Revenues, Expenditures, and Changes in Fund Balance—Governmental Funds (Year Ended December 31, 2012)

	General	Grant programs	Debt service	Capital projects	Other governmental funds	Total governmental funds
REVENUES						
Taxes	$26,836,116	$—	$—	$—	$—	$26,836,116
Licenses and permits	540,748	—	—	—	—	540,748
Intergovernmental revenue	8,629,774	7,236,075	—	—	963,451	16,829,300
Department earnings and program revenue	18,767,299	659,096	—	756,830	4,266	20,187,491
Fines and forfeits	2,109,236	—	—	—	—	2,109,236
Investment income	366,410	100,072	5,575	24,492	11,236	507,785
Miscellaneous	3,101,717	96,679	—	599,771	—	3,798,167
Total revenues	**$60,351,300**	**$8,091,922**	**$5,575**	**$1,381,093**	**$978,953**	**$70,808,843**
EXPENDITURES						
Current						
General government	$8,666,869	$832,967	$—	$—	$3,675	$9,503,511
Building and housing development	1,197,345	4,459,010	—	16,800	—	5,673,155
Public safety	28,436,434	2,365,532	—	—	—	30,801,966
Public works	5,375,162	—	—	—	912,198	6,287,360
Parks and recreation	3,725,868	205,836	—	—	—	3,931,704
Tourism	—	—	—	97,564	—	97,564
Capital outlay						
Infrastructure	—	—	—	2,245,948	—	2,245,948
Other	—	—	—	4,503,504	—	4,503,504
Debt service						
Principal retirements	764,306	185,000	9,812,151	302,248	—	11,063,705
Interest and fiscal charges	74,203	389,302	686,792	—	—	1,150,297
Total expenditures	**48,240,187**	**8,437,647**	**10,498,943**	**7,166,064**	**915,873**	**75,258,714**
Excess of revenues over (under) expenditures	12,111,113	(345,725)	(10,493,368)	(5,784,971)	63,080	(4,449,871)
Other financing sources (uses)						
Issuance of debt	—	—	—	2,400,000	—	2,400,000
Proceeds from the sale of assets	211,780	—	361,743	—	—	573,523
Transfers in	2,017,497	345,725	8,394,369	4,667,807	—	15,425,398
Transfers out	(15,018,460)	—	(84,887)	(606,160)	(65,590)	(15,775,097)
Total other financing sources (uses)	(12,789,183)	345,725	8,671,225	6,461,647	(65,590)	2,623,824
Net change in fund balances	(678,070)	—	(1,822,143)	676,676	(2,510)	(1,826,047)
Fund balances—beginning of year	14,272,057	—	1,976,214	1,491,167	320,790	18,060,228
Fund balances—end of year	$13,593,987	$—	$154,071	$2,167,843	$318,280	$16,234,181

The accompanying notes are an integral part of these financial statements.

earnings and program revenue into one category, showing $18,767,299 in fees.

The statement raises a question: How can the CAFR for the City of Fiesta be transparent to the public when it doesn't show how much money the parks and recreation department made and how much it spent? The answer is that the CAFR is not designed to do so. It is only designed to show the financial condition of the City of Fiesta. Because parks and recreation financial activities are combined with other departments, it is up to the public to ask for more information.

Under the FOIA, governmental units are required to provide the level of detail about finances that the public requests. But the fact is, few members of the public ever make such a request. They don't understand the financial reports in the CAFR of their local government, let alone wanting more information. It's important, though, for the leisure services professional to understand the financial reports. The GASB has designed the reports to be transparent, but the complexity of the reports has made them somewhat confusing.

Statistical Section

According to GASB, "there are fifteen statistical tables that a government should include in a CAFR unless the data are clearly inapplicable" (Granof and Wardlow 2003, p. 282). The statistical section supplies three important data. One is data to support the financial section of the report. The second is to show economic trends within the governmental unit, such as growth in the assessed valuation, construction revenues, or expenditures. The third is to present the type of financial analysis that financial analysts in the private sector provide for investors. Because the public and media are rarely skilled enough to provide it for governmental units, the governmental unit is expected by GASB to provide it for them.

The tables required are listed below:

- The general government functions provided by function for the last 10 years
- The general revenues of the government by source for the last 10 years
- Property tax levies and collections made by the government for the past 10 years
- The assessed and actual values of the taxable property within the government's jurisdiction for the past 10 years
- The government's property tax rates, including those of overlapping governments for the past 10 years
- Special assessments and billing collections of the government for the past 10 years
- The ratio of net general bonded debt to the government's assessed valuation and net bonded debt for the past 10 years
- The current computation of the legal debt margin
- The current computation of overlapping debt
- The ratio of the annual debt service for general bonded debt to general expenditures for the past 10 years
- Revenue bond coverage for the past 10 years
- The demographic statistics for the governmental unit
- The total property value, construction, and bank deposits for the past 10 years
- A list of the taxpayers who pay the most property tax
- Any miscellaneous statistics the governmental unit or its auditors think are important

For a CAFR to be awarded a Certificate of Achievement for Excellence in Financial Accounting by the GFOA, all of these data must be presented, a task which seems somewhat daunting. However, because governmental units maintain and share these records with each other over the years, it is only necessary to gather data for the fiscal year for which the CAFR is written. Creating the statistical section becomes more of an updating process. The section is typically unaudited by the government's CPA firm.

Understanding the CAFR

To help cut through the maze of accounting to get meaning from a CAFR, let's focus on a few understandable elements of the reports. One of these is the fund balance, and the other is cash.

The statement of revenues, expenditures, and changes in fund balance for the general fund of the City of Fiesta (table 10.5) was in excess of $13 million at the end of 2012, a reduction from the previous year's fund balance of over $14 million. That difference suggests the city is headed toward a weakened financial position. The same report shows that the combined balances of all funds declined by nearly $2 million over that period, more evidence of eroded fiscal strength.

The balance sheet (table 10.2) shows that the general fund had $4,669,898 in cash at the end of the 2012 fiscal year and all government funds had over $10 million. The cash position of Fiesta raises the issue of whether the city is solvent. The answer is that it depends on how much money the city needs to pay its bills in the near future. Most municipalities like to have cash on hand equivalent to three to six months of expenditures in the event of a catastrophe. The statement for revenues, expenditures, and changes in fund balance shows that the total annual expenditures for all governmental funds are $75,258,714, and $10,270,721 in cash in all governmental funds is less than three months' worth of cash reserves, suggesting that a catastrophe would create a cash shortfall.

What this means for the park and recreation department is that it is a department in a municipality that is at some financial risk. Because of the political dynamics discussed in earlier chapters, park and recreation services might be considered a luxury the city can't afford, particularly by fiscally conservative councilpersons. That is not to say that the park and recreation department is a risky venture, just that the financial position of the city and the political dynamics that exist in many municipalities make it a possibility.

Analysis of the CAFR suggests that one solution is for the parks and recreation department to become more dependent on program fees and less dependent on taxes. The statement of activities from the 2012 CAFR (table 10.4) shows the department only generated $175,629 in program fees. If the city gets into financial trouble and passes the pain down to the parks and recreation department, generating more program fees is an option worth considering.

As a leisure services manager, your understanding of how to read the CAFR of your municipality can help you anticipate and address the financial challenges you may face. The skill is useful not just when there are financial challenges but also when there are financial opportunities. In the case where a municipality carries large fund balances and cash reserves, you are well armed with the understanding that your municipality has access to financial resources to improve park and recreation department services.

SPECIAL DISTRICT CAFRS

Understanding leisure services government financial reports provided by special districts, such as park districts, recreation districts, forest preserve districts, or park and recreation districts, provides a different challenge than financial reports provided by general-purpose governments. Actually, they are easier to understand because providing leisure services is the special purpose for which the special district exists. The financial position of municipal park and recreation departments is much more difficult to discern within municipalities because of the comingling of departmental finances. For park districts, recreation districts, forest preserve districts, and park and recreation districts, there are departments, but they relate to the provision of leisure services.

Statements of Net Assets

A model for comparing the financial reports of special districts with those of municipalities providing leisure services is the Coast Community Regional Park District near Portland, Oregon. The Coast Community park district provides its CAFR on its website as a method of being as transparent as it possibly can.

The Coast Community Regional Park District presents a CAFR that is comparable to the City of Fiesta CAFR in every material way, including the presentation of its statement of net assets (table 10.6). The report shows the park district has over $554 million in net assets, of which nearly $138 million is in cash and investments.

Were these park and recreation services provided by the City of Portland instead of by a special district, the financial position of the park and recreation department would probably be buried in the general fund, comingled with police, fire, and other public safety services. As a special district, the financial condition of the governmental leisure services agency is clearer.

Statements of Activities

To analyze the cash position of the Coast Community Regional Park District, let's look at the statement of activities (table 10.7). Statements of activities for special districts use the same GASB format as do statements of activities for general-purpose county and municipal governments. The difference is that, as was the case for statements of net assets, the statement of activities is a summary report of multiple funds.

To understand how each of the funds performed, the statement of revenues, expenditures, and changes in fund balance must be compared against the balance sheet. The Coast Community statement of activities shows that, during the 2012 fiscal year, expenses exceeded program revenues by $79,773,720. That finding suggests that the remainder was made up by taxes, because the overall net assets for the year began at about $507 million and ended at nearly $555 million, an increase of about $48 million. To determine how each of the fund groups performed, see the Coast Community CAFR balance sheet (table 10.8).

To determine if $116 million on the balance sheet in cash and investments is sufficient to meet the standard of having three to six months of cash

Table 10.6 Coast Community Regional Park District Statement of Net Assets (December 31, 2012)

GOVERNMENTAL ACTIVITIES	
Assets	
Current assets	
Cash and investments	$137,821,322
Receivables	3,123,168
Prepaid items and deposits	9,299,931
Consumable supplies	432,582
Total current assets	150,677,003
Noncurrent assets	
Restricted cash and investments held by fiscal agent	140,486,773
Receivables	8,970,410
Deposits	8,140,262
Deferred charges	1,405,167
Notes receivable	40,262
Other assets	51,372
Net pension obligation asset—OPEB	3,868,635
Subtotal	162,962,881
Capital assets	
Nondepreciable assets	327,770,799
Depreciable assets, net of depreciation	141,036,552
Total capital assets	468,807,351
Total noncurrent assets	631,770,232
Total assets	**782,447,235**
Liabilities	
Current liabilities	
Accounts payable	2,667,882
Accrued payroll and related liabilities	4,059,845
Interest payable	2,366,832
Unearned revenue	5,950,205
Other liabilities	1,082,651
Accrued claims—due within one year	2,009,478
Compensated absences—due within one year	524,478
Long-term debt—due within one year	29,106,950
Total current liabilities	47,893,522
Noncurrent liabilities	
Accrued claims—due in more than one year	7,715,800
Compensated absences—due in more than one year	4,116,613
Long-term debt—due in more than one year	168,027,804
Total noncurrent liabilities	179,735,016
Total liabilities	**227,628,538**
Net assets	
Invested in capital assets, net of related debt	384,801,194
Restricted for	
Capital projects	8,948,410
Debt service	26,338,455
Nonexpendable endowments	3,052,658
Special projects	4,150,400
Net pension obligation asset—OPEB	3,868,635
Total restricted net assets	46,358,558
Unrestricted	123,658,945
Total net assets	**$554,818,697**

Table 10.7 Coast Community Regional Park District Statement of Activities and Changes in Net Assets (Year Ended December 31, 2012)

Functions/programs	Expenses	PROGRAM REVENUES: Charges for services	PROGRAM REVENUES: Operating contributions and grants	PROGRAM REVENUES: Capital contributions and grants	Total program revenues	NET (EXPENSE) REVENUE CHANGES IN NET ASSETS: Governmental activities
Primary government						
Executive/legislative division	$2,457,139	$700	$—	$—	$700	($2,456,439)
Finance/management services division	13,186,667	1,109,368	4,116	822,135	1,935,619	(11,251,048)
Human resources division	1,851,719	2,446	—	—	2,446	(1,849,273)
Land division	2,291,803	964,449	500	11,400,871	12,365,820	10,074,017
Legal division	1,572,650	387,650	—	—	387,650	(1,185,000)
Operations division	59,669,927	15,979,011	488,126	893,980	17,361,117	(42,308,810)
Plan/steward/develop division	6,457,765	(1,584,705)	—	4,409,399	2,824,694	(3,633,071)
Public affairs division	2,961,039	2,206	—	190,000	192,206	(2,768,833)
Public safety division	21,156,662	2,362,737	21,500	121,851	2,506,088	(18,650,574)
Interest on long-term debt	5,744,689	—	—	—	—	(5,744,689)
Totals	**$117,350,060**	**$19,223,862**	**$514,242**	**$17,838,236**	**$37,576,340**	**($79,773,720)**
		General revenues				
		General property taxes				95,015,571
		General obligation bond property tax				30,084,466
		Unrestricted interest				2,357,591
		Total general revenues				127,457,628
		Change in net assets				47,683,908
		Net assets, beginning of year				507,134,789
		Net assets, end of year				$554,818,697

Table 10.8 Coast Community Regional Park District Balance Sheet—Governmental Funds (December 31, 2012)

	MAJOR FUNDS: General fund	MAJOR FUNDS: Debt service fund	MAJOR FUNDS: Capital project fund	Nonmajor governmental funds	Total governmental funds
ASSETS					
Cash and investments	$787,986	$488,317	$18,416,245	$18,537,517	$116,240,721
Restricted cash and investments held by fiscal agent	196,703	27,161,473	113,128,597	—	140,486,773
Receivables					
Accounts receivable	2,387,949	—	4,691	9,520	2,402,160
Grants receivable	22,000	—	8,948,410	—	8,970,410
Interest receivable	485,511	1,968	38,785	—	526,264
Leases receivable	58,094	—	—	—	58,094

	MAJOR FUNDS				
	General fund	Debt service fund	Capital project fund	Nonmajor governmental funds	Total governmental funds
	ASSETS *(continued)*				
Prepaid items and deposits	8,913,026	—	8,140,262	—	17,053,288
Due from other funds	135,839	—	—	—	135,839
Consumable supplies	432,582	—	—	—	432,582
Notes receivable	—	—	—	40,262	40,262
Other assets	51,373	—	—	—	51,373
Total assets	**$91,481,719**	**$27,651,758**	**$148,676,990**	**$18,587,299**	**$286,397,766**
LIABILITIES AND FUND BALANCES					
Liabilities					
Accounts payable	$1,037,956	—	$1,264,607	$293,401	$2,595,964
Accrued payroll and related liabilities	3,690,563	—	174,534	169,921	4,035,018
Due to other funds	—	—	—	135,839	135,839
Deferred revenue	—	1,313,302	6,818,654	161,614	12,543,401
Deposits	480,058	—	—	—	480,058
Other liabilities	33,568	—	569,024	—	602,592
Total liabilities	**9,491,976**	**1,313,302**	**8,826,819**	**760,775**	**20,392,871**
Fund balances					
Reserved for:					
Encumbrances	979,916	—	7,382,958	11,282	8,374,156
Notes receivable	—	—	—	40,262	40,262
Debt service funds	—	26,338,456	—	—	26,338,456
Consumable supplies	432,582	—	—	—	432,582
Prepaid items and deposits	8,913,026	—	8,140,262	—	17,053,288
Other	—	—	—	4,172,619	4,172,619
Total reserved	10,325,524	26,338,456	15,523,220	4,224,162	56,411,363
Unreserved, designated in:					
General fund	22,235,891	—	—	—	22,235,891
Capital project funds	—	—	6,266,942	—	6,266,942
Unreserved, reported in:					
General fund	49,428,328	—	—	—	49,428,328
Special revenue funds	—	—	—	13,412,210	13,412,210
Capital project funds	—	—	118,060,010	—	118,060,010
Permanent funds	—	—	—	190,152	190,152
Total fund balances	**81,989,743**	**26,338,456**	**139,850,172**	**17,826,524**	**266,004,895**
Total liabilities and fund balances	**$91,481,719**	**$27,651,758**	**$148,750,990**	**$18,587,299**	**$286,397,766**

reserves to pay the bills, let's look at the statement of revenues, expenditures, and changes in fund balances (table 10.9). The statement shows the total expenditures to be over $161.6 million during the 2012 fiscal year. Considering the district has more than $116 million in cash and investments, it would be able to pay its bills for the first nine months of the fiscal year even if it didn't receive any money from taxes or program fees, which it will.

Basic analysis of the balance sheet and statement of revenues, expenditures, and fund balances suggests that the Coast Community Regional Park District is financially solvent. The statement of revenues, expenditures, and changes in fund balances also shows district tax revenues to be over $133 million, and combined with program fees, the total revenues for the district exceeded expenses by nearly $5 million, building fund balances.

Table 10.9 Coast Community Regional Park District Statement of Revenues, Expenditures, and Changes in Fund Balances (Governmental Funds for the Year Ended December 31, 2012)

	MAJOR FUNDS				
	General fund	Debt service fund	Capital project fund	Nonmajor governmental funds	Total governmental funds
REVENUES					
Property taxes and assessments	$95,015,571	$30,084,468	$—	$7,910,629	$133,010,668
Charges for services	10,041,082	—	46,201	72,398	10,159,681
Interest	1,857,565	131,820	300,873	531,686	2,821,944
Rents and leases	1,677,081	—	5,011	92,779	1,774,871
Grants	340,059	—	14,780,318	—	15,120,377
Regional parks foundation support	303,000	—	115,000	—	418,000
Other revenue	1,044,854	—	2,092,903	56,885	3,194,642
Total revenues	**$110,279,212**	**$30,216,288**	**$17,340,306**	**$8,664,377**	**$166,500,183**
EXPENDITURES					
Current					
Executive and legislative division	$2,183,146	$—	$—	$—	$2,183,146
Finance and management services division	7,041,969	10,282	5,856,850	534,620	13,443,721
Human resources division	1,882,568	—	1,525	—	1,884,093
Land division	2,276,215	—	164,585	201,623	2,642,423
Legal division	1,457,189	—	—	—	1,457,189
Operations division	46,530,383	—	1,939,350	6,449,263	54,918,996
Planning and development division	4,613,581	—	1,909,179	64,638	6,587,398
Public affairs division	2,883,098	—	11,762	260,170	3,155,030
Public safety division	19,761,020	—	1,022,122	—	20,783,142
Debt service					
Principal	684,809	25,990,000	—	—	26,674,809
Cost of issuance	—	737,549	—	—	737,549
Interest	109,257	6,148,200	—	—	6,257,457
Capital outlay	1,443,708	—	19,462,267	14,169	20,920,144
Total expenditures	**90,866,943**	**32,886,031**	**30,367,640**	**7,524,483**	**161,645,097**
Revenues over (under) expenditures	**19,412,269**	**(2,669,743)**	**(13,027,334)**	**1,139,894**	**4,855,086**
Other financing sources (uses)					
Proceeds from sales of property	150,487	—	—	—	150,487
Debt issuance	—	20,000,000	80,000,000	—	100,000,000
Premium on issuance of debt	—	8,264,230	—	—	8,264,230
Payment to escrow agency	—	(20,571,727)	—	—	(20,571,727)
Contribution from another fund	358,481	—	—	—	358,481
Transfers in	148,519	1,198,750	13,490,127	2,362,244	17,199,640
Transfers out	(11,033,473)	—	(3,556,941)	(3,883,660)	(18,474,074)
Total other financing source (use)	**(10,375,986)**	**8,891,253**	**89,933,186**	**(1,521,416)**	**86,927,037**
Net change in fund balances	**9,036,283**	**6,221,510**	**76,905,852**	**(381,522)**	**91,782,123**
Fund balances					
Beginning of year	72,953,460	20,116,946	62,944,323	18,208,046	174,222,772
End of year	81,989,743	26,338,456	139,850,172	17,826,524	226,004,895

Comparing the balance sheets of the City of Fiesta and the Coast Community Regional Park District, it is clear that the Coast Community park district is in a much better financial position. It is also clear that it is easier to understand financial reports of governmental leisure services agencies when the agencies are special districts instead of departments of municipalities.

MANAGING THE FINANCES OF GOVERNMENTAL LEISURE SERVICES

Although municipal leisure services departments are usually incorporated into the general fund and special districts have their own funds, they use the same tool to manage their financial resources: the budget and actual report. One difference is that a municipal department usually has a budget and actual report for each division and a special district usually has a report for each fund. Another difference is that special district funds are considered separate entities. That may not seem to make sense, but consider that entities are the repositories of taxes levied for specific purposes. A fund can have departments within in it, and the larger funds, such as the general fund, sometimes even have divisions within departments.

Either way, the process of managing revenues and expenditures is similar. Using the same methods as business and nonprofit organizations, the technique is to use the budget and actual reports to manage individual revenue and expenditure line items to make sure the bottom line comes in where you want it.

Budget and Actual Reports

It is one thing to read the financial reports; it is quite another thing to manage those reports. Managing the reports means managing the financial condition of the agency. If you work in a department of a municipality or some other general-purpose local governmental unit, the only authority you have is to manage the financial condition of your department within the general fund. Managing the finances of a park and recreation department of a general-purpose government is limited by the detail of financial reports provided to the manager.

An example of a report that is not particularly detailed is the monthly financial report of the City of Tangible, Kansas (table 10.10). The report shows only expense line items, including personal services (salaries and wages), material and supplies, other services and charges, and capital outlay. This minimal level of detail does not provide a leisure services financial manager much to manage. However, this report is only for public consumption. More detailed monthly financial reports are provided to management.

For example, the budget report of the Davidson Park District (table 10.11) for the Zone teen center reflects a department within the recreation fund. Since special-purpose districts have multiple funds, unlike leisure services departments of municipalities whose operations are buried in the general fund, many more details are available to Davidson Park District managers.

Reading the Budget and Actual Report

The detailed line-item budget and actual monthly report of the Zone is generated from a software program that creates revenue and expense categories. The budget column in the middle of the report reflects the annual budget for each line item. The total budgeted revenues for the Zone were $35,460 for the 2012 fiscal year. The total expenses for the Zone were budgeted at $43,235. Since the Davidson Park District fiscal year was from January 1 to December 31, the actual revenues for the fiscal year were $29,118.58 and the actual expenses were $46,714.44.

The monthly report shows a number of bases of comparison that can help the manager of the Zone manage the bottom line. The bottom line of the Zone was that it was budgeted to run a deficit of $7,775 for the year, but it actually lost $17,595.86, meaning that the department lost about $10,000 more than it was budgeted to lose. If other departments in the recreation fund had cumulative departmental surpluses of more than $10,000, the balance of the recreation fund would not decrease. But if other departments lost money as well, the recreation fund balance would decrease.

The monthly budget and actual report allows the manager of the Zone (as well as the financial manager of the park district) to track the progress the Zone makes each month to achieve its financial goal of keeping the bottom-line loss to $7,775 or less. The report does so by informing the manager that revenues are not being generated at the level they were budgeted. Then the manager can try to cut expenditures to keep the losses at $7,775 or less.

Table 10.10 City of Tangible, Kansas, Operating Funds: Statement of Appropriations Versus Expenditures and Encumbrances (Month Ended July 31, 2012)

Fund/object category	Annual appropriations	Current month expenditures	Year-to-date expenditures	YTD %Exp	Encumbrances outstanding	Remaining appropriations
FUND: 01 GENERAL FUND						
Parks and recreation						
Personal services	$2,902,878	$333,475	$333,475	11.49%	$13,404	$2,555,999
Material and supplies	414,122	28,633	28,633	6.91%	22,349	363,141
Other services and charges	1,179,102	83,882	83,882	7.11%	420,275	674,945
Capital outlay	74,570	—	—	0.00%	9,702	64,868
Division total	4,570,672	445,990	445,990	9.76%	465,730	3,658,953
Police						
Personal services	13,248,488	1,360,591	1,360,591	10.27%	—	11,887,897
Material and supplies	539,698	59,422	59,422	11.01%	37,630	442,646
Other services and charges	434,135	13,711	13,711	3.16%	17,001	403,423
Capital outlay	31,125	—	—	0.00%	16,340	14,785
Division total	14,253,446	1,433,724	1,433,724	10.06%	70,971	12,748,751
Fire services						
Personal services	9,608,469	1,046,369	1,046,369	10.89%	—	8,562,100
Material and supplies	211,266	4,469	4,469	2.12%	21,357	185,440
Other services and charges	167,244	8,608	8,608	5.15%	4,161	154,476
Capital outlay	58,400	—	—	0.00%	8,110	50,290
Division total	10,045,379	1,059,446	1,059,446	10.55%	33,628	8,952,305
Total for fund: 01 general fund	**$47,350,080**	**$4,639,292**	**$4,639,292**	**9.80%**	**$861,327**	**$41,849,461**
FUND 51: STORM WATER MITIGATION						
Storm water mitigation						
Personal services	$254,117	$27,894	$27,894	10.98%	$—	$226,223
Material and supplies	7,300	—	—	0.00%	2,118	5,182
Other services and charges	35,480	293	293	0.83%	1,025	34,162
Capital outlay	—	—	—	—	—	—
Division total	**$296,897**	**$28,187**	**$28,187**	**9.49%**	**$3,143**	**$265,567**
FUND 14: HOTEL MOTEL TAX						
Hotel motel						
Personal services	$—	$—	$—	0.00%	$—	$—
Material and supplies	—	—	—	0.00%	—	—
Other services and charges	1,740,000	60,000	60,000	3.45%	249,177	1,430,823
Capital outlay	—	—	—	0.00%	—	—
Division total	**$1,740,000**	**$60,000**	**$60,000**	**3.45%**	**$249,177**	**$1,430,823**

Table 10.11 Davidson Park District Budget Report—Detail (Month Ended December 31, 2012)

		REVENUE/EXPENSE			UNREALIZED		REVENUE/EXPENSE, PREVIOUS YEAR	
Account number	Description	This month	Year to date	Annual budget	Amount	%	This month	Year to date
REVENUE								
Revenues								
420100	General admission	$0.00	$0.00	$0	$0	0%	$0	$0
420455	Sponsor revenue	0.00	3,991.78	5,000	1,008	20%	0	5,000
420555	Program revenue	0.00	0.00	480	480	100%	27	27
420575	Special events revenue	261.00	3,581.37	4,500	919	20%	460	1,891
420580	Concert revenue	296.00	9,546.75	4,500+	5,047–	0%	2,196	3,885
420700	Pro shop sales	0.00	0.00	0	0	0%	0	0
	Total revenues	557.00	17,119.90	14,480+	2,640–	0%	2,683	10,803
RENTAL INCOME								
440000	Facility rentals	3,322.00	6,648.50	10,400	3,752	36%	321	5,632
440700	Birthday party rentals	85.00	798.00	2,430	1,632	67%	185	1,400
	Total rental income	3,407.00	7,446.50	12,830	5,384	42%	506	7,032
FOOD OPERATIONS								
450600	Concessions	165.32	3,022.99	6,000	2,977	50%	377	5,002
450700	Vending—soft drinks	27.68–	1,530.20	1,800	270	15%	20–	991
450800	Vending—general	20.95	108.50	350	242	69%	0	0
	Total food operations	158.59	4,661.69	8,150	3,488	43%	357	5,993
SHORTAGES AND OVERAGES								
460300	Short/over	2.25–	109.51–	0	110	0%	2	38–
	Total shortages and overages	2.25–	109.51–	0	110	0%	2	38–
MISCELLANEOUS INCOME								
470500	Miscellaneous income	0.00	0.00	0	0	0%	0	0
	Total miscellaneous income	0.00	0.00	0	0	0%	0	0
Total revenue		**4,120.34**	**29,118.58**	**35,460**	**6,341**	**18%**	**3,548**	**23,790**
EXPENSE								
Salaries and wages								
550300	Part time (PT)	2,928.51	24,667.51	26,900	2,232	8%	2,244	20,837
550575	PT staff—special events	157.50	4,155.38	575+	3,580–	0%	891	1,431
550700	PT staff—birthday parties	0.00	228.75	0+	229–	0%	19	19
550750	PT staff—facility rentals	30.00	2,034.00	1,040+	994–	0%	409	1,319
	Total salaries and wages	3,116.01	31,085.64	28,515+	2,571–	0%	3,562	23,606

(continued)

Table 10.11 (continued)

		REVENUE/EXPENSE			UNREALIZED		REVENUE/EXPENSE, PREVIOUS YEAR	
Account number	Description	This month	Year to date	Annual budget	Amount	%	This month	Year to date
SERVICES								
560030	In-service training	0.00	0.00	0	0	0%	0	0
560040	Dues and subscriptions	0.00	0.00	50	50	100%	0	0
560050	Advertising and publicity	0.00	0.00	1,000	1,000	100%	0	0
560060	Printing	0.00	0.00	0	0	0%	0	0
	Total services	0.00	0.00	1,050	1,050	100%	0	0
SUPPLIES								
570020	Office equipment/ furniture	0.00	0.00	0	0	0%	0	54
570080	Uniforms	0.00	0.00	300	300	100%	0	326
570100	Miscellaneous supplies	0.00	546.17	500+	46–	0%	0	350
570110	First aid supplies	0.00	0.00	200	200	100%	0	0
570390	Concession supplies	0.00	66.64	150	83	56%	0	40
570400	Recreation equipment	65.50	2,257.65	2,500	242	10%	0	859
570500	Pro shop purchased for resale	0.00	0.00	0	0	0%	0	0
570510	Food purchased for resale	379.85	2,450.55	2,500	49	2%	241	2,315
570525	Soft drinks purchased for resale	205.90	1,115.30	900+	215–	0%	0	702
570530	Vending purchased for resale	120.40	882.30	1,200	318	26%	0	695
570575	Special events	25.09	1,305.98	250+	1,056–	0%	32	95
570700	Birthday party supplies	92.97	470.83	1,160	689	59%	217	465
	Total supplies	889.71	9,095.42	9,660	565	6%	490	5,900
CONTRACTUAL								
580070	Repairs—equipment	0.00	198.50	0+	199–	0%	0	152
580080	Rental—equipment	0.00	0.00	0	0	0%	0	0
580150	Telephone	62.80	489.88	1,200	710	59%	41	124
580575	Special events	0.00	0.00	250	250	100%	0	0
580580	Concert expenses	1,425.00	5,845.00	2,360+	3,485–	0%	616	2,118
580754	Program expense	0.00	0.00	200	200	100%	0	0
	Total contractual	1,487.80	6,533.38	4,010+	2,523–	0%	657	2,394
CAPITAL/OTHER								
590060	Recreation equipment	0.00	0.00	0	0	0%	0	0
599999	Contingency	0.00	0.00	0	0	0%	0	0
	Total capital/other	0.00	0.00	0	0	0%	0	0
Total expense		5,493.52	46,714.44	43,235+	3,479–	0%	4,710	31,899
Net income/loss		1,373.18–	17,595.86–	7,775–	9,821	126%+	1,162–	8,109–
Total department revenue		4,120.34	29,118.58	35,460	6,341	18%	3,548	23,790
Total department expense		5,493.52	46,714.44	43,235+	3,479–	0%	4,710	31,899
Net department income/loss		1,373.18–	17,595.86–	7,775–	9,821	126%+	1,162–	8,109–

Skokie Park District Financial Statements

The Skokie Park District is a special-purpose district organized to provide parks and leisure services in the northern suburbs of Chicago. The park district has won several Gold Medal Awards for Excellence in Park and Recreation Management and more than 20 Certificates of Achievement for Excellence in Financial Reporting from the GFOA, both of which very few agencies can boast.

The FOIA, adopted by the federal government and affirmed by most states, requires that governmental units provide their financial statements to the public upon written request within seven working days of the request. Most (but not all) agencies comply with written FOIA requests, but only a small percentage of special districts go as far as the Skokie Park District does to make financial statements available to the public.

In the age of the Internet, it should be relatively easy for agencies to provide financial statements verbatim on the agency website, and that's exactly what the Skokie Park District does (Skokie Park District 2012a, 2012b). It posts its minutes from board meetings, planning documents, community surveys, and CAFR so the public will not need to submit FOIA requests to determine the financial position of the agency.

But almost no public leisure services agencies, including the Skokie Park District, regularly post the monthly budget and actual financial reports that are made available to agency management and board members. To obtain those documents, the public and media are still required to submit FOIA requests. Someday, that may change. In the meantime, unless they make a written request, the members of the public do not get to see what the board does.

References

Skokie Park District. 2012a. "Board Business." www.skokieparks.org/board-business.

Skokie Park District. 2012b. "Comprehensive Annual Financial Report." www.skokieparks.org/downloads/pdfs/CAFR.pdf.

But keeping losses down is more difficult than just waving a magic wand. Sometimes unforeseen expenditures must be paid. For instance, the line item of concert expenditures exceeded the budgeted expenses by $2,523, contributing to the actual expenses of the Zone exceeding the budgeted expenditures. It could be argued that cutting concert expenditures would have saved money, but such was not the case. Concert revenues were actually $5,047 higher than budgeted, making the net concert revenues positive by $3,701.75 instead of positive by $2,140 as budgeted.

How was that assessment made? If the actual concert expenditures of $5,845 are subtracted from the actual concert revenues of $9,546.75, the difference is $3,701.75. If the budgeted expenditures of $2,360 are subtracted from the budgeted revenues of $4,500, the difference is $2,140. In other words, by spending more money for concert performers than was budgeted, the revenues increased, allowing the net revenues to increase beyond the budgeted net revenues.

What contributed to the decrease in the Zone's revenues was the lower actual concession revenues of $3,022.99 compared with the budgeted amount of $6,000. But there were other declines in revenues that also contributed to reduced overall revenues for the Zone. A big one was facility rentals, which were budgeted at $10,400 but came in at $6,648.50, and birthday party rentals, which were budgeted at $2,430 but were actually $798. Sponsor revenue was also lower than anticipated, coming in at $3,991.78 compared with the budgeted amount of $5,000.

What the report does throughout the year is provide a basis of comparison with the budgeted amounts as well as the previous year's revenues and expenditures. A detailed budget and actual report, such as the one for the Davidson Park District Zone teen center, contains columns with historic data for comparison with the current fiscal year. The third column, which contains actual revenue or expenditure information for the current month, can be compared with the second-to-last column on the right, which shows revenue and expenditure data from the same month in the previous fiscal year. Likewise, year-to-date data are provided for the current and previous fiscal years.

Another element of a detailed budget and actual financial report in the public sector is the unrealized-amount column in the center of the Zone financial report and the percentage column detailing what percentage of revenues or expenditures have taken place for the year to date compared with the budgeted amounts. All of these columns of detail allow leisure services managers to make decisions that help them manage their statements of net assets and balance sheets and allow their statements of activities and statement of revenues, expenditures, and changes in fund balances to create fund entities that show the financial health of the agency to be solid.

Using the Budget and Actual Report as a Financial Management Tool

The detailed line-item budget and actual report gives public-sector managers the opportunity to understand what is taking place within their departments by revealing how each budgeted revenue and expenditure line item is faring. But how does the report permit leisure services managers to manage their finances? The answer is that it allows them to take **appropriate action**, defined as a decision to act based on the selection of the most rational solution to a problem.

Appropriate action varies from department to department and from line item to line item, which makes financial management in the public sector more complicated than in any other sector. Private-sector leisure services managers ultimately need to make sure their single-fund business entity makes a profit and creates equity in the fund. Nonprofit-sector leisure services managers need to make sure each of their funds breaks even. But public-sector leisure services managers are responsible for providing a level of detail that makes their job of managing finances much more complicated and consequential.

There are two reasons for this. First, multiple funds need to be managed to make the levying of the various taxes transparent. Second, the manager has many more leisure services offerings to administer than do business or nonprofit managers. Most leisure businesses offer a limited range of services, as do nonprofit organizations. Governmental leisure services offer a much wider range.

As an example, the budget and actual report of the Davidson Park District Zone teen center shows that the center offers a wide range of services just for teens, including drop-in services, concerts, birthday parties, and a multitude of special events. The budget and actual report for the Zone represents only 2 of more than 80 pages of budget and actual reports that the park district generates each month for the managers and supervisors who manage the various departments within the park district.

The task of managing each line item, therefore, is daunting. The Davidson Park District administrator has hundreds of line items to manage, each with a budgeted amount and various comparative data provided by each column category. It is a huge task to manage each one of them individually, particularly when there is little that can be done to increase revenues and decrease expenditures.

The key to reading a business balance sheet, a nonprofit statement of financial position, or a governmental statement of net assets, all of which reflect the financial condition of the entity at a given point in time, is to focus on a few important elements. The most important elements for a business are cash and equity. For nonprofits and governmental units, the most important elements are cash and fund balance.

For budget and actual reports, regardless of whether they are analyzed for business, nonprofit, or government entities, the most important element is the **net difference** between revenues and expenditures. The net difference does not necessarily mean that the

© Alan Heartfield/fotolia.com

Managing the leisure services offered by a park district can be complicated due to the many line items that provide detail on outdoor concerts and other events.

focus of the leisure services manager should always be on achieving revenue or expenditure predictions. Achieving the difference between budgeted revenues and budgeted expenditures is the goal.

In the example of the Davidson Park District concerts, the budgeted difference of $2,140 was the goal. There was no cause for celebration that the actual revenues of $9,546.76 exceeded the budgeted $4,500. Nor was there cause for despair that the actual expenditures of $5,845 exceeded the budgeted $2,360. The important number is that the actual difference of $3,701.75 exceeded the budgeted difference. In other words, the net income was higher than budgeted. In the case of the Davidson Park District budget and actual report, the leisure services manager needs to perform the calculations to identify these differences.

Another element of complexity is that the budget and actual report is not all that it appears to be. Budget and actual reports have budget line items that are accrued and others that are reported on a cash basis. Accruing the budget and actual report means reporting revenues and expenditures that are available and measurable (i.e., the financial manager is reasonably certain the revenues will be received or the expenditures will be paid).

For instance, in the case of revenues, when local governments send their property tax bills to property owners, it is reasonable to assume that most of them will be paid. Accruing tax revenues on the budget and actual report means calculating the percentage that will be paid and reporting the taxes as revenue even before property owners pay them. Likewise, for expenditures, when contracts with vendors are let or when purchases are made, it is reasonable to report them as expenditures on the budget and actual report, even though the governmental unit has yet to write the checks.

Everything else on the budget and actual report is mostly reported on a cash basis, making the report a combination of cash and accrual accounting. Sometimes there are revenues in the pipeline that need to be taken into consideration but that can't be accrued under GAAP. Likewise, there are times when expenditures in the pipeline can't be accrued. For instance, it is reasonable to assume that repair bills for the Zone teen center will need to be paid during the fiscal year. Even though the bills will fall within a reasonable range, repair expenditures cannot be accrued. On the other hand, sponsorship revenues can be accrued when sponsors commit to donating money, but it cannot be assumed that sponsors who committed the previous year will commit again. Since the manager cannot be certain, sponsorships for uncommitted donors cannot be accrued.

Cutting through the complexity of these nuances of accounting means that leisure services managers need to focus on a few important comparisons. In the case of the budget and actual report for the Davidson Park District Zone teen center, comparing revenues and expenditures for the same month in the current and previous fiscal years is important, as is comparing the year-to-date numbers for the current and previous fiscal years. The comparisons are important because they show short-term revenue and expenditure trends.

The usefulness of the budget and actual report in managing the financial health of departments within funds allows leisure services managers to manage the overall financial health of the fund itself. If departments exceed their budgeted difference goals, the financial health of the fund will improve, reflected in an increased fund balance and perhaps even more cash. Alternatively, if departments fail to meet their budgeted difference goals, the financial health of the fund will deteriorate, reflected in declining or negative fund balances and less cash.

At the end of the fiscal year, the budget and actual report final outcomes will be reflected in the statements of activities and revenues, expenditures, and changes in fund balances. These reports will summarize the combined outcomes of all the departments and funds that the leisure services agency oversees. If the cumulative effect is that the individual government entities and departments meet or exceed budgeted targets, the statements of activities and revenues, expenditures, and changes in fund balance will reflect well on the leisure services manager's overall financial management of the agency.

SUMMARY

Understanding the similarities and differences among the financial reports generated by business, nonprofit, and governmental leisure services agencies begins with knowing the oversight boards that require these reports: the FASB and the GASB. Understanding why these boards exist and that their prescriptions for financial reporting will change over time makes it important for leisure services managers to pay attention to the new rules that come from these boards.

Most recently, the GASB has required governmental units to provide a business-type statement of financial condition, called the *statement of net assets*, so lenders and bond rating agencies can better understand their financial condition. The statement of net assets is presented in a format similar to a balance sheet and is accompanied by a statement of activities, which is similar to the business income statement required by the FASB.

To manage the financial condition of a leisure services governmental unit, managers need to understand the complexity of that world. Governmental leisure services agencies provide a multitude of services that require monitoring hundreds of budgeted line-item revenues and expenditures. To help manage these line items, a budget and actual report is a useful tool that compares the month and year-to-date actual revenues and expenditures of the current year and the previous year.

The most daunting challenge is clarity in an environment of complexity. One way of achieving that clarity is to focus on important data, including the differences between budgeted revenues and expenditures, rather than achieving the line-item totals themselves.

Visit the Web Resource

For case studies, sample financial statements, key terms, and more, please visit the web resource at www.HumanKinetics.com/LeisureServicesFinancialManagement

chapter 11

Capital Financing and Construction Management

Learning Outcomes

After completing this chapter, students will be able to do the following:

- Identify sources of private-sector capital financing for businesses.
- Describe the ways that nonprofit organizations fund capital improvements.
- Recognize the various sources of capital financing for governmental organizations.
- Understand how local governmental organizations and special districts use referenda to finance capital improvements.
- Conceptualize how to manage construction projects and the associated consultants who help with the building of such projects.

By now, it should be clear that leisure services financial management is a complicated topic. It should also be clear that leisure services financial management requires not only an understanding of economics, finance, accounting, marketing, and fund-raising but also an understanding of political considerations, especially at the governmental level. In addition, there are two more financial topics that leisure services managers in all sectors must understand: capital financing and construction management.

Leisure services organizations need to have physical assets as sites for their activities. It is simply not possible for a leisure provider to offer services without physical assets. To offer swimming lessons, you need a swimming pool, lake, or other facility. To offer basketball leagues, you need a gymnasium or outdoor court. To offer softball leagues . . . well, you get the idea.

Building a recreational facility, such as a swimming pool, gymnasium, or softball field, requires assembling financial resources, gathering professional consultants to design and manage the project, and disbursing funds to the consultants and contractors who are involved in building or acquiring the capital asset. Managing these consultants and contractors is an essential part of managing the financial resources required to build the facilities.

This chapter focuses on the management of capital finance. It begins with options available to private-sector leisure services. It then considers how private-sector leisure services are different from nonprofit and governmental leisure services, describing how the capital finance process for the private sector is more straightforward than in the other sectors. In the private sector, costs are weighed against the benefits. If the benefits exceed the costs, it is logical for the capital improvement to be made; if not, the improvement won't be made.

The chapter then moves to the nonprofit sector. The methods of managing nonprofit capital improvements are not as straightforward as methods used in the private sector because many nonprofit leisure organizations have a fiduciary responsibility to serve indigents and do charitable work. Not every nonprofit client is charged for services, leaving a hole in the budget that can only be filled with donations. Capital improvements are not **cost-versus-benefit propositions** for nonprofit organizations, which means the feasibility of a project in the nonprofit sector involves more than just quantifying the costs and benefits.

For governmental units, the process is even more complex, as discussed in the next part of the chapter. Leisure services governmental units make their capital improvements within the maze of laws and regulations that protect the public from being exploited by public officials. For instance, there are public bidding laws, which do not apply to private or nonprofit organizations. Governmental units are usually required to accept the lowest bidder, whereas businesses and nonprofits can select whichever provider they want.

The differences among private, nonprofit, and governmental capital finance and construction management are great. Ignoring these differences has caused many leisure services professionals to transfer from one sector to another. Professionals who move from the nonprofit or governmental sector to the private sector cannot ignore the fact that every capital decision they make must have a profit motive. Leisure services professionals moving from the private sector to the nonprofit or governmental sector cannot ignore the fact that service plays a role in capital decisions along with consideration of the revenue streams that the capital improvement will need to bring with it. And, ignoring legal requirements can surprise leisure services professionals moving from the private sector to the public sector; there are personal criminal consequences for not following the law.

CAPITAL ASSETS FINANCIAL MANAGEMENT

Thus far, this textbook has considered financial statements for leisure services businesses, nonprofit organizations, and governmental units. All of those financial statements contained references to fixed assets and depreciation. But just understanding how fixed assets and depreciation are recorded on balance sheets is not sufficient for fully understanding how leisure services managers need to manage their capital assets. A few more terms need to be introduced.

To understand how capital assets, which are property such as real estate and equipment that is usually held for a long time, are acquired and developed, leisure services managers need to understand how to acquire sites for parks and facilities, how to build the facilities, how to pay for acquisition and construction costs, and how to manage the people who serve as consultants for capital projects. This chapter discusses these skills.

Capital acquisition and development differ greatly among the private, nonprofit, and public sectors. Capital acquisition is the purchase or construction of physical assets, namely land and buildings. In the private sector, capital acquisition is typically based on a risk–reward scenario. The development is always a risk due to the lack of a guaranteed revenue stream to pay back the capital borrowed to build a project. When the financing risk is manageable due to a solid cash-flow analysis or a proven product, there is an ability to make excellent returns and pay back the capital debt quickly and effortlessly.

In the past, it was easy to borrow capital from a **commercial lender**—a company, usually a bank, that lends money to businesses. Many projects were formulated on **speculative financing**, meaning there was a great deal of risk in making the loan. Speculative financing increases the risk of the project failing dramatically. Since loans are the preferred financing vehicle for capital projects in the private sector, it is important to bankers that loans will be repaid, suggesting that speculative financing is not the preferred way of doing business.

In terms of a building project, the private leisure services manager can select the contractor who best meets the given needs regardless of price. Private-sector projects are usually relationship driven and trust is a big factor in the decision-making process. If the project is exceeding its **financial projection** (estimates of its future financial performance), any cost overruns that affect the bottom line are usually passed on to the end user. In the private sector, the project decision makers are a smaller group, and thus decisions that affect the completion of a project can be made much more quickly. The decisiveness associated with private-sector projects makes them faster to complete and can beat a governmental project to the market by years.

Recruiting community volunteers to help build a new public playground can save money in the parks and recreation budget for capital development.

In the nonprofit sector, seeking funding for capital development is more difficult, because it is difficult to forecast the income a nonprofit will receive in order to secure competitive loans from lending institutions. That leaves donations as the primary way for nonprofits to secure capital for capital development. Securing donations, as was discussed in previous chapters, is a complicated process even for the most experienced nonprofit managers. In the end, the agencies that have developed a significant endowment for both capital and operations are the ones that can fulfill their primary mission. Bonds are another way to secure capital resources.

The building aspect of capital development can make for interesting architectural design and project management issues. Many nonprofits are governed by volunteer board members who pay attention to every decision surrounding finances. This sometimes leads to misunderstandings regarding project direction and the overall feeling of success surrounding a project. For instance, nonprofit board members often come from the construction field, housing industry, or banking sector, and they may have many suggestions about how to manage the project.

Government capital financing is in many regards the easiest financing model in terms of getting money, but spending capital is another story. Governmental units have a guaranteed revenue source in taxes. However, in many cases, there are more projects than funds available and the administrator or elected officials do not have the political will to spend limited capital on park and recreation facilities. Even worse, many governmental units do not prioritize capital spending based on a well-rounded public-input process, and they often spend money on the wrong projects. Finally, many small local governments do not spend capital at all on parks and recreation.

The entire capital planning and implementation process, from selecting the consultant to issuing construction contracts, is a tough process of negotiating procurement. The main focus is to find the lowest cost with an acceptable contractor. The contrast with the private sector, where cost is not the overriding factor, is clear.

The public bidding approach does not provide many opportunities for interaction among the project team members. This can lead to misunderstandings over the scope of construction work and increased costs through change orders. If the project team can work together, governmental obstacles can be minimized and a quality project that meets the capital financing criteria can be achieved. By using the competitive bidding process, particularly in lean economic times, governmental agencies can complete projects well under budgeted amounts. The primary vehicles for governmental financing to pay for capital projects are using cash on hand, paying as you go, and using bond proceeds.

To complicate matters further, in the public sector, referenda are often necessary to acquire funds for capital projects. Referenda are elections where the public votes whether or not to allow the governmental unit permission to borrow money for the project and pay it back through increased property taxes. Leading up to the election, political campaigns are conducted by the supporters and opponents of the project. The governmental unit itself is not permitted to participate in the political campaign, but it can orchestrate the messages of its supporters. Planning for referenda-based capital initiatives generally begins early. Referenda do follow a political process and require an understanding of public attitudes within the areas the governmental agency services.

Even if the capital project is justified, there is still the possibility that the referendum will fail. This can happen when there is a lack of appropriate responses to potential issues. The referendum campaign must gain public trust. If the referendum passes, the community will seek information on how the capital project is doing, so spending money wisely and delivering the project according to the public's perception are paramount for success. Many of these projects are funded with bond proceeds.

The subject of capital financing in leisure services is as important as any in this textbook. For privately owned businesses, capital financing goes to the core of the company business plan. For nonprofit organizations, capital financing is a donor-driven process with a level of political intrigue. For governmental units, capital financing is as political as it gets, requiring all of the skill sets that managers have developed.

SOURCES OF FINANCING FOR THE PRIVATE SECTOR

The easiest way to understand sources of capital financing for businesses is to revisit balance sheet accounting. As pictures of the financial condition of the business, balance sheets are also windows into the potential for businesses to acquire capital financing for their expansion and development. Balance sheets contain current and fixed assets, the total of which equal liabilities and equity. Creation of fixed assets requires cash, which can be acquired from operating profits, bank loans, the issuance of corporate bonds, or the issuance of new stock sold to investors.

To understand how leisure businesses would finance capital expansion, let's revisit the example of Sadie's Amusement Park. Let's assume that, after three years of operating her amusement park, Sadie has decided she needs to make an improvement so people won't get bored with the same rides each year. She wants to add a speedy roller coaster, which would cost $1 million to install. The roller coaster would bring new customers to the amusement park as well as provide repeat users with a reason to keep coming. Sadie did an analysis to show that if she built the new roller coaster for $1 million, she would increase her revenues by about $200,000 per year, suggesting that in five years the investment would pay for itself.

Cost-versus-benefit analysis is the reason businesses choose to make capital investments. They wouldn't do so without a payback. Sadie figures her payback period is five years, which means that she would make $200,000 profit off the investment every year after that. Of course, any investment involves risk, and Sadie's is no different. There is no guarantee she'll get $200,000 more each year; it's just an estimate based on surveys she has done of her customers and the community.

The reason Sadie is even considering expanding her business is that her original projections of revenue were fairly accurate. The amusement park made the profits she had predicted, giving her confidence that her roller-coaster projections would make a profit as well. Sadie's balance sheet for the fiscal year 2013 is her proof that she knows what she's doing. Her balance sheet (table 11.1) shows that she has accumulated cash reserves of $1.1 million by the end of the 2013 fiscal year.

The accumulation of that much cash provides Sadie with a capital financing option for her new roller coaster that is not available to less successful businesses. Sadie can take $1 million of her cash and spend it on the new ride. But paying for the roller coaster from the cash reserves would leave Sadie with only $550,000 in cash, about half the original amount. Having a small amount of cash would mean that a bad season could leave her with no cash at all. There are other choices she should look at, including acquiring more debt (bank loans) to build the coaster or taking on partners in the business by selling stock in her company. In either case, Sadie would be distributing the risk and holding on to her cash.

Of course, Sadie could employ a combination of the three options: spend some cash, secure more loans, and sell stock. But, for simplicity's sake, let's assume that she employs only one of those choices. To make her choice, she would need to decide how she wants her balance sheet affected.

The balance sheet comparison assumes that the investment in the speedy roller coaster is made on

Table 11.1 Sadie's Amusement Park Balance Sheet (December 31, 2013)

	2013	Cash	Debt	Equity
CURRENT ASSETS				
Cash	$1,100,000	$100,000	$1,100,000	$1,100,000
Accounts receivable	10,000	10,000	10,000	10,000
Inventories of supplies	50,000	50,000	50,000	50,000
Total current assets	$1,160,000	$160,000	$1,160,000	$1,160,000
FIXED ASSETS				
Equipment	$1,000,000	$2,000,000	$2,000,000	$2,000,000
Less depreciation	300,000	300,000	300,000	300,000
Net	700,000	1,700,000	1,700,000	1,700,000
Buildings	1,000,000	1,000,000	1,000,000	1,000,000
Less depreciation	300,000	300,000	300,000	300 000
Net	700,000	700,000	700,000	700,000
Land	1,000,000	1,000,000	1,000,000	1,000,000
Total fixed assets	2,400,000	3,400,000	3,400,000	3,400,000
Total assets	**$3,560,000**	**$3,560,000**	**$4,560,000**	**$4,560,000**
CURRENT LIABILITIES				
Accounts payable	$20,000	$20,000	$20,000	$20,000
Notes payable	0	0	0	0
Total current liabilities	$20,000	$20,000	$20,000	$20,000
LONG-TERM DEBT				
Loans	$2,000,000	$2,000,000	$3,000,000	$2,000,000
Less payment of principal	600,000	600,000	600,000	600,000
Total long-term liabilities	1,400,000	1,400,000	2,400,000	1,400,000
Total liabilities	**1,420,000**	**1,420,000**	**2,420,000**	**1,420,000**
Owners' equity	**2,140,000**	**2,140,000**	**2,140,000**	**3,140,000**
Total assets and liabilities	**$3,560,000**	**$3,560,000**	**$4,560,000**	**$4,560,000**

the first day of the new fiscal year beginning January 1, 2014. It shows that if Sadie spends $1 million of her cash on a new roller coaster, the construction of the coaster represents the conversion of one type of asset (cash) to another (equipment).

At the end of the fiscal year, December 31, 2014, depreciation of the roller coaster would begin, reducing the value of the new fixed asset by the percentage the IRS allows. Sadie's equity would be reduced accordingly, but hopefully the influx of new customers would more than make up for that depreciation.

Taking on a $1 million loan would increase debt by that amount and would initially have no effect on owners' equity. There would still be depreciation of the coaster at the end of the 2014 fiscal year, and there would be the added expense of interest payments on the loan. But Sadie would hope that both of these expenses would be covered by the increased revenues received from the new customers that a speedy roller coaster would bring in.

The third choice of selling $1 million in company stock has its benefits, too. There would still be depreciation on the coaster as an expense at the end of the fiscal year. However, since interest is not paid to equity investors, there would be no interest payment. But Sadie would have new partners in her business that would have a voice in how the business is run, something she may not want.

Spending existing cash, borrowing money, and selling stock to make capital improvements are the choices available to businesses, and each choice has consequences. Spending cash takes away the safety net for weathering economic recessions.

Borrowing money requires that interest be paid, which is an extra expense that can make a business less profitable. Selling stock means giving up a certain level of management control to stockholders, something that management may not be prepared to do.

HOW NONPROFITS FUND CAPITAL IMPROVEMENTS

In financing capital improvements, nonprofit leisure organizations face issues similar to those of private businesses in that they can spend their excess cash on the improvement or borrow money to pay for it. But there are a few differences between private businesses and nonprofit organizations.

Nonprofit organizations have no stockholders, so they can't sell stock to finance improvements. In addition, the cost–benefit concept does not always apply to nonprofit organizations the way it does to businesses. As required by the laws that permit nonprofit organizations to exist, providing services to the needy is more important than making a profit. Therefore, getting loans or issuing revenue bonds for projects where there is no expected stream of income to repay the bonds is not an option the way it is for businesses. Revenue bonds, bonds guaranteed by the revenue flow of the project, will be discussed later in the chapter.

Sources for financing capital initiatives change for the many nonprofits that have a charitable mission to serve the needy. For instance, if a nonprofit organization wants to build a revenue-generating facility that will be mostly self-supporting, such as a fitness center, it might have the option of going to a bank or other lender and borrowing the money. The lender would have reason to believe it will be repaid from revenue streams generated by the capital improvement. But when the intention of the nonprofit organization is to serve the needy, such as building an interactive children's museum intended to keep at-risk children off the streets, few lenders are willing to finance the project. The nonprofit organization can spend its excess cash to make the capital improvement, or it can solicit donations.

The other categories of nonprofit leisure services, such as country clubs or sport clubs, have the potential to generate a revenue stream, so they have the option of issuing revenue bonds. Whether a nonprofit organization has the option of spending its extra cash, borrowing money, or soliciting donations for capital improvements depends on its statement of financial position. As with the business balance sheet example for Sadie's Amusement Park, the statement of financial position determines the options available to the nonprofit leisure services organization.

Let's take another look at the Children's Discovery Museum of Recreation example from chapter 8. Assuming the museum continues its successful fund-raising efforts beyond the 2011 fiscal year and is able to accumulate an additional $500,000 in cash, the museum has the option of funding a $1 million interactive exhibit by using its cash or fund-raising, but probably not by borrowing. The 2013 statement of financial position (table 11.2) shows how the museum would be affected by spending cash or by fund-raising, assuming the capital improvement has been made.

The statement of financial position shows that when cash is used to finance the interactive exhibit, there is a considerable reduction in cash as an asset, but the total net assets doesn't change. Building the interactive exhibit using cash represents the conversion of cash to a current asset, but liabilities and total net assets are not affected at all.

Using a fund-raising campaign to finance the interactive exhibit results in substantial changes to the balance sheet. Up front, cash still needs to be used to pay for the construction costs, thereby reducing cash. The fixed asset is created, increasing fixed assets. And pledges are increased, reflecting the effect of fund-raising on the pledge assets.

On the other side of the balance sheet, unrestricted assets have declined by $1 million because cash has been spent. Restricted assets have been increased to reflect fixed assets being increased by adding the interactive exhibit to the total assets of the museum. Down the road, the accounting treatment of the pledge payments will restore cash to its original value of $1.18 million. As pledges are paid, cash increases and pledges decrease accordingly.

Because the statement of financial condition is a picture of the financial condition of the nonprofit organization at a given point in time, it behooves the manager to pay attention to its components. It's not a good thing to be short of cash. On the other hand, as chapter 8 considered, having too much cash could signal to the IRS that the nonprofit organization is more profitable than the law allows, although the IRS may not always be paying attention. Another issue with carrying too much cash is that if donors find out the nonprofit organization has that much money on hand, they

Table 11.2 Children's Discovery Museum of Recreation Combined Statement of Financial Position (December 31, 2013)

	2013	Cash	Donations
	ASSETS		
Current assets			
Cash and cash equivalents	$1,180,000	$180,000	$180,000
Short-term investments	1,400,000	1,400,000	1,400,000
Accounts receivable			
Clients	450,000	450,000	450,000
Pledges	3,250,000	3,250,000	4,250,000
Noncurrent assets			
Long-term investments	10,150,000	10,150,000	10,150,000
Land, buildings, and equipment	9,000,000	10,000,000	10,000,000
Less depreciation	(2,000,000)	(2,000,000)	(2,000,000)
Total assets	**$23,430,000**	**$23,430,000**	**$24,430,000**
	LIABILITIES		
Current liabilities			
Accounts payable	$250,000	$250,000	$250,000
Accrued expenses	50,000	50,000	50,000
Short-term debt	500,000	500,000	500,000
Noncurrent liabilities			
Long-term debt	1,000,000	1,000,000	1,000,000
Total liabilities	**1,800,000**	**1,800,000**	**1,800,000**
Net assets			
Unrestricted	10,080,000	9,080,000	9,080,000
Temporarily restricted	1,400,000	1,400,000	1,400,000
Permanently restricted	10,150,000	11,150,000	11,150,000
Total net assets	**$21,630,000**	**$21,630,000**	**$21,630,000**

have little motivation to donate for making capital improvements or supporting operations.

There are instances when nonprofit leisure organizations seek loans from banks or other lenders. A typical situation is where the organization has fallen short of its fund-raising goal. Another example is when the cost of the capital improvement has unexpectedly exceeded the amount of money raised. In either case, nonprofit organizations would be reluctant to give all the money back. Doing so would mean the capital improvement doesn't get made. It would also mean that future fund-raising efforts would be in jeopardy because future donors might lose confidence in the ability of the agency to raise enough money for the project, discouraging them from donating. To prevent that from happening, nonprofit organizations may secure bank loans to complete the project with the hope they can make up the cash deficit in the future, either through excess operating revenues or more fund-raising.

If a nonprofit leisure services agency requires a bank loan or sells revenue bonds, its statement of financial condition will be affected by an increase in long-term debt and a decrease in the unrestricted fund balance. The asset side of the statement of financial condition would not be affected at all.

Revenue bonds as sources of capital improvements are fairly rare for some types of nonprofits, particularly leisure services organizations. For other types of nonprofit organizations, such as nonprofit hospitals, revenue bonds are frequently used. The reason for the difference is the ability to pay—leisure services organizations have lower revenue streams than hospitals.

But revenue bonds are still a source of capital financing for the creation of fixed assets. As nonprofit leisure organizations focus on fee-supported services to make up for diminished funding from United Way and Community Chest, revenue bonds are increasingly being considered for capital improvements.

HOW GOVERNMENTAL UNITS FUND CAPITAL IMPROVEMENTS

As was the case for other finance and accounting issues, capital financing for governmental leisure services is more complex than in the other sectors. That's because governmental units have more options for financing capital improvement projects. They can use profits and donations, just as businesses and nonprofit organizations do, but the most common method of funding capital improvements is with tax monies.

Paying taxes is not optional for taxpayers, but governmental units can only collect tax money for capital improvements with the permission of the taxpayers themselves or their elected representatives. And since governmental units are mandated by law to follow certain rules of transparency that businesses and nonprofit organizations are not required to follow, the process of funding capital improvements with tax money is a lot more complicated than if profits or donations are used.

The way in which local governmental units are permitted to get additional tax money for capital improvements varies from state to state. There are states such as Illinois that require governmental units to have a referendum seeking voter approval before taxes are raised for capital improvements. There are states like Indiana and Wisconsin that don't require voter referenda but do require public hearings and the approval of common councils elected to levy taxes. **Common councils** are elected policymakers such as city councils, village boards, county boards, and park boards. All of this is done under the watchful eye of the media, including bloggers and taxpayer watchdog groups.

Most states require local governments to segregate their capital improvement monies into separate funds: a fund from which bond issue receipts are deposited and a separate fund to pay back the bondholders. A **bond issue** is when bonds are sold by a corporation or government agency at a particular time. They are identifiable by the date the bonds mature. The **bondholder** is the owner of a government or corporate bond. Being a bondholder entitles one to receive regular interest payments, if the bond pays interest (usually semiannually or annually), as well as a return of principal when the bond matures.

A few states allow bank loans to be made to the general fund of a municipality in order to make capital improvements. But for that to happen, the general fund must be able to repay the loan. Therefore, local governmental units are infrequent borrowers from banks. To repay bank loans, they would levy more taxes than needed to cover operating expenditures, and if they did that, taxpayer watchdogs would complain. Therefore, the primary source of funding capital improvements for government leisure services is an increase in property or sales taxes granted by the taxpayers or common councils with **home rule authority**. *Home rule* refers to the powers given to local government to prevent state government intervention with its operations. The extent of its power, however, is subject to limitations prescribed by state constitutions and statutes, such as population or approval by voter referenda.

Government Capital Fund Accounting

In most states, and according to the GASB, fund accounting for governmental units requires that monies received from the sale of bonds or loans must be accounted for in funds separate from those where the bonds are repaid. To clarify, if a governmental unit sells bonds to make a capital improvement such as the construction of a swimming pool, revenues from the sale of the bonds are shown, as are the expenditures to build the pool. The property or sales taxes received to repay the bonds are shown as revenues in a separate fund, as are the expenditures made to repay the bondholders. This transparency allows the public to see clearly that the money borrowed to make the capital improvement is only being used for that purpose and the taxes levied to repay the lender are being used for that purpose.

Each fund has its own balance sheet, a relatively brief statement that shows its assets and liabilities at the end of the fiscal year. The assets are usually limited to cash or investments. The other side of the balance sheet is usually limited to accounts payable and fund balance. Transparency is achieved through the statement of revenues, expenditures, and changes in fund balances.

Bonds

Governmental units, nonprofit organizations, and businesses sell bonds to fund capital improvements. The difference between the three sectors is not as much who purchases the bonds or how the bonds are accounted for as it is the source of repayment of the bonds. Leisure businesses repay their bonds from their revenue streams, nonprofits repay their bonds from revenues and donations, and governmental units repay their bonds from taxes.

These are not absolutes. There are governmental units that repay their bonds from revenue streams and operate like businesses. A good example is the Pleasant Prairie Parks and Recreation Department in Wisconsin. That department operates a $44 million indoor fitness, aquatic, ice, sport, child care, and therapeutic recreation facility that derives about $8 million per year in operating revenues, totally financing the bonds that built the facility. No tax revenues are used. But Pleasant Prairie is an exception. Most governmental units finance their capital improvements with general obligation property tax revenues or sales taxes.

Likewise, some nonprofit organizations sell bonds to finance capital improvements and repay them from revenue streams. But most do fundraising before they make capital improvements, paying for the improvements using donations derived from capital campaigns. Businesses have no tax option and rarely receive donations.

Corporate Bonds

Bonds are a major source of capital financing for leisure services businesses, nonprofit organizations, and governmental units. Several types of bonds are available to each sector. A corporate bond is issued by a corporation, typically in denominations of $1,000. The term is usually applied to long-term debt instruments, generally with a maturity date falling at least a year after the issue date. **Debt instruments** are paper or electronic obligations that enable the issuing party to raise funds by promising to repay a lender in accordance with the terms of a contract. Types of debt instruments include notes, bonds, certificates, mortgages, leases, and other agreements between a lender and a borrower. A **coupon** is a detachable portion of a bond that is given in return for a payment of interest, specifying when interest payments will be made to the bondholder. The bondholder is entitled to receive regular interest payments, if the bond pays interest (usually semiannually or annually), as well as a return of principal when the bond matures.

Sometimes, the term *corporate bond* is used to include all bonds except those issued by governments. Generally, though, it only applies to bonds issued by corporations. The bonds of states, local authorities, and international organizations do not fit in this category because they do not issue corporate bonds.

Corporate bonds are bought and sold, often on major stock exchanges. When they are traded, they are called *listed bonds*. The coupon, also known as the interest payment, is usually taxable. The tax rate on interest depends on the investor's personal tax bracket. Percentages can vary from 15 to 35 percent.

Sometimes the corporate bond coupon can be zero, meaning the bond pays no interest at all. The bondholder makes money because the bond has a discounted sale price with a higher redemption value. For instance, a bond might be issued at a value of $1,000 and redeemed at a value of $1,250 at its maturity date because the interest accumulates as part of the principal. These are called **zero-coupon bonds**. Some investors prefer this type of arrangement because interest is taxable at their earning levels but capital gains are taxable at fixed levels. Investors can save on their income taxes by holding zero-coupon bonds.

Despite being listed on exchanges, the vast majority of trading volume in corporate bonds takes place in decentralized, dealer-based, over-the-counter markets. Trading value depends upon the coupon rate of the bond and the going rate of interest at the time. Since the coupon of the bond cannot be changed, the trading value of the bond is what changes. Most bonds are initially sold at $1,000 values with an interest rate that is the going rate at the time of issuance. If the going rate of interest goes down, the value of the bond usually goes up, and vice versa.

An example is U.S. Treasury bonds. Let's say a $1,000 bond sold in 2001 and maturing in 2021 carries a 7 percent interest rate. If the interest rate for bonds in 2011 is 3 percent, the 2001 bond is worth more than $1,000. On the other hand, if a $1,000 U.S. Treasury bond sold in 2011 carries a 3 percent interest rate, but in 2014 interest rates go up to 5 percent, the bond is worth less than $1,000. The face value of the bond fluctuates as the going interest for bonds fluctuates relative to the interest the bond pays.

Some corporate bonds have an **embedded call option** that allows the issuer to redeem the debt before its maturity date. Other bonds, called *convertible bonds*, allow investors to convert the bond into equity. The embedded call option permits the corporate issuer to default on interest or principal payments, protecting the purchaser from losing the investment because the purchaser initializes a conversion to company stock. It may seem undesirable to own stock in companies that are at risk of defaulting on their bonds, but at least the conversion to stock postpones the total loss of the purchaser's investment.

Corporate bonds are rated by the risk that the company may not repay the interest or principal. Earlier, bond ratings were discussed for both corporate and municipal bonds. However, revenue bonds are not traded nearly as frequently as corporate or municipal bonds because they are a different animal altogether.

Revenue Bonds

Revenue bonds are similar to corporate bonds in that there is an expectation that the issuer will repay the interest during specific intervals and the principal at the end of the bond's life. The difference is that revenue bonds are not issued by corporations but by nonprofit organizations, governmental units, and other public-benefit agencies. The bond principal and interest payments for revenue bonds are guaranteed by the revenue flow of the issuing agency.

Municipal revenue bonds are somewhat different from those issued by nonprofit organizations. Municipal bonds are generally exempt from federal tax on their interest payments. But similar to corporate bonds or nonprofit revenue bonds, if the bond appreciates in value, the capital gain is taxable under federal income tax laws. For taxpayers who purchase municipal bonds issued in the same state in which they reside, interest payments are generally exempt from state and local taxes as well.

Revenue bonds are more frequently issued by nonprofit organizations than by governmental units. Because municipal bonds may be issued in one of two forms, revenue bonds or general obligation bonds, governmental leisure services have a choice of which to use to finance their capital improvements. Unless the leisure services agency is operating an enterprise fund, such as a golf course or other revenue-generating facility, there may not be enough revenue from operations to repay the bonds. In that case, a general obligation bond would be a better solution.

Governments that issue revenue bonds restrict the debt service to only the governmental enterprise that generates these revenues. **Debt service** is the series of payments of interest and principal required on a debt over a given period of time. The government itself does not pledge its own credit to pay the bonds. It is the taxpayers who pledge to repay the revenue bonds if the governmental unit fails to do so. In other words, taxpayers are obligated to pay these bonds off; hence the name *general obligation*.

When a municipality assumes liability for the debt service and the income from the project is insufficient, it is considered to be **double-barreled**, meaning the bonds will be repaid through two sources of cash flow: project income and tax revenue. These are municipal general obligation

© Jeff Clow - Fotolia

A governmental unit can finance capital improvements, such as the construction of a new swimming pool, in several ways, including bonds, property taxes, or sales taxes.

bonds as opposed to revenue bonds because they are ultimately backed by the issuer and its taxing power. The municipality guarantees that double-barreled bonds will be repaid with the faith and credit that the taxpayers will do so if the revenue streams from the project are not sufficient.

Before issuing revenue bonds, a nonprofit organization or governmental unit should conduct a feasibility study to compare the internal rate of return (IRR), or hurdle rate, of the project to determine if it is likely the bonds can be repaid from revenues. Feasibility studies examine similar projects to determine how they performed and whether it is likely the proposed project will perform well.

Municipal Bonds

Municipal bonds are similar to corporate and revenue bonds except they can only be issued by local governments or their agencies. Potential issuers of municipal bonds include cities, counties, redevelopment agencies, special-purpose districts, school districts, park districts, public utility districts, publicly owned airports and seaports, and any other governmental entity or group of governments below the state level.

Municipal bonds may be general obligations of the issuer or secured by specified revenues. Interest income received by holders of municipal bonds is often exempt from federal income tax and from the income tax of the state in which the bonds are issued, although municipal bonds issued for certain purposes may not be tax exempt.

Municipal bonds are sold to investors when they are issued. Investors may trade municipal bonds, just as they may trade corporate or revenue bonds. Municipal bonds are typically sold in $1,000 denominations with coupons payable at the going rate of interest at the time. However, when the interest is tax exempt at the state and federal levels, the going rate for municipal bonds tends to be lower than for corporate or revenue bonds. That is because the interest rate takes into consideration the fact that taxes will not be paid.

Typically, there is a bidding process for the sale of municipal bonds at the time of their issuance. Some states require that the bidding process be open to anyone, where the issuance is sold through an investment bank and competing banks submit sealed bids for the interest that they are willing to pay. The standard of practice is that the lowest bid is the one that the municipality accepts. But the lower the coupon rate, the more difficult it is for the investment bank to resell the bonds on the open market.

Municipal bonds can be issued in denominations higher than $1,000. If, for instance, a local bank is the low bidder purchasing the entire amount of the issuance, and it doesn't intend to resell the bonds, the governmental unit might be willing to issue a bond for the full amount. Some municipalities in smaller and rural communities do this routinely because local banks are willing to purchase the bonds and because the governmental unit would rather not deal with investment banks.

However, most local governments sell their bonds through investment banks. Full-service investment banks usually provide both advisory and financing services as well as the sales and research on a broad array of financial products, including equities, credit, rates, commodities, and their derivatives. The following are the largest full-service global investment banks, based on revenues and assets. These investment banks have been known to purchase large municipal bonds and corporate bond issues.

- Bank of America
- Barclays
- BNP Paribas
- Citigroup
- Credit Suisse
- Deutsche Bank
- Goldman Sachs
- HSBC
- JPMorgan Chase
- Morgan Stanley
- Nomura Holdings
- Royal Bank of Canada
- Royal Bank of Scotland
- Societe Generale
- UBS
- Wells Fargo

The authority for issuing municipal bonds varies from state to state. Some states allow elected officials to issue the bonds, but others require voter approval through referenda. It all depends on whether the state trusts its local governments to make the decision or whether the state trusts only the public to make the decision.

All states allow elected officials to issue bonds at certain levels in order to make capital improvements. It is just a matter of what level the state trusts them to do so. In some states, elected officials are only permitted to issue debt to make relatively small capital improvements, up to a few million dollars. In other states, local government units that have home rule authority can make whatever improvements they need, with the understanding that the elected officials will answer to the voters at election time.

FINANCING PUBLIC PROJECTS THROUGH REFERENDA

In states that require major capital improvements to have voter approval, municipalities, special districts, and county governments are required to begin the referenda process with an ordinance approved by the elected common council or board. Some states require that a petition drive be mounted, with a percentage of registered voters signing their names that they believe the **question** should be put on the ballot at the next election. Referenda are stated in questions that allow voters to vote *yes* or *no*. Whether a question is put on a ballot by ordinance or petition, the question on the ballot must state the dollar amount that the governmental unit wants to borrow, what it intends to spend it on, and how long it will take to pay the money back.

Some states, such as Missouri, allow the use of sales taxes to repay bonds that are sold to fund capital improvements. Other states, such as Illinois, allow the use of property taxes to repay the bonds sold to fund capital improvements. Sales and property taxes tend to be the most frequently used when referenda are required, but other funding sources can be used when referenda are not required.

In some states, such as Wisconsin, where common councils have the home rule authority to approve the sale of bonds for capital improvements, the common council can use its discretion as to how to repay the bonds. It can fund them from increased property taxes, sales taxes, or even state revenue sharing as well as any combination of the funding sources available to them.

For a referendum to pass, it must garner a majority of votes. A referendum question might be phrased as follows:

> Should the City of Newark issue $7,000,000 in general obligation bonds to construct a new swimming pool in Rogers Park, with the sale of bonds repaid over a 20-year period paid by an increase in property taxes?

The referendum question does not include all of the details relevant to the capital project, because doing so would require a long explanation and would be confusing. Most states believe that the public has a responsibility to stay informed about the major capital projects that local governments are considering and to require local governments to be transparent in their decisions.

The referendum question also does not include the rate of interest to be paid on the bonds that will be sold, because the governmental unit does not know what it will be. It also does not include the increase in property tax that each taxpayer will pay, because the governmental unit does not know that, either. All the governmental unit knows for sure is how much money it wants the voters to allow it to borrow, how long it will take to pay the money back, what tax will be increased to pay the money back, and what it will spend the money on. As part of transparency obligations, during the referendum campaign the governmental unit will provide scenarios of the financial impact on taxpayers, but ultimately it is the responsibility of the taxpayers to figure out what it will cost them.

Many of the voters' questions will be answered through the referendum campaign or by the media. The campaign and the media can help voters understand the issues because the actions of the governmental unit are open to public scrutiny and subject to public questions through FOIA and state **open meetings acts** or **sunshine laws**. These laws require government meetings, decisions, and records to be made available to the public.

Referenda Campaigns

Referenda to increase sales or property taxes to fund capital improvements are similar to election campaigns. They are contests between opposing points of view, with each vying for voter support. Those who want the referendum to pass argue their case, and those who don't argue theirs.

In general, political campaigns are determined by which side best gets its message out to the public and its supporters to the polls on election day. Motivation to go to the polls to vote for or against a political campaign is often determined by which side has made its case most effectively, motivating people to vote. It is great to have a message, but voter turnout is the key.

Effectively communicating with voters means having a compelling message, identifying the media to which the voters pay attention, and placing the message in those media. Communicating with

Politics of a Bond Referendum

Municipal park and recreation departments often fund their capital improvements through the sale of bonds, sometimes permitted by the city council and sometimes requiring referenda. When park and recreation capital improvements are funded by bonds authorized by the city council, the political will of the council is tested. When a referendum is required, public support of the park and recreation department is tested, and the department must make its case directly to the voters.

In Pflugerville, Texas, the park and recreation department exhausted its ability to fund park and facility improvements with operating or available capital funds. In May 2011, at a city council work session, the Pflugerville Parks and Recreation Commission recommended a bond referendum for November 2012. The park and recreation director provided a list of proposed capital improvements needed to maintain and improve the city's park system based on the five-year plan. These included improvements to parks, trails, and facilities.

According to news coverage, council members commented on the quality of the park system and the public's perception of the parks. One council member noted that there were plenty of parks but no sport complex. They agreed that some of the parks needed repairs and maintenance, and that overall the park system has the potential to get a grade of *A* but was not there yet.

Council members expressed concern about voter support for a bond referendum since one failed in 2008 for expansion of the Pflugerville Recreation Center and a new city hall. They thought November 2012 might be a good time and would generate a good turnout since it would be on the same ballot as the general election for the U.S. president.

"We had that election in May, which is kind of a boner thing to do," Councilman Wayne Cooper said. "Maybe November 2012 would be a great time if we're going to do it." He cautioned, however, that the economy might make any such referendum difficult. "[W]e need to make sure we do things we really need," Cooper said. "Keep in mind the community is a lot different than it was a year ago, than it was five years ago."

General comments about the commission's opinion will not be sufficient for a referendum to prevail, nor will rough estimates of the cost to fund those improvements to individual homeowners. More compelling arguments of need are required, as are testimonials from supporters. And a relative lack of resistance to a referendum would be nice as well. Otherwise full-blown political campaigns for and against the referendum will ensue.

References

Rasmussen, B. 2011. "Parks and Recreation Commission Recommends 2012 Bond Referendum." *Community Impact Newspaper*, May 10. http://impactnews.com/articles/parks-and-recreation-commission-recommends-2012-bond-referendum.

voters requires money for campaign literature, yard signs, billboards, and newspaper, radio, and television ads.

Getting voters to the polls on election day can be a function of setting up phone calling networks to encourage people to do their civic duty to vote. It can also be a function of providing transportation, especially for people who don't have their own. To accomplish this, the campaign needs a network of volunteer supporters to make phone calls and provide transportation to the polls.

Campaign costs to support referenda cannot legally be funded by tax money, because governmental units cannot spend taxpayer money to convince taxpayers to increase their own taxes. Nor can public employees actively support referenda; they are paid with tax money, so the same rules apply. But public employees can provide information about a referendum if they don't directly tell the public to vote for it.

If that seems like a distinction without a difference, it might be. The same is true with fundraising for referenda campaigns. Even though campaigns cannot be supported by taxpayer money, in many states it is not against the law for donors to include the architects, banks, and other potential beneficiaries of the referenda. Governmental leisure services units often pay architects and other consultants to do preliminary work on the project, such as developing concept plans. These consultants are among the first to contribute to referenda campaigns because they know that if the referendum is approved, their role in the development of the project will more than repay them for their contributions.

As for the campaigns themselves, they are similar to other political campaigns. There are campaign speeches, the news media get involved with editorials, and there is organized opposition. The opposition usually comes from taxpayer groups who oppose taxes in general, or sometimes from **NIMBYs** (**n**ot **i**n **m**y **b**ack **y**ard), people who live close to where the project will be constructed and don't want it in their backyard.

It is almost always easier to get taxpayers to oppose a referendum because, except for those who would use the facility, people usually don't favor increasing their taxes. That makes referenda campaigns uphill battles. For instance, 35 percent of community residents may use a swimming pool. To get a referendum passed to increase taxes to build a new swimming pool, a portion of the other 65 percent needs to be convinced to support it. This is not always an easy sell and is made even more difficult by tough economic times.

Unfair Competition Between Sectors

Because governmental units have the opportunity to get taxpayers to repay the debt for capital improvements, they have a competitive advantage over private businesses and nonprofit organizations. Private businesses can only finance their improvements by accumulating profits, borrowing money from investors or bondholders, or selling ownership in their companies. Nonprofits can only finance capital improvements through accumulated surplus revenues, revenue bonds, or donations.

For many years, business and nonprofit organizations have argued that it is unfair for taxpayers to fund government-provided leisure services because there is no capital cost to governmental units. To accumulate profits or repay bonds, businesses and nonprofit organizations need to charge higher prices to cover those costs whereas the capital costs of governmental units are covered by taxpayers.

The issue is especially sensitive when fitness centers or other revenue engines are considered by governmental organizations. Such facilities could be in direct competition with businesses or nonprofit fitness centers. An argument can be made that the governmental unit is using tax money to put a taxpaying business out of business.

Governmental leisure services units are forced concerns about unfair competition, particularly when it becomes an issue in a referendum campaign. There have been cases where fitness centers or other businesses feel threatened enough to contribute to the side opposing the referendum during the campaign.

Governmental units should consider whether asking voters for tax money to compete against businesses and nonprofit organizations is a good idea before they launch a referendum campaign. When common councils consider capital financing for facilities, leisure services managers can almost always be assured the issue will come up.

Approval by Common Councils

In states where referenda are not required to make capital improvements, such as Indiana or Wisconsin, elected officials have the authority to increase property or sales taxes without voter approval. Of course, voters still have the ability to remove elected officials from their positions at the next election, and officials often make the decision to support a capital improvement on that basis.

As discussed in previous chapters, some political ideologies believe that leisure services are a legitimate function of government and others do not. Common council members who do believe leisure services are a legitimate governmental function are more likely to be supporters than those who do not. In some ways, for a leisure services manager to gain approval through elected-official approval, the process is similar to that of a referendum. Both processes are inherently political. In discussing the matter with elected officials, leisure services managers are in effect campaigning for the improvement or at least lobbying for it. A case in favor of the capital improvement needs to be made, and sometimes opponents of the capital improvement will emerge to make arguments against the improvement. In the end, a majority of the elected officials will vote either for or against the capital improvement, sometimes because they were going to do so anyway and sometimes because the arguments were compelling.

The point is that leisure services capital financing for governmental units is more than a function of borrowing money or soliciting donations. Obtaining funding for capital improvements can be a very political process that can tear a community apart. It's not just a matter of costs versus benefits or whether the service would help people. At the governmental level, it can be a matter of political ideology, campaigns, or economic conditions that affect the behavior of voters or elected officials.

MANAGING CONSTRUCTION PROJECTS

The turnkey method of managing capital improvements might be a good option for large and complex projects, such as the construction of a new sports stadium.

Leisure services management includes a repertoire of financial management skills for capital projects, including the management of construction projects. Not only do leisure services managers need to understand how to acquire funds for capital financing, but they also need to administer the funds according to state laws and in a manner that gets as much bang for the buck as possible.

In managing construction projects, there are two ways to go. One direction is the **turnkey method**, where the business, nonprofit, or governmental unit puts itself completely in the hands of consultants, such as construction managers or architects, and has minimal contact with the consultant and building contractors until the end of the project, when it receives the keys. The other is the **in-house method**, where the organization serves as its own construction manager, hiring smaller consultants and construction companies to build the project. This is a hands-on approach where the leisure services manager is involved every step of the way.

Both methods have their adherents. Some leisure services managers prefer the turnkey method because it allows them to fulfill their other duties and because they don't know how to manage construction projects. Other leisure services managers prefer the in-house method because they believe they can build a facility cheaper than by paying a bunch of consultants and they will have more control over the project.

Architects

The standard playbook of many leisure services agencies, regardless of whether they are in the private, nonprofit, or governmental sector, is to hire an architectural firm and turn the project over to it. The leisure services agency generally signs a contract with the architectural firm for a percentage of the total construction costs, usually between 6 and 10 percent. Typically, the larger the project, the smaller the percentage, but such is not always the case. Some architectural firms have long-term relationships with leisure services agencies, and they take advantage of those relationships by charging a higher percentage on the contract.

Paying an architectural firm a percentage of the construction cost has its advantages and disadvantages, but from a financial standpoint, it mainly has disadvantages. If the architectural firm is being paid for its time and materials, it is difficult to estimate its costs during the beginning phase of the project, which eliminates the incentive of the firm to increase the cost of the project and provides an incentive for the firm to spend more time working on it. But if an architectural firm is paid a percentage of the project, there is an incentive for the project to be more expensive than the leisure services agency might have intended and less of an incentive for the firm to spend time working on the project.

One reason hiring an architectural firm is in the leisure services playbook is that it works. Architectural firms are experienced at designing and overseeing construction projects. They know how much it costs to build a facility because they have built them before. They know how to oversee contractors because they have overseen them before. It's easy to hire an architectural firm to manage the capital project. All the leisure services agency needs is the money.

When a leisure services agency does not have the money, or the project is relatively small, the agency may be forced to seek alternatives to the turnkey method. One of the options is to hire a **construction management firm**, which performs many of the cost-saving duties that a leisure services agency would do if the agency had the expertise or were large enough to do the project itself.

Construction management firms often have their own architects on staff. If they don't, they might have relationships with other architectural firms that can save the leisure services agency money. From a project design standpoint, it is cheaper and just as effective to limit the role of the architects to that of designing the project only. Construction management firms that have an architect on staff treat their work as a commodity. The same is true when they hire an architectural firm to provide the design.

Treating architectural services or any other services like a commodity means that the service is **flat-rate commissioned**. Rather than being paid a percentage of the total construction cost, the architectural firm is paid a flat fee for services. When architectural firms run turnkey projects, they treat the other consultants, such as engineers, as commodities.

Construction Managers

Construction management firms are emerging as the new paradigm of capital project development for leisure services, regardless of the sector. This approach was adopted first by the private sector as a way of maximizing financial resources, getting the most bang for the buck. The public sector is now seeing the cost-saving benefit as it becomes increasingly difficult to pass referenda or for common councils to approve bond issues for county and municipal leisure services departments.

In the public sector, construction managers are often able to arrange for private financing through

Lamp Incorporated

In 2007, the Huntley Park District in Huntley, Illinois, hired Lamp Incorporated as its project manager to replace the existing clubhouse at Pinecrest Golf Course. The process began with a meeting with the park district staff to determine the project budget and identify a project schedule. Because the busiest time of the golf course was between Memorial Day and Labor Day, Lamp needed to have the project documents completed and bid out with construction to begin the first Tuesday after Labor Day.

After Lamp established a total budget that was within the financial resources of the park district, Lamp developed a request for qualifications of architectural firms, reviewed them, and helped the district rank the firms. Once the firms were ranked, Lamp helped the park district staff interview the top four firms. Two firms were selected by staff for interviews with the park district board. Once the board selected a firm, Lamp helped the park district develop the architectural agreement.

During the design and preconstruction phase, Lamp worked with the design firm and Huntley Park District in budgeting and maintaining the schedule. Lamp made two presentations with the design team during this phase to show the park district board the design progress and budget maintenance. During this phase, the board was given the decision to either maintain a modest building and replace the irrigation system or upgrade the clubhouse and replace the irrigation system at a later date.

Once the architect completed the design documents, Lamp acted as the general contractor, soliciting subcontractors, reviewing the low apparent bidders, and making recommendations to the board for approval. Lamp prepared the agreements between the trade contractors and the park district, received their bonds, and made sure their insurance was in compliance with the documents.

To kick off the project, Lamp organized a building-breaking ceremony complete with a chrome-plated sledge hammer, which commissioners used to take whacks at the existing building. Demolition of the existing structure began the Tuesday after Labor Day and was completed by Memorial Day (9 months of construction). Lamp maintained the schedule and budget, processed pay requests, supervised construction, analyzed change order requests, and maintained the quality of standards the district was expecting. During this phase Lamp made presentations to the board on the progress and budget updates. Lamp also helped coordinate the building finishes, furnishings and equipment, and building utilities.

The park district was extremely happy with the entire project, especially since it came in under budget. The spring schedule for completion of the project was met and the park district was able to meet its golfing and banquet commitments.

public–private partnerships (PPPs). Then they develop the design plans for the facility; serve as project managers during the construction phase, overseeing the subcontractors; and turn over a completed and financed project to the leisure services governmental unit.

The way PPP financing works is similar to the way revenue bonds work. A feasibility study shows the possible revenue streams that the leisure services agency could generate by operating the completed facility. If it appears that enough money will be generated to pay the operating costs and the mortgage on the facility, the project goes forward. If the revenue streams appear too risky, the facility is seen as unfeasible and the project doesn't go forward.

The difference between PPP financing and revenue bonds is that, essentially, the private partner holds a mortgage on the facility with a **lien** on it—the right to keep property belonging to another person until a debt is paid. The lien is paid off over a specific time period, usually 20 years. During that time, the private partner is earning interest as well as receiving principal repayments. Revenue bondholders do not have the facility as **collateral** (assets that are pledged by a borrower to secure a loan or other credit and that are subject to seizure in the event of default). They just have a piece of paper that says they will be repaid. Municipalities often use PPP financing when they do not have access to capital funds in the short run but believe they will in the long run.

PPP financing is viable for governmental leisure units when there is revenue to be gained from operating the facility, such as a water park or golf course. It's also viable for other governmental enterprises such as public water and sewer systems because they generate substantial revenues from operations. But other governmental services such as public parks do not generate revenues, so PPPs are not viable options for them.

SUMMARY

Leisure services managers must understand capital financing because facilities are required to provide leisure services. Though private businesses, nonprofit organizations, and governmental units share similar challenges in constructing their leisure facilities, they face different challenges in acquiring funding.

Businesses have the option of spending accumulated cash profits on capital improvements. They also can acquire additional debt or sell equity in the company. Nonprofit organizations and governmental units cannot sell equity, but they can issue revenue bonds if there is an expectation that the capital improvement will generate enough money to pay operating costs in addition to the repayment of the bonds. Governmental units also have the option of going to the taxpayers for support.

Sometimes, using taxpayer money is considered unfair by existing businesses and nonprofit organizations, particularly during referenda campaigns. During these campaigns, voters are asked to approve the sale of municipal bonds to finance capital projects. Municipal bonds are issued at relatively low interest rates, and investors don't have to pay income tax on the interest repaid to them.

Bonds are available as a source of capital financing for businesses and nonprofits. Corporate bonds are available to businesses and revenue bonds to nonprofit organizations. Corporate bonds may pay various rates of interest or may be zero-coupon bonds based on the risk of the company repaying bondholders. In order for nonprofit organizations to issue revenue bonds, a feasibility analysis is performed to determine the likelihood of repayment. When the likelihood is low, which it is when the improvement is for charitable purposes, donations are the preferred method of financing capital improvements.

There are two preferred ways of approaching capital improvements for leisure services, regardless of whether the agency is a business, nonprofit organization, or governmental unit. One approach is the turnkey method and the other is the in-house method. Both have their adherents. Turnkey adherents often prefer to put themselves in the hands of their favorite architects, whereas in-house adherents often prefer to use construction managers.

Visit the Web Resource

For case studies, sample financial statements,
key terms, and more, please visit the web resource at
www.HumanKinetics.com/LeisureServicesFinancialManagement

chapter 12

Future Trends

Learning Outcomes

After completing this chapter, students will be able to do the following:

- Identify the latest transparency requirements of business, nonprofit, and public organizations.
- Learn how to keep apprised of changes in financial reporting requirements for all three sectors.
- Determine how changes in technology will affect leisure services.
- Understand how the continued focus on revenues will drive leisure services.

During the early 1800s, the public didn't care much whether corporate executives paid themselves vast sums of money. The public also didn't know that a substantial percentage of the money it donated to nonprofit charitable organizations went to administrative costs. And the public didn't know much about wasteful spending at the federal, state, and local government levels. But with the New York City media exposing Tammany Hall in the 1860s for all its corruption, and with the national media exposing corporate abuses in the early 1900s, transparency in both sectors has led to more ethical behavior on the part of government and corporate executives.

In the past 30 years, with the creation of CNN cable news in 1980, the subsequent creation of competing news outlets, and the growth of the Internet, the multitude of 24-hour news services, text alerts, and bloggers make it possible for the public to become aware of events occurring in the world very quickly. And since Twitter and Facebook alerts have become available on phones and other mobile devices, it is possible to be informed about events just seconds after they occur.

Sometimes it's good that people immediately know what's going on, but sometimes it unnecessarily scares them. For example, because many **AMBER alerts** are released to the public through the mass media, some parents are now afraid to let their children go anywhere alone, especially to parks. *AMBER* stands for America's Missing: Broadcast Emergency Response, and these alerts are media announcements that a child has been reported missing and that everyone should keep a watchful eye for the child and the abductor. The alerts have been extremely useful in saving children, but they have their downsides, too. For one, parental fears about children playing outside have contributed to childhood obesity and have increasingly isolated children from outdoor environments. Little research has been done on whether children staying inside has reduced the rate of abductions, but according to Project America, kidnappings between 1982 and 2000 increased by 468 percent. In addition, the likelihood of being kidnapped is much higher among teens and young adults, suggesting that adults are more at risk of being kidnapped than children. And of the children who are kidnapped, Project America reports that 49 percent are kidnapped by family members and 27 percent by acquaintances (Project America 2012).

Sometimes the unintended consequence of today's mass information culture is that people live in fear more than they should. Public awareness of problems can make people worried about venturing outside, and the same can probably be said about financial management. In the days before 24-hour news services, the public wasn't as aware of how much waste, fraud, and corruption there is in the financial world. But for the past 30 years, there have been multiple stories about how greedy business executives can be, how much money is spent on the administration of nonprofit organizations, and how lazy and corrupt public officials can be. These financial AMBER Alerts, so to speak, have caused public outrage, which has led to Federal Trade Commission (FTC) and Federal Communications Commission (FCC) regulations making businesses more transparent, IRS regulations making nonprofit organizations more transparent, and FOIA and open meetings legislation making government more transparent.

In Illinois, for instance, the importance of the public's right to know has led the legislature to expand the Open Meetings Act that applies to local governments. Now some of the personnel records of government employees are available, including not only their pay and benefits but also personal information. The intent of the law is to discourage nepotism or other favorable hiring and promotional practices as well as to provide information about employee pensions. As a result, the news media have been able to shine light on numerous abuses that have taken place in hiring, promotion, and employee benefits, discouraging future abuses.

Transparency laws may have led to the public helping police catch the perpetrators of crime in the financial world, but they have also had unintended consequences, just as AMBER Alerts have had for kidnapping. One unintended consequence is that it is now much more difficult, time consuming, and expensive to manage the finances of leisure services organizations in all three sectors. In addition, news stories about financial corruption have dampened the willingness of the public to fund governmental services.

TRANSPARENCY REQUIREMENTS

Transparency requirements are essential if investors in the private sector, donors in the nonprofit sector, and taxpayers in the public sector are going to determine if their investments, donations, and taxes are being used as promised. All three sectors have transparency requirements designed to reassure investors, donors, and taxpayers that their money is indeed being used as promised. Although transparency systems are not perfect, leisure services financial management is far better off with systems in place. Without them, it would be the Wild West all over again.

Private-Sector Requirements

In many ways, the business world is still the sector with the least amount of transparency. Unless a company is publicly traded, its financial statements are a private matter between the company and the IRS, state, and local tax-collecting agencies.

Income tax records are protected. The financial condition of a privately owned company is nobody else's business, according to confidentiality provisions. These privacy provisions apply to the details contained in a tax return; audit, collection, and investigative reports; information given by the taxpayer related to tax liability; information provided by an individual on behalf of the taxpayer related to the taxpayer's financial affairs; information furnished in or extracted from the federal tax return, federal audit or investigation report, or revenue agent's report; or any vital piece of information available from the IRS, which includes data in the form of a tape, information on whether a taxpayer has filed income tax returns or not, and information on tax returns that are generated and processed electronically (Public Records Guide 2010).

Publicly owned companies are different. Because publicly owned businesses have stock that is traded on stock exchanges, they have greater transparency requirements under FTC regulations. These regulations require that balance sheets and income statements be made available to the public so that potential buyers and sellers of corporate stock and bonds can know the financial condition of the company. This level of transparency is becoming more open and obvious as time goes on.

During the economic downturn beginning in 2008, the U.S. government loaned money to certain banks and lending institutions as well as two domestic automobile manufacturers, General Motors and Chrysler. While using taxpayer money to get back on their feet, several boards of these corporations voted to pay their executives huge bonuses for doing a good job. Almost immediately, the media picked up on these bonuses and informed the public that this was occurring, causing public outrage.

Lending institutions such as Fannie Mae and Freddie Mac, which hold over $5 trillion in mortgage loans, were exposed as having paid 12 executives $13 million in bonuses. The issue was exacerbated by the fact that Congress had spent $170 billion in taxpayers' money to bail out the lending institutions (Boak and Williams 2011).

With the public outcry for more accountability, the FTC and FCC began looking at ways to limit executive bonuses, or at the very least, tax them. The public mood led Congress to introduce bills to either limit executive compensation or to stop providing taxpayer assistance to failing businesses. In response to the Fannie and Freddie controversy, legislation has been introduced to eliminate executive bonuses or tax them. The political consequences could lead to greater or lesser regulation of businesses, but if history is a teacher, the trend is probably toward greater regulation.

Greater regulation has been the overall trend since the Great Depression. When lesser regulation is tried, the economic results are usually unsatisfactory, as exemplified by the housing market crash in 2008, argued by some to have been caused by deregulation of the banking system. Because Democrats controlled Congress at the time of the crash, the response was greater regulation. Republicans, on the other hand, argue that lesser regulation leads to greater job growth and opportunity, and their inclination is to reduce regulation, as occurred during the Reagan administration.

Greater government involvement in business, not lesser involvement, is the most likely prediction for the future. In the short run, some Republicans may take us back to an era of less governmental involvement for a while, but when businesses are regulated less, they tend to exploit that opportunity, usually with negative outcomes. Although there have been short-term declines in the regulation of business, the long-term trend has been increased regulation; growth in the FTC is a testimony to that trend. Therefore, over the long run businesses can expect more government involvement, and more involvement means more transparency will be required.

For leisure services managers, greater government involvement and greater transparency mean more reporting requirements. More financial statements will be made public. Tax returns will be more complicated in order to reassure tax-collecting agencies that deductions are legitimate and that the pay of publicly traded executives is available for scrutiny.

Greater transparency will mean that investors and consumers will have the ability to question the decisions that corporate executives make, including pricing decisions, the structuring of corporate debt, the issuance of new stock, and even the way in which products are marketed and sold. With more transparency, just about every decision executives make will be open to scrutiny.

Nonprofit-Sector Requirements

In light of the United Way scandal of the 1980s, when it was revealed that much of the money donated to the national organization was spent on executive pay and perks (Baker 2008), the IRS has added a layer of reporting to the tax code for nonprofit organizations. Form 990 now requires that nonprofit organizations report executive pay and provide details on their charitable work to justify their nonprofit status. Each year requirements are added to the 990 that focus on having the reporting process provide more information to justify nonprofit status. And, of course, the 990s of nonprofit organizations are available to the public and media under the FOIA and also online on websites such as www.guidestar.org.

States charter nonprofit organizations, and they have their own reporting requirements. Some state departments of revenue or secretaries of state require that nonprofit organizations provide the minutes from their meetings and detailed justifications of executive pay and charitable work. In an effort to be transparent, the public can access

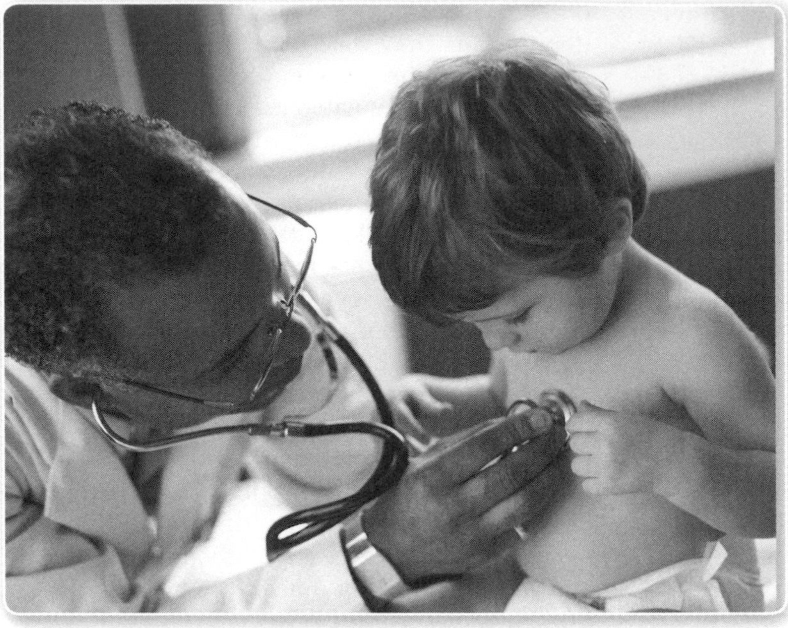

To justify their tax-exempt status, state and federal nonprofit hospitals increasingly must document their charitable work and executive pay, making the jobs of hospital administrators more complicated.

these records of how the nonprofit organization makes its decisions as well as how it raises and spends its money.

What this means to nonprofit leisure organizations is that their financial reporting requirements are becoming increasingly complicated and transparent to the public. In the past, the public had to take the word of nonprofit organizations that they were doing charitable work. Today and in the future, nonprofit organizations will need to prove it. This is not a bad trend, but it makes the job of nonprofit managers more complicated.

Nonprofit hospitals take in billions of dollars from patients, insurance companies, and government providers, and at the same time they fulfill their charitable obligation by providing free and discounted care to the poor. Nonprofit hospitals compete with for-profit and government-run hospitals, and they are also getting into the fitness business by opening first-class health and wellness centers that can be seen as competition for private and YMCA fitness centers. The IRS and state regulators are increasingly looking at the amount of charity care nonprofit hospitals provide and questioning whether it's enough to justify tax exemption.

In Illinois, for example, two fairly wealthy nonprofit hospitals, Edward Hospital in Naperville and Northwestern Memorial Hospital in Chicago, have had their state tax-exempt status revoked by the Illinois Department of Revenue, setting off intense lobbying efforts by the Illinois Hospital Association. At the federal level, nonprofit hospitals are now required to provide much more detail on their charitable activities through Schedule H of IRS Form 990. Again, this trend is not necessarily bad, but it makes the job of nonprofit hospital administrators more complicated.

Because of health care reform passed by Congress in 2009 and decreased funding from the federally subsidized Medicare and Medicaid programs, more and more hospitals will be looking at the potential revenue stream of providing medically managed fitness programs. These programs could also help reduce the long-term costs of managing chronic conditions such as diabetes as well as the health insurance costs of hospital employees. The entrance of hospitals into the fitness field will likely affect the private, government, and nonprofit fitness center industry.

In *Megatrends*, Naisbitt argued that other states should pay attention to what happens in California because eventually it will happen everywhere else in the country (Naisbitt 1982). The earlier reference to Proposition 13 (chapter 2), where local parks and recreation agencies were used as the whipping boy for local governments in order for citizen taxpayer organizations to receive reductions in property taxes, has been at issue in other states since that time. In Illinois, property tax caps were adopted by the legislature in 1991, 1995, and 1997. Other states have adopted similar measures.

What does this mean for the future? As in the private sector, leisure services managers of nonprofit organizations will need to maintain an awareness of the changing environment of reporting their financial activities to the federal and state governments. Nonprofit agencies will also need to make sure that their executive pay, which will be reported by the media, is in line with public expectations. Bad publicity is bad for business, but it's especially bad for nonprofit organizations that depend on the goodwill of the public for donations. Transparency requirements lift the veil on financial management and are a potential threat to maintaining public goodwill. Nonprofit leisure services managers have to be attentive on both fronts.

Governmental-Sector Requirements

Transparency requirements for governments are applied for the same reasons they are applied to business and nonprofit organizations: to give the public a better opportunity to make informed electoral decisions. Episodes of news shows such as *60 Minutes* are rife with stories about insincere efforts made by elected officials to improve transparency, mainly to get themselves reelected. In a November 2011 story, for instance, *60 Minutes* exposed insider trading by members of Congress that resulted in them getting rich on information they were privy to as elected officials. As a result of this broadcast and other media reports, a bill that had been languishing in Congress remarkably passed both the Senate and the House almost unanimously in February 2012. Because the House version was watered down from the Senate version, the final bill has yet to be negotiated in a conference committee.

A *New York Times* article quoted Senator Charles E. Grassley (R-Iowa), who wrote the bill's proposed disclosure requirement for firms that collect political intelligence regarding potential financial investments. Grassley criticized House Republican leaders who, he said, "wiped out any chance of meaningful transparency for the political intelligence industry." He said he would fight to restore the requirement (Pear 2012).

The issue and the debate illustrate that when government transparency requirements are placed upon governments, it's a self-regulating process. Rather than reporting to another government

Predicting the Future

John Naisbitt distinguished himself as an economics visionary with his book *Megatrends* in 1982, which sold 9 million copies in 58 countries. He revised his predictions in 1990 and again in 2000. In 2009, Naisbitt published *China's Megatrends: The 8 Pillars of a New Society*, drawing on his scholarly work in the Far East.

Naisbitt studied at Harvard, Cornell, and Utah Universities and was an executive for IBM and Eastman Kodak. In the political arena he was the assistant secretary of education under President John F. Kennedy and served as special assistant to President Lyndon Johnson. He left Washington in 1966 and joined Science Research Associates. In 1968, he founded his own company, the Urban Research Corporation, as well as the Naisbitt China Institute, a nonprofit research institution studying the social, cultural, and economic transformation of China. He also taught at a number of Asian universities.

All of the *Megatrends* books focused on predictions of how the world would evolve based on evidence that important trends had already begun and would become even more important. An important premise of the books was that the United States is between two eras, the old industrial age and the new information age. Naisbitt predicted that we would become a global village due to our linkages via computers and the Internet. Such an assertion may not seem that futuristic today, but it was in 1982. The Internet didn't exist then, except for in the military, making Naisbitt very forward looking in his day.

In relation to leisure services, Naisbitt predicted in 1982 that the way we worked was changing. What he left unsaid was that the way we used our leisure time would inevitably change as well—if people used the Internet in their work, they might use it in their play as well.

Naisbitt predicted that, because society uses technology in its work, people will seek other people during their leisure. Naisbitt called that trend *high tech/high touch*, suggesting human beings need to be with each other socially, not just see each other on a computer screen. Naisbitt said that people who understand this will prosper, and such has been the case for leisure services professionals.

References

Answers.com. 2012. "John Naisbitt." Accessed January 29, 2012. www.answers.com/topic/john-naisbitt.

eNotes. 2012. "*Megatrends* by John Naisbitt." www.enotes.com/megatrends-salem/megatrends.

Naisbitt, J. 2012. "Biography." Accessed January 29, 2012. www.naisbitt.com/biography.html.

agency, it becomes a matter of the government reporting directly to the public.

Again, the problem usually begins with executive pay and perks. In California and Illinois during 2010, much publicity was given to how city councils and park district boards gave city administrators and park district managers big pay increases at the end of their careers so they could reap large amounts of money in their pensions when they retired. Publicity was also directed at how these same administrators and managers were rehired at half pay from the same governmental units, with their half pay and pensions exceeding their pay during their active career. In Illinois, the *Chicago Tribune* cited officials at the Glencoe and Fox Valley park districts for taking excessive liberties with the pension system and their severance packages (TribLocal 2010).

This created public outrage that could only be quelled by greater transparency. The transparency took the form of expanded state open meetings and the FOIA. In Illinois, for instance, the personnel files of all public employees can be requested under the state freedom of information legislation. These files were previously considered confidential to protect the employees, but largely because of the pay and retirement abuses and the need to appease the public, the legislature changed the law. Now, because public employees are paid with tax money, the public has been given the right to see what it is paying for (Sunshine Review 2012).

In Florida, it has been state law for over 30 years that the media and public have the right to know who is applying for management positions in local government, even before the governmental unit has had the opportunity to interview them. The result is that the local media often conduct background checks of their own with the media in other communities before the governmental unit has the opportunity to do a background check. Thus, many candidates for management positions in local governments have been tarnished by the media before being given serious consideration by the local government to which they were applying. And, of course, highly qualified candidates have declined to apply for positions in local government to avoid the resurfacing of some controversial issue in their past.

In the case of public meetings, most states give elected boards the right to go into executive session to discuss matters of personnel, pending contracts, litigation, or land purchases. However, states such as Illinois, which once only required elected boards of local governments to take minutes from these sessions, now require executive meetings to be video or audio recorded. If there is a question that topics not covered by the executive-session exemptions were covered in the session, the public can ask the court to review the recordings to determine if violations of the state's open meetings act occurred.

And then there's the matter of communication between public officials. Under the FOIA, all forms of written and electronic communication are available to the public upon request. If, for instance, a community wants to build a new aquatic center, letters and e-mails exchanged among elected officials, staff, and private vendors are public information and available upon request.

In government, especially at the local level, it's all about how the government spends taxpayer money. In the United States, transparency means showing how tax money is spent wisely. Leisure services managers in the public sector need to realize that they are living in a fishbowl, and the glass is becoming clearer with each successive year. Any mistakes that get made are subject to immediate scrutiny.

ONLINE SCRUTINY

In addition to transparency, the online environment provides opportunity for public comment across all three sectors. People rate businesses and organizations and discuss their experiences online, especially when they feel they have been treated poorly. Websites like yelp.com, CruiseCritic.com, and TripAdvisor.com are examples. And any organization with a website that allows for feedback offers an opportunity for public comment.

For public sector leisure services agencies, newspaper coverage of board meetings and other activities can generate public criticism (and sometimes praise) through letters to the editors or online comments, which are just part of the territory of the public sector (although they can be difficult for public officials to endure). Public officials are public figures. The rules of slander and libel are different for them; they only apply when there is malicious intent by the slanderer. But maliciousness is subjective, and it's difficult to prove when the burden of proof is on the victim.

Calls for the resignation of public officials are common, and most newspaper editors do not think this type of comment is malicious. The problem is that the calls for resignation affect the willing-

Increased scrutiny of leisure services events and administrators can raise public awareness of financial accountability and can also generate public criticism.

ness of public officials to take action. For instance, fewer and fewer leisure services managers are asking elected officials for the money to build new facilities because they know they will be criticized or even asked to resign by bloggers who are opposed to spending tax money on such frivolous things.

In Naperville, Illinois, for instance, between 2001 and 2010, the park district had six different executive directors, all of whom were taken to task by bloggers and newspaper columnists. Sometimes the board members and staff were accused of misappropriation of public funds for such expenditures as going to state and national conferences, activities in which agencies all over the country participate. Other accusations of misappropriation of funds included awarding bids to the second- or third-lowest bidders for construction projects, which is not permitted in Illinois. In other words, sometimes the media were correct in their judgments, and sometimes they were unfair.

With the advent of online news and loss of print advertising dollars, community newspapers, especially, used the practice of allowing anonymous comments to drive consumers to their websites, giving online advertising more value. This practice, however, generated local criticism, especially from community leaders and public officials, and eventually the practice changed to require that commenters register their names, addresses, and phone numbers.

For example, the *Daily Chronicle* in DeKalb, Illinois, now identifies comments with the first name, last initial, and town in which the commenter lives, and comments are available online for only one week. The registration page on the *Daily Chronicle* site states, "Your first name, last initial, hometown, and username will appear with your comments" (www.daily-chronicle.com/user/register.xml).

Blogging is another form of making opinions and experiences available to a wide online public. *Blog* is short for *weblog* and is like an online diary on specific topics, often generating online responses from people with shared interests. Hobbies, politics, travel, health, and fitness are common topics. These blogs have expanded the amount of information and points of view available to the public. Today, there are millions of **bloggers** with their own websites expressing their opinions. Not all of them provide what would be considered verifiable information by academic standards, but they do provide information of a sort.

Whether leisure services managers in the public sector like it or not, online newspapers and bloggers have added a level of transparency that didn't exist before. Newspapers and bloggers have made leisure services administration in the public sector more challenging for managers, but they have increased accountability to the public. The question is, does fear of being criticized affect the behavior of leisure services managers in the public sector? Will leisure services managers of the future stay indoors where it's safe, so to speak, just like parents who are afraid of the dangers outside for their children?

CHANGES IN FINANCIAL REPORTING

Financial reporting requirements are a moving picture, changing as new information becomes available and as problems are identified. Since the private and nonprofit sectors are under the FASB, changes in FASB guidelines are especially relevant to them. And since public-sector accounting is under the GASB, changes in GASB guidelines are relevant to them. It is not always important for leisure services managers to understand the reasons for the changes, although sometimes it helps if they do. But it is vital for managers to pay attention to inevitable changes that they will need to comply with.

FASB Requirements

Since its founding in 1973, the FASB has had the task of developing accounting standards for business and nonprofit entities. And the FASB hasn't sat idly by since that time, as shown by its stated mission. Officially, its mission is "to establish and improve standards of financial accounting and reporting for the guidance and education of the public, including issuers, auditors, and users of financial information" (FASB 2012) with the following five goals:

1. Improve the usefulness of financial reporting by focusing on the primary characteristics of relevance and reliability and on the qualities of comparability and consistency.
2. Keep standards current to reflect changes in methods of doing business and in the economy.
3. Consider any significant areas of deficiency in financial reporting that might be improved through standard setting.
4. Promote international convergence of accounting standards concurrent with improving the quality of financial reporting.
5. Improve common understanding of the nature and purposes of information in financial reports.

Except for the second goal, all of these goals contain the word *improve*, suggesting that leisure services managers in the private and nonprofit sectors can expect that the FASB will be constantly looking for ways to improve financial reporting.

For instance, in 1984 the FASB created a task force called the **Emerging Issues Task Force (EITF)** to serve as a shield against interest groups. This group was created to provide timely responses to financial issues as they emerge, especially ones that are controversial. Comprising 15 people from both the private and public sectors as well as representatives from the FASB and an SEC observer, the EITF helps the FASB consider the course of action it should take. If the EITF reaches a consensus on an issue, it pronounces it an *EITF issue* and the FASB defers to the task force by considering the pronouncement as valid and including it in GAAP.

For instance, the housing market crash starting in 2007 caused lending institutions and investors to ask the EITF to reconsider the pronouncement that certain assets be valued at their historical cost rather than their market value. The EITF is considering that request and will come out with a rule that could affect all business and nonprofit entities, including leisure services entities. The question is, if fixed assets are valued at other than their historical cost, who gets to decide what their value should be, and can investors trust that those values will be accurate?

This suggests that leisure services managers in the private and nonprofit sectors need to pay attention to the issues being considered by the EITF as well as the FASB. Otherwise, they could be surprised by rulings and pronouncements and could be ill prepared to implement them. Professional publications regularly report on the issues being considered and give professionals time to express their opinions before the EITF or FASB makes its rulings. Leisure services managers need to consider how a potential pronouncement will affect the financial position of their business or nonprofit organization.

Financial accounting in nonprofit organizations is prescribed by the FASB, but there are times when the GASB guidelines apply to GAAP. Included among these guidelines is the valuation of fixed assets. Unlike businesses and like government agencies, fixed assets are not depreciated. Nonprofit leisure services managers need to pay attention to both sides of the street, so to speak.

GASB Requirements

Since governmental units need to primarily pay attention to GASB rulings and pronouncements, their focus should be somewhat simpler than that of nonprofit organizations. However, similar to the FASB, the GASB is constantly looking for ways to make governmental reporting more businesslike. Its mission is to establish and improve standards of state and local governmental accounting and financial reporting. The result has been information to guide and educate the public, including issuers, auditors, and users of financial reports. Leisure services managers in the public sector need to pay attention to GASB issues and the pronouncements it makes.

GASB Pronouncements

In the first decade of the 21st century, the GASB made 23 pronouncements (Putnam 2011):

1. Recipient Reporting for Certain Shared Nonexchange Revenues—an amendment of GASB Statement No. 33 (April 2000)
2. Basic Financial Statements—and Management's Discussion and Analysis—for State and Local Governments: Omnibus—an amendment of GASB Statements No. 21 and No. 34 (June 2001)
3. Certain Financial Statement Note Disclosures (June 2001)
4. Determining Whether Certain Organizations Are Component Units—an amendment of GASB Statement No. 14 (May 2002)
5. Deposit and Investment Risk Disclosures—an amendment of GASB Statement No. 3 (April 2003)
6. Budgetary Comparison Schedules—Perspective Differences—an amendment of GASB Statement No. 34 (May 2003)
7. Accounting and Financial Reporting for Impairment of Capital Assets and for Insurance Recoveries (November 2003)
8. Financial Reporting for Postemployment Benefit Plans Other Than Pension Plans (March 2004)
9. Economic Condition Reporting: The Statistical Section—an amendment of NCGA Statement 1 (May 2004)
10. Accounting and Financial Reporting by Employers for Postemployment Benefits Other Than Pensions (June 2004)
11. Net Assets Restricted by Enabling Legislation—an amendment of GASB Statement No. 34 (December 2004)
12. Accounting for Termination Benefits (June 2005)
13. Sales and Pledges of Receivables and Future Revenues and Intra-Entity Transfers of Assets and Future Revenues (September 2006)
14. Accounting and Financial Reporting for Pollution Remediation Obligations (November 2006)
15. Pension Disclosures—an amendment of GASB Statements No. 25 and No. 27 (May 2007)
16. Accounting and Financial Reporting for Intangible Assets (June 2007)
17. Land and Other Real Estate Held as Investments by Endowments (November 2007)
18. Accounting and Financial Reporting for Derivative Instruments (June 2008)
19. Fund Balance Reporting and Governmental Fund Type Definitions (March 2009)
20. The Hierarchy of Generally Accepted Accounting Principles for State and Local Governments (March 2009)
21. Codification of Accounting and Financial Reporting Guidance Contained in the AICPA Statements on Auditing Standards (March 2009)
22. OPEB Measurements by Agent Employers and Agent Multiple-Employer Plans (December 2009)
23. Accounting and Financial Reporting for Chapter 9 Bankruptcies (December 2009)

Adapted from North Dakota University Systems. Available: http://ndus.edu/uploads/resources/2614/04-gasb-update.pdf

Some of these pronouncements are innocuous enough, such as pronouncement 12 regarding the recording of termination benefits for public employees. But others have had great impact on how financial statements are presented. One example is Statement 34, which created statements of net assets and statements of activities in CAFRs that have a businesslike presentation, something that was completely new to governmental financial reporting at the time.

If paying attention to what the FASB is doing is an important task for leisure services managers in the private sector, paying attention to what the GASB is doing is equally as important for leisure services managers in the public sector. The good news is that for financial reporting to become more transparent to a public that doesn't understand complicated accounting reports, it is important that FASB and GASB financial reports be less complicated.

That seems to be the intent of the FASB and particularly the GASB. The inclusion of GASB Statement 34 created statements of net assets that are simpler and similar to corporate balance sheets. The bad news for leisure services managers in the public sector is that the traditional GASB combined balance sheets are still required in annual financial reports, the conversion of one to the other adding a layer of complexity to the job of public-sector managers.

CHANGES IN TECHNOLOGY

Technology has affected leisure services in a number of ways, such as in the immediacy of registration and payment for services and in allowing greater transparency. In the public sector, city council meetings are broadcast on local television stations, just as Congressional meetings are on C-SPAN. Governmental units like to think this makes them look more open and transparent to the public, but often it makes them look ridiculous because governmental meetings are often slow and boring in reality and attendees say things that aren't always accurate or intelligent.

Similarly, in an effort to be more transparent to the public, board meeting minutes are posted on governmental websites, and sometimes their financial statements are, too. With the creation of simpler financial reports, it's now easier for the public to assess the financial position of those governmental units willing to place their financial records on the Internet, and it's only a matter of time until state legislatures require local governments to post their financial reports.

In the private sector, the financial statements of publicly traded companies are available on the Internet, providing immediate access to the financial position of companies. Equities and bonds are traded online, as are all forms of financial instruments. In fact, corporate securities can be traded automatically by instructing a trading software program to buy and sell at certain prices.

Now decades old, the personal computer is used for financial purposes in all sectors. Almost any leisure services agency that is up to speed, regardless of whether it is a business, nonprofit, or governmental organization, now allows service users to register and pay their fees online with a debit or credit card.

The cutting edge of technology is smartphones, tablets, and similar small devices, which are evolving to take the place of personal computers. Golf courses, for instance, allow golfers to reserve tee times online. Museums that charge admissions and have limited numbers of tickets sell them online. All of this can be done from a smartphone. But whether program or service registration takes place from a home computer or from a phone, the ability to register and pay is more immediate and the implications of immediacy challenge the creative thinking of leisure services managers.

The fact that most young people acquire their cell phone numbers when they are preteens and later move away from home with those same phone numbers creates challenges at another level. Leisure agencies that attempt to do planning and gather public opinions using surveys and telephone polls are forced to use the more primitive methods of mail surveying and door-to-door data gathering if they want to include young people in their research. Using area codes to create databases for telephone polling is becoming an

© Stephen Coburn - Fotolia

Leisure activities must change to keep up with advancements in technology. Children often grow up with smartphones, handheld videogames, and other devices that draw their attention away from outdoor recreation choices.

ineffective way of identifying residents of a community or demographic.

Many leisure agencies are publicizing their services using social networking applications, such as Facebook, Twitter, and LinkedIn. Tweets posted on these social networks pop up on the screens of smartphones as soon as they are posted, making people aware of what agencies are doing. But none of this is particularly enlightening to students in the leisure services field; they are very much aware of how technology works. What they might not be aware of, though, is how technology is changing leisure.

It's not just the examples of video games or the Internet that show how leisure activities are changing. More important, young people are more likely to have grown up indoors and thus are less likely to participate in outdoor recreation. A 2003 outdoor recreation study (RoperASW 2004) showed that the older people are, the more likely they are to participate in outdoor recreation. Conversely, the younger they are, the less likely they are to participate.

FOCUS ON REVENUES

Revenues derived from user fees have not always been important to the public and nonprofit sectors. In the 1800s and early 1900s, with government services supported by taxes and nonprofit services supported by donations, recreation programs were often free. Perhaps the precipitating event that changed the nature of revenue generation for public leisure services was Proposition 13 in California, where severe cuts were made in the ability of local governments to generate property tax revenue, forcing them to charge fees instead (California Tax Data 2012).

For nonprofit organizations, the national trend in fund-raising, particularly since the 2007 economic downturn, has been down (Tascarella 2011). To survive, nonprofit organizations have been forced to focus more on the revenues they can generate from services.

Revenues in the Public and Nonprofit Sectors

The private sector of the leisure services economy has always focused on revenues. The survival of businesses depends on understanding customers' needs and delivering products or services to customers for a fair price. Fair price can be determined as the cost of producing the product plus a reasonable profit, or it can be defined as whatever price the market will bear.

The nonprofit sector of the leisure services economy tries to follow the lead of the private sector by charging a fair price for a product or service, usually defined as the cost of producing the product plus the cost of the administrative overhead to deliver the product. It is less common that the nonprofit sector charges whatever the market will bear, but previous chapters showed it's not unheard of. The YMCA fitness center example in previous chapters is a case in point. However, if nonprofit leisure agencies charged whatever the market would bear for services, it would be more difficult for people to justify donating money to the agencies.

Sometimes the public sector doesn't even charge what it costs to produce the service. This is often because political forces oppose charging a fair price for the service. Previous chapters have discussed how elected officials might think charging a fair price will interfere with their ability to get reelected and how interest groups can manipulate elected officials to keep their program fees low. Either way, governmental leisure services can fall back on taxes, so a cost-based or market-based model for fees and charges is rarely warranted.

The continuing focus on revenues should not be much different than it has been in the past for the private sector. But, if history is any indication, the focus on revenues will increase for governmental units and nonprofit organizations. At the governmental level, recent political gains by antitax candidates have put people in office who believe smaller government is better than bigger government. For instance, the Tea Party movement, which began in early 2010, was successful in electing 89 new representatives to Congress and changing several Democrat governorships to Republican control in November 2010. With national, state, and local debts growing at an alarming rate, antitax groups have morphed into antispending groups.

History has shown that government-sector leisure services have been a tough sell from the beginning. During the formation of the Central Park Commission, the New York Legislature bought into the idea of a special-purpose government that provided parks only when it was argued that the parks would pay for themselves. At the turn of the 20th century, there was a nationwide movement to create a national park system. But with huge federal deficits, not much has been done to expand that system since the early 1990s. It hasn't helped that children don't spend much of their time outdoors lately. Park expansion at the local level has slowed as well.

Facility-based recreation services have seen an increase, though. The number of publicly owned and operated outdoor aquatic centers has increased during the last 20 years, as has the number of indoor recreation centers. At the local level, these outdoor aquatic and indoor recreation centers have been funded by property and sales taxes, but for the most part, they have been designed to be self-sustaining in supporting their operational costs.

With donations falling off precipitously during tough economic times, nonprofit leisure services organizations have seen contributions fluctuate. For nonprofit organizations, the solution has been to focus more on program fees, relying on donations to defray capital costs rather than operating costs.

Entrepreneurism has always been the economic engine of the American economy. It would, therefore, make sense that entrepreneurism would be the salvation of leisure services in the public and nonprofit sectors as well. If entrepreneurism is in the future of public and nonprofit sectors, though, leisure services managers in the public and nonprofit sectors will need to understand what managers in the private sector understand: Fees for services are derived from meeting human needs, and human needs can't be met unless you know what they are.

Market Research

For user fees to be king in the public and nonprofit sectors, leisure services managers in these sectors need to understand how private organizations survive in a world without tax money or donations. They need to understand that they are slaves to their customers, and customers do not just walk through the door. They have to be identified and interviewed, and their needs have to be determined. Entrepreneurs need to find out what customers want and how much they are willing to pay for it. Then entrepreneurs need to build models and test them to see if their market research was correct.

If leisure services professionals in the public and nonprofit sectors think that market research is a lot of work, that's because it is. But what choice do entrepreneurs have? Either they go out and get customers into their businesses, or they starve.

Many public and nonprofit leisure services managers don't think that the situation is that dire. They believe that plenty of people still need their free or low-cost services. For instance, Milwaukee County Parks charged a mere 75 cents for admission to its swimming pools until 2007, largely because of the view of county commissioners that there were many low-income people who couldn't afford to pay more than that. But the policy overlooked the people who could pay more, depriving the park system of needed revenues to support pool operations.

Previous chapters have discussed how nonprofit leisure services managers already know they need to focus more on customer needs. But managers in the public sector are only starting to figure out that customers are king because fees are king. In both sectors, though, too little solid market research has been done to identify who the kings are and how much they're willing to pay.

Statistical Polls and Surveys

Political polling has been around since the 1920s, when it was first used to determine whether people would vote for a candidate. Early polling was often highly inaccurate, as exemplified by Thomas E. Dewey's predicted victory over President Harry Truman, where the *Chicago Tribune* erroneously predicted Dewey to be the winner. Polling is still an imperfect science, as the media learned in 2000 when Al Gore was predicted to have defeated George W. Bush in Florida. Nevertheless, polling is now used for market research in all sectors as a tool of business, attempting to determine whether consumers will purchase certain products or services.

The technique is straightforward enough. A random sample of a population is selected and telephone numbers identified. Then a pollster calls them and asks a few questions, recording the responses on paper or in a computer program. Since 2010, polling has been expanded to cellphone polling and e-mail questionnaires, and it can be done on smartphones as well. Companies such as the Public Research Group are using multilayered techniques to identify voter sentiments and have used the same techniques for market research and donor solicitation.

The questioning process usually begins by asking respondents whether they are familiar with the political candidate, product, or service, usually followed by some behavior questions. In political polling, this might include questions about membership in a political party, whereas for business polling, questions usually involve the products that respondents use.

In political polling, respondents are then asked whether they plan to vote in the next election and who they're going to vote for. In business polling, respondents are asked whether they would purchase a certain product and how much they would pay. Both polls end with demographic questions about the age and gender of the respondent. The demographic questions are used to build profiles of voters or consumers to determine if different groups exhibit different behaviors.

Surveying is similar but involves a different methodology. Surveys are longer with more detailed questions. They are usually administered by creating a database of addresses. From this database, a random sample is selected and the sample respondents are sent questionnaires with a self-addressed, stamped return envelope. Surveys can also be sent electronically to the e-mail addresses of a random sample of respondents, assuming the population from which the sample is drawn contains everyone in the target population.

Online surveys are also used as a market research method with the understanding that not everyone may have a computer or choose to visit the website. Researchers understand that the sample is not random and so it cannot be generalized back to the total population of the targeted population, unless, of course, the targeted population is just the people who visit the website.

When polling and survey data are gathered, researchers convert the responses to numeric values. A *yes* response may take the value of 1 and a *no* the value of 0. Then statistical averaging can be applied to see what percentage of people responded affirmatively to a question and what percentage responded negatively. The same methodology can be applied to gender, where a female respondent might have the value of 1 and a male 0.

The purpose of collecting statistical data is to create statistical averages and percentages about what portion of respondents would vote for a certain candidate or purchase a certain product or service. Using other statistical techniques, it can be determined, for example, if females would behave differently than males or older people would behave differently than younger people. These are the techniques used in the nationwide RoperASW survey on outdoor recreational behavior that was discussed earlier.

Interviews and Focus Groups

Statistical polling and surveying has limitations. One of them is that although many questions can be asked, the responses are limited to certain choices. A methodology that some political analysts and market researchers prefer to use in conjunction with statistical analysis is the qualitative approach of interviewing people individually or in groups, usually called *focus groups*. The interview technique can provide insights not available in surveying and polling, but data analysis of the results is somewhat more complicated and subjective.

When people are interviewed, their responses either need to be recoded manually, by taking notes, or electronically, by making video or audio recordings. When interviewers rely on taking notes, it is possible to miss some responses or misinterpret what the respondents said. When recording respondent interviews, there is less chance of mistaking what was said because the interviewer can revisit the response. In any case, the process is time consuming and, as such, most researchers limit their sample size because of cost and time constraints.

Data Analysis

If the purpose of market research is to determine what products or services people will buy and how much they will pay for them, it is essential to analyze the data using techniques that provide meaningful information. For the two methodologies, statistical surveying and polling and qualitative interviewing and focus groups, there are different ways of analyzing the data. And yet if the analysis is done properly, the same findings should be apparent from both.

Statistical analysis, where numbers are considered as percentages or averages, provides measures of central tendency and dispersion that are clear and understandable. For instance, it might be shown statistically that a higher percentage of females and younger children would use a new aquatic facility compared with males and older children. When the qualitative interview and focus-group responses are analyzed, the same findings should be apparent from responses, although there might be far fewer interviewees than there were survey respondents. The difference is that the interviewees have the opportunity to explain why females and younger children would use the aquatic facility.

Both qualitative and statistical methods of data analysis seek themes in the responses. The themes might tell market researchers why consumers prefer one product or service over another or why the image of one product or service is more appealing than another. All of this helps market researchers understand what they can do to make their product more appealing so they can sell more of it and make more revenue.

Government and nonprofit leisure services organizations do far too little market research. Part of the reason is that it is difficult, time consuming, and expensive. Another reason is that there is little motivation for them to do so. But with changes in the ability of governmental units to tax and with declining donations on the horizon, governmental and nonprofit leisure services managers would be well advised to emulate the techniques used by their counterparts in the private sector. The day will come when their livelihoods depend on it.

SUMMARY

As a leisure services manager, it should come as no surprise that the world is an ever-changing place and that those who embrace change will inherit the future. Beginning with the movement toward greater transparency caused by public discontent from stories in the 24-hour media, managers need to pay attention to the pronouncements coming from the FASB and the GASB, even when they are only in the discussion phase.

Future pronouncements will lead to changes in reporting procedures, particularly in the public sector, where even personnel records will no longer be private information. And the pay and benefits of administrators and managers in all three sectors of the leisure services economy will be subject to public scrutiny in the future.

Changes in technology also are part of your e-future. Children are staying inside their homes more because parents are afraid for them to go to the parks, and video games and smartphones seem to be outcompeting traditional recreational activities.

Political and economic changes are taking place that are affecting how leisure services are delivered and funded. Among them is an antitax movement that affects the level of tax support that governmental leisure services agencies can expect to receive. Recent declines in the economy are also affecting the amount of donations that nonprofit organizations can expect to receive.

Because of these challenges, nonprofit and government leisure services organizations need to adopt more businesslike revenue-generating techniques if they expect to prosper. Businesses find it important to conduct periodic market research using techniques with which government and nonprofit organizations need to be more familiar. Statistical polling and surveying is one technique; customer and focus-group interviews are another.

As a leisure services professional, you need to develop your management skills, particularly as they relate to financial management. Understanding financial reports is part of it, and understanding what people want to do with their leisure time is another.

Visit the Web Resource

For case studies, sample financial statements, key terms, and more, please visit the web resource at www.HumanKinetics.com/LeisureServicesFinancialManagement

Glossary

accountancy—Recording the acquisition of materials, keeping track of inventories, measuring output, analyzing the cost of goods sold, and managing the profitability of the company.

accountants—The people overseeing or participating in the maintenance of the financial reporting system of an entity.

accounting—Defined by AICPA as "the art of recording, classifying, and summarizing in a significant manner and in terms of money, transactions and events which are, in part at least, of financial character, and interpreting the results thereof" (Accountingexplanation.com 2011).

accounts—Places in the books of an entity to record assets, liabilities, income, and expenses.

accounts payable—Monies owed to other companies for products or services your company purchased from them.

accounts receivable—Monies owed to the company by other companies or individuals that are customers.

accrual accounting—Business accounting method where transactions are recorded as they are incurred, whether or not cash has been received or checks written. Also see *full accrual accounting*.

Adam Smith—A Scottish economist who believed markets should be left alone by governments as much as possible, commonly referred to as *laissez-faire capitalism*.

altruism—The unselfish concern for the welfare of others.

AMBER alerts—Media announcements that a child has been reported missing and that everyone should keep a watchful eye for the child and the abductor. *AMBER* stands for America's Missing: Broadcast Emergency Response.

American Institute of Certified Public Accountants (AICPA)—The professional organization of CPAs.

American Society of Public Administration (ASPA)—The first professional organization representing public administrators; serves academic, federal, state, and county professionals.

Andrew Jackson Downing—Editor of *The Horticulturalist* magazine in New York and a landscape designer, he had traveled extensively in Europe and was surprised at how much more livable European cities were compared with American cities. He convinced the New York Legislature to permit the creation of Central Park.

annual financial report (AFR)—A report that public corporations must provide to shareholders to describe their operations and financial conditions.

appreciate—When assets become more costly to replace as the years pass because their value increases.

appropriate action—A decision to act based on the selection of the most rational solution to a problem.

assets—The property, buildings, equipment, goodwill, or other measurable holdings of an entity.

auditors—CPAs who perform random checks of transactional entries and the resulting balances to determine if financial statements are fair representations of the financial position of an entity.

autonomy—The ability to act on your own.

average shareholders' equity—Calculated by adding shareholders' equity at the beginning of a time period to the shareholders' equity at the end of that time period and averaging the total.

average total assets—The five-month mean average of a company's total assets.

bad debt—Money owed to a business that the business knows probably won't be repaid.

balance sheet—A report that provides a picture of the financial condition of an entity at any given point in time, including its assets, liabilities, and equity for a fund.

bankrupt—The financial condition under which total liabilities are worth more than total assets and the balance sheet doesn't balance.

behavioral science—A subset of social sciences involving the study of actions and reactions of humans and animals.

bloggers—People who post articles or respond to media articles online.

bondholder—Owner of a government or corporate bond. Being a bondholder entitles one to receive regular interest payments, if the bond pays interest (usually semiannually or annually), as well as a return of principal when the bond matures.

bond issue—When bonds are sold by a corporation or government agency at a particular time and are identifiable by the date the bonds mature.

bond ratings—A rating system ranking the probability that the borrowing business, nonprofit, or governmental organization will be able to repay the bondholders.

bonds—Loans in the form of a contract that the government or businesses enter into with a bondholder that specify the interest rate and amount of the loan to be paid back over a specified length of time.

bookkeeping—Formal record-keeping process to track expenses, income, and profits.

books—The place where accountants maintain the financial records of the entity; could be on paper or in electronic files.

bottom line—Net income after taxes.

bridge loan—A short-term loan used until permanent financing is secured or the obligation is met.

budget—An accounting document that predicts how much money an entity will receive and how much it will spend over a given period of time; a plan for taking in revenues and expending them in such a way that there is always something there. In microeconomic terms, budget plans organize spending for the fiscal year.

budget and actual reports—Financial management tools that track revenues and expenses, showing the line-item budgeted amounts with the actual amounts of revenues and expenses to date.

budgetary and fiscal compliance—When financial resources gathered by the governmental unit are used in accordance with the governmental unit's budget.

budgeting as an art—Where experience causes financial managers to become more accurate at predicting revenues and expenditures over time.

business model—A plan for generating income to support a product or service.

business sense—Ability to figure out how to make a profit providing products or services.

calculated risks—Risks that entrepreneurs take when they think they have an idea of the probabilities of success.

capital acquisition—Purchase or construction of physical assets, namely land and buildings.

capital assets—All tangible property that cannot easily be converted into cash and that is usually held for a long time, including real estate and equipment.

capitalism—An economic system where individuals can accumulate wealth through private ownership of property and businesses.

capital needs—Money needed to cover operations.

capital resources—Money available to purchase capital assets.

cash-basis accounting—Accounting method similar to what individuals do in their personal checkbooks, where only what is received or paid is recorded; records of transactions where money has actually been received or disbursed.

cash cow—A very profitable department to be milked for all it's worth.

cash-flow budget—Also called *cash budget*, the cash-flow budget is a prediction of future cash receipts and expenditures for a particular time period, usually in the short-term future. The cash-flow budget helps the business determine when income will be sufficient to cover expenses and when the company will need to seek outside financing.

cash ratio—Cash plus cash equivalents plus invested funds divided by current liabilities.

Central Park—The first park in the United States, credited with starting the leisure services profession.

certified public accountants (CPAs)—Professional accountants who have passed qualifying examinations demonstrating their knowledge in the field of accounting, allowing them to be auditors of other accountants.

charitable status—The status enjoyed by some nonprofit organizations that means that people may donate to the organization and deduct the donations from their gross income when they file their tax return.

collateral—Assets that are pledged by a borrower to secure a loan or other credit and that are subject to seizure in the event of default.

commercial lender—A company, usually a bank, that lends money to businesses.

common councils—Generic term for elected policymakers such as city councils, village boards, county boards, and park boards.

communism—An economic system where the government owns all property and businesses and all citizens work for the government.

competition—Occurs when two or more businesses, nonprofit organizations, governmental units, or any combination of the three attempt to sell their products or services to the same customers.

compound interest—Interest calculated on the initial principal and the accumulated interest.

comprehensive annual financial report (CAFR)—The financial report that public sector (government) entities are required to compile.

conservative approach—Used in budgeting to mean that expenses and revenue are not expected to increase.

consistency—When a business has fixed a method for the accounting treatment of an item, it enters all similar items in exactly the same way.

construction management firm—Performs many of the cost-saving duties that a leisure services agency would do if the agency had the expertise or were large enough to do it itself.

cooperative competition—Business competition that benefits customers with lower prices, better products or services, and greater availability, generally increasing the marginal utility to customers.

corporate bonds—A form of debt generally sold to private investors rather than lending institutions. Corporate bonds pay a fixed interest rate to the holder, usually at a lower rate of interest than a bank loan.

cost of goods sold—The amount of money a company spent to buy raw materials and produce a product or service. Includes the direct costs of producing the product or service but excludes the indirect costs such as overhead or other expenses.

cost-versus-benefit propositions—Techniques for determining the feasibility of a project or plan by quantifying its costs and benefits.

coupon—A detachable portion of a bond that is given up in return for a payment of interest. The coupon or coupon rate of a bond is the amount of interest paid per year expressed as a percentage of the face value of the bond. It is the interest rate that a bond issuer will pay to a bondholder.

coupon rate—Interest rate that bonds pay.

credits—Entries on the right side of double-entry bookkeeping accounts that represent the reduction of an asset or expense or the addition of a liability or revenue.

cross-sectional research—Research where increases and decreases in member satisfaction can be measured.

current assets—Assets that would take the company a modest amount of time to convert to cash.

current liabilities—Money the company owes to individuals or entities that typically needs to be repaid in less than five years.

current ratio—Current assets divided by current liabilities.

debits—Entries on the left side of double-entry bookkeeping accounts that represent the addition of an asset or expense or the reduction of a liability or revenue.

debt instruments—Paper or electronic obligations that enable the issuing party to raise funds by promising to repay a lender in accordance with the terms of a contract. Types of debt instruments include notes, bonds, certificates, mortgages, leases, and other agreements between a lender and a borrower.

debt ratio—Total liabilities divided by total assets to determine if debt is too high in relation to owner's equity.

debt service—Series of payments of interest and principal required on a debt over a given period of time.

debt-to-equity ratio—Total liabilities of a company divided by shareholder equity.

dedicated tax source—Property, sales, excise, or other taxes that can only be spent for a sole purpose, such as park and recreation services.

default rates—The percentage of borrowers who are not able to repay the loans.

deficit spending—When the government spends more than it has, financed by borrowing rather than taxation.

defined annual income—Pension plan primarily available to government employees that guarantees a certain level of annual income upon retirement.

demographics—Key attributes, characteristics, or statistics of a certain group or population.

depreciation—Concept that some fixed assets, such as buildings and equipment, get used up and lose their value; decrease or loss in value of fixed assets because of age, wear, or market conditions.

depreciation value—Calculated by subtracting the salvage value from the original cost and dividing the remaining value by the number of years of expected life.

destructive competition—Occurs when businesses seek to destroy each other so that the winner can take all by creating a monopoly.

development director—Person in an organization who has the full-time responsibility of cultivating (developing) prospective donors and harvesting their donations.

dichotomy of politics and administration—A way to separate the process of making policy from the process of implementing policies.

Dillon's rule—Local governments can only levy what taxes states permit and nothing else.

direct competition—Similar businesses in the same market.

direct costs—The cost of materials to produce a product or service.

discounts—Decreases in the full value of principal and interest that the borrower would pay on a loan.

donation exchange—Where people give money and only receive a good feeling in return.

donor base—A group of people within a community who are regular contributors to community charities and nonprofit organizations.

donor cultivation—Term used in fund-raising to describe relationship building, the foundation upon which most fund-raising takes place.

double-barreled—When a municipality assumes liability for debt service and the income from the project is insufficient.

double-entry bookkeeping—Process of writing down transactions in chronological order in a journal and then posting the transactions to accounts in the ledger.

due diligence—Doing research to determine facts about a business that are backed by evidence.

earnings yield—The quotient of earnings per share of stock divided by the share price of that stock.

economic model—A way of generalizing a complex economic concept or behavior expressed in the form of an equation, graph, or illustration for the purpose of predicting the future.

economics—The social and behavioral science of not only how markets work but also how economic forces influence human behavior.

economists—People who attempt to understand the present and predict the future of the economy in the same way meteorologists predict the weather, by gathering data and building models.

embedded call option—Allows the issuer to redeem the debt before its maturity date.

Emerging Issues Task Force (EITF)—Task force created to provide timely responses to financial issues as they emerge, especially issues that are controversial.

endowment fund—Groups of investments that provide a fairly steady stream of dividends to the nonprofit organization, smoothing out the effects of donations that rise and fall as the economy rises and falls; permanently restricted money set aside solely for generating income that can be used for scholarships or capital projects.

enterprise fund—Used in the public and nonprofit sectors to account for operations financed primarily through user charges or fees.

enterprises—Business ventures.

entity—A legal vehicle, such as a business, nonprofit organization, or governmental unit, established to carry out specific purposes; an accounting unit.

environmentalists—People who work to protect the environment from destruction or pollution.

equity—Also called *stock shares* of ownership in a business, which can be bought and sold by investors wishing to trade them for speculation; whatever amount is left over after the liabilities are subtracted from the assets, typically the value of the entity to the owners.

equity contributions—Capital and start-up costs of new businesses funded by the owner or the owner's family.

ethics—Codes of conduct that professions create based on their fundamental understanding of right from wrong. Ethics is all about making the right decision in the face of political and moral dilemmas.

excess revenue over expenditures—How government and nonprofit agencies describe their profits.

expected life—How long the asset will be useful.

expenditure budget—A budget that includes spending data.

expenditures—Term used by government to describe expenses as the extinguishment of cash resources.

expenses—Money leaving the entity for any purpose that decreases the entity's equity.

fair price—The price at which supply and demand are in equilibrium.

Federal Reserve Board—A seven-member board that oversees the U.S. banking industry, establishes monetary policy (namely interest rates and availability of credit), and monitors the economic health of the country.

Federal Reserve System—Created by Congress in 1913 as the central banking system for the United States, it is governed by a board that regulates interest rates and other monetary policies. All banks are members of the Federal Reserve, and the Federal Reserve supervises and regulates the banking industry.

fiduciary—The legal or ethical relationship of confidence or trust between two or more parties, usually related to the management of money or property.

finance—The study of investing and borrowing money.

financial accounting—The accounting technique used for generating reports for investors, donors, the general public, and the governmental units that tax businesses in the private sector.

Financial Accounting Standards Board (FASB)—A board that establishes rules that govern business accounting.

financial autonomy—Financial independence.

financial markets—Where investors go to invest their money in businesses that they think will yield them a profit.

financial projection—Estimates of the future financial performance of a project.

financial ratios—Relative magnitude of two selected numerical values taken from the financial statements of a business.

fiscal year—Budget year that begins when the business cycle for the entity logically begins or ends; the period in which an organization determines its financial condition, which may or may not be the same as the calendar year.

fixed assets—Assets that depreciate; excludes land, which does not depreciate.

flat-rate commissioned—Rather than being paid a percentage of the total construction cost, the architectural firm is paid a flat fee for services.

forecasting—A basic level of research is conducted to draw logical conclusions.

Franklin Delano Roosevelt—The 32nd president of the United States who applied Keynesian economics to the Great Depression by creating the CCC and other federal programs that built and improved state, federal, county, and municipal parks all over the country.

Frederick Law Olmsted—Noted park designer and the first superintendent of the Central Park Commission, he oversaw the successful construction of the park. He was also able to influence the creation of three park districts in Chicago and the planning of several cities, and he was the designer of the 1893 World's Columbian Exposition in Chicago.

Freedom of Information Act (FOIA)—A federal law that says that all governmental records must be made public on demand.

free enterprise system—Few restrictions are placed on business activities and ownership and government restrictions are minimal.

full accrual accounting—Depreciates assets whereas modified accrual accounting doesn't depreciate them during their useful life but extinguishes them when assets are taken offline; records of transactions that are available and measurable.

full disclosure and materiality—All information and values pertaining to the financial position of a business must be disclosed in the records.

fund—A group of accounts within an entity for a specific purpose.

fund balance—Term used in government accounting instead of *equity*; the net worth of a fund, measured by total assets minus total liabilities.

fund-raising—Process of soliciting and gathering monetary contributions or donations of other resources by nonprofit or governmental agencies.

fund-raising consultant—A company hired to oversee the fund-raising effort but not specifically raise funds itself.

game the system—Understanding and manipulating the rules to achieve selfish ends.

general funds—Groups of accounts, usually segregated by state departments, where the funding comes from a multitude of revenue sources.

general ledger—The main accounting record of businesses that use double-entry bookkeeping; sometimes called the *nominal ledger*.

generally accepted accounting principles (GAAP)—The rules by which transactions are recorded and reports are prepared.

general obligation bonds—Where the principal and interest from the bonds are repaid from the revenue streams that the facility provides.

going concerns—Entities that accountants believe will likely be in existence within the next 12 months.

government accounting—The technique used by governmental units that collect taxes and must remain transparent in the ways they spend the public's tax money.

Governmental Accounting Standards Board (GASB)—Board that establishes rules that govern accounting practices of governmental agencies.

governmental unit—A legal entity established by political processes that has legislative, judicial, or executive authority over other institutional units within a given area. Governmental units typically have taxing powers or rely on tax collection to support operations.

Great Depression—Economic depression in the 1930s when unemployment reached 25 percent and government intervention became politically popular.

greed—Excessive desire to acquire or possess more than what one needs or deserves, especially with respect to material wealth.

gross profit—Calculated by subtracting the cost of goods sold from the revenues.

gross profit margin—Calculated by dividing the dollar amount of the gross profit by the revenues, which produces a percentage.

growth stage—The stage in which the demand for a product or service is increasing and producers are able to develop economies of scale, driving down production costs.

hard sciences—Sciences, including physics, chemistry, and microbiology, that begin with theories that can be tested as hypotheses and from which conclusions become laws.

home rule—A local government can levy whatever taxes it wants except for those that the state limits or prohibits.

home rule authority—Powers given to local government to prevent state government intervention with its operations. The extent of its power, however, is subject to limitations prescribed by state constitutions and statutes, such as population or approval by voter referenda.

horticulturalists—Experts in the science of cultivating plants.

income—Money coming into the entity from any source that increases the entity's equity.

income after taxes—How much money is left after income taxes are paid to the IRS and to the revenue service of the state in which the business is incorporated.

income before taxes—How much money the company has made after all of its revenues and expenses have been considered.

income statement—A report that provides a picture of the income and expenses of an entity during a certain time period for a fund.

incremental budgeting—Projected revenues and expenses are generally based on historical data, particularly from the previous year, and adjusted according to anticipated changes in the marketplace or economy.

indigent citizens—Citizens who are poor.

indirect competition—Other businesses or activities that compete for potential customers' time and money.

indirect costs—Costs of doing business besides materials; includes labor, equipment, rent, and utilities.

individualistic cultures—Cultures of states that tend to accommodate interest groups, where the values, beliefs, and traditions are such that it is every man for himself and it would be irrational for anyone to act otherwise.

inflation—The devaluation of currency.

inflation rate—The annual percentage increase in the price of goods and services.

inflows and outflows—Money moving in and out of accounts, derived from revenue streams created and expenses.

in-house method—Where the organization serves as its own construction manager, hiring smaller consultants and construction companies to build the project. This is a hands-on approach where the leisure services manager is involved every step of the way.

in perpetuity—For life or, in some cases, forever.

interest—The cost that borrowers pay for the use of the lender's money, usually expressed as an annual rate.

interlocking directorates—Corporate board members who either serve on other boards or who are managers of other corporations in various industries.

International City/County Management Association (ICMA)—Professional organization of city managers.

interperiod equity—When a governmental unit has sufficient revenues to pay for the services it provides.

inventory—The supplies and materials a company has on hand to manufacture its products or provide its services.

inventory shrinkage—Reduction in the value of inventory due to unexplained reasons.

investment appreciation—The increased value of the endowment fund investment portfolio.

investment proceeds—Earnings from investments.

iron triangles—Permanent alliances among three groups: interest groups, elected officials, and bureaucrats; very strong alliances.

John Maynard Keynes—An economist who sought to improve on the economic theory of Adam Smith without going as far as Karl Marx. He recognized that during economic downturns, government needs to stimulate business via deficit spending.

journals—Books or electronic files that record transactions in chronological order.

Karl Marx—A 19th-century German philosopher who became a political and economic revolutionary with his theory that business profits are accumulated as unpaid wages to workers.

Keynesian economics—John Maynard Keynes' economic theory that when the economy is weak, the federal government can and should do more.

labor theory of value—The economic principle that suggests that labor costs are more relevant in estimating the cost of a good or service.

laissez-faire—One of the guiding principles of capitalism, it says an economic system should be free from government intervention and driven only by market forces.

layer-cake federalism—A term used in political science to show there are distinct separations of the powers of the federal government, state governments, and local governments.

ledgers—Includes the general ledger or nominal ledger, which are books or electronic files where specific accounts are recorded.

leisure—The time when people can play, but it is not playing in and of itself.

leisure services—A multitude of pastimes that afford relaxation and enjoyment, usually provided by business, nonprofit, and governmental agencies.

leisure services administration—Management of leisure services agencies, involving the management of people and money.

leisure services financial management—The administration of accounting and reporting systems upon which leisure services agencies rely.

lending market—The banks and lending institutions available to finance debt.

letter of transmittal—A document from the chief administrative and chief financial officers of the governmental unit summarizing what the governmental unit did during the fiscal year.

leveraging assets—Borrowing money to create more total assets in order to generate more goods or services and hence more profit.

liabilities—Loans or other short-term or long-term debts owed by the entity to other individuals or organizations.

lien—The right to keep property belonging to another person until a debt is paid.

linear thinking—Only considering one variable.

line-item accounts—Account categories that are reasonably descriptive, such as accounts for electricity expenditures.

line items—Individual listings in a budget for categories of expenses or revenues.

lines of credit—Loans that are drawn as the company needs the money, with repayment dates depending on the amount used.

liquidity—The ability to convert assets to cash.

liquidity ratios—Ratios that measure a company's ability to pay off its short-term debt obligations. This is done by comparing the company's most liquid assets, those that can be easily converted to cash, with its current liabilities.

liquidity risk—The ability of investors to take their money out of an investment at a moment's notice; it considers the cost to the investor and how that affects the actual interest earned compared with the interest promised.

loan contract—Written agreement between the lender and borrower that spells out the terms of a loan.

longitudinal research—Research conducted over time, with periodic cross-sectional analysis.

long-term debt—Money owed that is paid back over a five-year period or longer.

loss leaders—Products or services sold at a loss to attract customers; the strategy is that once customers are in the store, they will buy other products that are profitable for the store to sell.

macroeconomics—The study of large economies that exist at the world, national, state, and regional levels.

management accounting—A method of accounting used to generate cash-based expense and income reports so managers can determine whether the revenues generated by services are at least covering costs.

marble-cake federalism—A term used in political science to show there is a mixing or overlap of the powers of the federal government, state governments, and local governments.

marginal utility—Economic principle that holds that the use of a good or service is what determines its value, not the cost of the labor to produce the good or service.

marketing approach—Businesses focus on the customer, because it is the transaction between the business and the customer that provides the business its lifeblood.

marketing budget—The marketing budget is an estimate of the funds needed for promotion, advertising, and public relations in order to market the product or service.

market introduction stage—The stage in which a product or service is new and unfamiliar to most potential customers, costs to produce the good or service are high and demand is low, and customers have to be prompted to purchase it.

Marxism—A political and economic system that advocates class struggle to create historical change to replace capitalism with communism.

matching concept—The business concept that expenses must be matched with revenues.

maturation stage—Stage in which the demand for a product or service has peaked and prices are so low that some producers are no longer able to make a profit and thus drop out of the market.

mean—The statistical average.

median—The middle of the range in data analysis.

membership model—Where people pay to join the agency and pay no additional fees for using certain services.

microeconomics—The branch of economics focusing on the study of smaller economies, such as local or organizational markets.

mission—The general purpose for which an organization exists.

missionary work—Converting people to an idea before converting them to the specific institution.

mission program—A program operated as part of the mission of a leisure services organization.

models—The use of data to create simple or complex formulas to predict future outcomes.

modified accrual accounting—Records of transactions that are available and measurable but do not depreciate fixed assets, recording them in different funds; government accounting method where revenues are recognized in the period they are available and measurable and expenditures are recorded in the period where the associated liability has occurred.

mom-and-pop business—A small business, usually owned by one or two people (i.e., husband and wife) with a small number of employees and relatively low volume of sales.

moralistic cultures—Cultures of states that tend to minimize the influence of interest groups, where the values, beliefs, and traditions are such that it is important to act on behalf of the general welfare of the populace.

moving averages—Statistical averages within a range of dates that are updated each year by adding the most recent value and deducting the least recent value.

municipal bonds—Can only be issued by local governments or their agencies.

municipal park and recreation departments—Departments in cities, villages, or towns that oversee park and recreation services operations.

National Recreation and Park Association (NRPA)—The national professional organization for park and recreation professionals and agencies.

net assets—Difference between assets and liabilities of a nonprofit agency.

net difference—Achieving the difference between budgeted revenues and budgeted expenditures is the goal of leisure services managers.

net income—The amount of money left after all direct and indirect expenses have been subtracted from total revenues.

net income after taxes—Money left after income taxes are paid to the IRS and to the state revenue service in which the business is incorporated.

net profit margin—Calculated by dividing the dollar amount of the net income after taxes by the total revenues.

net receivables—Payments owned to a business minus bad debt.

New Deal—President Franklin Roosevelt's programs and policies designed to promote economic recovery and social reform during the 1930s.

NIMBYs—People who live close to where the project will be constructed and don't want it in their backyard (i.e., **n**ot **i**n **m**y **b**ack **y**ard).

noncompensation—One should show the full details of the financial information and not seek to compensate a debt with an asset or a revenue with an expense.

noncurrent assets—Generally called *fixed assets*; the value of the land, buildings, and equipment owned by the company.

nonoperating income and expenses—Derived from sources of revenue outside the core business of the company.

nonprofit accounting—Provides documentation to the IRS that proves the organization is reinvesting profits back into the organization and at the same time demonstrates to donors how money is being used.

nonprofit organizations—Organizations that are exempt from paying taxes under IRS tax code 501(c).

nonprofit sector—Organizations and agencies that are restricted by federal tax code from distributing profits to board members. Organizations in the nonprofit sector rely on members, volunteers, and donors to carry out their missions and to raise funds. Nonprofit sector organizations do not collect taxes and often do not pay taxes, unlike public and private sector organizations.

obsolescence—When something becomes outdated or old-fashioned to the point of not being useful.

open meetings acts—State and federal statutes requiring that government meetings, decisions, and records be made available to the public. Also called *sunshine laws*.

operating budget—A plan for the total revenues and expenses of the organization, typically on a departmental basis.

operating income—Calculated by subtracting overhead from gross profits.

operating margin—Calculated by dividing the dollar amount of the operating income by the revenues, yielding a percentage.

opportunity costs—Lost revenues from not being in a position to take advantage of a business opportunity.

organizational chart—A picture of the hierarchy of the organization, including the lines of authority and responsibility.

overhead expenses—Indirect costs or fixed expenses of operating a business; costs that are not directly related to the manufacturing of a product.

padding the budget—The process of increasing expenditure requests in excess of the minimum an agency needs in order to fund unforeseen expenditures.

park districts—Special taxing districts providing parks and recreation.

Pendleton Act—Congressional action in 1883 that created the civil service system in order to reform governmental hiring practices and eliminate political patronage dating back to the 1820s.

pension—Steady streams of income that are paid to retired public employees.

periodicity—The concept that each accounting entry should be allocated to a given period and should be split accordingly if it covers several periods.

permanence of methods—Allows the coherence and comparison of financial information published by the entity.

pledges receivable—Donation commitments made to a nonprofit organization that have not been received yet.

political machine—Group that controls the activities of a political party.

political patronage—The system of giving favors to those who support a particular political party or elected official; favors include appointments and contracts.

political process—Resolving important issues as a group through the use of influence.

politics—The acquisition and use of power to determine outcomes; determining who gets what, when, and how.

portfolio—Record showing all the investments by name that have been bought and sold on behalf of a business or nonprofit agency.

price–earnings (P/E) ratio—The price of the stock divided by the earnings per share of stock. P/E ratios are part of the family known as *multiples*.

price point—A point on a scale of possible prices at which something might be marketed.

primary fund-raising—When organizations conduct their own fund-raising campaigns, sometimes competing for donations against other fund-raising efforts.

principle of continuity—When stating financial information, one should assume that the business will not be interrupted.

private company—A company with a sole proprietor or equity owners. Private companies are not obligated by law to show their financial reports to anyone other than the owners, namely the stockholders.

private sector—The portion of the economy where businesses operate.

production budget—A budget that estimates the number of units that must be manufactured to meet the sales goals. The production budget also estimates the various costs involved with manufacturing those units, including labor and material.

profit—Surplus revenue.

program fees—Revenues generated from fees for leisure services.

project budget—A prediction of the costs associated with a particular company project. These costs include labor, materials, and other related expenses. The project budget is often broken down into specific tasks, with task budgets assigned to each.

promissory notes—Unsecured agreements between banks and companies where companies receive a fixed amount of money and they agree to repay principal and interest at designated periods.

Proposition 13—Referendum on the California ballot in 1978 that severely reduced the property taxes that local governments could levy.

proprietary funds—Government enterprises requiring funds that segregate revenues and expenses; also called *enterprise funds*.

prudence—Showing reality as it is; one should not try to make things look prettier than they are.

public choice—Political science term that describes the belief that governments should only provide public safety services, and they should not provide other so-called nonessential services, such as parks and recreation.

publicly held companies—Companies that sell stock to investors in a stock market; they must show their financial statements to both stockholders and potential stockholders.

public–private partnerships (PPPs)—Where the construction manager arranges for private financing through a private partner that holds a mortgage on the facility.

public sector—The government, supported by the public through property taxes.

quasi-businesses—Organizations that make a profit but reinvest that money into the expansion of the organization.

question—Voter referenda are stated in the form of a question that allows a yes-or-no vote.

quick ratio—Cash and equivalents plus short-term investments plus accounts receivable divided by current liabilities.

rate of return—Also called *return on investment*; refers to the percentage of money earned on the investment described in terms of how long it will take to recoup the investment.

reciprocal—Calculated by reversing the two numbers, making the numerator the denominator and the denominator the numerator.

recreation—A pastime, diversion, exercise, or other resource affording relaxation and enjoyment, suggesting recreation is an activity; a leisure activity.

referendum—A vote on a question on the ballot that asks voters if they are willing to increase their own property, sales, excise, or other tax or change some other public policy.

regression models—Models that consider several variables to determine the relationship between a dependent variable and one or more independent variables.

regularity—Conformity to enforced rules and laws.

remedial action—Fixing something that is not working.

reserve fund—An account set aside to meet unexpected costs in the future. It may be restricted to a certain purpose or used as a savings account for general future purposes.

return on assets—Net income divided by average total assets.

return on equity—Net income divided by average shareholders' equity.

return on stockholders' investments—Also called *return on equity*; the rate stockholders earn, determined by the dividing shareholders' equity into net income.

revenue bonds—Issued by nonprofit organizations, governmental units, or other public-benefit corporations with payment guaranteed by the revenue flow of the issuing agency.

revenue budget—A budget that consists of revenue receipts of government and the expenditure met from these revenues. Tax revenues are made up of taxes and other duties that the government levies.

revenue engine—Very profitable services where the fee structures for programs generate substantially more in revenues than the programs cost to provide.

risky proposition—An investment where you can make or lose a lot of money.

rule of ten—When building a relationship with a potential donor, the development manager should never bring up money until she has had at least 10 meetings with that person.

sale of debt—Financing a business by getting a bank loan to be paid back with interest.

sale of equity—Financing a business with co-owners or partners.

sales budget—A budget that estimates future sales, often broken down into both units and dollars, used to create company sales goals.

salvage value—The value of a fixed asset at the end of its useful life.

saturation and decline stage—The stage in which the demand for a product or service is in decline, producers are struggling to survive, and no one seems to be able to make a profit.

secondary fund-raising—When another nonprofit organization, such as United Way, Community Chest, or Community Foundation, takes on centralized fund-raising to avoid competition for donations to support community services.

service efforts, costs, and accomplishments—Citizens have the right to know these things about governmental units.

short-term debt—Bank loans or other debt to be repaid within five years.

short-term investments—Investments that mature or expire in one year.

sincerity—The accounting unit should reflect in good faith the reality of the company's financial status.

slack—Money that is hidden in a budget for discretionary use by financial managers by underestimating revenues or overestimating expenditures.

social engineering—The process of manipulating the way people behave in order to bring about positive change.

social science—The study of human society that includes the fields of sociology, anthropology, economics, psychology, political science, education, and history.

soft sciences—Social sciences; human beings are involved and thus findings are not as predictable as in hard sciences.

sole proprietor—The only owner of a business.

special-purpose district—Taxing unit created by legislation or voter approval for a special purpose such as parks and recreation.

special taxing district—A geographic area within which the property owners pay a tax to support a service or improvement specific to that area.

speculative financing—Loans made to risky businesses where it is highly likely that the business will fail, but if it succeeds, the return on investment will be great.

state boards of accountancy—Nonprofit agencies that are independent of state government or are departments of state government.

statement of activities—A report for local government agencies that shows revenues, expenditures, and changes in fund balances; the FASB term for income statements in nonprofit accounting.

statement of financial position—The FASB accounting term for balance sheets in nonprofit accounting.

statements of net assets—Financial statements that show, in a businesslike presentation, the financial condition of a governmental unit; similar to business balance sheets or nonprofit statements of financial position.

statements of revenues, expenditures, and changes in fund balance—Financial statements that summarize the financial activities that led to changes in the balance sheets of a governmental unit over a fiscal year.

stock—Equities, or certificates of ownership in a company.

stock price—The market value of a share of common stock on any given day.

sunshine laws—See *open meetings acts*.

surplus money—Profit. Nonprofits call this money *excess revenue over expenditures*.

SWOT analysis—The process of evaluating the strengths and weaknesses of an organization and its environmental opportunities and threats.

T-account—A visual aid used by accountants to illustrate the effect of a journal entry on the general ledger accounts. Debit amounts are entered on the left side of the *T* and credit amounts are entered on the right side.

Tammany Hall—The New York City political machine that ran the city between the 1850s and 1880s.

taxation exchange—Where people pay taxes to governments and in return receive services that they may or may not use.

taxes—Required payments to government used to provide public goods and services for the benefit of the local community, state, or nation.

tax-free municipal bonds—Bonds used to raise money for improvements in infrastructure or other aspects of the municipality or governmental unit; they are tax free, meaning the lenders or bondholders pay no income tax on the interest earned.

tax levy—The amount of taxes to be collected or raised.

temporarily restricted funds—A group of funds required by the FASB, often used to accept donations for capital projects.

Theodore Roosevelt—The 26th president of the United States; during his terms the federal government led the expansion of the national park system and attempted to break up monopolistic industries that benefited the industrialists who came to be viewed as robber barons.

time value of money—The expected deterioration of the value of money over time due to inflation, which is the reduction of goods and services that a fixed amount of money will purchase. A fundamental idea in finance is that the money one has now is worth more than the money one will receive in the future. Because money can earn interest or be invested, it is worth more to an economic actor if it is available immediately.

total assets—The sum of all subcategories of assets, representing the worth of the company.

total liabilities—What the company must repay in the short or long term.

toxic assets—When the value of a loan is significantly lower than shown on the balance sheet.

traditionalistic cultures—State cultures that tend to entrench the influence of existing interest groups, where the values, beliefs, and traditions of the state are such that it is important to continue the status quo.

transactions—Deals or business agreements; exchanges or trades, as of ideas, money, or goods; or the transfer of funds into or out of accounts.

transparency—The concept that the entity is not hiding anything, namely its financial position, from those who would be hurt by its misrepresentation; laws adopted at the federal, state, and local levels that require most information to be made public, meetings to be announced and take place in public, and bidding to be competitive by individuals or companies doing business with governmental units.

turnkey method—The leisure business, nonprofit, or governmental unit puts itself completely in the hands of consultants, such as construction managers or architects, and has minimal contact with the consultant and building contractors until the end of the project, when it is handed the keys.

unrestricted funds—Funds typically used for operating purposes, often repositories for mission program revenues, revenue-engine program memberships and fees, and unrestricted donations.

value exchange—Where people trade their money for a product or service that has value.

variance analysis—The line-item comparison of budgeted revenues and expenses with actual revenues and expenses, where the analysis attempts to determine why there is a difference.

venture capitalists—Investors willing to take risks that banks and other lending institutions aren't willing to take.

zero-based budgeting—A budgeting methodology with no assumptions of incremental changes in base line-item revenues and expenses; every line item in the budget is required to prove that there is a reason it should exist and show how it contributes to the bottom line of the company.

zero-coupon bonds—Bonds that pay no interest at all. The bondholder makes money because the bond has a discounted sale price with a higher redemption value.

Bibliography

Accounting Coach. 2012. "Accounting Principles." Accessed January 29, 2012. www.accountingcoach.com/online-accounting-course/09Xpg01.html.

Accountingexplanation.com. 2011. "Accounting as a Business Language." www.accountingexplanation.com/accounting_as_a_business_language.htm.

Advisory Commission on Intergovernmental Relations. 1964. *The Problem With Special Districts in America*. Washington, DC: U.S. Government Printing Office.

Allen, K.R. 2006. *Launching New Ventures*. New York: Houghton Mifflin.

American Institute of Certified Public Accountants. n.d. "AICPA Code of Professional Conduct." www.aicpa.org/Research/Standards/CodeofConduct/Pages/default.aspx.

American Institute of Certified Public Accountants (AICPA). 2012. "Frequently Asked Questions about the AICPA." Accessed January 29, 2012. www.aicpa.org/About/FAQs/Pages/FAQs.aspx.

American Society for Public Administration. 2012. "Code of Ethics." www.aspanet.org/public/ASPA/Resources/Code_of_Ethics/ASPA/Resources/Code%20of%20Ethics1.aspx?hkey=acd40318-a945-4ffc-ba7b-18e037b1a858.

Anderson, V.T. 1986. *A Comparative Analysis of Operating Budget Income Sources of Local Public Leisure Service Delivery Systems in West Virginia, With Emphasis on Self-Generated Revenue*. Morgantown, WV: University of West Virginia Press.

Angle, J. 2011. "Lawmakers Confront Executives Over Fannie Mae and Freddie Mac Bonuses." *Fox News*, November 16. www.foxnews.com/politics/2011/11/16/lawmakers-confront-executives-over-fannie-mae-and-freddie-mac-bonuses/.

Babcock, R.F., and W.U. Larsen. 1990. *Special Districts—The Ultimate in Neighborhood Zoning*. Cambridge, MA: Lincoln Institute of Land Policy.

Bailey, T.A., D.M. Kennedy, and L. Cohen. 1998. *The American Pageant* (11th edition). Boston: Houghton Mifflin.

Baker, N. 2008. "The 1992 United Way Scandal: A Case of Failed Leadership." http://userwww.sfsu.edu/~nbaker/documents/united_way.pdf.

Bannon, J., and W. McKinney. 1980. *White Paper: A Study and Analysis of Illinois Park Districts*. Champaign, IL: University of Illinois Press.

Barbaro, M. 2007. "As a Director, Clinton Moved Wal-Mart Board, but Only so Far." *New York Times*, May 20. www.nytimes.com/2007/05/20/us/politics/20walmart.html?pagewanted=all.

Barlow, E. 1977. *Frederick Law Olmsted's New York*. New York: Praeger.

Bazley, J.D., L.A. Nikolai, and H.D. Grove. 1977. *Financial Accounting: Concepts and Uses*. Boston: PWS-Kent.

Beattie, A. 2012. "Market Crashes: The Dotcom Crash." Accessed January 29, 2012. www.investopedia.com/features/crashes/crashes8.asp#axzz1fEfeonfw.

Bellis, M. 2012. "The History of Commercial Deodorants." About.com. Accessed January 29, 2012. http://inventors.about.com/od/dstartinventions/a/deodorants.htm.

Bingham, R.D., E.W. Hill, and S.B. White. 1990. *Financing Economic Development*. Newbury Park, CA: Sage.

Blair, J.P. 1995. *Local Economic Development*. Thousand Oaks, CA: Sage.

Blinn, S.R. 1977. *The Professional Preparation of Municipal Recreation and Park Executives*. Boston: Boston University.

Boak, J., and J. Williams. 2011. "Fannie Mae, Freddie Mac Executives Get Big Housing Bonuses." *Politico*. www.politico.com/news/stories/1011/67292.html.

Board Source, Knowledge Center. 2012. "Can Nonprofits Make a Profit?" Accessed January 29, 2012. www.boardsource.org/Knowledge.asp?ID=3.115.

Bollens, J.C. 1957. *Special Districts in the United States*. Berkeley, CA: University of California Press.

Bollens, J.C., and H.J. Schmandt. 1975. *The Metropolis: Its People, Politics and Economics*. New York: Harper & Row.

Botkin, R., and M.A. Kanters. 1990. *Benefits of Illinois Park District Leisure Services*. Macomb, IL: Western Illinois University Printing.

Bowen, W.G., T.I. Nygren, S.E. Turner, and E.A. Duffy. 1994. *The Charitable Nonprofits: An Analysis of Institutional Dynamics and Characteristics*. San Francisco: Jossey-Bass.

Brayley, R.E., and D. McLean. 2008. *Financial Resource Management: Sport, Tourism, and Leisure Services*. Champaign, IL: Sagamore.

Brewer, G.D., and P. deLeon. 1983. *The Foundations of Policy Analysis*. Homewood, IL: Dorsey Press.

Brinberg, D., and J.E. McGrath. 1997. *Validity and the Research Process*. Beverly Hills, CA: Sage.

Bromage, A.W. 1962. *Political Representation in Metropolitan Agencies*. Ann Arbor, MI: Institute of Public Administration, University of Michigan.

Brown, D. 1980. *A Presentation of the Oral Testimony Received At Hearings of the Special District Subcommittee*. Springfield, IL: League of Women Voters.

Buchanan, J.M., and R.D. Tollison. 1972. *Theory of Public Choice: Political Applications of Economics*. Ann Arbor, MI: University of Michigan Press.

Burns, K. 2009. "The National Parks: America's Best Idea: John Muir." www.pbs.org/nationalparks/people/historical/muir/.

Burton, T.L. 1971. *Experiments in Recreation Research*. Totowa, NJ: Rowman & Littlefield.

Butler, G.D. 1976. *Introduction to Community Recreation*. New York: McGraw-Hill.

Cairns, M. 1997. "The History of Illinois Park Districts." *Illinois Parks and Recreation* (July/August): 23-27.

California State Controller's Office. 2003. "State of California Accounting Standards and Procedures for Counties." www.sco.ca.gov/files-ARD/manual_cntyman.pdf.

California Tax Data. 2012. "What Is Proposition 13?" Accessed January 29, 2012. www.californiataxdata.com/pdf/Prop13.pdf.

Campbell, D.T., and J.C. Stanley. 1963. *Experimental and Quasi-Experimental Designs for Research*. Chicago: Rand McNally.

Cape, W.H., L.B. Graves, and B.M. Michaels. 1969. *Government by Special Districts*. Manhattan, KS: Government Research Center Press.

Chadwick, B.A., H. Bahr, and S. Albrecht. 1984. *Social Science Research Methods*. Englewood Cliffs, NJ: Prentice-Hall.

City of Harrisburg, Pennsylvania. 2008. "Comprehensive Annual Financial Report." http://harrisburgcitycontroller.com/wp-content/uploads/2010/01/2008_CAFR.pdf.

Collins, M.F., and I.S. Cooper. 1998. *Leisure Management Issues and Application*. London: Wallingford.

Consensus Economics. 2012. "Consensus Forecasts." Accessed January 29, 2012. www.consensuseconomics.com.

Cook, C. 1972. *A Description of the New York Central Park*. New York: Benjamin Blom.

Cook, T.D., and D.T. Campbell. 1979. *Quasi-Experimentation Design and Analysis for Field Settings*. Chicago: Rand McNally College.

Cooter, R., and T. Ulen. 2000. *Law and Economics*. Reading, MA: Addison-Wesley.

Dess, G., G.T. Lumpkin, and A. Eisner. 2011. *Strategic Management: Text and Cases*. New York: Irwin Professional.

Diamond, J. 1997. *Guns, Germs and Steel: The Fates of Human Societies*. New York: Norton.

Dickason, J.G. 1983. "The Origin of the Playground: The Role of the Boston Women's Clubs, 1885-1890." *Leisure Sciences* 6: 83-98.

Dickinson, M.M. 1978. *The History of the Illinois Association of Park Districts, May 1928-October 1978*. Springfield, IL: Illinois Association of Park Districts.

Downs, A. 1994. *New Visions for Metropolitan America*. Washington, DC: Brookings Institution.

Driver, B.L., P.J. Brown, and G.L. Peterson. 1991. *Benefits of Leisure*. State College, PA: Venture.

Dye, T.R. 2000. *Politics in States and Communities*. Upper Saddle River, NJ: Prentice Hall.

East Bay Regional Recreation and Park District. 2010. "2009 Comprehensive Annual Financial Report." Accessed January 29, 2012. www.ebparks.org/about/budget#cafr.

Eckart, W.J., Jr. 1993. *The Impact of Professional Preparation on Municipal Budgets in Parks and Recreation*. Hartford, CN: University of Connecticut Press.

Edginton, C.R., S.D. Hudson, and S.V. Lankfor. 2001. *Managing Recreation, Parks, and Leisure Services: An Introduction* (2nd edition). Champaign, IL: Sagamore.

Edginton, C.R., D.J. Jordan, D.G. DeGraaf, and S.R. Edginton. 2002. *Leisure and Life Satisfaction*. Boston: McGraw-Hill.

Edginton, C.R., and J.G. Williams. 1978. *Productive Management of Leisure Service Organizations*. New York: Wiley.

Elazar, D.J. 1970. *Cities of the Prairie*. New York: Basic Books.

Emanuelson, D.N. 2002. *A Comparative Analysis of Illinois Park Districts and Illinois Municipal Parks and Recreation Departments*. DeKalb, IL: Northern Illinois University.

Emanuelson, D.N. 2007a. Autonomy, Professional Training and Revenues. *Illinois Park & Recreation* (May/June): 30-33.

Emanuelson, D.N. 2007b. "The Case for Park Districts." *IMPACT: The Official Publication of the Wisconsin Park & Recreation Association* (Winter): 26-27.

Encyclopedia of Children and Childhood in Society. 2012. "Playground Movement." Accessed January 29, 2012. www.faqs.org/childhood/Pa-Re/Playground-Movement.html.

Fahrion, K.A. 1984. *Development and Powers of Illinois Park Districts*. Springfield, IL: Illinois Legislative Council.

Farlex. 2009. "Investor Advisor." http://financial-dictionary.thefreedictionary.com.

Federal Accounting Standards Advisory Board (FASAB). 2008. "2008 Pronouncement as Amended." www.fasab.gov/accounting-standards/authoritative-source-of-gaap/accounting-standards/archived-versions/pronouncements-as-amended/2008-pronouncement-as-amended/.

Federal Accounting Standards Advisory Board (FASAB). 2011. "FASAB Facts 2010." www.fasab.gov/wp-content/uploads/2011/03/FASAB_FACTS_03_2011.pdf.

Federal Accounting Standards Advisory Board (FASAB). 2012. "Accounting Standards." Accessed January 29, 2012. www.fasab.gov/accounting-standards/.

Financial Accounting Standards Board (FASB). 2012. "Facts about FASB." Accessed January 29, 2012. www.fasb.org/facts/.

Finkler, S.A. 2001. *Financial Management for Public Health, and Not-for-Profit Organizations*. Upper Saddle River, NJ: Prentice Hall.

Flickinger, T.B., and P. Murphy. 2004. *The Park District Code*. Springfield, IL: Illinois Association of Park Districts.

Foster, K.A. 1997. *The Political Economy of Special Purpose Government*. Washington, DC: Georgetown University Press.

Friedman, T.L. 2007. *The World Is Flat: A Brief History of the Twenty-First Century*. New York: Picador/Farrar, Straus and Giroux.

Golembiewski, R. 1984. *Public Choice Theory in Public Administration*. New York: Garland.

Goodnow, F.J. 1900. *Politics and Administration: A Study in Government*. New York: Russell and Russell.

Government Accounting Standards Board (GASB). 2012. "Facts About GASB." Accessed January 29, 2012. www.gasb.org/cs/BlobServer?blobcol=urldata&blobtable=MungoBlobs&blobkey=id&blobwhere=1175821770571&blobheader=application%2Fpdf.

Granof, M.H., and P.S. Wardlow. 2003. *Core Concepts of Government and Not-For-Profit Accounting*. Hoboken, NJ: Wiley.

Greve, F. 1997. "Park Perks Come With the Territory." *Chicago Tribune*, November 26, 1, 25.

Gulick, L.H., J.D. Mooney, and L. Urwick. 1937. *Papers on the Science of Administration*. New York: Institute of Public Administration, Columbia University.

Halsey, E. 1940. *The Development of Public Recreation in Metropolitan Chicago*. Chicago: Chicago Recreation Commission.

Harper, J. 2009. *Planning for Recreation and Parks Facilities: Predesign Process, Principles and Strategies*. State College, PA: Venture.

Harrigan, J.J., and R.K. Vogel. 2003. *Political Change in the Metropolis*. New York: Longman.

Hawkins, R.B. 1973. *Public Choice: A Program to Reform and Revitalize Local Government in California*. Sacramento, CA: State of California Printing Office.

Hawkins, R.B. 1976. *Self Government by District: Myth and Reality*. Palo Alto, CA: Hoover Institution Press.

HealthBridge. 2012. "HIE Services." Accessed January 29, 2012. www.healthbridge.org/index.php?option=com_content&task=view&id=83&Itemid=54.

Hendon, W.S. 1981. *Evaluating Urban Parks and Recreation*. New York: Praeger.

Henry, N. 2001. *Public Administration and Public Affairs*. Upper Saddle River, NJ: Prentice-Hall.

Hoovers. 2012. "Six Flags Entertainment Corporation." Accessed January 29, 2012. www.hoovers.com/company/Six_Flags_Entertainment_Corporation/hrcjri-1.html.

Howard, D.R., and J.L. Crompton. 1980. *Financing, Managing and Marketing Recreation and Park Resources*. Dubuque, IA: Wm. C. Brown.

Human Kinetics, ed. 2006. *Introduction to Recreation and Leisure*. Champaign, IL: Human Kinetics.

Humke, R.P., and J. Brademas. 1976. *Organizational Alternatives in Hoffman Estates, Illinois*. Champaign, IL: University of Illinois.

Hurd, A.R., R.J. Barcelona, and J.T. Meldrum. 2008. *Leisure Services Management*. Champaign, IL: Human Kinetics.

Ibrahim, H. 1991. *Leisure and Society: A Comparative Approach*. Dubuque, IA: Wm. C. Brown.

Illinois Association of Park Districts. 2001. *The Park District Advantage*. Springfield, IL: IAPD.

Illinois Auditor General, William G. Holland. 2012. "Public Documents." Accessed January 29, 2012. www.auditor.illinois.gov.

Illinois Municipal League. 2000. *Illinois Municipal Directory*. Springfield, IL: Illinois Municipal League.

IMDb.com. 2012. "Memorable Quotes for *Wall Street*." Accessed January 29, 2012. www.imdb.com/title/tt0094291/quotes.

Indiana State Board of Accounts (SBOA). 2012a. "About SBOA." Accessed January 29, 2012. www.in.gov/sboa/.

Indiana State Board of Accounts (SBOA). 2012b. "Cities and Towns." www.in.gov/sboa/2435.htm.

Internal Revenue Service (IRS). 2012a. "Exempt Purposes—501(c)(7)." Accessed January 29, 2012. www.irs.gov/charities/nonprofits/article/0,,id=226376,00.html.

Internal Revenue Service (IRS). 2012b. "Exempt Purposes—501(c)(3)." Accessed January 29, 2012. www.irs.gov/charities/charitable/article/0,,id=175418,00.html.

Internal Revenue Service (IRS). 2012c. "Examples of Tax-Exempt Social and Recreational Clubs." Accessed January 29, 2012. www.irs.gov/charities/nonprofits/article/0,,id=226377,00.html.

Internal Revenue Service (IRS). 2012d. "Forms and Publications." www.irs.gov/formspubs/index.html.

International City/County Management Association (ICMA). 2012. "ICMA Code of Ethics." Accessed January 29, 2012. http://icma.org/en/icma/ethics/code_of_ethics.

Kaszak, N.L. 1993. *Handbook of Illinois Park District Law.* Springfield, IL: Illinois Association of Park Districts.

Kennedy, P. 1998. *A Guide to Econometrics.* Cambridge, MA: MIT Press.

Kraus, R.G. 1987. *Research and Evaluation in Recreation, Parks and Leisure Services.* Columbus, OH: Horizons.

Kraus, R.G., and L.R. Allen. 1996. *Research and Evaluation in Recreation, Parks and Leisure Services.* Scottsdale, AZ: Gorsuch Scarisbrick.

Lewis, P.H. 1961. *1820-1960 Study of Recreation and Open Space in Illinois.* Champaign, IL: University of Illinois.

Linder, D.O. 2011. "Al Capone Trial (1931): An Account." http://law2.umkc.edu/faculty/projects/ftrials/capone/caponeaccount.html.

Lohman, J. 2009. "Per Capita State Bond Debt for 50 States." www.cga.ct.gov/2009/rpt/2009-R-0009.htm.

Lutzin, S.G. 1979. *Managing Municipal Leisure Services.* Washington, DC: ICMA Press.

Maddala, G.S. 1983. *Limited-Dependent and Qualitative Variables in Econometrics.* New York: Cambridge University Press.

Mancuso, A. 2011. *How to Form a Nonprofit Corporation in California.* Sacramento, CA: Nolo Law for All.

Manta. 2012. "United States Companies." Accessed April 3, 2012. www.manta.com/mb.

McGuire, F.A., R.K. Boyd, and R.E. Tedrick. 2004. *Leisure and Aging: Ulyssean Living in Later Years* (3rd edition). Champaign, IL: Sagamore.

McLaughlin, C.C. 1983. *The Papers of Frederick Law Olmsted: Creating Central Park, 1857-1861.* Baltimore: Johns Hopkins University Press.

McNamara, R. 2012. "John Muir, Naturalist Whose Writings Inspired the Conservation Movement." Accessed January 29, 2012. http://history1800s.about.com/od/americanoriginals/a/johnmuirbio.htm.

Meier, K.J., and J. Brudney. 2001. *Applied Statistics for Public Administration.* Fort Worth, TX: Harcourt College.

Milakovich, M.E., and G.J. Gordon. 2004. *Public Administration in America.* Belmont, CA: Thomson Wadsworth.

Mills, G.E. 1991. *Buying Wood and Building Farms: Marketing Lumber and Farm Building Designs on the Canadian Prairies, 1880 to 1920.* Ottawa: Environment Canada, Parks Canada, and National Historic Sites.

Mitchell, J. 1999. *The American Experiment With Government Corporations.* Armonk, NJ: M.E. Sharpe.

Mobley, T.A., and D. Newport. 1996. *Parks and Recreation in the 21st Century.* Myrtle Beach, SC: Leroy Springs and Company.

Mood, D., F.F. Musker, and J.E. Rink. 1995. *Sports and Recreational Activities.* Boston: WCB McGraw-Hill.

Mull, R.F., B.A. Beggs, and M. Renneisen. 2009. *Recreation Facility Management: Design, Development, Operations, and Utilization.* Champaign, IL: Human Kinetics.

Naisbitt, J. 1982. *Megatrends.* New York: Warner Books.

Nalbandian, J. 1991. *Professionalism in Local Government.* San Francisco: Jossey-Bass.

National Park Service (NPS). 2012. "Budget Systems." Accessed January 29, 2012. www.nps.gov/applications/budget2/index.htm.

National Recreation and Park Association Video Series. 1997. *The Legends of Parks and Recreation Administration.* Arlington, VA.

Nobelprize.org. 2012. "Nobel Peace Prize 1931: Jane Addams Biography." Accessed January 29, 2012. http://nobelprize.org/nobel_prizes/peace/laureates/1931/addams-bio.html.

Nolo Law for All. 2012. "Tax Concerns When Your Nonprofit Makes a Profit." Accessed January 29, 2012. www.nolo.com/legal-encyclopedia/taxes-nonprofit-corporation-earnings-30284.html.

Nonprofits Assistance Fund (NAF). 2006. "The Nonprofit Budgeting Process." www.nonprofitsassistancefund.org/clientuploads/MNAF/ArticlesPublications/BudgetingProcess.pdf.

Nonprofits Assistance Fund (NAF). 2012. "Home Page." www.nonprofitsassistancefund.org.

Norton, W.W. 1990. *Central Park: The Birth, Decline, and Renewal of a National Treasure.* New York: Prentice-Hall.

"Oasis of the Seas: Is a Combination of Arts, Science and Technology." n.d. *The Reader's Eye.* www.thereaderseye.com/oasis-of-the-sea-is-a-combination-of-arts-science-and-technology/.

Oklahoma Teachers Retirement System. 2010. *Comprehensive Annual Financial Report for the Fiscal Year 2009.* Accessed January 29, 2012. www.ok.gov/TRS/documents/2009CAFR.pdf.

Olmsted, F.L., Jr., and T. Kimball. 1973. *Frederick Law Olmsted: Landscape Architect.* New York: Benjamin Blom.

Orfield, M. 1997. *MetroPolitics.* Washington, DC: Brookings Institution.

Osborne, D., and T. Gaebler. *Reinventing Government.* New York: Addison-Wesley.

Ostrom, V. 1973. *Understanding Urban Government: Metropolitan Reform Reconsidered.* Washington, DC: American Enterprise Institute for Public Policy Research.

Pear, R. 2012. "House Passes Bill Banning Insider Trading by Members of Congress." *New York Times.* www.nytimes.com/2012/02/10/us/politics/house-passes-bill-banning-insider-trading-by-members-of-congress.html.

Platt, R.H. 1996. *Land Use and Society: Geography, Law, and Public Policy*. Washington, DC: Island Press.

Powell, W.W., and R. Steinberg. 2006. *The Nonprofit Sector: A Research Handbook* (2nd edition). New Haven, CT: Yale University Press.

Prater, C. 2010. "What the New Credit Card Law Means for You." www.creditcards.com/credit-card-news/help/what-the-new-credit-card-rules-mean-6000.php.

Project America. 2012. "Crime: Crime Rates: Kidnapping." Accessed January 29, 2012. www.project.org/info.php?recordID=158.

Public Records Guide. 2010. "Information About Income Tax Records." http://publicrecordsguide.com/income-tax-records.html.

Putnam, R. 2011. "Recent GASB Pronouncements." North Dakota University System. http://ndus.edu/uploads/resources/2614/04-gasb-update.pdf.

The Quotations Page. 2012. "Quotation Details: Will Rogers." Accessed January 29, 2012. www.quotationspage.com/quote/659.html.

Rainwater, C.E. 1922. *The Play Movement in the United States*. Chicago: University of Chicago Press.

Riess, S.A. 1996. *City Games: The Evolution of American Urban Society and the Rise of Sports*. Champaign, IL: University of Illinois Press.

Riley, J. 2012. "Political Culture of the United States." Accessed January 29, 2012. http://academic.regis.edu/jriley/421elazar.htm.

Robyn, M., and G. Prante. 2011. "State-Local Tax Burdens Fall in 2009 as Tax Revenues Shrink Faster Than Income." www.taxfoundation.org/research/show/22320.html.

Rogers, E.B. 1987. *Rebuilding Central Park*. Cambridge, MA: MIT Press.

Rokkan, S., S. Verba, J. Viet, and E. Almasy. 1969. *Confluence: Comparative Survey Analysis*. The Hague: Mouton.

Roper, L.W. 1973. *A Biography of Frederick Law Olmsted*. Baltimore: Johns Hopkins University Press.

RoperASW. 2004. "Outdoor Recreation in America: Recreation's Benefits to Society Challenged by Trends." www.funoutdoors.com/files/ROPER%20REPORT%202004_0.pdf.

Rosenweig, R., and E. Blackmar. 1992. *The Park and the People: A History of Central Park*. Ithaca, NY: Cornell University Press.

Ross, B.R., and M. Levine. 2001. *Urban Politics*. Itasca, IL: F.E. Peacock.

Roth, R. 2012. "Financial Ratio Tutorial." *Investopedia*. Accessed January 29, 2012. www.investopedia.com/university/ratios/.

Rubin, H.J. 1983. *Applied Social Research*. Columbus, OH: Charles E. Merrill.

Sawyer, T.H., and O. Smith. 1999. *The Management of Clubs, Recreation, and Sport*. Champaign, IL: Sagamore.

Schuyler, D., J.T. Censer, C. Hoffman, and K. Hawkins. 1992. *The Papers of Frederick Law Olmsted: The Years of Olmsted, Vaux, and Company*. Baltimore: Johns Hopkins University Press.

Searle, G.A.C. 1975. *Recreation Economics and Analysis*. New York: Longman Group Ltd.

Sessoms, H.D. 1993. *Eight Decades of Leadership Development*. Arlington, VA: National Recreation and Park Association.

Shivers, J.S. 1967. *Principles and Practices of Recreational Service*. New York: Macmillan.

Shivers, J.S., and J.W. Halper. 1981. *The Crisis in Urban Recreation*. East Brunswick, NJ: Associated University Press.

60 Minutes. 2011. "Congress: Trading Stock on Insider Information?" November 13. www.cbsnews.com/video/watch/?id=7388130n.

Small Business Administration (SBA). n.d. "Prepare Your Business Finances." www.sba.gov/category/navigation-structure/starting-managing-business/starting-business/preparing-your-finances.

Smith, S. 1975. "Similarities Between Urban Recreation Systems." *Journal of Leisure Research* (July): 270-281.

Standards for Excellence Institute. 2011. "The Standards for Excellence Code." www.standardsforexcellenceinstitute.org/dnn/TheCode.aspx.

Standeven, J., and P. DeKnop. 1999. *Sport Tourism*. Champaign, IL: Human Kinetics.

Stetzer, D.F. 1975. *Special Districts in Cook County*. Chicago: University of Chicago.

Sullivan, A., and S.M. Sheffrin. 2003. *Economics: Principles in Action*. Upper Saddle River, NJ: Pearson Prentice Hall.

Sunshine Review. 2012. "Illinois Freedom of Information Act." Accessed January 29, 2012. http://sunshinereview.org/index.php/Illinois_Freedom_of_Information_Act.

Tascarella, P. 2011. "United Way of Allegheny County Bucks National Trends With Fundraising Efforts." www.bizjournals.com/pittsburgh/print-edition/2011/06/10/united-way-of-allegheny-fundraising.html.

Taylor, F. 1911. *The Principles of Scientific Management*. New York: Harper-Norton.

Themed Entertainment Association. n.d. "Welcome to the TEA Website." www.teaconnect.org.

Theobald, W.F. 1979. *Evaluation of Recreation and Park Programs*. New York: Wiley.

ThinkExist.com. 2012. "Chris Rock quotes." Accessed January 29, 2012. http://thinkexist.com/quotes/chris_rock/.

Tillman, K.G., E.F. Voltmer, A.A. Esslinger, and B.F. McCue. 1996. *The Administration of Physical Education, Sport, and Leisure Programs*. Boston: Allyn and Bacon.

TribLocal. 2010. "Retirement Perks Cost Town Millions." *TribLocal Skokie*, September 17. http://triblocal.com/skokie/2010/09/17/retirement-perks-cost-towns-millions.

van der Smissen, B., M. Moiseichik, V.J. Hartenburg, and L.F. Twardzik. 2000. *Management of Park and Recreation Agencies*. Ashburn, VA: National Recreation and Park Association.

Veal, A.J. 1987. *Leisure and the Future*. London: Allen and Unwin.

Vickerson, R.W. 1975. *The Economics of Leisure and Recreation*. New York: McMillan.

Washington State Board of Accountancy. 2012. "Board Purpose." Accessed January 29, 2012. www.cpaboard.wa.gov.

Washington State Parks. 2012. "State Parks Fees." Accessed January 29, 2012. www.parks.wa.gov/fees.

"Washington State Parks to Charge Fees Starting Friday." 2011. *King 5 News*, June 30. www.king5.com/news/State-park-fees-in-effect-starting-Friday-124778979.html.

"Why Mealtime Matters." n.d. http://poweroffamilymeals.com/Mealtime_Matters/.

Wild, R. 2012. "How to Define a Bond as a Financial Tool." *Dummies.com*. Accessed January 29, 2012. www.dummies.com/how-to/content/how-to-define-a-bond-as-a-financial-tool.html.

Wilson, W. 1887. "The Study of Administration." *Political Science Quarterly* 2 (June): 197-222.

Wolman, H., and A. Levy. 2010. "Government, Governance, and Regional Economic Growth." *GW Institute of Policy Working Papers*. www.gwu.edu/~gwipp/Governance%20and%20Government%207-7-11.pdf.

Yahoo Finance. 2012a. "Six Flags Balance Sheet." Accessed January 29, 2012. http://finance.yahoo.com/q/bs?s=SIX+Balance+Sheet&annual.

Yahoo Finance. 2012b. "Six Flags Entertainment Corporation Income Statement." Accessed January 29, 2012. http://finance.yahoo.com/q/is?s=SIX.

Yoder, D.G., D. Zoerink, and K.D. Adkins. 2000a. *An Analysis of the Role and Impact of Park Districts, Forest Preserves, and Conservation and Recreation Agencies in Illinois*. Macomb, IL: Western Illinois University.

Yoder, D.G., D. Zoerink, and K.D. Adkins. 2000b. *The State of Illinois Park and Recreation Agencies and Beyond*. Macomb, IL: Western Illinois University.

Index

Note: The letters *f* and *t* after page numbers indicate figures and tables, respectively.

About the Author

David N. Emanuelson, PhD, has three decades of experience working in the leisure services, serving for 12 years as department head of two parks and recreation departments in Illinois and Indiana and 20 years as a park district executive director in Illinois.

Emanuelson also taught courses in parks and recreation administration, public administration and political science for 14 years. Before retiring, Emanuelson held the post of assistant professor at George Williams College of Aurora University, teaching administration, financial management, commercial recreation, facility management, and the economics of parks and recreation. Emanuelson currently works as a consultant in the leisure service industry.

In 2003, he received the Gold Medal Award for Excellence in Parks and Recreation Management and has received nine consecutive Certificates of Achievement for Excellence in Financial Accounting. He is a member of the National Recreation and Park Association, Illinois Park and Recreation Association, Wisconsin Park and Recreation Association, Midwest Political Science Association, and the honorary fraternities Rho Phi Lambda, Pi Alpha Alpha, and Beta Gamma Sigma.

Emanuelson worked closely with his wife, Sharon, on the creation of this book. They reside in DeKalb, Illinois, and enjoy traveling, boating, water sports, and golf.

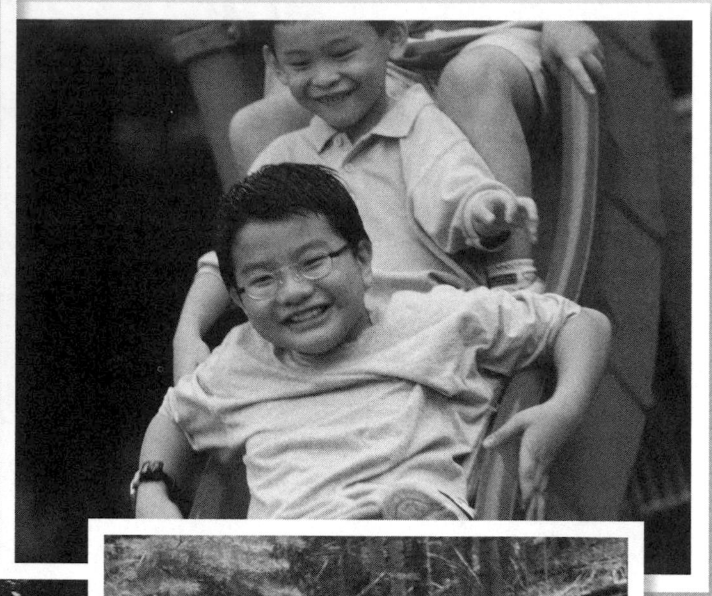